"The Word

MADE ▽ FRESH

A down to Earth version of The New Testament

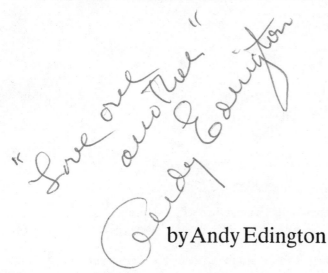

by Andy Edington

EAKIN PRESS ★ Austin, Texas

VOL. II
The New Testament
Second Printing

Copyright © 1988
By Andy Edington

Published in the United States of America
By Eakin Press, P.O. Box 23069, Austin, Texas 78735

VOL. I   ISBN 0-89015-681-6
VOL. II   ISBN 0-89015-682-4
2 VOL. SET   ISBN 0-89015-683-2

Dedication

This book is dedicated to the great cloud of witnesses who have surrounded my life, including my family; my wife Marguerite, daughter, Rita, son, David, plus my parents, brothers, a sister, grandchildren, nephews, nieces, those here and those who have gone before, a host of friends, including preachers and teachers — they are all in the book.

All of these influences, plus the energy to do the work, have been undergirded and made both strong and binding by a Word, a Name, and a Sign.

FOREWORD

More than two centuries have elapsed since old Johannes Bengel gave this advice to people who would study his edition of the New Testament in Greek: "Apply your whole self to the text; the whole matter apply to yourself." *The Word Made Fresh* gives the reader a delightful opportunity to enjoy the fireworks that crackle and flash when Andrew Edington applies his whole self to the Bible and the whole Bible to himself.

No one knows better than Andy Edington that the Word of God is never stale, as if it were our job to make it fresh. But he knows better than most of us how stale we can make the Bible seem when we read it with dull and unimaginative hearts. He knows especially well how a wrong sense of the holiness of Holy Scripture can keep us from seeing how deeply it plunges into the ordinary fabric of human life, where the Holy Lord is always challenging us, loving us, and calling us to be his kind of people. And he knows that God is always ready to make His Word fresh to us when we give our whole selves to the reading of Scripture and apply the whole matter to ourselves.

The Word Made Fresh is neither a commentary nor a new translation. It is not, above all, a substitute for reading the Bible in one of the excellent modern translations that tries to give us the most accurate possible rendering of the best Hebrew and Aramaic and Greek manuscripts of the Biblical text (such as the *RSV, The New English Bible, The Jerusalem Bible).* What Andrew Edington has done in *The Word Made Fresh* is to give us his own paraphrase of Scripture as it impacts on his own life and changes the way he looks at himself, at us, and at our contemporary world. It is not the work of a professionally trained Biblical scholar, even though countless hours of devoted study and rich experience have gone into its preparation. It is instead a layman's challenge, full of genuine humor and much wisdom, to come always fresh to the reading of the Bible. As such it is a hymn of praise to the Lord who makes all things fresh.

James A. Wharton
Austin Presbyterian Theological Seminary

CONTENTS

AUTHOR'S COMMENT

The Word Made Fresh is being republished in two volumes, covering all sixty-six books of the Bible, and re-published with a slightly altered format.

This publication is made possible because of the interest and vision of MeJ and John O'Neal, who have felt that *The Word Made Fresh* is a vehicle for developing an interest in the Bible among those whose exposure to the Bible has been either quite limited or non-existent, as well as being a treatment of the Biblical word that might stimulate new thought areas for those people who are already conversant with the Bible.

It is my hope that every time a 12-year-old or a disadvantaged person, or anyone else receives a new and helpful insight into the word of God through *The Word Made Fresh* that the Lord will add a new blessing into the lives of MeJ and John O'Neal.

Andrew Edington

MATTHEW

The lineage of Christ is established from the line of Abraham and includes such well-known names as Isaac, Jacob, Boaz, David, and Solomon.

Many generations later there was a couple, Mary and Joseph, and at the beginning of their marriage it developed that Mary was with child, the seed of life having been implanted by the Holy Spirit as an act of God. Joseph, the husband, was disturbed over the pregnancy of his wife, since he knew he had not touched her, and he thought he would hide her out for awhile.

An angel of the Lord, however, appeared to Joseph and assured him that his marriage was all right and that the pregnancy of Mary was of the Lord. The angel also told Joseph that the child would be a boy and that his name should be Jesus, for he would save the people from their sins.

All of these things were necessary in order to fulfill the prophecies of old which said "A virgin shall be with child, and the child be named Emmanuel, which is a word meaning, 'God with us.'"

Joseph believed the angel and was relieved of his anxieties and became a husband to Mary.

Now when Jesus was born in Bethlehem of Judea in the days of Herod the king there came wise men from the east to Jerusalem saying, "Where is the child that is born to be king of the Jews? We have read this message in the stars and we wish to worship the child."

Word of this inquiry reached Herod, the king, and he assembled the chief priests and a few of the leaders of the Jewish people and demanded that they tell him where the child was born.

The church leaders told him that the prophets of old had always said that the king would be born in Bethlehem in Judea.

One of the spokesmen quoted one of the prophets saying "You town of Bethlehem, in the land of Judah, you are far from the least of the places in Judah, for from your town will arise a governor that shall rule the people of Israel."

Herod then arranged a secret interview with the wise men and asked them all manner of questions about their star reading and then he said to them, "Go to Bethlehem and look for this child, and when you have found him, come back here and tell me where he is; as I would also wish to go and worship him."

When the wise men left the king and hit the road, the star which they had seen in the east went before them and it remained high in the heavens directly over the place where the child was. The wise men were elated over this strange and wonderful phenomena.

When the wise men arrived at the dwelling they saw the young baby and Mary his mother, and they went down on their knees and worshipped. They also presented their gifts of gold, and frankincense, and myrrh.

The wise men were warned of God about Herod, however, and they were not stupid enough, being wise men, to return to Herod, but went home another way.

The angel of the Lord appeared then to Joseph in a dream and warned him to take the child and Mary to Egypt and get the child out of the jurisdiction of Herod until the matter had been forgotten. Joseph then took Mary and Jesus to Egypt and remained there until he had heard of the death of Herod. This, too, was a fulfillment, for a prophet had said "Out of Egypt shall I call my son."

When it dawned on Herod, however, that the wise men had made a nut of him, he was greatly peeved and ordered the slaying of all the children in Bethlehem and the surrounding area who were two years old and under, which he figured would be the age range in which Jesus would be.

This also fulfilled a prophecy spoken by Jeremiah who said "In the land there will be heard a lamentation, and weeping, and great mourning, for it will be the Jewish mothers weeping for their children."

When Herod was dead, however, and Joseph knew of this, he obeyed the angel who again appeared in a dream to him and told him to return to the land of Israel. Again being warned of God to stay away from the capital, Joseph took his family aside in Galilee, and made a home in the city of Nazareth, again fufilling a prophecy that said "He shall be called a Nazarene."

Chap.

3

Not long after this there appeared a wilderness preacher known as John the Baptist, and his great theme was 'Repent, for the kingdom of heaven is at hand.'

Now this John was the fulfillment of the prophecy of Isaiah, who said, "The voice of one crying in the wilderness, saying 'prepare for yourselves a way of the Lord and straighten out your lives.' "

John was a real wilderness preacher, wearing camel's hair and leather shorts, and he ate the food of the wilderness, mainly honey and locusts.

The people came from all the surrounding area, from as far away as Jerusalem, to hear him preach, and many repented and were baptized, confessing their sins.

When some of the technical minded church leaders appeared, however, he got tough with them in his speaking and denounced them with such words as "You descendants of snakes, who has managed to scare you a bit? You'd better bring some real evidence of repentance when you come here. You can't get by just saying that you are descendants of Abraham. If God wishes to do so He could raise up children in the line of Abraham from the stones you see around you."

"Talk will do you no good anymore." continued John, "but you had better start producing some good works. All the trees that don't start bearing good fruit will be cut down. It's just that simple. Now I can baptize you with water, but there is one coming far greater than I, whose shoes I'm not worthy to lace, and He shall baptize you with the Holy Spirit, and with brand new enthusiasm.

"I'll tell you something else. He'll stir things plenty. His fan will separate the wheat from the chaff, and the wheat will be saved and the chaff destroyed. Now you begin to think about which you'll be!"

Finally, one day, Jesus himself appeared at the Jordan River and asked John to baptize him.

"No, sir." said John. "It is I that needs the baptizing. You baptize me."

"Let's just do it my way this time, John. It is necessary that it be this way."

Then John baptized Jesus, and when Jesus left the water the heavens opened and the Spirit of the Lord descended as a dove and appeared above him and rested upon him, and a voice from heaven came forth saying "This is my beloved son, in whom I am well pleased."

Chap.

4

Sometime after this Jesus entered the wilderness for a period of meditation in order to decide how to best go about the business of fulfilling his mission in life.

It was customary to fast and pray during such a period and Jesus did this.

The first plan for his life that Jesus contemplated was what might be called a suggestion of the devil. The idea was to use the power of God, which Jesus had, to turn all the stones into bread, feed everybody free, and be a big hero.

Jesus replied to this idea by saying "Bread is not enough for a man's life. Man must also have the word of God. Something solid on which to base his life."

Later in his meditations the tempting idea of protecting health and the body occurred to him. Why not just order the angels to look out for everybody so no one would so much as stump his toe?

Jesus immediately recognized this as a temptation and rejected the thought.

Finally, the tempting thought came to just take over the world and run it. To use the power of God to put down evil and bless the good. All Jesus would have to do would be to worship power and become a universal Marshall Dillon.

Christ refused to accept this as a proper mission, stating that "You are to worship God, and God is the only one you are to serve."

The angels of God then appeared to him and prepared him for his mission of teaching.

News came to Jesus at this time that John the Baptist had been put in jail; so he departed from Nazareth and went to Galilee, which also fulfilled the prophecy that stated that "the people of Galilee who live in great darkness will see a great light, so that those who are depressed and feel hopeless, will also begin to perceive that there is light and hope."

Jesus began at this time his full ministry, saying "Repent, for the kingdom of God is available."

Jesus also began to recruit some workers. When he was walking by the sea he saw two brothers, Peter and Andrew, who were casting their nets for mullet.

Jesus said to them "Come with me. You are casting for fish, and I will put you to casting for me. It is far more interesting and satisfying to cast for men." Peter and Andrew left their nets and followed Jesus.[1]

Later Jesus saw two other brothers in a boat with their father and he spoke to them the same way and they left the boat and their father and followed Jesus.

Jesus then began to teach in the synagogues, whenever possible, and he preached often, telling the good news of the Kingdom of God, and he began healing all kinds of diseases and all manner of ailments, many being psychological.

Of course, word began to spread about his healing ability, and people came with all manners of aches and pains, many mental cases, and many with varied diseases and torments. It was not long before a great many people began to follow him, coming from Jerusalem, Judea, and even from across the Jordan.

Chap.

5

Seeing a crowd on one occasion he climbed up a hill and began to teach them saying:

"The basis for all happiness is laid on a person's willingness to be humble before God, recognizing the need for God, and therefore being willing to seek God's way for life.

"It is a great blessing to grieve or mourn and then through prayer receive comfort. The true knowledge of a refuge in God comes only to those who have need.

[1]The old man left in the boat probably had a few comments to make about the younger generation.

"Particularly happy are those who bend to God's will, for they learn thereby to control the earth.

"Happiness is a great search. The seeking itself is pleasure, and God fills abundantly the life of one who hungers and thirsts for righteousness. Spiritual growth is a reward in itself.

"Happy is the merciful person, for not only does he receive mercy, but he is not burdened with the judgments and condemnations of his fellow man.

"Joyful is the person who understands God, but to comprehend God requires purity of heart and mind. Sin and evil are like dark glasses, while goodness clears a person's vision.

"Happy are those who are working toward peace, who actually remove prejudice and hate from their minds, for these are the people who become truly God's children.

"Happiness must be willing to stand a test. The happy person has a sense of values that is impregnable and is capable of withstanding persecution or scoffing.

"People actually are like salt. It is fine as long as it has its zest, but when the saltiness is gone, it is no good anymore, and it must be thrown out, where it will be stomped.

"You people also have the chance to be the light of the world. You must be like a city set on a hill to be seen of men. Don't hide your goodness, but let it shine. Like a candle. Don't put a candle under a bucket, but put it on a candlestick and let it light up the house.

"Let your light so shine before men that they may see your good example, and they will glorify God because of you.

"Now don't get the idea that I've come to destroy the old law or change the word of the prophets. I have not come to destroy, but to explain, make relevant, and complete the law and the prophets. Basically, there is no change to be made in the law of God until everything is finished in accordance with God's plan.

"In fact, whoever breaks even the smallest of God's commandments and teaches others that this is all right, shall be listed last in the kingdom of heaven, but the person who observes the word of God himself and teaches others to do likewise, shall be a great one in the kingdom of heaven.

"Actually, your understanding of life must exceed that of the technical churchman, or you won't even get into the kingdom at all.

"For example: The old law said 'Thou shall not murder, for a murderer is in danger of final judgment,' but the law has a fuller meaning than that, for it means that you should not desire to murder. You have no business losing your cool and popping off at another person.

"In fact, if you come to worship, or to pray, and when you kneel you remember that you have a grudge, get up and go first and get straight with your fellowman, get rid of any hate or enmity that you have, then come to God in worship or in prayer.

"If you have difficulty with another person you should attempt to get it amicably worked out very promptly as it might grow and become more and more involved and then finally when it has reached serious proportions it might turn out that you were the one in the wrong. Then you will be held accountable.

"Another example of the law is found in the words 'You shall not commit adultery.' The complete part of this law which I reveal to you is that you should not look on a woman with lustful desire in your heart, for you are then thinking adultery even though you may not do it.

"If you are having trouble with a habit the best thing to do is to get rid of it. It would be better to lose an eye or give up seeing if all you can see turns to evil thoughts, or to lose a hand if it is causing you to be violent. You see, it is better to lose one part of the body, than for one part to result in the degradation of the whole body.

"The customary law among you people has been that if a man wanted to get rid of his wife he merely wrote himself a bill of divorcement and that was that. You have a greater family obligation than that, for you have no right to divorce unless your wife has already broken the family unity by joining herself to another man. The man who is responsible for the wife leaving is also an adulterer.

"The traditional law among you has also established the validity of certain statements if sworn 'by heaven' or 'by God.' This is not the proper use of the law. It is better not to always be affirming 'on a stack of Bibles' or the like, but so live that your word is good, and all you need to say is yes or no, and everyone will know that you mean it.

"There is also among you a tradition that arranges for revenge in the form of an eye for an eye and a tooth for a tooth, but you should learn to accept insult or adversity without revenge. If somebody considers that you owe him a shirt give it to him, and throw in a tie for good measure. If a man needs help give him help and more so, for if he needs you to walk with him one mile, go with him two.

"Learn to be a giver. Be willing to loan your possessions to be used for others' pleasure.

"The old-timey philosophy of life was easy, for it is said 'love your friends and hate your enemies.' Now I bring a fuller and straight from God admonition, which is 'love your enemies.' Make friends of them. Actually try to make happy even the people who curse you, and you should do good deeds to people who have no use for you, and the hardest and maybe most important, pray for them who take advantage of you. Suddenly then you become a child of God.

"Have you noticed how free of prejudice God is? He sends the sun to shine on the good and the bad, and he sends the rain on the just and the unjust.

"Be reasonable now, if you love just those who love you, what accomplishment is this? Even the mafia feels this way. If you are nice only to those who are nice to you, what credit is that, even the heathens and the politicians do this.

"Why not try to be as nearly like God as possible?

Chap.
6

"Again, I emphasize, be a giver, not that you may be noted and admired as such by men, for if you are rewarded for such by men, it is not necessary for God to reward you, and it is preferable to be rewarded by God.

"In short, don't make a big thing over your generosity, sounding trumpets and waiting for a crowd to gather to announce your kindness. This kind of giving has a reward, but it is earthly and shallow, but giving quietly and graciously so much so that you hardly know yourself how generous you are being, and your Father in Heaven, who knows all things, will reward you in His way.

"Let me tell you something now about private prayer, when you as one person are in the presence of the Lord God of Hosts. Pray in private. Don't stand on the streets or in some public place so that everyone will see that you are praying. The people that put on a show with their prayers have a reward but it is earthly. When you pray, find a secret place, and pray in secret. The Lord will reward you, and this He will do openly. You do not need to nag God with a bunch of repetitions in prayer either. In fact, he knows what you want and what you need before you ask him; so don't be like the show-offs.

"As a sample or suggestion let your prayer run something like this:

Our Father, who art in heaven, hallow it be thy name, thy kingdom come, thy will be done on earth as it is in heaven; give us this day our daily bread and forgive us our debts as we forgive our debtors, and lead us not into temptation, but deliver us from evil, for thine is the kingdom and the power and the glory forever, Amen.

"Note the point on forgiving. It is simply an arrangement the Lord has made for He will forgive you as you forgive the people who have offended you.

"You are also called upon to exercise self-denial and self-discipline, but it must be genuine. There is some reward in merely talking about self-denial and giving the appearance of being this way, but you should seek to please God in this, and not merely for appearance's sake.

"Don't be a money grabber, a hoarder, or the type that does not know how to give. In the first place, there is no real security on earth. Thieves, moths, and floods can ruin you. Also if you store up treasures you get to thinking and worrying about the treasures too much. If you want real treasure store them in the heavenly kingdom in the form of good deeds, and good thoughts, and friendly service.

"Learn to to look for the good. If you are always looking for the bad aspects finally these things infiltrate the whole person through the eye. What a dark, miserable place inside you are if everything looks dark and miserable to you.

"No one can work for two bosses at the same time, or he will compare them, and prefer one to the other; so you can't be your own boss and at the same time serve God. Assuming that you choose God, then your way of life is clear.

"Do not be anxious or worried, about what you will eat or what you will drink, nor for your body, what you will wear. What you really are is far more important than what you eat, drink or wear.

"Take the birds. You don't see them fanning nor selling nor running stores, but the Lord gets feed to them. Don't you think you're worth more than a bird to God? Work, but don't worry.

"You can't get taller by worrying about being short.

"Clothes don't mean so much. The lilies are admired just as they are, and Solomon with all his dough couldn't outdress the lily. Don't worry so about your clothes, for if God was so careful to clothe the grass which sometimes lasts only a few days, be assured that He will clothe you, you people with your little faith.

"Again, I say, don't be so anxious, worrying about what you will eat or drink or wear, for your Father knows you need these things.

"The big thing is to seek the kingdom of God and the understanding of it, then all the secondary things will take their place; so do not be anxious for tomorrow but let tomorrow look out for itself. There are enough problems today.

Chap.

7

"It should interest you to know that you are not appointed judges of your fellowman. Actually, if you insist on judging, you will be judged the same in return. Furthermore, you generally will be treated in the same manner that you treat other people.

"Why be one that can find a speck in your neighbor's eye and you cannot see the whole splinter that is in your own eye? What brass you must have to try to correct your brother all the time, when you are yourself full of errors. You had better get yourself straight first, then maybe you can be of some help to your brother.

"There is no point in your wasting good teaching and true inspiration on insensitive and antagonist people. It would be like insisting on putting a pearl necklace on a pig.

"Ask God when you have a need. God will give. Search for his kingdom and you will find it. No one is ever turned away. The searchers always find and to those that knock he opens the door of his kingdom.

"What man is there who will give his son a stone when he has requested bread, or a snake when he has asked for fish? If man, being human, knows to give good things to his son, how much better does God know to give good gifts to those that ask him?

"In dealing then with your fellowman you should think of doing for him those things that you would normally care to have him do for you, which is a good summary of the law and the prophets.

"The way that I teach is a narrow way in that it is well defined. It is not easy to follow the straight path, but it is the way to a full and eternal life, while the undisciplined way is a way to destruction and death.

"I want to warn you about false teachers. They will look good and sound good, but inside they are wolfish. The way to tell them is by their results, just like you tell a good tree because it produces good fruit, a diseased tree produces a bad fruit. Eventually, the bad trees or the false teachers will be cut down and destroyed. You can tell the good ones by their fruit.

"The payoff is not found in lip service. There will be some who are always saying 'Lord this, and Lord that' who will never enter the kingdom for the kingdom is for those who put my teachings into practice, for this is the will of my Father.

"In the day of judgment there will be many saying 'have we not preached in your name, and denounced evil, and even done some good works?'

"At that time I will say to this bunch 'I never knew you. You have had the wrong attitude all along.'

"To those who hear what I am teaching and do something about it, I would say such a person is similar to a sensible man who built his house upon a rock and the rains came and the winds blew and beat upon the house but it fell not for it was founded upon a rock.

"But to those who hear my teachings and do nothing about them, I consider them similar to an unreasonable man who built his house upon the sand; and the rains came and the wind blew and the house fell. It was a total collapse."

As Jesus ended these sayings the people were astonished, for they had never heard such sound doctrine and they sensed that He spoke as one having complete authority.

After the teaching session from the hilltop many people began to follow him, and a leper came and worshipped him and said, "If you want to, you can cleanse me."

Jesus said "I don't want publicity so don't go around telling people, but go to the health officer and present yourself and pay your just fee, as this is the custom when you are healed."

When Jesus came to a seaside resort[1] a high ranking Roman officer came to him and said, "Lord, my orderly is at home sick and in great pain."

"I will come and heal him" said Jesus.

"Lord, I am not worthy enough to have you as a guest in my abode. I am a man of authority myself, and I understand giving orders, being accustomed to exercising authority over soldiers; so I recognize your supreme authority and all you have to do is give the order for healing."

Jesus was joyfully astonished and said, "So much faith I have not seen anywhere. There will be a strange gathering of people of the kingdom of heaven. Many shall miss it for lack of faith, and there shall be weeping and gnashing of teeth among them. You, my good officer, you may go now. Your faith has made the healing possible and at this very moment your servant is well."

Later Jesus came to Peter's house and saw Peter's mother-in-law sick and running a fever. Jesus touched her hand and the fever left her, whereupon she got up and fixed coffee for everyone.

That evening there were brought to Jesus many with various problems and difficulties, and he cleared their minds and healed their bodies. This also was the fulfillment of the prophecy saying 'He took our infirmities and carried away our sickness.'

When Jesus saw that there were too many people for the accomodations, he ordered the disciples to cross the sea with him. A scribe, who was present, stepped forth then and said "Master, let me go, I will follow you anywhere."

"Let me caution you," said Jesus, "that although foxes have holes and the birds have nests, the son of man has no place to stay."

Another follower spoke out saying "I'm willing to go, but first I need to go and bury my father."

"Don't make excuses or put your decision off. Follow me and let the spiritual dead ones left behind bury the dead."

Jesus then entered the ship and his disciples followed him. There arose a great storm on the sea and waves began to wash over

[1]Capernaum

the ship, but Jesus remained asleep.

Some of the disciples came to him, however, and awakened him saying "Lord save us or we will all perish at sea."

"What are you afraid of?" asked Jesus. "Do you have so little faith?"

In a few minutes Christ arose and ordered the winds to cease and there was a great calm on the sea.

The men in the ship were amazed and asked each other what manner of man was this that the wind and the sea obeyed him.

When the ship landed on the other side and they were once again on land there came two crazy men, maniacs who were living among the tombs.

When the maniacs saw Jesus they called out to him asking if he had come to increase their torment. A good distance away, but in sight, were a bunch of wild pigs, and the lunatics cried that they would rather join the wild pigs. Jesus then ordered the pressures that were causing the lunacy to depart to the pigs and as a result the herd of pigs ran madly to a bluff and then into the sea. The keepers of the pigs went back to town and reported the incident.

The townspeople came out then to see Jesus and asked him to leave the area and let them and their livestock alone.

Jesus adhered to their request, and entered a ship and returned to his own community.

Chap.

9

After arriving in his own area, the people brought a man sick of the palsy to him. Jesus was pleased with the faith of the friends of the man, and so he said to the palsied man "Thy sins are forgiven."

Immediately one of the Religious Scholars objected to Jesus using the authority of God.

Jesus sensed this and so he said "Which now is easier, to say thy sins are forgiven you or arise and walk? Just so you will know for sure that the son of man has the power to forgive sins, I will demonstrate."

Then to the palsied man Jesus spoke and said "Arise, get off the stretcher, and go home." The man did as he was told. The people who witnessed this marveled and praised God for making such power available to a man.

As Jesus departed he saw a man named Matthew, who was at the custom office desk collecting taxes, and Jesus said "Follow me." The man immediately arose and followed Christ.

It also happened that as they were sitting around eating, many ordinary people and many questionable characters sat down with Christ and his disciples.

Some of the hierarchy of the church saw this and they asked some of the disciples, "Why does Jesus associate with such low class people?

Jesus overheard them and he turned to them and said "The person that is well does not need a doctor, but only the sick. Just think about that a little. I want to see mercy exercised, not sacrifice, and I have come not for those who already understand, but I am come for the lost and for the sinners."

"Furthermore," he continued, "while the bridegroom is around and the party is going all should rejoice and be happy. It is when the bridegroom is gone that things will get tough. Also you can't patch pants forever, anymore than it is wise to put a clear drink in a dirty bottle. It is better to get new bottles."

While he was still speaking there came to him one of the local dignitaries saying "My daughter has just died. Come and touch her that she might live."

Jesus immediately arose and followed the man. As he was walking a woman with a circulatory problem touched the hem of his garment, for she had reasoned that if she could touch Jesus she would be well.

Jesus, when he saw her, turned to her and said "Lady, be of good cheer. Your faith has made you well." At this moment the woman was healed.

When Jesus arrived at the dignitary's house the funeral home people had already taken charge and were playing the funeral music.

Jesus said "Step aside. The girl isn't dead, but is asleep." The funeral director and the pallbearers all laughed. After Jesus had asked to have them removed from the house, he went in and took the girl by the hand and she arose and walked out front. The report of this was spread around widely.

After leaving this place, two blind men followed Jesus and began calling forth "Thou descendant of David, have mercy upon us." They even followed him into the house to which he was going. Jesus then spoke to them and said "Do you believe that I have the power to restore sight?"

"Yes," they immediately answered. Then Jesus touched their eyes and told them that their faith was sufficient for healing, and immediately their eyes were opened. Jesus asked them, however, not to publicize the matter. Their joy was too much, however, and they told of their experience wherever they went.

On another occasion, sometime later, the disciples brought a dumb man to Jesus. This man was possessed with a devil or an impediment that prevented his speaking. Jesus removed the obstacle. The people again were astonished.

The technical churchmen were not happy with this and accused Jesus, intimating that it took a devil to catch a devil.

Jesus continued to move about, however, teaching and preaching and healing people of many varied diseases.

As Jesus observed the multitudes he was moved with

compassion toward them, and felt that they were as sheep with no shepherd, and that they were without purpose in life.

This caused Jesus to say to the disciples, "The harvest is plentiful but the laborers are few. Pray the Lord of the harvest that he may send more laborers."

After the twelve particular disciples had been chosen Jesus called a meeting of them and instructed them in the power through faith that was made available to them in the area of healing diseases, counseling, and relieving tensions.

The twelve men present were Peter, Andy, Jim, John, Phil, Bart, Tom, Matt, Jimmy,[1] Si, Ted, and Judas. These are the twelve that Jesus sent forth and he ordered them to begin their preaching to the lost ones among the house of Israel and not to start on the Gentiles or the Samaritans.

"Tell them," said Jesus, "that the kingdom of God is available. Heal the sick, cleanse the lepers, raise the dead, and cast out the demons that cause mental illness. You have received abundantly yourselves; so give abundantly of yourselves.

"Don't take a lot of baggage or worry about money. Let the people you serve help you and pay your way. When you visit a community learn of a good family and stay with them.

"If you enter a home and you are graciously received, bless that home, but if they should shun you, leave the place alone. When you leave give the discourteous people the sign of your displeasure, which is shaking your feet at them. What's more, if a place treats you poorly the Lord himself will tend to that place in the day of judgment.

"I know," continued Jesus, "about the problems you will face. You are as sheep being thrown to the wolves; so be as wise and understanding as possible, and be yourself as harmless as doves.

"You need to be careful with legalistic type men. These men will trap you into statements that will get you brought before the church court, and they will send you to jail or beat you, and all because of me. You will even possibly be delivered to governors or kings, which you must use as an opportunity to witness. When these occasions arise don't worry then about what to say as I shall see that you are inspired in your speech, for the spirit of God will come upon you at such times.

"This announcement of the kingdom which you are making is a whole new ball game in this world and it shall cause much strife so that families will be divided in their opinions and children shall even oppose their elders and death will come to many because of this, and you and your kind will be hated, but the faithful will be amply rewarded in the end.

[1]Son of Alphaeus

"Don't hesitate to run. If they get after you too hotly in one city run full speed to another and there will still be places to go and proclaim the gospel even when I come the second time.

"Don't let all the devilish people bother you in your faith. Even though they do not know it, they are all servants of God. In time God will attend to the disciples of the devil and the things they are getting by with now will be brought up against them.

"Even though all I say is not clear to you at first, preach what I teach you and light will begin to come, for you and the hearers.

"Don't be anxious about those who try to make life tough for you or who want to whip you; they can do only limited harm. The real danger is the one who can influence your inner thoughts and desires, for this can lead to destruction of body and soul.

"The sparrows that you see are considered almost worthless by man, but God knows when even one is lost. In fact the very hairs of your head are numbered; so don't be afraid of life, for God considers you of great value.

"Be certain that anyone who testifies of me before other people will find that I will testify for him in the day of judgment, and he who ridicules me or rejects me before men, the same person will find me not knowing him when he appears before my Father.

"The revolutionary teaching that I proclaim is not always a peaceful matter, for it will cause divisions among people, and great arguments, and violence. In fact, a person who chooses his own family or friends in preference to me is not worthy of me.

"To be worthy of me a person must assume great responsibilities, but a person who looks out only for himself shall lose his life, but he that is willing to give up his own interests in my behalf shall find a new and wonderful life.

"Anyone who receives graciously a person who speaks forth for God shall receive the same reward as the prophet receives. There shall even be rewards for those who do as little as give a cup of cold water to a child, provided it is given with a good attitude."

Chap.

11

After giving these instructions to the group at the leadership school, Jesus departed and began teaching and preaching on his own.

John the Baptist was at this time in prison and he began to wonder about the kingdom and what he was doing in jail; so he asked two men to go to Christ and make sure that he had baptized the real messiah.

"Are you the true savior that was to come or not?" bluntly asked one of the men when the two saw Christ.

"Stay around a few days," said Jesus, "and then go and tell John that you have seen blind receive their sight, and the lame walk, that you have seen lepers cleansed, the deaf to hear, the dead raised, and the disadvantaged have had the good news preached to them. You have my blessing if you understand this and relate it properly."

After the two men left, Jesus turned to the multitude and talked to them asking them about their relationship with John the Baptist.

"What did you expect to see," asked Christ, "when you all went into the wilderness? The wind blowing the reeds? or did you expect to see a fancy dude? or maybe a prophet? I tell you, when you saw John the Baptist you saw more than a prophet. For you saw the one of whom it is written 'Behold I send my messenger before thy face, who shall prepare the way for you.'

"I tell you people, that of all the people that were ever born or will ever be born, there is none greater than John the Baptist. Yet even his greatness is nothing compared to that provided in the kingdom of heaven.

"Nothing will ever be settled until the words of the prophets and of John have been fulfilled.

"Do you know what you really resemble? You are similar to children playing games. You don't seem to understand at all the real purpose in life.

"For instance, John came observing all the correctness of liturgy and strict obedience to custom, and you called him a fanatic, and the son of man came enjoying life, and you call him such names as 'big-eater,' 'wine drinker,' and a friend of ruffians. It takes a long time for wisdom, though, to assert itself."

Jesus then began to rebuke places where his preaching had produced such meager results.

"Woe unto you, Baltimore,[1] and woe unto you Los Angeles,[2] for if the great works which were done in your cities had been in Kerrville[3] or Citronelle,[4] they would have reformed. I tell you Kerrville and Citronelle will be a lot better off in the day of judgment.

"And New York,[5] which is exalted to the skies, will be brought to nothing, for if the mighty works done there had been done in Madrid,[6] it would survive, but I tell you it will go better for Citronelle in the day of judgment than for New York."

This brought on a batch of questions, in answer to one of which Jesus said, "I am thankful to God that He has chosen to hide many things from the intellectuals and yet revealed many of these things to simple people. I know the Father knew what He was doing.

"The Father has revealed all things to me. No one really knows me except God, and no one really knows God except me, and then to those to whom I reveal the Father.

[1]Chorazin
[2]Bethsaida
[3]Tyre
[4]Sidon
[5]Capernaum
[6]Sodom

"Come to me all of you who are worn out and frustrated, and I will give you rest. Take my responsibilities upon you, learn of me, for I am simple and not difficult to know, and in me you will find great satisfaction, for my obligations are easy and my requirements are not too tough."

Not long after this Jesus was walking with his disciples on Sunday and as they passed through a corn field some of the disciples picked a few ears to eat.[1] When this was called to the attention of the technical churchmen they immediately noted that this violated the law of the Sabbath day and they called this to Jesus' attention.

"What about David? Is it not recorded that David and those with him ate on the Sabbath when they were hungry? In fact he even went and ate the communion bread that was in the church.

"Did you also not know that on the Sabbath priests could do as they wished in the sanctuary?

"I must tell you that my presence here makes this a more important place than the temple. On top of all this, if you knew what God meant when he said 'I prefer mercy to sacrifice' you would not be blaming these guiltless men.

"In fact I am the Lord of the Sabbath day."

A few minutes after this Christ entered one of the synagogues and there was a man there with a deformed hand, and so these same precise-minded men asked Christ if it was in order to heal people on the sabbath day.

"Let me answer you with an illustration," said Christ. "What man among you, if he had one sheep and that sheep falls into a pit on Sunday will not get to work and lift the sheep out? Actually, it is perfectly proper to do good things on the sabbath day."

Following these remarks, Christ turned to the crippled man and said, "Stick out your hand."

The man obeyed and the hand became perfectly normal.

This sent the technical churchmen into a committee meeting, to devise strategy to get rid of Jesus.

Jesus then left the immediate area and many people followed him, and he continued to heal and to help, but he again asked the people not to make a big thing over the healing.

This also was a fulfillment of the prophecy which said, "My chosen one, in whom I am greatly pleased, shall possess my spirit, and he shall be helpful even to the Gentiles, and he shall not be contentious, nor a great complainer, nor shall he be a big voice in the streets. He will not so much as bruise a reed or play pranks, but he shall in the end be victorious. The Gentiles will learn to trust him."

There was then brought to him a person who was deaf, dumb,

[1]Perfectly legal.

and blind, and Jesus healed him, and saw that all his senses were restored.

The people were amazed and began to ask if this was the son of David, the long awaited messiah.

Some of the more skeptical church leaders, however, expressed the idea that it took a devil to handle a devil. Jesus sensed their opposition and their feelings and spoke to them saying, "Every organization that is divided against itself will fold up, and the same goes for a city or a family. If the devil casts out the devils, then Satan is divided against himself; so how then shall Satan's kingdom survive? If I cast the devils out by the power of Satan, what power do you use to get the job done? These very acts and attempts of yours stand in judgment against you.

"But if I heal by the power and spirit of God, then you should recognize that the kingdom of God has come close to you.

"It's just like taking over a strong man's house. The first thing you'd better do is bind the strong, then you can have his house. In other words, if you're not with me, you're against me, and if you are not working with me you're wasting your time.

"All manner of sins will be forgiven, but refusal of anyone to recognize or accept in any way the spirit of God, such a one is in a hopeless condition, for he has closed off the chance for light.

"It is quite simple. A tree must be made good to bring forth good fruit, while the corrupt tree brings forth contaminated fruit. A tree then is known by its fruit.

"The trouble with you hate mongers is that you are evil, and therefore have no chance of speaking good, for the mouth finally gives forth the contents of the heart.

"In people, then, a good man brings about good things while a bad man brings about trouble, strife and pain.

"Watch your lip, for every careless word that you speak will be mentioned at the time of judgment, for this will be one basis for judgment."

"Why don't you show us some private wonder or fantastic miracle?" asked a representative from the church study committee.

"Only agnostics seek a sign, but there shall be no sign more than those already given, such as in the account of Jonah. Jonah was 3 days and 3 nights in the whale and the son of man shall be 3 days and 3 nights hidden from those on earth. The men of Nineveh who repented will be able to criticize the present generation; for they repented at Nineveh and you are not repenting, and one greater than Jonah is here preaching to you.

"The Queen of Sheba could easily criticize you fellows, for she came all the way from the deep south to listen to Solomon, and you have a chance now to listen to one greater than Solomon.

"Repentance, however, is not enough by itself. It is like a man who has cleaned all the trash out of his house and he simply makes more room for dirt; so that the last state of the man is worse than the first. Repent, and then work, or you will be one of the wicked generation."

While Jesus was talking to these people a messenger came and told him that his mother and brothers were outside waiting to see him.

Jesus said "Who is my mother? and who are my brothers?" So saying he stretched forth his arms to all the people and said, "See, you are my mother and my brothers, for whoever does the will of my father immediately becomes my mother, or my sister, or my brother."

Chap.
13

That very day Jesus went out and sat by the seaside but the people crowded around him so he couldn't see the water so he got in a dinghy boat and talked from there to the people sitting on the shore. Jesus told the people stories that were really glimpses of the way life operates.

For instance, he said that there was a man once upon a time who went forth to plant seed and he scattered the seed in every direction, being a kind of love life type. Consequently some seeds fell by the wayside and the sparrows, red birds, and titmouse types had a ball.

Some of the seed fell on stones where there was no dirt and although the seeds sprouted there was no place for the roots so the sun scorched them and they perished.

Some of the seeds fell among thorns and Johnson grass and were choked without a chance. Some of the seed fell on good ground and grew and brought forth good fruit, the amount depending on the quality of the soil.

Jesus suggested to the listeners that they do a little thinking about the story.

Some of the disciples, knowing nothing at all about teaching, criticized Jesus for telling stories and asking people to think for themselves as they wanted Christ to simply give them a factual manual.

Christ reminded the disciples that merely because they had had an opportunity to learn by association and divine inspiration, that this is not available to everybody. Christ even cautioned them that spiritual knowledge must be increased and one who becomes satisfied with his own soul's progress stands in danger of losing all.

Jesus explained that not everyone has an open mind or is receptive to organized teaching, but that most people will listen to a story, and then some day it may soak in and be meaningful. Jesus reminded them that this was what the prophets had long ago said would be the case.

Jesus said that he was sympathetic to these people and understanding of them, for they had predetermined not to listen or change, and only subtle teaching would begin to make a dent. Just be thankful for your open-mindedness and your willingness to learn.

In fact, you have no idea how fortunate you are. During all the history of the whole world there will be only you few who will see the things you will see and directly hear my words, and the prophets and righteous men of old have yearned for this and many to come will wish they could have been in your sandals.

Take this story that I have just told of the sower. The seed is the word, the good news of God's love and care, but it is snatched away from some because they pay no mind to its presence.

There are those who receive the word and it seems worth keeping, but hardheadedness, and custom, and convenience give it no place to grow, and it dies for lack of depth, for it cannot stand any adversity or pressure.

Then there are those who receive the word but they're enmeshed in too many pleasures. The ball games, golf, girls on the beach, boat trailers, bowling leagues, bunny girls, and if you have all these at once it is difficult for the word to grow.

Now when the word finds a person who will provide an opportunity for growth, then the word becomes predominant, and great things begin to happen, depending on the native talents of the receiver of the word.

"Master, what is the kingdom of heaven like?" asked one of the group.

"Well," Christ said, "since we're talking about seed, it is like a man who plowed a field and sowed good seed in it, but while his fence riders were smoking and drinking coffee or goofing off an enemy came and sowed some sorry seed in the field.

"When the crop began to grow it was obvious that there were lots of weeds among the good fruit trees.

"The servants came then to the master and said that something was rotten in Denmark, for the field was full of both good trees and sorry stuff. The owner immediately knew that Pedro's bad boy had done this.

"The servants suggested that they go at once and pull up all the bad young shoots.

"The wise owner said 'No. Just let things ride. Perhaps you may mistake a good young shoot for a dead one. Wait until they grow to full manhood and are producing fruit, then I'll tell you to gather the unproductive and burn them, but the others will come into my kingdom.' "

"You mean that's all there is to the kingdom, Master?" asked another.

"No," Jesus replied, "for the kingdom has many aspects, one is like a mustard seed which a man took and planted in his field. As you know it is the smallest and least likely looking seed of them all, but give it time and it grows and it becomes a huge tree, and the birds light in it, and gives protecting shade.

"I'll tell you another thing about the kingdom of heaven. It is like a small dash of flavoring or a leaven which a cook puts in meal and before long the whole barrel of meal is tasty."

Jesus spoke thus simply to the people and he did not confuse or confound them, or leave them with charts or diagrams. All this too was fulfillment of the prophecies of old.

After this Jesus dismissed the crowd and went indoors with the disciples. One of the disciples said "Master, we aren't much on thinking ourselves. How about explaining the story about the tares in case somebody asks us?"

"Well," Christ said, "the man who sowed the good seed is the Son of man, the planner and planter of life. The field is the world. The good seed are those who become the children of God and the weeds are the choosers of evil. The sower of the evil seed is the devilish ideas of evil. The harvest comes at the end of the world and the angels are the harvesters. As the weeds are gathered and burned so shall it be at the end of the world.

"The angels of the son of man shall go forth throughout all the universe and gather all things that are offensive and all workers of evil and they shall be destroyed in pain and agony.

The righteous shall then shine forth like the sun and shall be aware of being in the kingdom of the Father. Now you boys listen to that, let it sink in, and teach it."

"But not to end on a gruesome note," Christ continued. "Let me also point out to you that the kingdom of heaven is like treasure hidden in a cave or a field. A fellow one day finds this treasure, and he immediately sells all that he has and purchases the ground where the treasure is. You'll have to meditate a little with that one."

"But here's another. The kingdom of heaven is like a merchant who is a pearl expert and he wants to find the best one of all. One day he finds this wonderful pearl, so he gives up everything to get it. Of course, he knew what he wanted, and he knew it when he saw it.

"So much for the farmers and the merchants. Now you fishermen listen. The kingdom of heaven is like a net that is cast into the sea and brings in all kinds of fish. When the net is full it is dragged ashore. The good legal fish are kept and the suckers and rough fish are thrown away. That's the way it is going to be at the end. The angels at the end are going to sever the wicked from the just and the wicked shall be cast into eternal separation from God and goodness."

"Did you understand all that?" asked Jesus.

"We sure did," they replied.

"Then remember this," said Jesus, "everyone who is carefully instructed in this manner better start house cleaning, and separating the good things in his life and doing away with the evil."

Then Jesus left. A few days later he came to his own community and he began to teach Sunday School, and the people were astonished.

Some began saying such things as "How come he's so suddenly smart?" or "Isn't he the carpenter's son who married Mary?", "Isn't he the brother of James, Joe, and Si?" "Ain't he got sisters here, too?" "Who does he think he is to teach us?"

Jesus said, "A prophet may have great honor, but rarely at home."

Because of their lack of belief, Jesus did very few good works there, and he left soon.

Chap. 14

About this time King Herod, who had no great I.Q. and who was also basically insecure, heard of the fame of Jesus and decided that he was John the Baptist, raised from the dead and he was terrified. For it was Herod who had put John the Baptist in prison because John had accused Herod of trifling with another man's wife. Herod had not executed John for fear of the multitudes with whom John was popular.

At a big birthday party, however, Herodatus had her daughter Sluzzy do a special dance for Herod, which started with seven veils and ended with none. Herod immediately offered to pay well for the performance. Sluzzy asked her Mother, who was also her agent, what she should ask and the mother suggested the head of John the Baptist, without the body being attached.

Herod did not care for this arrangement, but everybody gave him the "you promised" routine and so he ordered John beheaded.

The disciples were permitted to have the body for burial, though the head of John was brought to Herod on a tray, making a very poor centerpiece.

When Jesus heard of this he went apart in sorrow, but the multitudes followed him anyway. When Jesus saw the crowds again he had compassion on them, and healed many.

As the day crept into later afternoon some of the disciples began to get hungry and suggested that there be a break for the people to return to their homes for food and to provide the disciples a chance to eat without a bunch of hungry people staring at them.

Jesus said "Feed them."

"But, Master," said one of the disciples, "the only one who has offered to share is a small boy with a small lunch of corn bread sticks and sardines."

"Bring these to me," said Jesus.

Then Jesus turned to the crowd and said that they should sit down and be comfortable and then Jesus took the small lunch and blessed it, and gave some portion to each of the disciples and told them to pass the food among the people. Everyone ate and was satisfied and the litter bug representative from each of the twelve tribes went about and collected the refuse and leftovers. There were about 5,000 people including the women and the children at this gathering.

Jesus then asked the disciples to row themselves across the lake and leave him to himself. Jesus then dismissed the multitudes and went apart into one of the hills to pray and be alone.

The disciples, however, began to have trouble with their dinghy as the waves arose and the boat began to ship water. Knowing of the storm and their distress, late in the night, Jesus walked on the water to their aid. When the disciples saw Jesus walking on the water it scared the very goose grease out of them.

Jesus spoke calmly unto them however saying "Cheer up. It is I. There is no reason to be afraid."

Peter said, "If it is really you, let me walk on the water, too, that's bound to be something else!"

And Jesus said, "Come."

Peter climbed out of the boat and began to walk on the water, for of course he could not swim. After taking a few steps though he began to see the waves and the white caps and said to himself 'I must be nuts'; so he began to sink, calling forth to Christ "Save me, save me!"

Immediately Jesus stretched forth his hand and lifted him saying "How short-lived your faith is and why do you doubt so the presence of my power?"

As Jesus entered the ship the sea began to subside. The disciples were awed at this incident and they used this as an occasion for worship.

The boat finally landed at St. Petersburg[1] and when the word of Christ's presence became known all the elderly, and infirm, and diseased trooped into the area, and some only seeking to touch the hem of his garment. As many as touched him or received his touch were made whole.

Chap.

15

Then there came to Jesus certain manual-minded churchmen of some importance in Jerusalem and they asked Christ, saying, "Why is it that some of your followers do not observe all our traditions or adhere to our styles? In fact, some of them eat without washing their hands."

[1]Gennesaret

"Why do you, my good fellows, fail to pattern your styles and traditions on the commandments of God?" said Jesus. "For instance, God said to honor your father and mother, and that it was a sin even unto death to use your parents for your own good. Yet you have developed a tradition that makes gifts to your parents tax deductible. You have even paid sums or made arrangements with your parents to be free of them; so you have developed a tradition contrary to the spirit of the commandment of God. No wonder that wise prophet Isaiah said of people similar to you, that you draw near to God with your mouth, and you speak beautiful phrases of worship, but your heart is far from God. What you do is teach the regulations of man as if they were the doctrines of God."

Then Jesus moved his place of teaching so that he might speak to the multitudes and he taught them many interesting things.

"For instance," said Christ "it is not that which goes into a man's mouth that causes trouble, but what comes out of it."

Immediately some of the disciples came forward and said "Master, you've made a lot of the leadership school graduates unhappy."

"Don't worry, boys," said Christ "every plant that my heavenly father has planted shall not be disrupted. Just don't worry about misinformed or prejudiced people. It is like the blind leading the blind, and ususally the whole bunch falls in a ditch."

"I don't understand what you mean," said Peter.

"Well, Peter, certainly you understand that if you eat spinach, chew it and digest it, then you later excrete it, and no harm is done. This is natural and the plan of God. If you gulp it down and then in misery later spit it out, this is a harmful thing to you and others. If you receive an evil thought then, swallow it and let it go through you and pass away. Evil thoughts, however, of murders, adulteries, thefts, false witnesses, and blasphemies, if you keep and dwell on these things will defile a person. Now isn't it kind of silly to worry about washing your hands before meals?"

Jesus then left this area and went into the cities of Tyre and Sidon where there was much slave trading. While there a woman came to Jesus in great distress and said that her daughter was a really mixed up kid. Jesus paid no attention to her.

In a few minutes the disciples came to Christ and asked him to please get rid of the woman as she was driving them nuts.

"At present, I am only working with the lost sheep of the house of Israel," replied Christ.

The woman would not be driven away and she implored Christ to help and she prayed to him.

"Why should I give bread prepared for the special people to dogs?" asked Christ.

"Dogs must live also, Master, even if it be the crumbs of the tables," said the woman.

"Gracious lady," said Christ, "your faith is exceedingly great. Your request is fulfilled and your daughter is even now free of her difficulty."

Jesus then left this area and returned to the sea of Galilee, and climbed a small hill on the seacoast and sat down.

Great multitudes soon began to gather, a vast number of the blind, the dumb, the crippled and many others, and they implored Jesus to help them, and he healed them.

The curious crowds were astonished when they saw the blind receive their sight, the lame walk, and they heard the dumb speak; and many began to glorify the God of Israel.

Then Jesus summoned his disciples to him and said that he was sorry for these poor people, many of whom had not eaten for three days as they were often too far from their homes or villages to get food.

One of the disciples said, "But, Master, you certainly don't expect our little itinerant church to feed this gang."

Jesus said, "How much food do you have for yourselves?"

"Seven loaves of bread and a fair size string of fish," replied the treasurer.

Jesus then requested the multitude to sit down and he took the loaves and the fishes and he blessed them and then asked his disciples to begin to distribute them among the people. Everyone present managed to get something to eat and the girl scouts cleaned up the litter which filled about seven baskets.

There were about 4,000 people present and he dismissed them and then entered one of the little boats and journeyed to Point Clear, Alabama.[1]

Chap.
16

Once again some of the more professionally minded among the church leaders came to Christ and asked him for some great flashy show of his power.

In a rather droll manner Jesus spoke to them saying, "When you look up at twilight and see a red sky, you say 'it's going to be a pretty day tomorrow.' Then when morning comes you say that the sky is getting red and dropping and that it will soon storm. How stupid can you get? You can read the signs of weather and not the signs of life which is all around you.

The wicked and the evil want their kind of sign, but the sign that has been given was the sign of the prophet Jonah." Jesus then left them and with the disciples crossed the sea of Galilee.

When the group arrived on the other side it suddenly occurred

[1]Magdala

to them that no one had thought to bring the lunch.

Jesus said to them, "Don't fall for the subtle teachings of the know-it-all crowd."

The disciples then began to discuss among themselves what Jesus meant, and also what they were going to do about lunch.

Jesus listened a bit in amusement and then said, "What little faith you have. You're worrying about lunch when only a few days ago we fed 5,000 people. Or what about the time we fed the 4,000? Don't you understand? I'm not a baker talking about bread, evaluating the whole wheat against the rye, I'm telling you to beware of the doctrines of the know-it-alls. Some of you just think about eating too much."

Later in the week Jesus and his disciples journeyed to New York[1] and while sitting there gazing out on the water pensively he turned to the disciples and said, "Who do men around generally say that I, the son of man, am?"

"I have heard some say you are John the Baptist returned from the dead," said one of them.

"I hear some say you are Elijah returned," replied another.

"I've heard people say you were Jeremiah or one of the other prophets," said Matthew.

"Whom do you say that I am?" asked Christ.

Peter immediately spoke forth and said, "Thou art the Christ, the son of the living God."

"Blessings on you, Peter," said Christ, "for you did not reason this out for yourself, but it was revealed to you by the Lord himself. You have made a fundamental statement. It connects you with the basis of the kingdom, for upon this truth the very church of Christ shall be built and its progress shall be such that as it moves on its way and no gates of evil can ever eventually stop its triumphant progress."

"Furthermore," continued Christ, "I give unto all of you who stand on this truth the privilege of opening this way and this kingdom to others, and I will support your promises in my name in the kingdom that is mine, and I will refute those who refute your witness."

"At present, however," Christ said, "you are not to announce that I am the son of God, and the Saviour of the world."

Following this teaching session Jesus began to gradually reveal to his disciples how the kingdom must begin and make its laborious progress. He pointed out that he must be arrested in Jerusalem, and suffer many abuses before the church courts, and be killed, and to be raised from the dead.

Peter immediately objected to this and said that no one would harm Christ as long as Peter was on hand to fight.

"Don't tempt me, Peter. This is the way of violence and evil and

[1]Capernaum

is self-destructive. You are talking like an ordinary man and not as one who is beginning to draw near to God."

Jesus then turned to all of the disciples and said, "If you are to follow me you must learn self-control, and you must select problems to solve and burdens to carry. The more of your own self-interests you give up the more of a real life you will find, if you do this for my sake. How useless for a man to gain the whole world and lose himself. Who in his right mind would trade his very soul for anything?

"For one of these days the son of man shall come in a great blaze of magnificent glory of the Lord himself, and with a host of angels, and then everyone will be rewarded according to his works. In fact, some of you standing here will so grow in your lifetime in this available kingdom that death will have no recognition to you for you shall join me as naturally as if we meet on the street."

Chap.
17

About a week later[1] Jesus took Peter, James and John apart from the others and they went up on top of a hill and the appearance of Christ became completely spiritual so that his face shone as a bright light and his garments white as bright snow, and there appeared on either side of him Moses and Elijah and they talked with Christ.

Then Peter said, "Lord, this is a tremendous experience for us. Let us make three historical markers here, one for you, and one for Moses, and one of Elijah."

Even as Peter finished speaking, however, a bright cloud descended close overhead and a voice from the cloud said, "This is my beloved son, in whom I am well pleased, hear him."

This scared the willie-nillie out of the disciples and they fell on their faces.

Jesus said, "Get up boys and don't panic." And when they arose there remained only Jesus, and he was returned to his terrestrial body.

As they were coming down the mountain Jesus instructed them to tell this account to no one until after his resurrection.

One of the disciples then said, "But we were always taught that Elijah had to come again before the Messiah and restore order in preparation."

"Well, actually," said Jesus, "he did come and very few paid any attention to him and they booted him about something awful. The same type of thing shall happen to me also."

The disciples then understood that John the Baptist had been the man to whom he referred.

When Jesus arrived at the bottom of the hill a man came to him

[1]I sometimes think Christ did a little fishing for a few days.

and said that his son was nutty and that the disciples had not been able to help at all.

Jesus then said somewhat sadly, "How long does it take for you fellows to learn? I wonder sometimes if you'll ever graduate. Bring the boy to me."

Jesus dealt immediately with the problem that had the boy confused and he left Jesus completely cured.

Promptly one of the disciples came up and said, "Why couldn't one of us do that?"

"There are two reasons," Christ replied. "In the first place you do not have enough faith. You still have lingering doubts. If you had the pure faith of a mustard seed you could move mountains. Nothing is impossible with the pure power of God.

"In the second place, however, this type of mental ailment is most difficult and can be cured only by prayer and great willingness for self-sacrifice."

Later in the week as they were sitting by the shores of Galilee Jesus suddenly said to them, "I am going to be betrayed into the hands of men and they shall kill me, but I shall arise on the third day."

The disciples were exceedingly sorrowed by this, for they were not prepared to accept the glory of the resurrection promise.

After this, the group came again to Key West and the Internal Revenue man came to Peter and asked if Christ had paid his taxes.

Peter said, "Yes, he has paid his taxes."[1]

When they came indoors, Christ said to Peter, "What do you think? Do tax collectors collect from their own children or from strangers?"

Peter said, "They collect from strangers."

"Then the children are free," said Christ. "But, Peter, let us not offend the system, even if it be a bit stupid or irregular. Go down to the water's edge and cast your hook into the sea and reel in the first fish that strikes, no matter how small. When you open the mouth of this fish to get your hook you will find a coin. Take the coin to the Internal Revenue and pay both our taxes."

Chap. 18

The disciples then came to Jesus and said, "Do they have elections in the kingdom of heaven? Who gets to be the greatest?"

And Jesus seeing a little child nearby called to him and let him stand in the midst of the disciples and said, "Greatness has no place in the kingdom of heaven. In fact, until you develop a simple, trusting attitude as this little child you can't even get into the kingdom. Once, however, you have mastered the humble simplicity of a little child, you are then already great.

[1] I think Peter was trying to be protective.

"Incidentally, be particularly noticeable of the young. When you interest a young one in me you are blessed by me, but if your example misleads a young person who already has started on the road with me, it would be better for you to have a bank vault tied around your neck and for you then to be thrown in the deepest part of the ocean.

"Now I know that difficulties will arise in the world, but woe to those that deliberately cause them. I would suggest strongly then that if you have a bad habit, get rid of it, don't explain it. It would be better to be one legged than always kicking old ladies in the shins.

"If you have an eye that sees evil and desires it, it would be better to have it removed, than to let it contaminate your whole being.

"Let me then emphasize this matter of the very young and innocent. Each one of them has an angel close to the Father, watching each of them. I am here to save everyone that might be lost.

"I can tell you don't understand me very clearly. Let me put it this way. If a man has a hundred sheep and one of them strays away, doesn't he leave the 99 and go into the hills and seek the lost one? And if he finds that sheep he rejoices greatly and is far more excited over the finding of the lost one than over the 99 that are safe. I tell you, the Father in heaven, is exceedingly anxious to save each one that goes astray.

"Let me make now a practical suggestion about dealing with people. If a person has wronged you do not publicly denounce him or talk about him, but go to him privately and discuss the error. If this doesn't do any good go again with one or two others and seek to reason with the man.

"If it is a reasonably grievous error, and he will not listen to any of you, then report the matter to the church. If you handle this man in this considerate way and prayerfully pronounce judgment, your judgment shall be supported in the kingdom of heaven.

"It might also interest you to know that if two of you conscientiously and unselfishly agree on a matter and shall go to the Father, the matter will be handled. For where two or three are gathered in my name in pure worship, I am there."

Peter then said, "Master, I'm a little quick with my temper. You have told me to learn to forgive a man's offense against me. Wouldn't forgiving him about 7 times be enough?"

"No, Peter. It would be nearer seventy time seven, and since you don't know your multiplication table very well, I'm saying you never quit forgiving.

"There is so much to tell you about the kingdom of heaven. For instance, it is in a way like a king who decided to run a security test on his servants. In checking he found that one of his servants owed him $11,500 and had never even paid any interest.

"The king then said, 'We'll just sell him and his family and get what we can out of the deal and be rid of him.'

"The servant than begged the king to keep him and promised to begin to repay the loan; so the king had compassion on him and said, 'I'll just forgive the whole debt and let you start all over again.'

"That same servant, however, went out and found a maintenance man who owed him $10, and he took him by the throat and demanded his money. The poor man did not have $10 and he fell down and pleaded with the servant for mercy and told him that he would shortly be able to pay. The servant, however, had the maintenance man cast into prison.

"Some of the other workers came and reported this to the king and the king sent for the servant and he chewed him out saying, 'You are a bitter ole baddy, and a bum. I forgave you all you owed and you immediately exercised punishment instead of compassion on your debtor. To put it mildly I'm mad. I'm turning you over to the toughest collecting agency in town until you've paid back every cent.'

"Now, boys, if you from your hearts do not forgive everyone their trespasses my Father in heaven is going to deal with you like the king did with the mean servant."

Chap.

19

Jesus then took another trip, this time going around the sea of Galilee and crossing the Jordan and coming to the coast of Sea Island, Georgia.[1] As usual, great multitudes followed him and he healed them of their infirmities.

This non-structured approach to religion kept bugging a lot of the liturgically frozen churchmen and so they devised some trick questions, one of them being, 'Is it lawful for a man to put away his wife for just any ole reason?'

Jesus answered them and said, "You are trying to make a specific out of a generality. Do you not know that God in the very beginning made men and women, and he didn't make them alike, but he did make them to complement each other. When a man and a woman marry they establish a new basic unit of life, which is a family, even if they have no children. If this marriage is entered into properly, under God's guidance and blessing, he makes one unit of the two, and what God has put together man should make no effort to break it apart."

"Well, then," said one of the more crummy ones, "why did Moses give permission for a man to write a bill of divorcement?"

[1]Judea

"It was because of expediency. Moses didn't want some fine ladies to have to live with some of you pig-headed and hardhearted characters. Even so, this divorce business is not the general intent of the Lord in the beginning. In fact, unless your wife is completely unfaithful to you, you should stick together. If an unfaithful partner moves around marrying others, the unfaithfulness is contaminating to any with whom an unfaithfully divorced person may marry."

"Since a man may not always know about such things, is it better not to get married at all?" asked one of the disciples.

"The generality I have given you cannot be specifically applied to everyone. Some people, for instance, will not even understand what I'm talking about. Did you not know that there are some men who are born impotent and some women frigid? Did you not know that there are some men who are made impotent by violent, or punitive, or sometimes well intentioned but misguided men? The idea is for everyone to strive as best he can in his own capacity and knowledge, and more earnestly toward the kingdom of God."

A nursery school teacher saw Christ and immediately brought the children to him while she went for coffee. The disciples tried to disperse the children, but Jesus said, "Permit them to come to me, for these represent the innocence and freedom of the kingdom of heaven."

Christ then touched each one in turn and blessed them.

Not long after this a rather important type of person came to Jesus and said, "Good teacher, I am enjoying life. What can I do to live forever?"

"First be careful with semantics. There is none completely good except God. As a starter though, you might keep the commandments of God."

"Which ones do I have to keep?"

"You must not commit murder, or adultery, or steal, or lie, you must respect the family unit as represented by your mother and father, and should be as concerned for your neighbor as you are for yourself."

"I have observed everyone of these things from the time I was a small boy."[1]

Jesus then said, "You are almost perfect and ready for eternal life. Go home, sell all your stock, give away your golf clubs, dismiss your servants, and turn your savings account over to the church, get your toothbrush and hair brush and follow me."

The young man left greatly depressed, for he was in a high tax bracket.

Jesus then said to his disciples, "I feel deeply sorry for the rich for it is more difficult for them to enter the kingdom than for others, for they have so much to sacrifice. It is as difficult as for a camel,

---

[1]Personal opinion—he had forgotten the one on telling a lie.

who doesn't like to kneel anyway, to get on his knees and crawl through a small slit in a wall.[1]

When the disciples heard this they were amazed[2] and said, "Who then can be saved?"

Jesus said, "Don't worry about the details, just be certain that nothing is impossible with God, though many things seem impossible to men."

Then Peter said, "We have given up our fishing, our beer parties, everything, and we have followed you. What's in it for us?"

"For you who have followed me," said Christ, "in re-creation time when I shall sit on my throne of glory, you shall have thrones of judgment of your own, and everybody else, now and in the future who has forsaken his plans, or his family ties, or lands, or business opportunities for my sake shall receive 100 percent reward and everlasting life.

"But there are some folks who think they are at the top who are going to be at the bottom, and some of those judged inconsequential by man shall be very high in my eternal kingdom."

Chap.

20

"Fellows, the kingdom of heaven about which you are so curious is different, and I know it is hard for you to understand. For instance, it is like the owner of a big vineyard and when he noticed that the grapes were ripe he went to the employment office in town and inquired about laborers. He agreed to pay each one $10.00 for the day's work. A few hours later the owner realized that there were not enough laborers and the grapes would spoil and so he went back to town to hire more laborers. The owner promised to give the laborers what he thought was right, and so some more men went to work.

"The owner came to town again when there was only a little over an hour left for working and he saw some men idle.

"The owner said, 'Why are you not working?'

" 'Nobody has offered us a job,' they replied.

" 'Well, come with me to my vineyard and work what time is left and I'll pay you what I consider right.' The men then came to work.

"At the end of the day the laborers lined up to receive their pay and the lord of the vineyard instructed the treasurer to pay each man $10.00 apiece, from the first to the last.

"When the men who had worked all day perceived that they received the same reward as those who had worked only one hour, they immediately began to gripe to high heaven, form unions, and denounce the lord of the vineyard.

[1] Scholars like to play with this. Help yourself.
[2] They did not know any scholars.

"The lord of the vineyard calmly spoke to them saying, 'Friend, I acted only according to our agreement. I fulfilled my agreement with you. If I want to deal equally with others in my own way what affair is it of yours? Simply because you make selfish distinctions is no reason for me to do so. I tell you it is difficult to understand the spirit of the kingdom of heaven.' "

Jesus and the disciples then headed for Jerusalem and enroute they stopped at a Dairy Queen and chatted. Jesus said to them at this time. "We are going to Jerusalem. I will be betrayed and placed at the questionable mercy of the church courts and they shall see that I am condemned to die. They will, of course, arrange for the Gentiles to do this, and I shall be beaten, and crucified, but I shall arise again."

As they drew nearer to Jerusalem they passed near the home of Mr. Smith,[1] and Mrs. Smith, the mother of James and John, came to Christ and knelt at his feet and said, "I know you are going to be a king. My two sons are good boys and I want you to let them have little thrones, one on each side of you."

Jesus said, "Typical mother, you don't have any idea of what you are asking or what is good for your sons."

Jesus turned to James and John then and asked, "Are you able to take the type of punishment that will be mine or be submerged into the dark waters of death that shall be mine?"

The brothers answered together, "We certainly are."

"All right, you asked for it and you shall get it, you will be discomforted and persecuted, but the relative positions in the kingdom of heaven are in the hands of the Father; so forget that."

The other disciples, of course, didn't like this attempt at promotion,[2] but Jesus comforted them and calmed them down saying, "Every day and age has its establishment of authority, and promotions, and power structures, but it is not to be that way among you and my true followers. If a man among you wants to be great let him be a person of service, and the more you serve the nearer you come to being a chief."

"Just as with me. I did not come to be the recipient of kindness, but the extender of kindness, and to finally give my life in exchange for the lives of others."

The group continued on its journey and as they approached Jericho there were two blind men sitting by the wayside and they heard some of the people saying that Jesus was passing nearby. Immediately they began shouting, "O, Lord, thou son of David, have mercy on us." The crowd tried to make them hush, but Jesus stopped and called out to them saying, "What do you want me to do for you all?"

[1] Zebedee

[2] Probably had been wanting to ask themselves.

"Lord, open our eyes," they both said in unison; so Jesus had compassion on them and touched their eyes and immediately their eyes received sight, and they began to follow Jesus.

As they drew near to Jerusalem near the Mount of Olives just outside the city limits, Jesus told two of the disciples to go into one of the suburban markets and that they would find a burro and a donkey there tied near the market. Jesus told the men to untie them and bring them to him. Jesus also told them that if the owner or some busybody asked them what they were doing to simply tell them that the Lord had need of transportation.

All this was done to make valid the old prophecy that said that the Saviour would come in a simple manner, riding on a lowly beast of burden.

The disciples did as Jesus commanded and they placed their own garments on the two animals as a sign of their commitment and Jesus sat upon one of the animals and began his entrance into the city.

Many people began to throw their garments in his path, and to cut palm branches and place them on the road ahead of him.

The people then began to cheer him saying, "Hip-hip Hurrah!, Hail the King!," Blessed be the son of David!," "Great is he that cometh in the name of the Lord!"

And when Jesus came into the city of Jerusalem itself many people began to ask what in the deuce was going on and who in thunderation was this man that so many are cheering.[1]

Some of the people said, "This is Jesus, a prophet, who comes from Nazareth."

When Jesus came to where the temple was he went in and he denounced the people who were using the temple for their own gain, and he drove out the merchants, and overturned the tables of the money changers, and knocked down the booths of those that sold sacrifices and he said forcibly unto them, "It is decreed by God that my house shall be called a house of prayer and you have made it a den of theives."

Then came the lame and the blind into the temple to him and he healed them.

Many of the established church leaders saw the wonderful things that he did and they heard the people shouting his praises, even the children, and they didn't like this at all.

One of the more pompous types asked Jesus, "Do you hear what the children are yelling?"

"Yes," replied Jesus. "Have you never read that out of the mouths of babes and sucklings has God often produced wisdom and insight?"

[1]This was not during the football season.

Jesus then departed and left Jerusalem, going to Bethany, which was only a very short distance away.

In the morning Jesus returned to Jerusalem and on the way he passed a fig tree and decided to eat a fig. While examining the tree he found there was not a fig on it, and he spoke to the tree and said, "You're a fraud," and immediately the fig tree withered away.

When the disciples saw this they said to Jesus, "What goes on here?"

Jesus said, "I am still trying to teach you faith. Acutally, if you have enough faith you can not only wither a fig tree prematurely but you could move a mountain and cast it into the midst of the sea. In fact, all worthy things that you shall ask in real pure prayer, believing without blemish of duty, it will be done."

Jesus returned again this day to the temple and he began teaching some of the people that were there. Shortly some of the officers of the church came to him and asked if he had a teacher's certificate or a permit to teach.

Jesus said, "Let us exchange questions. I will tell you on what authority I teach and do things you have witnessed if you will tell me if the baptism of John was from heaven or from men."

The officers then called a study committee together and they reasoned that if they replied that the baptism of John was from heaven then they would have to explain why they did not believe John. If, however, we say the baptism of John was of men, the people will get sore and we won't be reelected church officers.

As a result they said to Jesus, "We cannot say."

"Then I will not tell you of the source of my authority, " replied Jesus.

"But let me give you fellows something to chew upon a bit. Let's suppose there was a man with two sons and he came to the first one and said, 'I want you to go and work in the vineyard,' but the son said he wouldn't go as he had a touch of bursitis. But shortly he changed his mind and went and worked hard in the vineyard.

"Then the father went to the second son and asked him to work and he said, 'Sure, Pop, I'll get right with it.' However, he didn't go at all.

"Now which of the two would you say did the will of his father?"

They immediately replied, "The first son."

"You think about this fellows, for I say there will be harlots, and despisers of religion, and thieves that will repent and enter the kingdom of heaven ahead of you. For John came and made a great number of the so-called wicked repent and they went to work, and you heard John and never changed a bit.

"Let me worry you with a little more thinking stuff. There was a man who had a big ranch, and a big vineyard, and a winepress, and he decided to go on an extended trip; so he built walls, and towers, and fortifications around the place and then left them under the care of an overseer.

"When the harvest time came, the owner sent three of his servants to bring back a portion of his fruit. The overseer beat up one of them, stoned another, and executed the third.

"This did not set very well with the owner so he sent a larger number of servants on the next fruit acquiring mission and they received the same treatment.

"Finally, the owner sent his son, thinking certainly he will be properly treated.

"When the overseer saw the son coming, however, he thought now is the chance for the big deal. We will kill the son, who is the only heir, and then the ranch and everything will be ours forever; so they took the son and killed him and threw him out of the vineyard.

"When the Lord of the vineyard himself comes, now what do you think will happen to the overseer and his helpers?"

"That's easy. He will miserably destroy the wicked overseer and his helpers and he will get somebody else to run his ranch."

"Don't you remember your scriptures? Do you remember the part about the stone which the builders rejected has become the foundation stone itself? This is the Lord's doing, and it is a mystery to you. But I tell you that the kingdom of God which you think you control will be taken from you and it will be given to the people who return the fruit to the owner.

"You may not understand this, either, but if you butt against the stone that is the foundation you'll be broken, and if it falls on you you'll be crushed."

It occurred, of course, to some of these phony purveyors of religion that Jesus was talking about them, but they were afraid to arrest him or attack him because the people supported Jesus and considered him a prophet.

Chap. 22

"There is so much to tell you men about the kingdom of heaven that I must continue to illustrate. It is, for instance, like a certain king that arranged for a marriage for his son and he sent his servants out to issue the invitations orally. Those first invited declined.[1] The king then sent forth another group of servants and told them to tell the people that he had already put the barbecue on, plus spareribs, and everything was ready for the wedding, but it seemed that there were other things to do, a ball game, a bird hunt, a big sale in the making, and some of the invited guests got sore at the servants for nagging them and punched some of them in the nose.

"Now this did not set well with the king and he sent first his own strong armed men to punish the violent ones, and then he sent other servants in to all various places of the world and invited them,

[1]Probably the husband came to the door.

disregarding their social status, or their behavior pattern, or their ethnic background, and many of these came to honor the occasion and marriage of the son.[1]

"One fellow, however, came just to eat and already had his napkin under his chin. The king said to him, 'What do you mean coming in here this way?' Being only interested in himself, he was dumbfounded.

"The king said, 'Throw him out. Bind him hand and foot and toss him into eternal separation from the place of the king, and he can join the others that are weeping and gnashing what teeth they have left.'

" 'You can see by this,' said the King, 'that eventually all will be invited, but not everyone by a long shot will come into the kingdom.' "

This caused some of the rigid minded churchmen to appoint a committee, whose purpose was to devise a way to trap Jesus into saying something illegal or anti-church.

Sometime later the committee sent a representative to join with one of the civic clubs that was going to question Jesus, the first question being subtly put,[2] "We know you are a true master teacher, that you teach the way of God absolutely accurately, and we also know that you are without prejudice, making no distinction between one person or another; now tell us, what do you really think, should we be paying all these taxes to that big stinker Caesar?"

Jesus, of course, saw through their cagey trap and he said, "Why are you phonies trying to get me into trouble? However, let me see one of the coins with which you pay taxes." They brought him a $5 gold piece.

Jesus said, "Whose picture is this on the coin, and whose mark of ownership is on the other side of it?"

They said, "Caesar's."

Jesus said, "Then it must be his. Give it to him, but give to God the things that are God's."

This answer flat stumped them, and they left mumbling in their beards.

The same day there came a committee from an organization that did not believe in the resurrection of the dead.

"Master, in case you didn't know it, Moses said that if a man die without having any children, his brother shall add the widow to his household and attempt to enable her to have children. Now we heard of a family that had seven brothers and the eldest died without children and left the widow to the second brother. The second brother died without children and left the widow to the third, the

[1]Could be the marriage of Christ to the One great Holy Church. [2]Possibly graduates of the Watergate experience.

third died and on down she went until all seven brothers were dead.[1] Finally the seven-times-a-widow died. You say there is a resurrection of the dead. If so, then whose wife shall she be in the resurrection?"

Jesus said, "You neither know the scriptures nor understand the power of God. Everyone in the resurrected world is an angel of the Lord in an incomprehensible type of freedom where the structures of marriage and such do not exist.

"But don't miss the point of the idea of the resurrection. Do you not know that God said I am the God of Abraham, and of Isaac and of Jacob? God is not the God of the dead, but of the living."

The people hearing this were absolutely astonished.

When the Phariss Liturgical Club had heard that the Sadducee No-Future Club had been baffled, the PLC group sent their lawyer to ensnarl him in a legality.

"Master," the lawyer graciously asked, "which is the most important law that we have?"

Jesus said to him, "That you shall love thy Lord thy God with all your heart and with all your soul and with all your mind, this is really the first and great commandment, but it is incomplete without the second which is that you are to love your neighbor as yourself."

Now the PLC group believed that a messiah, the Christ, was to come someday and that he would be a man, a descendant of David; so Christ turned to give the smart aleck a little dose of his own medicine,[2] and he said, "The Christ who is to come, whose son is he to be?"

"The son of David," one of them replied.

"How then do you account for the fact that David refers to him that shall come as his Lord, saying, 'The Lord said unto my Lord, sit on my right hand while I make your enemies your footstools.' If David then calls him Lord, how is he his son?"

No one could answer this. and they quit their questions.[3]

Chap.
23

Then Jesus spoke to the disciples and to the multitude and said, "Let me tell you something about the Pharisee Legalistic Group. They teach exactly properly the teachings of Moses so you listen to them and you do what they propose that you do, but just don't do like they do, for they do not practice what they preach.

"They assign extremely difficult tasks to good church members and do none of these things themselves. The only time one of them does something worthwhile he does it in order that he might receive some recognition. They also particularly care to adorn themselves with all manners of symbols of authority and distinction, and they like to sit at the head table and introduce the speaker, and they

---

[1]Sounds odd, but don't forget Peaches Browning. [2]For instructive purposes.
[3]I think one of the PLC suggested they better go and have a few beers.

particularly enjoy being called important titles such as 'Worthy Grand Arch Duke.'

"Actually there is only one great title and that is 'Father,' and that is for the Lord God himself, and similar unto it is the title 'Christ,' and that is reserved solely for me. But if you want greatness be one who serves, and if you want to be exalted be willing to do even the most menial of jobs and the Lord will tend to the exaltation.

"Really, I'm ashamed of some of you phoney intellectual church leaders. You confine the kingdom of heaven within such strict bounds that no one can get in and you don't even go in yourselves.

"You foreclose a mortgage on a poor widow's house and compensate for it by having a long prayer in her behalf.

"You search everywhere for someone dedicated in a different way and you connive to shift his dedication to your own silly framework, and the poor fellow winds up twice as bad as he was.

"You are a bunch of blind guides. A poor penitent person who binds a contract under oath in the temple you disregard, but if he puts up enough collateral you welcome him as a debtor.[1]

"Don't you know that truth is better than gold? You even determine guilt as innocence at the altar by the gold that is placed there. Do you think the gift is greater than the altar? Don't you nuts know that he that puts his confidence in the altar and in the temple is putting his trust in God?

"I grant that you do some good. You distribute some of the tithe money to the poor and do a little charity work, but you completely neglect the real important matters of justice and mercy and faith. You need to do both matters, neither to the neglect of the other.

"You goofs! You'll spend five hours debating an inconsequential matter at a church and then in two minutes decide to change the whole structure.

"I'll say one thing, you look good on the outside. Your ears are clean and the garments pressed, but inside you are a complete mess. Clean your hearts first, and then someday later send your shirt to the laundry.

"When I see you fellows I'm reminded of a cemetery. The outside is beautiful white marble, but under are decayed bones. Really, this beautiful outside is the way you appear to most men and you get by with it.

"You also are great ones for glorifying the prophets and you talk of how you would have prevented men like Jeremiah from being put into jail, but you are exact replicas of the people that did these things. I'm sorry really to say this to you, but you can go to hell!

[1]Kinda makes you think of some Banks.

"I send you prophets and teachers and writers and you crucify them, and beat them, and run them out of town. It is fellows like you who have caused all the violence since the slaying of Abel right up to the time last week you killed a man in the temple. Every generation can observe these things."

Then turning away a bit and looking lovingly at Jerusalem Jesus said, "O Jerusalem, Jerusalem, in whom the prophets and the teachers I have sent have been stoned, how often have I longed to magically gather you under my protection and care as a mother hen does her chicks, but you would not respond. How desolate you inevitably must be. Your chance has gone. The next time that I come it shall be in such power and glory that you shall call forth 'Blessed is He that cometh in the name of the Lord.'"

Chap.
24

Jesus then departed from the temple but the disciples took him and wanted to show him some of the other temples, and the new fellowship hall, the bell tower, the patio with the bird bath and Jesus then said to them, "None of these things will last forever."[1]

Later Jesus was sitting in one of his favorite spots, the Mount of Olives, and the disciples came to him and requested a private and executive session.

"Master," one of them said, "let us in on the real secret. When are all these things going to happen? What will be the sign, will we have fifteen minutes warning before the second coming and the end of the world?"

"Look, fellows," said Jesus, "don't be fooled or panicked by all this. There will be some claiming to be me, and there will be people who believe them.

"There are many years yet to come and much will happen; there will be wars and talks about wars; don't get all steamed up over such unfortunate things, for this is part of the road that people must travel to the end. Nation will rise against nation and combinations of nations against combinations of nations, and there will be famines and pests and pollution, and earthquakes, in various places. This is just almost only a beginning of the history of man.

"Many of my followers will be persecuted and killed, and many nations shall spurn and detest what you teach for my sake and in my name. There will be many who won't be able to stand the pressures, and they shall betray each other and become bitter against one another; and false prophets shall take advantage of the situation to glorify themselves and to deceive people. Wickedness shall often seem to be the predominant factor and those that are lukewarm in any cause will fail, but those who are faithful shall be saved.

"It is going to take quite awhile though, as the good news of the

[1]My interpretation:"don't be too proud of temporary values."

availability of this kingdom which I have been proclaiming shall be preached all over the whole world to give a chance to every nation. Sometime after this will the end come.

"When you begin to be aware of the abomination of desolation spoken of by David, the prophet, get in church as fast as you can.[1] At this particular time there will be no place for unimportant details like waiting to put on clean socks or get a set and shampoo, nor if you're working in a field don't bother to go home to shower and change clothes. Since there will be much panic pregnant women will have more problems as will those with small children, but it is hopeful that this occasion will not be in the winter time nor on the sabbath day, for part of the panic will be occasioned by the tribulation, the worst distrubance in history. The time of this great difficulty, however, shall be shortened so that the saints of the Lord may not perish.

"Immediately all kinds of rumors will begin to be circulated. Some will say Christ is here again, or he just landed in Alaska; believe it not for there shall be false Christs and false prophets and they shall do all kinds of attention-attracting things, which will deceive all but the true believers.

"I am telling you these things ahead of time. Pass the word down the years, remember that if they say 'he is here,' or 'he is in the desert,' don't go forth on a chase. If they say 'he is in a secret hiding place,' believe it not, for as the lightning comes out of the east and shines across the heavens to the west; so shall my second coming be. Like eagles to a carcass, you'll know where to come.

"Another thing to remember is that immediately following the days of tribulation,[2] there will be a period of complete darkness day and night, there will be meteor showers, and even the collision of some heavenly bodies, and then shall appear the sign of my coming, and all the people of the world will gasp, and they will all see me coming in the clouds of heaven with great glory and unbelievable power, and the Lord God himself shall send a host of angels to proclaim the arrival with their trumpets, and they shall gather all the believers from the four directions all over the earth and from all the heaven, from one end to the other.

"You still, of course, want to know when this will happen. Well, look at a fig tree, when its branches are tender and puts out new leaves you know spring is near; so when you begin to see all these things I've been telling you, you will know for sure that the end is near. I even tell you that this earth and the existing structure of it as you know it will not be demolished until all these things have come to pass.

"What I tell you is absolutely true. Heaven and earth may pass away before my words won't.

[1]I do not know what this means. [2]World War 3? or 4? or 5?

"But no one knows the day nor the hour, not even the angels of heaven, only the Father.

"The end will come when man is somewhat on the downbeat, as he was in the days of Noah, when there was attached greater emphasis on eating and drinking, and having big weddings and big parties, and the people were not even aware of their misplaced values until the ark started floating, and the flood swept them away. My second coming will also be something like this.

"It will happen so fast that two people will be working side by side and one will be saved and the other will perish, and two women will be chatting as they come out of the supermarket, and one will be taken and the other abandoned.

"The best advice I can give you is to be ready at any time. It really has to be this way, for if a man knew his house was going to be robbed at a certain hour he would be already sitting there with his shotgun to prevent it. You just better be ready anytime, for you'll never guess the time of the second coming.

"How happy then is a wise and faithful person who has been caring for others and when the Lord comes he finds this faithful one doing his service. I tell you the Lord will make for him a reward beyond his dreams.

"On the other hand, if a man thinks that he will mistreat people for his own benefit for awhile, thinking that the day of judgment is a long way off, and he spends his time eating and drinking and carousing to no purpose, the Lord is going to slip up on that character and he shall toss him into the tank with the hypocrites and there shall be no pleasant sounds in that place.

Chap.

25

"But let us talk some more about the kingdom of heaven that is all around us. It is like ten cute young girls waiting to be invited to a big party. Five of the girls were wise and five were foolish. The foolish ones were concerned only with their immediate looks and were not worried about anything else, but the wise ones had fresh garments ready, and had thought considerably about the matter of preparing for a party which might be now or it might be tomorrow. Finally all ten of the girls went to sleep and suddenly here came the host inviting them to the party. All the young girls jumped up and yelled 'yippee,' but the foolish said to the wise, 'We left our flashlights, we didn't bring evening clothes, and we have no lipstick.'

" 'That is a shame,' replied the wise young ladies, 'but we have prepared for this and we are not merchants with extra stock. You had better run to a drive-in grocery and see what you can do.'

"While they were gone to purchase lights and ornaments, the party assembled and the door was closed. When the foolish ones finally returned with the proper equipment the doorman would not let them in and said that he did not remember them.

"In short, fellows, prepare yourselves at once for the kingdom," said Jesus, "for you know not the day nor the hour when suddenly you are faced with the Lord of life at the entrance to his kingdom.

"Now here is another angle for you to consider about the kingdom. It is similar to an important man who decided to take a long trip and he summoned his three employees and he turned his possessions over to them. To one of them he gave approximately $50,000 of money and things, and to another he gave $20,000, and to a third he gave $1,000 having distributed the responsibility in proportion to the abilities of the three persons.

"The employee with the $50,000 went to work and invested the money and made some good trades and doubled the amount so that he had $100,000, and the employee with the $20,000 did the same and doubled his original amount, but the fellow with the $1,000 went and put it in his mattress and laid down on it most of the time.

"Now after a couple of years the owner returned and requested an accounting. The first employee stepped forward and said, 'President Jones, you entrusted me with $50,000 and I have put it to work and here I bring you $100,000.'

"The president said to him, 'My good man, you have been wise and faithful with the relatively small responsibility that I gave you and so I am going to promote you to a much larger and more favorable position. Enter into the great joy of my kingdom.'

"The man who had been given the $20,000 then stepped forward and said, 'I too invested and worked and I have doubled what you left in my care and here is $40,000.'

" 'Well done,' said President Jones, 'you are a wise and faithful servant. You have proven that you can handle small things, I will now place you in a greater position. Enter into the joy of my kingdom.'

"Then stepped forward the employee who had received $1,000 and he said, 'President Jones, I know that you are a strict and careful man, accomplishing things that didn't seem possible, as well as being a keen judge of other's abilities; so I was afraid of making a mistake and I took your $1,000 and put it in my mattress and sat on my tail all the time you were gone.'

" 'You are a wicked and thoughtless employee,' roared President Jones. 'You know that I believe in getting things done and you should have at least done all you could with what you had. As a result I'm taking away even the $1,000 you kept and giving it to a real worker. Every person who uses whatever ability he has as best he can for my sake shall be abundantly blessed, but as for you and those like you, you are to be cast into eternal separation from my kingdom.' "

Apparently one of the disciples then asked Jesus again about the scene at the day of judgment, for Jesus said, "When the King of kings shall come in all his glory and all the hosts of the angels shall be with him, then He shall sit on the throne of glory, and before him shall be gathered all the peoples of all the nations and he will separate them like a shepherd divides the sheep from the goats, and he shall place the sheep on his right hand and the goats on his left hand.

"The King shall then say to those on his right hand, 'Come you happy people. Bless you, and move into the kingdom which the Lord has prepared for you from the very beginning of creation. When I was hungry you fed me, when I was thirsty you gave me something to drink and when I was a stranger you were nice to me. When I needed clothes you clothed me, when I was sick you did what you could to heal me, and you even visited me in jail.'

"Then these good people will begin to say, 'That sounds mighty nice but we never saw the Lord; when could we have fed you, or given you something to drink, or bought you a shirt, or put witch hazel on a bruise, or visited you in prison?'

"The King then shall kindly say, 'When you did one of these things to even the least important and most undeserving person you could find, you did it to me.'

"Then shall the King turn to those on the left hand and he shall repeat the same thing in the negative to the effect that when he was hungry they did not feed him, thirsty they gave him nothing to drink, without clothes they ignored him, sick, they let him look out for himself, and in jail, well they never even passed by the area.

"At once, of course, those on the left shall become defensive and say, 'We never saw you, Lord. How could we see you hungry when we never saw you, or thirsty, or any of all those other things you mentioned?'

"Then the King shall reply and say, 'Everytime you passed a chance to feed a hungry person, or treat a wound or share your water or visit a poor fellow in jail, you missed a chance to do it for me.'

"Then shall the King say, 'Those on the left are to be cast into the everlasting separation but those on the right enter into an eternal life of unbelievable joy.' "

Chap.
26

Jesus said then to the disciples, "I have had to cram a good deal of teaching into a short time for the feast of the passover is only two days away and after that I am to be betrayed and crucified."[1]

Now the top echelon among the Jews who controlled all Jewish matters met to discuss some way of having Jesus legally killed. The name of the Chairman of the Board was Slick Faustus.[2]

One of the rulers pointed out that it would be dangerous to do anything against Jesus on a holiday when the people were

---

[1] I still think that the disciples actually doubted this.　　　　[2] Caiaphas

everywhere.

In the meantime Jesus had moved to the outskirts of the city in the suburb of Bethany, and was having a meal there with Simon the leper.[1]

While the group, including the disciples, were eating a woman walked in uninvited and took a box of precious ointment which represented her life's savings, and poured it on Jesus' head as he ate.[2]

The disciples were immediately annoyed and in great righteous sounding tones bemoaned the waste of the valuable oil. It was even suggested that the oil might have been sold and the money used to help with the Benevolent Budget.

Jesus said to them, "Why are you so upset with this woman? What she has done is a great act of real worship. You will always find benevolent needs in the world, but not always a fitting time and way to worship. Actually this ointment she had saved for her own body at her death, and she has given it to me for my death. Do you know how marvelously important this thing is that she has done? Well, I'll tell you, that wherever in all the world forever that the good news of my kingdom is preached there shall be told this incident, in her honor, and as a memorial to her sense of true worship."

Later, probably the next day,[3] Judas, one of the twelve, went to the Ruler's Council of the Jews and agreed to initiate a citizen's arrest on Jesus for $2,500. Since they agreed, Judas then began to figure on a time and place that would be safe for him and that would get the job done.

When the day came for the passover the disciples asked Jesus where they should gather for the feast of the passover.

"Go to the city to the house of a man named Mark[4] and say that Jesus says his time has come and that he would like to keep the passover at Mark's house with his disciples."

The disciples did as Jesus requested and the passover supper was prepared and Jesus came and sat down with the twelve about twilight.

"I regret to say it," Jesus mentioned, "but one of you will betray me."

This upset the disciples considerably each began asking, "Is it I?"

"Just one of you that is eating with me, for the son of man goes as the prophets foretold, but woe to the one who is the betrayer, it would have been better for him if he had never been born."

Judas then, fearful that he had already been spotted, said to Jesus, "Are you talking about me?"

Jesus said, "You are the one talking."

[1]This was considered socially improper. [2]No doubt causing the oil to drip into the bar-b-que sauce. [3]If curious, consult a scholar.   [4]John Mark's father, according to Dr. Weatherhead, who heard it from somebody else.

And as they were eating, Jesus took bread and blessed it, and broke it, and gave it to the disciples, and said, "Take, eat, this is representative of my body."

Then he took the cup, and gave thanks, and gave it to each of them and said, "All of you take a drink from this cup,[1] for this symbolizes my blood which is to be shed for remission of sins. This will be my last drink of wine until that day I will drink with you in my Father's kingdom." Then the group sang a hymn and went out to the Mount of Olives.

"Unfortunately, all of you are going to get disturbed and upset because of me tonight. Just remember that it is similar to the old saying that when the shepherd is knocked cold the sheep scatter. But soon I will arise, and I will meet you in Galilee."

"Not me, Master," said Peter, "when trouble comes to you that's right up my alley and I'll stick right by you."

Jesus said, "Peter, you mean well with all your big talk, but before the rooster crows in the morning you will have already denied your association with me three times."

"Wrong again, Master. They can kill me, but I will never deny you." At once all the others chimed in saying the same thing and gave the pledge of allegiance.

Jesus then came to the beautiful garden spot called Gethsemane and he asked the disciples to sit down while he went apart and prayed. He did ask Peter, James and John to go with him, and it was with sadness for Christ knew what was to come.

Jesus said then to the three of them, "Sit here and be alert, for I am approaching the time of trial and death, and I want to pray before I am disturbed."

Jesus then went a little deeper into the garden and prayed saying, "Father, if it is possible, relieve me of this task, but if not I will do thy will exactly as you think best."

After this prayer he returned to where he had left James, John and Peter, and all of them had gone to sleep.

Jesus turned to Peter and said, "What a brilliant group of watch dogs. You couldn't stay awake an hour.[2] This is a good example of the danger of life. You have to always be alert for temptation, for often the spirit is willing, but the flesh is weak."

Jesus then went apart for a second time to pray and say, "I know, Father, that this duty must be done. I have my answer, thy will be done."

Jesus returned again and the three men had all gone back to sleep. Jesus then departed for the third time and again in prayer he prepared himself for doing God's will.

Jesus returned then to all the disciples and told them they had just as well keep on sleeping, as his prayer time was completed and

[1] I expect it will be found and used as an instrument of peace. [2] If they'd been in the Cossack army they would have been executed.

the hour was at hand when the son of man would be betrayed into the hand of sinners.

Not long after this he awoke the disciples and said that it was time to get up as the betrayer was approaching. At this point Judas arrived accompanied by a bunch of fellows with barrel staves, sticks, and stones, as well as with the dignitaries for high church council. Judas had arranged with the group that he would indicate the wanted man by kissing him on the cheek. Judas then came to Christ and said, "Hello, Master," and kissed him on the cheek.

Jesus said to Judas, "Friend, do you really know what you are doing?" Then the group came forward and seized Christ and began to take him away. One of the disciples then promptly pulled out his trusty fishing knife and took a whack at the nearest fellow, and cut the ear off one of the servants of the high priest.

Then Jesus calmly said, "Put your knife up. Violence just produces violence. In the first place, don't you know that I could pray to the Father and he would instantly dispense an army of angels that would gobble this crowd up in a minute. The Scriptures, however, must be fulfilled, for this is the plan of God."

Jesus then turned to the multitude and said, "Isn't it a little weird? You come as if you were after a mad criminal and yet only a few days ago I was daily in the temple teaching and you didn't lay a hand on me. Why the sudden change? Of course, this too is to fulfill the plan of God."

The group that arrested Jesus then took him to Slick Faustus where the Board of Trustees was already in session awaiting the arrival of Christ.

The rulers had attempted to bribe some witnesses to give false testimony against Christ, but they couldn't find any that would take the money until very late when finally they found a couple of professional liars.

The testimony of the witnesses was symbolically accurate but intentionally slanted, for one of them said, "This man Jesus said that he was capable of tearing the temple down in three days and rebuilding it."

Ole Slick jumped up and shouted to Christ, "What do you say to that?"

Jesus simply looked him calmly in the eye and said nothing.

"Then answer this, by God," bellowed ole Slick "Are you or are you not the Christ, the son of the living God?"

Jesus said, "Apparently you're going to do most of the talking, but just for the record, boy, the next time you see me I will be on the right hand of power, coming in the clouds of glory."

Then Slick, the high priest, started shredding Kleenex and gnawing on his robes and he blurted forth, "This man hath spoken blasphemy. We don't need any more witnesses. You have all heard the blasphemy, now what do you say?"

"He is guilty of death," said the rulers.

Then to ease their tensions they began to spit on Jesus[1] and strike him, slapping him in the face, and yelling, "How about a prophecy now? Can you tell who hit you the last time?"

Now Peter, who of course was not permitted into the judgment room, was sitting outside the building and a girl who was taking advantage of the crowd gathered to sell hot coffee said to Peter, "You are one of the ones that was with Jesus in Galilee."

"You're nuts," said Peter, "you just saw somebody that looked like me."

Peter moved away from this spot and another girl came by and said to some of the people standing around, "This big fellow here was with Jesus in Galilee."

Again Peter denied his relationship, coloring this denial with some of the curse words he had learned in his early fishing days.

Not long after this a couple of other people said that they thought Peter was connected with Christ because of his accent. Then Peter really blew his cool and began to curse and swear and declared that he didn't even know Christ.

Then out of the early morning twilight came the crowing of a rooster and Peter suddenly remembered what Christ had said and went out and wept bitterly.[2]

Chap.
27

First thing in the morning the Jewish rulers met to consider how they might legally condemn Christ to death. They decided that the death penalty would have to come through a Roman court on a basis of treason; so they bound Christ and delivered him to Judge Bean.[3]

Then Judas, when he realized what he had done, regretted his actions, and brought the $2500 back to the church office saying, "I have sinned and betrayed an innocent man."

"Tough stuff, man, but you can't unscramble these eggs[4]" replied the elders and the priests.

Judas then threw the money down on the temple steps and went out and hanged himself.

The chief priests picked up the money but said that it would mean a re-trial and undo the whole plan if they put the money back in the treasury; so they appointed a committee which decided to use the money to buy land in which poor people could be buried. It is still a symbol of unrighteousness. This action fulfilled exactly the prophecy of Jermiah who had said that the value placed upon Christ by the people would be used as a means of purchasing a potter's field.

[1] If I had been God, this is about where I'd knocked some heads flying. [2] A little man weeping is not so bad, but a big one somehow impresses me more. [3] Pontius Pilate [4] It can't even be done today. There is no un-mix master.

While all this was in progress, Jesus appeared before Judge Bean
and the Judge said, "Are you King of the Jews?"

Jesus said to him, "No comment." Then he was accused of
treason by the priests and the elders and he didn't even answer.

Bean said, "Don't you hear all these terrible things these people
are saying about you?" Jesus never batted an eye nor said a word,
and ole Judge Bean marveled at his calmness.

It so happened that at this time each year it was customary for
the Judge to release one prisoner as a gesture of recognizing the week
of celebration. The worst prisoner that Bean could think of was a
fellow named Dillinger[1] and so he thought he could diplomatically
get out of the chance of antagonizing the Jewish leaders by saying,
"All right, I'll release either Dillinger or this Jesus who is called the
Christ. What is your choice?" Judge Bean had already sensed that the
charges against Jesus were phoney.

Judge Bean sat down then on the judgment seat to await the
answer from the Jews. About this time a messenger came from Mrs.
Bean saying that his wife was certain that Jesus was innocent, that
she had dreamed it,[2] and that Bean should turn Jesus free.

In the meantime the elders and the priests had circulated among
the crowd and secured a few shills with a few bribes, so that when
Bean asked about the release there were various shouts of "Free
Dillinger!"

"What then," said Bean, "shall I do with this man Jesus?" And
the same ones called forth, "Crucify him, crucify him!"

Bean said, "But what has he done?"

"Crucify him, crucify him," and they began to raise signs and
demonstrate.

Bean then saw that it was an unreasonable situation with which
he did not care to cope, and so he secured a ceremonial bowl of
water and in the presence of all he washed his hands and said, "This
man is innocent, and I clean my hands of any part of this injustice."

"We'll take the blame," cried the crowd, "and pass it on down
to our children."

Then the officials released Dillinger, and the bailiff beat Jesus,
and he was then turned over to the soldiers who were assigned to
handle crucifixions.

The soldiers stripped him, and put upon him a mocking robe of
authority, and they made a crown of thorns for his head, and they
put a seaweed in his right hand and they began to make fun of him,
bowing to him and saying "Hail, King of the Jews."

After they had mocked, and spit upon him, they removed the
mocking robe of scarlet authority and they put his own simple robe
back upon him and they led him away to be crucified.

Enroute to the place of crucifixion, the soldiers noticed a big

[1] Barabbas

[2] She probably had been joining some of his followers and hearing him.

man watching among the spectators and they summoned him to help carry the cross of Jesus.

When the procession arrived at the hanging tree[1] they gave Jesus a drink of vinegar mixed with pickle juice[2] and when he tasted it he refused to drink it. Then they crucified him.

As the custom was, the squad of soldiers assigned to the job, shot dice for the robe of Christ and other garments, as the prophet had said, "They parted his garments among them and cast dice for this possession."

The soldiers then sat down and watched him. As was also customary, the accusation was written on a sign placed over his head, and in his case it read, "This is Jesus, the King of the Jews."

There were two thieves at the same time crucified with Christ being in the middle. Some of the onlookers began to make fun of Jesus, jesting him about his ability to destroy the temple and build it back in 3 days. Others mocked him saying that it would appear that the Son of God could easily get down off a cross.

The chief priests and elders also got into the act in their manner of insolent logic saying that he was apparently able to save other people why couldn't he save himself.

In fact, one of them said, "If you'll just come down from the cross unharmed we will join your movement ourselves."

Another said, "He trusted so much in God, why doesn't God do something for him now?"

The thieves also began to get in on the griping.

Then suddenly there came a darkness over the whole land for three hours and Jesus cried forth in his pain, "My God, my God surely thou hast not forsaken me?"

Some of those standing by said that they couldn't hear for sure but they thought that Jesus was calling for some help from Elijah. One of the men there then went and took a sponge with some juice on it and gave it to him to drink.[3] The others said, "Don't help him. Let's see if ole Elijah comes down to do something."

At this moment Jesus died, and suddenly the veil of the temple was rent from top to bottom, and the earth shook, and huge rocks were split down the middle, and many graves were opened and the bodies of some of the saints which were in them came out of the graves and went into Jerusalem and appeared to many people.[4]

Now when the senior officer in charge of the crucifixion and soldiers saw the earthquake and the many accompanying things, they were terrified and said, "Truly this was the Son of God."

There were many women present, though at a respectable distance, most of whom were followers of Christ, and among them was Miss Alabama[5] and Mary the mother of James and John.

[1] A place called Golgotha. [2] Nobody has ever been that thirsty. [3] A form of vinegar wine. [4] And scared the goose grease out of most of them. [5] Mary of Magdala.

At evening time there came a very important businessman named Big Joe[1] who was also a disciple of Christ and went to Bean[2] and requested the body of Christ. Bean immediately arranged for this to be done.

When Big Joe had taken the body and wrapped it in accordance with the custom and knowledge of that day he laid it in the tomb which he had previously prepared for himself and he had a great stone rolled to the door for the sepulchre, and he departed, but Miss Alabama and the other Mary stayed by the sepulchre.

The next day the hierarchy of the synogague was still worrying and they came to Judge Bean and they told him that Jesus said that he would rise again in three days, and they wanted none of this.

The committee chairman spoke forth and said, "Order immediately that the sepulchre be under constant guard for fear some of his followers steal the body and claim that he has risen, and then we'd be worse off than we already are."

Bean said, "You have your own temple guards, assign them to the job."

As a result, the guards were posted, the sepulchre was sealed, and security was established.[3]

Chap.
28

After the sabbath day had passed[4] Miss Alabama and the other Mary came at the crack of dawn and as they were near an earthquake came, or so it seemed, for the angel of the Lord descended from heaven and rolled back the stone with a mighty force, and then sat on the huge boulder. The look of the angel was like lightning and clothes like purewhite snow, and the brave temple guards protecting the tomb fainted dead away.

The angel spoke to the ladies calmly, however, and said, "Fear not, for I know you have come to honor Jesus who was crucified. He is not here. He is risen. Come and I will show where his body lay, then go promptly[5] and tell his disciples that he is risen from the dead and that he will go to Galilee and meet them there, and there you will see him."

The girls departed immediately with a mixture of fear and great joy and ran to bring the good news to the disciples.

As they departed, however, Jesus met them and said, "Hello." At once they fell at his feet and worshipped him.

Then Jesus said to them, "Don't be afraid or get all emotional about this. Go tell my close associates to go on to Galilee and I will meet them there."

---

[1]Joseph of Arimathaea [2]For he had influence. [3]Man and his idea of security is still a major weakness. [4]A day ended at dawn of the next day. Also no visiting in cemeteries, etc., on Sunday. [5]Possibly not a necessary remark.

While the ladies were doing this, the guards finally came to and reported to the chief priests what had happened. Immediately the chief priest called an emergency committee meeting of the rulers in executive session and they took large sums of money[1] and gave the money to the soldiers and bribed them to report that the disciples had stolen the body of Jesus. They even promised the soldiers that they would see that Judge Bean didn't investigate it.

As a result, the soldiers took the money and did as they were told to do, and the word of this leaked out and became common knowledge among the Jews.

Then the eleven disciples went into Galilee to a favorite place on a mountain side and Jesus appeared there to them. Most of the disciples worshipped him, but some couldn't believe their eyes.

Then Jesus said to them, "You must understand that all power is given to me in heaven and on earth and I commission you and all those who come after you in the years to come to go into all the world and to teach all nations, baptizing them in the name of the Father, and the Son, and the Holy Spirit. I want you also to teach them everything that I have taught you, and I will be with you always no matter where you go, and even until the end of the world."

---

[1]Even though not in the church budget.

MARK

The good news about Jesus Christ, the Son of God, begins as the prophets, speaking of John, write 'Behold, I send my messenger to prepare the way, a voice crying in the wilderness, urging repentance.'

John fulfilled this prophecy, baptizing those who came to him, preaching repentance to the many who came from all over the Jordan area to hear him. John dressed in camel skins and he received the confessions of the people before he baptized them.

John lived a wilderness life and existed on wild honey[1] and locusts. The theme of the preaching of John was the announcing of the coming of the Messiah, one mightier than John, a savior who John said was so great that John was not worthy enough to untie his shoes.

John preached also saying, "I baptize you all with water, but the coming real One will baptize you with the Holy Spirit."

One day Jesus appeared and requested that John baptize him. When Christ came forth from the water the heavens opened and the spirit of the Lord descended on him as softly as a dove lighting on a limb.

A voice from heaven then was heard saying, "This is my beloved son and I am well pleased with him."

Immediately following this occasion Jesus went into the wilderness for a period of meditation in order to determine His plan of action.

During this period, Jesus lived alone and was served by the angels of God as he prayed and meditated.

Not long after this, John was put in prison. Jesus then came to Galilee and began his career by preaching the good news of the kingdom of God, declaring that the kingdom of God was available, and that those who repented and believed could become immediately active in the kingdom.

While Jesus was walking along the beach of Galilee he saw Simon and his brother Andrew casting their nets, for they were commercial fishermen.

Jesus spoke to them and in closing said, "If you will come with me I will show you how to catch men." As a result, both men left their trade and followed Jesus.

As Jesus continued walking the shores of Galilee he saw the Smith boys,[2] James and John, and they were repairing their nets, for they too were commercial fishermen. Jesus talked with them and they left their business and went with Christ also. Mr. Smith was left with only his hired help.[3]

[1]Prevents allergies - try it.   [2]Zebedee boys
[3]Old man Zebedee probably wasn't too happy at this point.

The first missionary trip was to New York,[1] and there Jesus taught in the church during the open pulpit period. Jesus was an immediate hit and the people were astonished, for he presented new ideas and spoke with real authority, not as if he were one of the teachers reading from printed material.

In the church that day was a man who was some kind of psycho.

"Why don't you leave us alone?" he yelled at Christ. "Are you here to change our lives? I know you are the only son of God."

"Cool it, my friend," calmly said Jesus. Then Jesus ordered the upset feeling to leave the man, and with a loud shout the man was free of his trouble.

Naturally, this put tongues to wagging plenty, and the people were amazed.[2]

Many began to think about the new ideas proposed by Christ and they were greatly impressed that the evil spirits listened to his commands. As a result, the fame of Christ began to spread.

After the service, Jesus, accompanied by Simon, Andrew, James, and John, went to the home of Simon and Andrew and on arriving learned that Simon's mother-in-law was running a high fever.

When Jesus was told of this he went to the lady, took her by the hand, and lifted her to her feet. The fever immediately left her and she went straight to the kitchen to fix coffee and refreshments.

That evening people came from many nearby spots with all kinds of ailments and Jesus healed them all with his touch. To those afflicted with an evil spirit Christ cleansed them, but always ordered the evil spirit to refrain from announcing Christ, as he was not yet ready for this to occur.

Early the next morning, before the others were awake, Jesus went apart in a solitary place to pray and prepare for the new day.

Simon and the others found him before very long and one of them said, "Everybody in town is asking for you."

"Well, let's go to another town and preach there." As a result, Christ went from town to village in Galilee, healing and teaching.

On one occasion a leper came to him and kneeling down said, "If you want to do so, you are capable of healing me."

Jesus was moved with compassion, and so he put out his hand and touched the man and said, "I will heal you. You are now well." As soon as Jesus spoke the leprosy disappeared. Christ then instructed the man and dismissed him saying, "I would rather that you not blab this healing all over town, but it is necessary for you to go to the health officer and be taken off quarantine, and to pay there at the church your cleansing fee. Moses established this procedure."

[1]Capernaum   [2]There were no doubt also some who thought this was staged.

The man couldn't contain himself, however, and he went around telling so many people that Jesus had to leave town because of the crowds; so he stayed in a rural area and let the people come to him.

Again Jesus came to New York and the word of where he was staying leaked out. As a result so many people came to the house that there wasn't room for everyone. Jesus taught them as best he could under the circumstances.

Several fellows had a sick friend whom they were carrying as the man was too sick to walk. Not being able to get into the house for the people, the friends opened a hole in the roof and lowered their buddy down in front of Christ.[1]

When Jesus saw the obvious dedication and faith of the men, he turned to the sick one and said, "Your sins are forgiven you."

There were some strongly orthodox church people present, however, who immediately began to wonder how Jesus considered it within his authority to forgive sins.

Jesus sensed this, of course, and spoke to these people saying, "Why are you perturbed about authority? Which statement is most authoritative, 'Your sins are forgiven you" or 'Arise and walk for you are healed'?

"Well, just so you will know about my authority, I am telling this sick man to get up and go, for he is healed."

The man immediately arose and went out carrying the folded stretcher with him. All the people were amazed, and most of them glorified God.

From here Jesus went to the beach and there he taught the people who came to him. As Jesus was walking along he passed the Customs Office booth and Matt[2] was working there. Jesus spoke to him and Matt immediately quit bookkeeping and came with Christ.[3]

At meal time many people surrounded Christ, sinners, unbelievers, agnostics, Texans, and so some of the extremely technical churchmen asked among themselves about the kind of company Christ was keeping.

Jesus spoke to them kindly but firmly saying, "People who are healthy don't need a doctor, but the sick do. I did not come to earth to gad about with the righteous, but to call sinners to repentance."

"What about the observance of church customs? The disciples of John and of the Pharisees all fasted, why don't your disciples?"

"Why should the people fast in honor of the Lord when the Lord is with them, no more than wedding attendants refrain from eating cake with the bridegroom?

[1]I bet there was no insurance on the roof, either. [2]Levi, known as Matthew [3]This quitting bookkeeping had to be the easiest one.

"The day will come, however, when I won't be here, then you can return to fasting procedures.[1]

"You are supposed to be sensible in life. You wouldn't sew new cloth on an old garment or put new wine in old bottles.[2] In other words, you just have to adjust to change and get with the program."

A few days later Jesus and his disciples were passing through a cornfield on Sunday and the men picked some corn and ate it.[3] Naturally, the fault finders became active and said to Christ, "Why do your disciples break the law of Sunday?"

"Do you remember what David did? You are always using him as an example. Well, when he was hungry on Sunday he ate the communion bread and drank the wine. Sunday was made to be helpful to man, for rest and refreshment. What is more, I am the Lord of the Sabbath Day, and anything done with me is proper."

Chap.

3

On another occasion Jesus entered the church and there was a man there who had a deformed hand. Since it was Sunday the local critics watched to see if Christ would heal on Sunday, as they wanted to accuse him of breaking the laws of Moses.

Jesus spoke to the man and said, "Step forward, please."

Then Jesus turned to the curious critic committee and said, "Is it illegal to do good on the Sabbath or bad? Is it against the law to kill or to save life on Sunday?" Naturally, this shut the committee up tight.

Jesus was saddened by the lack of compassion on the part of these so-called leaders, and he turned to the man and said, "Stick out your bad hand."

The man did as Jesus ordered and the hand became immediately normal.

This so flustered the antagonistic leaders in the area that they decided to go the Mafia[4] and try to get a contract out on Christ. Jesus departed to the coast and a large throng followed after him. People everywhere began to hear of the great deeds of Christ and they traveled from everywhere to find Jesus and see for themselves.

As a consequence, it was necessary for Jesus to get in a skiff as protection from the throng for He had healed many, some being healed by simply touching Christ's robe, and often a psycho called forth declaring Jesus to be the Son of God.[5]

Jesus later climbed a hill and summoned selected ones to his presence and there he ordained the twelve and bestowed on them power to heal and to help mental cases.

[1] I strongly believe we should fast periodically.
[2] The word to me is that the bottles bust.
[3] Legal. Farmers left grain in the fields for travelers.
[4] Herodians
[5] Christ didn't particularly care for this as he wasn't ready to declare himself.

Simon was nicknamed Peter, and called Rocky, while James and John were named the Sons of Thunder.[1] The others of the twelve were Andy, Phil, Bart, Matt, Tom, Jimmy[2] Ted and Si.[3] Judas was also ordained, and he was the one destined to betray Jesus.

Later they all went to lunch but the multitude of people swarmed around Jesus to the extent that the disciples thought they would be forced to rescue him.

The hot-shot temple teachers from Jerusalem who had come to check on Jesus began to say that Christ was a high-ranking devil and that was why he could order the devils to leave people.

Jesus asked them, "How can Satan throw out Satan? A house divided against itself shall not survive; so how can Satan be against Satan? It is exactly like going into a strong man's house. Unless you are able to tie securely the strong man, you can't enter his house and take his goods.

"I tell you," continued Christ, "that all the many sins that men commit can all be forgiven, except the sin against the Spirit of God."

Jesus said this because these arrogant men had denounced the Holy Spirit of God which was in Christ.

Not long after this, the mother of Christ and a couple of his brothers sent word to him that they were on the outside of the crowd and would like to see him.

Jesus said, "Who is my mother, or my brothers?"

Then looking at the crowd gathered around him Christ said, "You are my mother and my brothers and my sisters. In fact, anyone who does the will of God is my mother and my close kinsperson."

Chap.
4

Once again Christ began teaching by the seaside and was forced to get into a small boat because of the press of people. On this occasion Jesus taught the many people using parables.

"There was a man," said Christ, "who went out to plant seed, and as he scattered it, some fell along the side of the path and various birds came and ate the seed. Some of the seed fell on very hard ground, and it grew but having no roots it didn't last very long, for the sun burned it, and it withered away.

"Some of the seed fell in the thorns, and the thicket choked off the chance of growth. Some of the seed, however, fell on good ground, and it grew and prospered and multiplied. Now, think about that a little."

A little later when there were only a few people around Christ, one of the men said, "Would you mind explaining the parable you told us?"

---

[1]Boanerges   [2]Son of Alphaeus   [3]Simon the Caananite

"You fellows are on the inside of this movement and you will learn a great deal from your association with me, but the parables are a means of teaching many people now and in the future. Everything I say or do is aimed at the conversion of people.

"You ask about the parable I told you not long ago? Well, the sower represents the word of God. Sometimes the word falls by the wayside and Satan eats it up, then there are those who are similar to the stony ground for they are interested for a short time, but tire of obligations and have no depth of feeling.

"There are also those that find that the cares and excitement of the world chokes out the word and they are too busy to nourish the word. Fortunately, there are those who receive the word and love it, who use the word, who take it to others.

"This is the sensible way. Surely if you have a candle you don't put it under the bed and light it, but you put it on a candlestick where it will shine out for all the room.

"God doesn't intend to hide anything forever. The word is for use. Think about this a little."

"There is an interesting balance in life," continued Christ. "If you criticize other people you will in turn be criticized. The more you want to learn, the more you will get to learn. You are to use for God the attributes that he has given you, or you will finally lose everything that God has given to you."

"Take the kingdom of God," said Jesus, "for it operates in the same manner as a man who plants his field. There is no way for him to fully understand how the seed grows, how first comes the blade, then the ear, and finally the whole corn. When the time comes for harvesting, then shall the farmer gather the good grain. Get that?"

"Another way of putting it," spoke Christ, "is to say the kingdom is similar to a grain of mustard seed, the tiniest seed you nearly ever saw. When it grows, however, it becomes such a large thing that birds can roost in the branches."

This is the way Jesus taught. Sometimes privately he said things to the disciples that he didn't say in public.

In a little while Jesus suggested that they get in two or three boats and cross the lake; so Jesus entered one of the boats and went to sleep on the stern. While crossing the lake a storm arose and the boat seemed as if it would capsize.

One of the disciples then awoke Christ and said, "Master, don't you care what happens to us? We can't swim, and we will all drown."

Jesus then spoke to the wind and to the sea and told them to smooth it; so there was a sudden calm.

"Where is your faith?" asked Christ. "Why are you so easily terrified?"

The men then began to talk among themselves and say, "What gives with this Jesus? Who is he? Imagine a man who orders the wind and the sea and they obey him."

Finally they crossed the lake and arrived in New Orleans.[1] No sooner had Christ left the ship than a lunatic came running toward him, a crazy man who lived in a cemetery and was too strong to be held in chains.

The wild, demented man fell at Jesus' feet and worshipped him.

"I know you," cried the looney one, "You are Jesus, the Son of God. Release me from torment, please."

"Come out, you unclean and evil spirits," ordered Christ.

"What is your name?" asked Jesus.

"I am called Legion, because I am many times crazy. Please don't do away completely with all my feelings."

There was a herd of swine feeding nearby and the devils that tortured Legion asked to be put in the swine rather than being banished. Jesus agreed to the arrangement, and the tormenting devils left Legion and entered the swine herd, spooking them so that they jumped off a cliff into the sea and drowned.

The men who were responsible for the swine went and reported this in town and everywhere.[2] As a result, quite a number of people came out and saw Legion sitting in the presence of Jesus, clean and properly clothed, in his normal mind, and they were greatly impressed.

Word of this spread around and soon a group representing the Swine Co-Op came to Jesus and asked him to please leave the area.

Jesus then returned to the ship. When Legion asked if he could go with Christ, the master said, "Not this time. Return to your home town and there witness to the great things the Lord has done through you."

The man did as he was told and began telling all about Jesus in Sibley, Louisiana.[3]

When Jesus arrived on the opposite side of the lake he was greeted by one of the church leaders, a man named Barclay,[4] who fell at Jesus' feet and said, "My little girl is about to die. Please come and touch her that she may live."

Jesus went to Barclay and many people followed so much so that there was some pushing and shoving and crowding. A woman who had a circulatory problem and who had been to many doctors, and was still getting worse, came and reached out and touched the robe of Jesus.

The woman had said to herself that if she could but touch the robe of Jesus she was sure that she would be cured. It was true, for as she touched His robe, she was healed.

Jesus felt the loss of power or the extension of goodness that had left him and he asked, "Who touched my robe?"

---

[1]Land of the Gadarenes   [2]Maybe the owner had swine insurance.
[3]Decapolis   [4]Jairus

"Just about everybody," said one of the disciples. "There are so many people that many brush against you."

The woman then, in fear and trembling, came to Jesus and said, "I am the one that touched the robe."

"Your faith has made you well, young lady," said Jesus. "Go in peace and continue to be well."

While Jesus was talking to the young lady a messenger came from Barclay's house saying that it was too late, the daughter was dead. Jesus heard this message being given to Barclay.

"Be not afraid, Barclay. Believe in me," said Christ.

Jesus would not allow anyone except Peter, James, and John to go with him. When Jesus arrived he found the house in a hub-bub, with people crying and wailing.

"Why all the noise?" asked Jesus. "The little girl is only sleeping." Following which remark a bunch of the people snickered and made fun of Jesus' comment.[1]

Jesus soon cleared the room of everyone except the mother and father, and then Jesus approached to where the young girl was stretched out and he took her by the hand and said, "All right, honey, it is time to get up."

Immediately the girl arose and walked, like a twelve year old Girl Scout should.

Jesus requested that the astonished witnesses would please not make too big a thing over the matter and suggested that the girl might enjoy a little ice cream.

Chap. 6

On the next little trip Jesus and his disciples returned to his own area and began to teach in the church there. The local people began to wonder about Jesus.

"What goes on here?" asked one of the local persons. "Who does this fellow think he is to be teaching us strange ideas?"

"As far as I know," replied another local yokel, "This fellow is the son of Mary and Joseph. In fact, he has a couple of sisters living here now." Obviously, some of the people didn't care to listen and were offended.

Jesus perceived this and he said, "It is unfortunate, but true, that a prophet may be honored in many places, but not in his home town." Because of this attitude, Jesus was able to do very little healing, though he continued to teach in the nearby villages.

Not long after this Jesus assembled the twelve and told them to go out in his name in pairs and to teach, giving to each of them the power to cast out devils.

Jesus also instructed them saying, "You are not to carry a lot of luggage. You do not need money or food, just one coat, and sandals

---

[1]The Funeral Home Director also took a dim view of this statement.

for your feet. As you work as a missionary stay where you are wanted. If anybody gives you the lip and tells you to split, leave at once, but not before you have shaken your foot at them. I tell you that in the day of judgment things will go better for Sodom and Gomar than for the place that gives you trouble."

As a consequence, the disciples left in pairs and began preaching repentance, in some instances casting out devils and in many cases healing the sick.

King Herod heard of Jesus and the wonders of his healing and teaching and Herod immediately concluded that he was John the Baptist come back to haunt him. Some of Herod's buddies said, "Naw, this man is old Elijah, or some prophet returned, don't worry."

"Not so," said Herod. "It is John returned. I feel it in my bones."

Herod was the one who had put John in prison for criticizing Herod's stunt of stealing his brother's wife. The wife, Sugar Liz,[1] was particularly peeved over the matter and wanted to have John executed but Herod would only consent to a jail term.

Herod was afraid of John, for Herod knew John was a just and holy man and Herod liked to hear John preach.

On the occasion of a big party celebrating Herod's birthday Sugar Liz had arranged for one of her chorus girl protegees to do a special dance. The girl made such a big hit with Herod that he blurted out in his enthusiasm, "Sweetie, I'll pay you any fee you ask. You were sensational."[2]

The girl immediately went to her agent, Sugar Liz, and said, "What shall I ask, a mink stole?"

"No, honey. Tell him you want the head of John the Baptist," said Sugar Liz.

"Just the head?" asked the girl.

"Yes," said Sugar.

As a result, the dancer came to Herod and told him that she wanted the head of John the Baptist, and on a silver tray.

Herod did not care for this suggestion, but he kept his word and delivered the head of John on a silver platter.[3]

When the disciples learned of this they came and claimed the body of John and gave him a Christian burial.

The apostles came to Jesus and reported all these matters. Jesus said to them, "You boys have been real busy and need a rest so we will go to a remote place for some rest."

When they departed for some privacy, many people began to follow, and Jesus was moved with compassion for the people and their problems.

---

[1]Heroditas   [2]Entertainers in those days were paid after performances.
[3]I think Sugar Liz kept the silver platter.

Jesus had been teaching and healing most of the day and there was a large crowd present; so one of the apostles said, "Master, the day is moving along, everybody is hungry, we are pooped. Please order the people to go home and eat and let us get our rest."

"If the people are hungry, feed them," replied Jesus.

"Where will we get $2,500 to provide hamburgers and shakes for everybody?" asked the disciples.

"What do you have available?" asked Christ.

"Five loaves of bread and two small fish," was the reply.

"Divide the crowd into regular groups of 50 and 100," said Jesus.

When this was done, Jesus took the loaves and the fish and raised his eyes toward heaven and asked for a blessing, and then he broke the loaves and divided the fish and began to pass the pieces to the disciples, who began to pass food around the crowd, and before long about 5,000 were fed and the clean-up group of church young people gathered all the scraps.

Immediately after this Jesus ordered his disciples to get into the boats and cross over to Destin[1] while Jesus dismissed the crowd. Then Jesus went into the hills to pray.

Toward sunset, Jesus was on the shore while the disciples were in the ship and Jesus saw them straining at the oars and having a lot of trouble for a storm had arisen and they were rowing against the wind.

After Jesus had allowed them to sweat it a bit, he came toward them walking on the water. At first they thought they were seeing things and cried out in panic.

Jesus spoke to them saying, "Cool it, boys. It is I. Don't be so scared." Jesus then joined them and the sea became calm and they were completely astonished by all that they had seen. For some reason the feeding miracle had not impressed them so much, but this walking on the water was something else.

The ship landed at St. Petersburg[2] and word of the arrival of Jesus quickly was spread throughout the area. As a result, the sick, the lame, and the blind came from everywhere, and Jesus went about the area teaching and healing.

Chap.

7

Some of the more straightlaced and pious-posing of the church leaders then came from Jerusalem to check on the activities of the new movement forming around Jesus.

The first thing these men noticed was that the disciples didn't wash their hands enough before eating.[3] The strict church people were very strong on the handwashing process as this was a tradition.[4]

[1]Bethsaida   [2]Genneseret
[3]They were accustomed to losing Brownie points maybe.
[4]It was a healthy practice also. They didn't know this.

"Why is it, Jesus," asked one of the leadership crowd, "that your disciples don't wash their hands always before eating?"

"You know, your own prophet Isaiah really had you persons tagged when he said 'These people honor God with their lips but not with their hearts. They worship God in vain, for they teach the commandments of people.' Washing hands, like washing pots and pans, is a device of man, which you treat as being more important than the will of God.

"Moses, for instance, said that you are to respect and deal fairly with your mother and father. Yet if some of you are caught taking things from elderly parents you say that the things will be yours soon anyway because of inheritance. You miss the whole spirit of the commandment. That is just an example of how you twist things to your own benefit."

When Jesus then had assembled a group around him interested in learning, he spoke to them, saying, "It is not what goes into a person that defiles him, but what comes out. I suggest that you think that statement over a bit."

When Jesus had withdrawn into a house the disciples came to him and said, "What did that mean about what went into a man couldn't defile him?"

"Sometimes you fellows seem a bit thick. Don't you know that whatever goes into a man enters his stomach, then goes out through his bowels. It doesn't affect his heart or his real self. It is evil thoughts, and hateful ideas that come from the heart of a man, when these things go forth they really hurt. It is evil things that makes an evil man."

From here Christ went to Miami[1] and Miami Beach[2] and tried to hide out for awhile, but it didn't work.

A certain woman had a daughter who was a hellion and the lady wanted Christ to remove the evil spirit. Now the lady was a Greek.

"The children should be helped first. It is certainly unfortunate that some people will feed dogs and let the children starve."

"I agree," said the lady. "At our house the dogs get the crumbs the children let fall on the floor."

"For this good statement thank you, and at this moment the devil has departed from your daughter."

When the lady arrived home she found her daughter well and relaxed.

After leaving this area, Jesus again turned toward the Sea of Galilee, passing by Sibley, La., again en route. It was here that a young man was brought to Jesus who had an impediment in his speech. Jesus took the young person aside, stuck his fingers in the boy's ears, and then touched his tongue, and then raising his eyes to

[1]Tyre   [2]Siddo

heaven, Jesus said, "Open the passages." At once the boy's ears were opened and his tongue freed and he began to speak plainly.

Jesus suggested that there be no big talk about these healings, but the more he asked them not to tell of these healings the more they told of them, recounting the times that he made the deaf hear, the blind to see, the lame to walk, and the dumb to speak.

On another occasion Jesus turned to one of his disciples and said, "These people have been following me around for three days and have had practically nothing to eat. If I send them home, some of them will poop out en route."

"How can we produce bread for them here in the wilderness?" asked the disciple.

"How much bread do you fellows have?" asked Jesus.

"Seven loaves," was the reply.

Jesus then asked the people to sit in an orderly manner, and when he had blessed the bread and a few fish which someone donated, the food was passed throughout the crowd and there was some left for the litter committee. There were close to 4,000 people present on this occasion.

Jesus then joined the disciples on board a sloop and went to Cape Cod.[1]

Some of the troublesome church leaders then came to Jesus, asking him technical questions, urging him to give them a sign of power,[2] tempting Christ.

"Why do people always want some type of show?" asked Christ, who was somewhat disgusted. "Anyway, there will be no exhibition for this crowd," said Jesus, and he left with the disciples to cross the lake again in a ship.

The disciples, as usual, were hungry and in their willingness to serve the crowd they had failed to do any eating themselves, although one of them had kept one loaf of bread, just in case.

"Don't you boys be influenced by the Pharisees, the formality crowd, nor be influenced by Herod, who represents the military or the power structure."

The disciples didn't get the drift of this and decided Jesus was talking with them this way to make up for no bread.

"Why are you boys worrying about bread? Are you really that stupid? Don't you have eyes to see and ears to hear? When I divided the food among 5,000 weren't there 12 bags of scraps and when I did it with the 4,000 weren't there 7 bags of scraps? Haven't you figured out yet how unimportant food is or how complete is the power of God in me?"

Finally, they came again to New York and there a blind man was brought to Jesus. Then Jesus took the blind man by the hand

[1]Dalmanutha

[2]Most of us would have given a sign, such as putting both their ears on the same side of their heads.

and led him to the edge of town where Jesus moistened his fingers and placed them over the eyes of the blind man.

"Do you see anything?" asked Christ.

"I see men, and they appear as trees walking."

Jesus then put his hands on the man's eyes and when he looked this time he could see everything clearly.

Jesus said to the man, "You can go home now, but please don't blab about this healing all around town."

The disciples and Jesus then went toward Savannah, Ga.[1] and as they were walking along Jesus asked them, "Whom do persons say that I am?"

"Some say John the Baptist," replied one.

"Some say Elijah or one of the prophets," put in another disciple.

"Whom do you say that I am?" asked Christ.

"You are the Christ!" said Peter.

"That's right," said Christ, "but I am not ready for you to start telling this to other people."

Jesus then began to teach the disciples, telling them that as the Saviour he must suffer many things, that he would be rejected by the organized church, that he would be killed and then in three days rise from the dead.

Peter didn't like this seemingly defeatist talk and said, "It is not so. We won't let them do those things to you."

"You must be quiet, Peter. You are tempting me to misuse my power and you are thinking on worldly matters, while I am thinking only of the plan of God."

Jesus then spoke specifically to his disciples and said, "If anyone chooses to follow me, such a person must exercise self-control, take upon oneself a share of life's responsibilities, and put my cause first. For a person who is only interested in one's own life will surely lose it, but who ever gives of one's own life freely for others because of me and the good news of God's love, then that person has saved their own life forever.

"Actually what good does it do a person to accumulate all kinds of possessions and lose his soul? What value could a person possibly put on their own soul?

"Anybody who avoids me and my teaching and acts as if ashamed of religion, then when that person stands in the presence of the glory of God and the angels, I will act ashamed of that person and will not acknowledge such a one to my Father."

Chap.
9

Jesus continued teaching the disciples and he said to them, "Actually, there are some of you here who will live long enough to

[1]Caesarea

see the power of God at work in his kingdom on this earth, and you will have greater understanding of this."

Six days later Jesus took Peter, James, and John and went to a secluded spot on a mountain and in their view Jesus was transformed into his heavenly appearance, and his cloak became a radiant white, even whiter than snow, and there appeared beside him Moses and Elijah, and they were conversing with Jesus.

Peter was astounded, as were James and John, but Peter blurted forth, "Master, it is a great treat for us to be here."

Not knowing what else to say, Peter then suggested that they build three churches and name one for Moses, one for Elijah, and one for Jesus.

There was the presence of a cloud over the three and a voice from heaven spoke saying, "This is my beloved son, hear him."

All of a sudden the cloud disappeared and only Jesus remained with the three disciples.

As they were returning down the mountain Jesus instructed the three not to report what they had seen until after he had risen from the dead. Privately, thereafter, the three disciples began discussing among themselves what was meant by the expression 'rising from the dead,' for this was a new doctrine.

Later they asked Jesus saying, "Why is it that the interpreters of the scripture tell us that Elijah must come first and restore matters, then that the Saviour comes and must undergo suffering, and be killed?"

"Elijah has already come, and he has been mistreated, just as the scriptures said."

When they returned to the main group of disciples there was a big crowd around them and some religious experts examining them. When the people saw Jesus they ran to him and welcomed him.

"Why do you question these associates of mine?" Jesus asked the church reporters.

One from the crowd of people then spoke and said, "I have brought my son who has a speech block, occasionally having short fits, he foams at the mouth[1] and I asked your disciples to cure him and they could not do it."

"How short of real faith and understanding you are. How long will it take to teach you? However, bring the young man to me."

When they brought the young boy to Christ, the youngster had a seizure and fell on the ground.

"How long has the boy had this?" asked Jesus.

"Since he was a child," replied the father. "There have been some bad times, like the time he fell in the fire, and again in the water. If you can help us, Jesus, please have compassion, and do something."

[1]Probably epilepsy.

"If you believe, then you must know that anything is possible with God."

"I believe, Lord, I believe," said the father as the tears fell, "and even help any need I have for stronger belief."

As the people began to press forward, Jesus commanded the devilish spirit to leave the boy, and not to return. The boy was immediately in quick pain, and then quietly relaxed in sleep, looking so peaceful that some thought he had died.

Jesus then took the boy by the hand and helped him to his feet.

When Jesus and the disciples were back at the motel that evening, they asked him why it was that they had been unable to help the boy.

"The boy was very, very sick, and to cure him took a great deal of prayer and a history of fasting, and such power is not easily attainable."

After this they left the area and went through the section around Galilee on the quiet as Jesus wished to spend more time instructing the key disciples.

"Be prepared for some tough times," said Jesus. "In fact, I will become the victim of man's unkindness to man. I must be killed, but I will rise on the third day."

The disciples did not understand at that time what Jesus meant. They came to New York again and sitting around that evening Jesus said to the disciples, "What have you been yakking about among yourselves today?"

They didn't answer, for they were ashamed to admit that they had been discussing who among them was the greatest or would receive the greatest recognition when Jesus established his kingdom.

"Let me tell you something about my kingdom," said Christ. "The person that is ambitious to be first will be last."

Then Jesus called to a small child and when Jesus had put his arm around the child he said, "Anytime you concern yourself with the welfare of one of these little ones, you are doing it for me. This means that you will also be accepting the one who sent me."

John then spoke and said, "Jesus, in town today I saw a fellow who was preaching and healing in your name, but since he was not one of us I hushed him up."

"You were wrong, John," said Jesus, "for no one can do things in my name and be against me. If he is not against me, he is for me. In fact, anyone who gives just a cup of water for my sake, such a person does not go unrewarded.

"It is really trouble for anyone who mistreats or misleads one of the little children. In fact, he'd be better off if he had a huge stone tied around his neck and he was thrown into deep sea.

"Don't let any relationship, any possession, or any part of you be the cause for your downfall. If your sports car is always getting you into evil, it would be better to live without it and walk. If everywhere you look you see opportunities to do evil, you'd be better off blind. A one-eyed man in heaven is a lot better fixed than a 20-20 vision man in hell.

"Everybody is going to be tested and tempted in some form. You are also challenged to add flavor to life; so there must be some goodness in you developing so that you can add it to life. Be kind and have peace among yourselves."

Chap.
10

Jesus next visited the shores along the upper part of the Hudson[1] River and the people followed him as usual, and so he began teaching again.

One of the legal-minded churchmen came to Jesus and said, "Is it lawful for a man to get rid of his wife?" The question was simply an attempt to embarrass Jesus.

"What did Moses say?" asked Christ.

"Moses said it was all right as long as you wrote out a statement of divorce," was the reply.

"Yes," said Jesus, "Moses wrote this regulation because he knew what a hard-hearted bunch some of you fellows were. You should remember, however, that the basic plan of God was the creation of male and female, and the system called for a person to separate from the parents and to join with a member of the opposite sex in order to begin a new family. The married couple then are to become one independent family. Man has no business tampering with this basic plan."

Later some of the disciples began to question Christ further in this matter. "It is not proper for a person to be party to the breaking up of a family, whether the woman leaves the man or vice the versa, it is preferable that the two remain together as a family," said Jesus.

Some people then brought some little kids to Jesus for him to touch and bless, but the disciples tried to protect Jesus from "the little brats."

Jesus did not care for their interference and he spoke firmly to the disciples, saying, "Permit little children to come to me, don't stop them, for it is their style of innocence that is a major part of the kingdom of God. In fact, anyone who approaches the kingdom with any motive except the simple yearning of a small child, shall never really be a part of the kingdom."

Jesus then took the children one by one and blessed them.

On a later occasion a grown person came to Christ and asked, "What shall I do in order that I might live forever, good Master?"

"Why do you call me good? There is only one completely good and that is God. No doubt, though, you know the commandments about such things as adultery, stealing, lying, deceitful business practices and the like."

[1]Jordan

"Master, I have always observed all the commandments. I really try to be good."

Jesus was greatly impressed by the man and he said to him, "You are almost perfect. You lack only one thing, so go sell all your possessions and give the money to the Benevolent Budget, thereby building a nice big treasure for yourself in heaven. Then you should assume the responsibility of being a Christian witness and follow me."

The man left very sad for he had great possessions and no desire at all to conduct a garage sale.

Jesus looked at his disciples and then said to them, "It is exceedingly tough for a rich man to be part of the kingdom of God. Riches are a great diversion and only those who can get down humbly on their knees like a camel and be able to get through the eye of the needle can get into the city of God."

They wondered then among themselves as who could be saved, for everyone had some possessions about which they greatly cared.

"With men it is impossible, but on God's level all things are possible; so calm down a bit and don't panic."

"We have left all we had," said Peter, " and we are following you."

"Let me assure you that any person who sacrifices by leaving friends, families or glorious plans and follows me for my sake or as a witness for the good news, such a person shall be rewarded, even on this earth, in spite of tough persecutions, but such a person shall also acquire eternal life.

"There will be some surprises. Some that think they are first shall be last."

The group then headed for Jerusalem and the disciples were getting nervous in the service. Jesus then continued to instruct them, saying, "We are now going to Jerusalem. I will be arrested there, turned over to the church courts, condemned to die, then transferred to the civil authorities. During this time I will be mocked, people will throw old tomatoes at me, and then I shall be killed and rise again on the third day."

James and John later came to Christ and said, "We would like for you to do us a favor."

"What is it?" asked Jesus.

"We would like to be your number one and number two boys when you set up your kingdom."

"You fellows don't know what you're asking, of course. I'll tell you this, you will get to face the great problems and be subject to the rigorous pressures that come with Christian leadership, but as to the top ranking spots, those are designated by God and I'm not free to tell you who gets these posts."

The other ten didn't like this power play by James and John and began to grumble.

Jesus called the group together to calm them and said, "In civic life there are rules and people in authority, but in the kingdom of God the leaders are those that serve, and greatness is given to those that minister; so who would try to be chief gets busted to private; so seek to serve, and in this way you can become a chief.

"As for me, I came not to be served, but to serve, even to the point of giving my life that believers might live."

The next trip was to Mobile[1] and there were many people around the gates of the city begging. One of them was Blind Tom[2] and when he was told that Jesus was near he began to yell out, saying, "Jesus, son of David, have mercy on me."

As usual, some of the people around him began to tell him to hush, but also as usual, the fellow just yelled all the louder. Jesus stopped and asked that Blind Tom be brought to him, and Tom arose and headed toward where he had heard Jesus.

"What do you want?" asked Jesus.

"I want to see," replied Blind Tom.

"All right," said Jesus, "Your faith has made you well." Immediately he could see.

Chap.
11

When the group arrived at the Mount of Olives very close to Jerusalem, Jesus asked two of the disciples to go to a nearby little hamlet and he told them that they would find there a young donkey tied to a tree and that they were to untie him and lead him back to where Jesus was.

"If anybody asks you what you are doing," said Jesus, "just tell them that the Lord needs the donkey and there will be no problems."

The disciples did as they were asked and they found the donkey and untied him.

A couple of checker players were sitting nearby and one of them said, "What are you birds doing untying that donkey?"

"The Lord has sent for the donkey," replied the disciples. This satisfied the checker players.[3]

The disciples returned to Jesus with the donkey and put some of their clothes on the donkey's back as a makeshift saddle.

In this manner began the triumphal entry into Jerusalem and many people cut palm branches and threw them in the path as an acknowledgment of their appreciation of Christ.

Some onlookers called forth loudly, "Hosanna! Hosanna! Hurrah for the one who comes in the name of the Lord! Hurrah for the kingdom of David! Cheer the one who represents God!"

Jesus then entered Jerusalem and went to church, returning in the evening to San Angelo.[4]

[1]Jericho [2]Bartimeas
[3]It has never been hard to satisfy checker players anyway. [4]Bethany

On the way to Jerusalem the next morning Jesus was hungry, and when he saw a fig tree with leaves on it he went to pick some figs, but it was barren.

The disciples heard Jesus condemn the tree and order it never to produce again.

On entering Jerusalem again the group came to church and there found the church being used as a market place for selling the gifts of the day before, and there was trading, money changing, and much noise. Jesus then drove the merchants from the building, not even giving them time to take their pots and pans with them.

Jesus then spoke with authority saying, "The scripture says that the house of God is to be a house of prayer for all nations, and some people have made of it a place for thieves and sharpies."

The church authorities were greatly disturbed over the incident and the loss of revenue it entailed and they began to plot against Jesus for his popularity with the people was making him a threat to their rule.

The next day on returning to Jerusalem the disciples noticed that the fig tree to which Jesus had spoken had already started to die.

Peter said, "Master, the tree that you condemned is already withering away."

"You should have such faith in God, Peter. I tell you," continued Christ, "that anyone who has complete faith and trust in the Lord, can order a mountain to disappear into the sea. Anything is possible for a person of complete belief.

"You should have the same feeling about prayer. If you pray in complete faith, you will receive whatever you request.

"You should also enter into prayer having first forgiven anyone anything that might have been done to your detriment and God will be equally beneficient to you. If you don't forgive others, however, don't expect God to forgive you."

On the next jaunt into Jerusalem there came to Jesus a group of church politicians and they asked Jesus, "By what authority do you do and say the things you do?"

"All right," replied Christ, "I will tell you about my authority if you will tell me if the baptism of John was from heaven or was it simply a civil matter?"

The politicians reasoned that if they said the baptism was from heaven Jesus would then say, 'Then why didn't you believe John?' They also reasoned that if they said it was a civil matter there would be trouble with their constituents, all of whom believed John was a great prophet.

Finally one of them said, "We don't know."

"Then I will not tell you about my authority," said Jesus.[1]

---

[1] I really get a thrill out of Jesus handling the city slickers.

Jesus then began to teach them using stories[1] as a basis for his comments.

"There was a certain person," said Jesus, "who planted a vineyard and fixed a fence around it, built a watch tower, and generally set up a good operation; then leased it and went on a cruise.

"When it was about harvest time the owner sent his real estate agent to collect the percent of yield of the crop. The vineyard keeper just had the man beaten and sent away with nothing.[2]

Later on the owner sent another agent[3] and this one was treated to stone throwing, kicked around a bit, and sent away. The owner kept finding new agents willing to try to collect, but they were all beaten or killed.

"Finally, the owner sent his only son, and thought that of course they wouldn't dare do anything to him, but the lease holders decided to kill the son and then claim the land.

"What do you think the owner is going to do when he comes? Well, he is going to destroy the lease holders and give the land to others.[4] The scripture says that the stone which the builders tossed away has become the head of the corner. This is the Lord's way; isn't it a wonderful promise?"

The crummy politicians wanted to harm Christ then, but they were afraid of the interference of the people, for the money grubbers knew to whom Jesus was referring in the vineyard story.

As a result, this group employed a couple of church lawyers and a few Watergate Plumbers to try to catch Christ in some illegal action or statement that was cause for arrest.

Consequently, the paid slicky snoopers came to Christ and said, "We know you are honest and truthful, and that you teach the truth of God even if it were to get you into trouble. Solve a problem for us. It is lawful and proper to pay taxes to Caesar? Shall we pay or not?"

Jesus knew them for snakes, of course, and he said, "Why are you trying to trap me? Anyway, bring me a coin."

Holding up the coin which they brought, Jesus asked, "Whose picture is this?"

"It is Caesar's," they replied.

"Then if the coin is his, go on and give it to him, but be equally careful to give to God the things that are his."

Everyone was tremendously impressed with this masterful handling of a difficult situation.

The next crowd to take a run at Jesus was the Association of Super-Professors.[5] These heavy-minded persons did not believe in the resurrection.

[1]Or parables [2]Life is tough sometimes on agents.
[3]He hadn't heard what happened to #1.
[4]It may be that if we don't shape up the earth might go to the Martians.
[5]Sadducees

One of these profs said, "Moses wrote in the commandments that if a man dies he leaves his wife to his brother, if the wife has no children, then the brother can give the children deal a try.

"Suppose there were seven brothers, and the first died and left the wife to the second. The second died and left the wife to the third, and on down until all seven brothers were dead. Finally Killer Lou[1] died and went to heaven. Whose wife shall she be?"

"You meatheads neither know the scriptures nor the power of God. In the life to come there is no marrying but everyone is free like an angel.

"What is more, have you not read in the scriptures how God spoke to Moses and said, 'I am the God of Abraham, Isaac, and Jacob.' God then is not the God of the dead, but of the living, and therefore in this thought concept there is no death."

One of the newspaper reporters was impressed with the way Jesus answered the difficult questions; so he decided that he had might as well ask a question himself.

"Which of the ten commandments do you rate as the most important?" queried the press.

Jesus said, "The Lord our God is one Lord, and you shall love the Lord with all your heart, with all your soul, with all your mind, with all your strength, and this is the first, but equal to it is the commandment to love your neighbor as yourself. There is no greater commandment."

"You are right, teacher, for surely there is one God and no other, and to love Him completely with soul, mind, and strength, and then to love your neighbor is certainly superior to merely participating in some purely liturgical service."

"You are pretty sharp, friend, and you are beginning to get the feel of the kingdom of God."

After that most of the persons zipped their lips for they perceived the wisdom of Christ.

Sometime later Jesus was in the church and during the open discussion period commented on the fact that the press referred to Christ as the son of David.

"David himself, inspired by the holy spirit, said 'The Lord said to my Lord, sit on my right hand until I have all your enemies packed down under your feet.' If David then called him Lord," continued Jesus, "how can some of you say he is David's son?" This exchange made a big hit with the ordinary folk.

"Be on the look-out for some of the pious sounding big shots that enjoy getting all dressed up and having people bow and scrape to them in the supermarket. They are the kind that want to be given plaques and sit on the 50 yard line, and yet they switch from taking advantage of widows to reciting long prayers. In the judgment, they are going to get it worse than anybody."

[1]The girl in the case.

Jesus then moved to a corner of the church and began to watch the people bring their offerings and put them in the plate at the front of the church.

In a few minutes, a poor widow came and tossed in ten cents. Jesus then turned to his disciples and said, "That lady has made the biggest gift so far. You see, she gave a large portion from what very little she has, while the others have been giving small portions of great possessions."

Chap.

13

As they were leaving the church one of the disciples turned to Christ and said, "This is an impressive building, don't you think? Look at the huge stones of which it is made."

"You're impressed by these buildings?" asked Christ. "Don't be misled by appearances. In time, there won't be one stone here left on top of another."

Later that evening as Jesus sat on the Mount of Olives, Peter, James, John and Andrew came to him and wanted to know when the end of the world would be and when Christ's kingdom would be the only one.

"Try not to be fooled," spoke Jesus. "Down through the years there will be many who come claiming to be the Messiah and seeking to take over the world.[1]

"You can count on there being a bunch of wars, and a lot of rumors about wars. Nation will rise against nation, organization against organization, there will be earthquakes, famines, and all types of troubles.

"You can count on some personal problems, also.[2] You will be criticized, beaten, placed in awkward positions, some of these things being opportunities to witness.

"The good news has to reach everyone in the world, somehow. Incidentally, when they put you on trial and ask embarrassing or puzzling questions, don't worry, for the holy spirit will come to your assistance in your time of need.

"There are plenty of difficulties ahead in the world, churches shall be divided, dissension shall exist within families, and Christians, Jewish or otherwise, shall be hated in many places. The persons that are undaunted shall be saved.

"When the time comes for the abomination of desolations spoken of by Daniel,[3] appearing where you'd never think it possible, then head for the hills!

"When the big disturbance comes, look for a safe place, with the hills being the best bet. Don't stop to find your seven iron, or take anything from the deep freeze — just run, boy, run! It would be good

[1] I think Hitler was the worst of the ones I've met.
[2] Inflation, arthritis, etc.
[3] No one has ever given me an acceptable explanation of this. Persecution of the Jews, concentration camps, 3 day virus?

to pray that the trouble doesn't come in wintertime, or that you are living in the deep south when it does hit.

"There shall be a period of maximum tribulation, distress, and lack of order. In fact, except that the Lord has agreed to make the period pretty short, no one could survive all the trouble, but for the sake of the believers, the Lord has shortened the days of tribulation.

"Don't fall for a bunch of rumors. There will be people saying 'Christ is in Kansas,' or 'Christ has landed on the West Coast,' or the like, but forget it. There will be fake Christs, and some of them will be able to do neat tricks.[1] It won't be easy to sit tight and keep the faith, just remember I am telling you well ahead of time.

"After the big time of tribulation there will be darkness as if there were a long eclipse of the sun and moon, there will be lots of shooting stars, and the space vehicles shall get tilted.

"At this time, God will send his angels and they shall gather the Lord's chosen ones from all over the world, and from all the parts of the heavens where those who have already died are busy.

"When will this be? Well, learn from a fig tree. When the branch is tender and puts out leaves you know it's spring and summer is near; so when you see all these things I've described happening you can know that that time is near. All these things will happen during this phase of God's creation.

"Heaven and earth as you know them will be replaced, but the words of truth which I speak are eternal.

"As for the exact time, don't try to synchronize your watches. No one knows exactly, the angels don't know, the Son of God doesn't even know, only the Father knows.

"Be on your toes, though. Pray and be prepared. For the Son is like a man who has gone on a long journey and left the keeping of the house to his servants, as I am leaving the stewardship of the earth to you. Be careful. You have no idea when I, your Master, will return, morning, noon, or night. You certainly don't want me to return and find you goofing off; so let your key word be 'Watch'! There's no telling when I shall return."

Chap.
14

As the celebration day for the Passover was only two days away, the controlling faction among the Jewish leaders plotted ways of eliminating Christ, but they agreed that on the actual day of the Passover the people would be in no mood to permit anything to happen to Jesus.[2]

In the meantime, Jesus was in Mobile having lunch with Simon, the leper, and there approached him from the street[3] a woman with an alabaster box full of a precious oil and she poured the oil on Jesus' head.[4]

[1] Like sit on a throne in the Astrodome and Guru it.

[2] Being a holiday, all the ordinary and working people would be in the crowd—they loved Jesus.

[3] They ate outdoors on patios.   [4] Some dripped into the bar-b-que sauce?

At once some of the practical-minded disciples objected, mumbling to each other that she could have given them the oil, let them sell it, and then they could give the money to the poor.[1]

Jesus said, "Cool it, boys. Leave the lady alone. She has done what she considers a good deed and an act of worship. Don't be too worried about the poor as they are part of life and you can always be helpful to them. You will not always have me here, though. This lady has performed a beautiful act of worship, so much so that wherever in all the world the good news is preached and taught, what this person has done will be told as a memorial to her."

That evening, or the next day, Judas, one of the selected twelve, went to the chief priests of the church and agreed to make a citizens arrest on Jesus. An agreement was made on the price of the act and then Judas began to scheme as to the best way to betray Christ and not get caught.

The next day[2] the disciples asked Jesus where he wished to celebrate the Passover feast.

Jesus then turned to two of the disciples and said, "You all go into the city and you will see a man carrying a pitcher of water. Follow him to the home where he works. When you get there ask for the owner of the house.

"When the good man who owns the house comes to see you say to him 'The Master would like for you to show us the guest room as he wishes to eat the Passover with his disciples at your home.'

"The man will then show you a large upper room with a table and benches and there you can arrange for the meal."

The two disciples went into the city and everything was exactly as Jesus said it would be. That evening Jesus arrived with the twelve.

As they were eating the Passover Jesus said, "One of you here will betray me."

This created a stir and several immediately said, "Is it I?"

"It is one of you that joins me in this meal. It is necessary that I go, but woe to that one who is the betrayer. He will wish that he had never been born."

As they ate Jesus took a piece of bread and blessed it and then broke it, and gave a piece to each one present.

"Take this bread. Eat it. It is my body."

Then Jesus took the cup[3] and when he had given thanks he passed the cup around the table for each man to take a sip, and they all drank of it.

"This is my blood of the new testament," said Jesus, "Which is shed for many. I tell you that I will no more drink of the fruit of the vine until I drink it in the new kingdom of God."[4]

---

[1]Middle East oil problems again.
[2]Maybe the day before or the day after.
[3]Some day we will find the cup.
[4]Wine in heaven? Why not?

At the end of this ceremony the men sang a hymn and all departed for the Mount of Olives.

Either en route or after they arrived Jesus spoke to the twelve and said, "All of you will be greatly disturbed tonight because of me. Just as the prophet said, 'The shepherd is smitten and the sheep scatter.'

"However, after I have risen I will go to Galilee and meet you there."

"Not me, Master. I am not going to scatter or back down from anything," said Peter.

"You mean well, Peter, but before the rooster gets to crow twice you will have denied me three times."

"Not so! If I have to die, I will do it for you!" strongly spoke Peter, and the others affirmed the same for themselves.

There was a little knoll on Mount of Olives[1] and when they came there Jesus said to the disciples, "Sit here while I go apart to pray. Peter, you and James and John come with me."

After going a very short distance Jesus said, "I am worn out, for I am approaching my death. Stay here and keep watch."

Jesus then went forward a bit and kneeled down and prayed to the Lord that if there were some other way to get the job done he would like to know about it.[2] "Nevertheless, Father, you know what is best, and I will obey your will."

Jesus then came back to the three and they were asleep. Jesus spoke first to Peter and said, "You're the big talker, but you couldn't even keep watch for an hour? Let this teach you to be constantly alert, and pray that you not be tempted, for though the spirit is often willing, the flesh is weak."

Jesus then stepped aside again and prayed to God as he had previously. When Jesus returned the second time the three were asleep again, and they were too ashamed to even make excuses.

The third time the same thing occurred and Jesus said, "Sleep on, and take your rest. The time has come for your Master has been betrayed and turned over to the sinners. Let's go, for the betrayer approaches."

While Jesus was speaking, Judas appeared and with him a group with swords and clubs, furnished by the Jewish leaders.

Now the betrayer had told the vigilantes that he would point out the one to be arrested by a kiss on the cheek.

Judas then approached Jesus, kissed him on the cheek, and said, "Master, Master."

At once the vigilantes seized him and began to take him away. One of the disciples then pulled out a fishing knife and took a swipe at one of the church representatives, cutting off his ear.

[1]Gethsemane
[2]I presume that later Jesus told them what he had prayed.

Jesus then said, "Are you come out at night to arrest me as if I were a common thief? Why didn't you arrest me when I was teaching Sunday School?" The scriptures, of course, had to be fulfilled.

At this point the disciples took to their heels. A certain young man, however, followed Jesus,[1] but the vigilantes snatched away his robe and left him a streaker.

The citizens arresting group then took Jesus to the church headquarters where the big shots were all assembled.

Peter followed this procession, keeping well out of sight. Peter stayed well outside the headquarters, warming himself by an open fire.

The church court leaders then began to try to locate some witnesses to testify against Jesus, but they drew a blank.

Soon, however, there came forth some witnesses who had been bribed.

"We heard Jesus say that in three days he would destroy this church building which is man-made, and then build another that is not man-made."

Some of the witnesses said that wasn't exactly what had been said, and there was disagreement among the witnesses.

The senior judge then spoke to Christ and said, "What have you got to say? Will you answer these charges?"

Jesus remained silent.[2]

"Are you Christ, the son of the Blessed Lord?" asked the senior judge.

"I am," answered Jesus, "and you will see me sitting on the right hand of all power and coming in the clouds of heaven."

Then the judge tore his robe in rage and said, "That tears it. What need we with more witnesses? You have all heard the blasphemy. What do you think?"

They all agreed that Jesus should be executed. Then some began to make sport of Jesus and bait him to perform some magic tricks, or to prophesy.

As Peter was hanging around outside one of the car hops who was going around selling coffee came to him and said, "This fellow here was one of the followers of Jesus."

"You're nuts, girl. I don't know what you're talking about." Peter then went out on the porch, while in the distance a rooster crowed.

Another girl who was socializing around the crowd then saw Peter and said, "Here's one of the followers."

Peter denied this association again. A third time, when accosted by some men, Peter strongly denied any connection with Jesus, for

---

[1] I have always thought this was Mark.
[2] This has to be the toughest thing to do.

the men had singled him out because of his southern accent.[1] Peter
even cursed[2] in his strong denial.

The rooster crowed again. Peter remembered then the saying of
Christ and remorse began to get to him; so he went apart and wept
bitterly over his failure.

Chap.

15

The next morning the leaders of the Jews in Jerusalem held a
conference and determined that since they did not have the right to
execute they would refer Jesus to the Roman ruler, Pontius Pilate,
since Rome used capital punishment.

"Are you the king of the Jews?" Pilate asked Jesus.

"Yes," said Jesus.

The chief priests then accused Jesus of many things, but he
refrained from replying.

Pilate then said, "Don't you care to speak in your own behalf?
Haven't you heard all these weird charges?"

Jesus did not answer and Pilate was greatly impressed with his
self-control.

Each year at the Passover time it was customary for the Roman
government to release a Jewish prisoner as a goodwill gesture to the
Jews. There was in prison at this time a man named Killer Cade,[3] but
when the people began to yell for the release of a prisoner Pilate said,
"Would you be pleased if I released to you the King of the Jews?"

Now Pilate knew that the chief priests had framed Christ and he
was aware of their trickery in stirring the crowd to release Killer
Cade instead of Jesus.

"What shall I do then with this man you call King of the Jews,"
asked Pilate.

"Crucify him!" yelled some of the crowd.

"What has he done?" asked Pilate.

"Crucify him, crucify him!" continued the chant of the mob.

As a result, Pilate released to the people Killer Cade and ordered
that Jesus be prepared for crucifixion, the first step being the
receiving of lashes.

Jesus was then led into the open area in front of the palace,
where he was put in a mock purple gown and a crown of thorns was
placed upon his head. The unruly mob then began to clamor and
shout saying, "Behold, the King of the Jews!"

The crowd made great sport of Jesus, bowing to him in
mockery, and spitting on him.

After a short spell of this, one of the attendants removed the
purple robe and put Jesus' own robe back upon him and they led
him forth to be crucified.

[1]Galilean
[2]Some old fisherman language that came back to him.
[3]Barabbas

There was a large dark-skinned man standing on the curb watching the procession and the soldiers ordered him to come forward and carry the cross for Christ. The man was named Simon and he was in town on business from North Africa. The man had two sons, one was Ruff[1] and one Alex.[2]

The procession finally arrived at Hill of Skulls.[3] Jesus was offered a drink of wine, but refused it.

As soon as Jesus was crucified, his belongings were divided among the soldiers using dice as a means of deciding who received what. This was about the third hour of the morning.

Over the cross on which Jesus was crucified there was written 'The King of the Jews.'

Along with Christ there were crucified two others, one on each side of Jesus. This fulfilled the prophecy which said, 'He was numbered with the transgressors.'

Some of the crowd even at the crucifixion were taunting Christ, saying such things as "You can destroy the temple and build it in three days, why don't you save yourself and come down from the cross?"

The chief priests also commented among themselves saying, "He saved others, why can't he save himself?" Some said, "Let Christ descend now from the cross and we'll join his side ourselves." Also the ones crucified with him railed at him.

About the sixth hour a darkness came over all the land and lasted for three hours. About the ninth hour, Jesus cried out in agony, "My God, my God, why have you forsaken me?"

Some of the people who heard the cry thought that Jesus was calling on Elijah and one ran and filled a sponge with vinegar and raised it to Christ's lips on a bamboo pole, saying to the crowd, "Let's keep him alive and see if Elijah will come and help him."

Then Jesus gave one cry and died. Instantly, back in Jerusalem, the veils of the temple split from top to bottom.

The centurion in charge of the execution when he heard Christ and saw the glory of his death solemnly said, "Truly this man was the son of God."

In the background there were at a distance some of the women, Mary, the former Miss Alabama, Mary the mother of Joe, and Sally.[4] There were other women also who had been in the group following Jesus in his ministry.

At sundown there was the beginning of the day known as Preparation Day, for that was the day before the Sabbath.

Joseph of Arkansas,[5] a prominent merchant and follower of Christ, came to Pilate on Preparation Day and claimed the body of Christ.

---

[1]Rufus [2]Alexander [3]Golgotha [4]Salome [5]Arimathea

Pilate checked to make certain from the centurion that Jesus was dead, and when he was certain that Christ was dead he gave the body to Joseph.

Joseph then purchased fine linen and had the body carefully wrapped and laid the body of Christ in the family sepulchre which had been cut from the solid rock, and then had a huge stone rolled to seal the tomb. Now Mary, the pretty one, and the Mary who was the mother of Joe watched and marked the spot of the grave.

Chap.
16

When the period for observing Sunday was completed, pretty Mary, Mary the mother of James, and Sally had collected their various spices and little flowers to come to the tomb.

On arriving they were astonished to see that the stone was rolled away, for it was a huge stone. As they entered the tomb they saw a young person sitting on the right side, clothed in a long white robe, and they were scared stiff.

"Don't be afraid," the young person said, "for I know you are looking for Jesus who was crucified. He is risen. He is not here. You can see where he was, though. You go on along now and tell the disciples, as well as Peter, that Jesus has gone to Galilee. You will see him there exactly as he told you that you would."

The ladies left in a panic, trembling and amazed. They never said anything to anybody at first, for they were really terrified.

Now Jesus first appeared to Mary, from whom he had cast out seven devils. Mary then immediately went to the mourning disciples and told them that Jesus was risen. The disciples didn't believe her.[1]

Next Jesus appeared to two of his former followers as they walked and when they told the disciples they didn't believe them either.

Finally, Jesus appeared to the eleven as they were eating and he chewed on them a bit in a kindly fashion for their unbelief and hardness of heart.

Jesus then said to them, "Now you know that it is true; so go into all the world and preach the good news to every creature, and whoever believes and is baptized shall be saved, but the ones that do not believe are condemned.

"You will be able to tell the believers, for they shall have power to beat the devil, to cast his crowd out, they shall speak with a new force and inspiration. Some will be able to handle serpents, and others will be immune to disease, and they shall be able to heal by laying hands on the sick."

---

[1]Not the only ones who have taken too lightly some female remarks.

Sometime after this, the Lord ascended and took his rightful place on the right hand of God.

The disciples then went forth and preached everywhere, the Lord working with them all the time, and confirming their preaching with signs that God lives and acts.

Many others have written down the various matters seen and doctrines heard, in which we believe completely, but since it all seemed quite clear to me from the first I heard, I will recount the whole matter to you, Theo,[1] as best I can with real accuracy.

During the reign of Herod there was a minister known as Father Zack[2] and his wife was called Betty.[3] The two of them were very righteous and followed strictly the teachings of the holy book.

The couple had no children although they had been married a number of years.

On one occasion when Father Zack was conducting a church service, a portion of which called for the burning of incense behind the curtain and not in view of the praying congregation, there appeared to Zack an angel of the Lord. Zack was at once scared stiff.

The angel said, "Don't panic, Zack. You may think it's about time, but the Lord has heard your prayer and your wife Betty will soon become pregnant and give birth to a son, and you are to name him John. There will be an occasion of great joy when your son is born and many shall celebrate, for your son will be great in the sight of the Lord. Your boy will be a teetotaler, and from the very beginning shall be full of the spirit of God. Your son will change the lives of many and win them to the Lord.

"Your boy will have the power and spirit of Elijah, he shall persuade fathers to be more concerned with their children, and disobedient adults will he lead to new paths of wisdom, and other things will he do to prepare the people for the coming of the Lord."

"You've got to be kidding," said Zack. "I am a little old, and so is my wife. We have passed the best time to have children."[4]

"I am Gabriel," said the angel, "and I come from standing in the presence of God. I was sent by God to tell you these things. As a result of your unbelief, you are to remain dumb and not able to speak until what I have told you comes true."[5]

When Zack came from behind the curtain and appeared before the people he was unable to speak and he signaled to them that he was dumb.[6]

As soon as Zack finished the proper observances at the church he returned home and not long after this Betty became pregnant.

Betty removed herself from all social activities for about five months and rejoiced in her unexpected condition.

[1]Theophilus [2]Zacharias [3]Elizabeth [4]A very unscientific comment.
[5]This also meant no blabbing about it around town.
[6]Local diagnosis was probably "a stroke."

About six months after the temple incident, Gabriel appeared in Nazareth, a town in Galilee, and there presented himself to a young lady named Mary, who was a virgin and engaged to marry a boy named Joseph.

Gabriel, sent from God, came to Mary and said, "Good morning. You are indeed the most highly favored lady in the world, for the Lord is with you, and has chosen to particularly bless you above all other women."

Mary was greatly puzzled by this unusual little introductory speech.

"Don't be disturbed, Mary," said Gabriel, "for you are in good standing with the Lord. You will become pregnant and give birth to a son and his name shall be Jesus. He shall be the greatest.

"Your son will be called 'Son of the Almighty' and he shall be given the throne of David, and he shall reign over the multitude of believers forever, and the extent of his kingdom shall be indefinite; so that it will have no end."

"How can this be since I am a virgin?" asked Mary.

"The Holy Ghost will come upon you, and the power of God shall activate you, and the holy child born to you shall be the son of God."

"As a matter of information, your cousin Betty, who is normally a little beyond the regular years for having babies, is now pregnant in the sixth month. With God, you see, nothing is impossible."

"I am a servant of God," said Mary. "May these things come about as you have said." The angel then departed.

Mary shortly then went to visit Betty and Zack. When Mary spoke to Betty the babe in her womb jumped, and Betty was filled with the Holy Ghost.

At once Betty said to Mary, "Most happy and honored are you above all women, and blessed is the son who will come to you. How honored I am that the mother of my Lord comes to visit. I knew as soon as you spoke, for the son I carry jumped with joy within me. Blessings on you, Mary, for you believed and you will surely see the performance of the things you have been told."

"My soul worships God," said Mary. "My whole spirit rejoices in God my Saviour, for he has looked down on little ole me, and yet from now on generation after generation will call me blessed. The holy God has done great things to me. The Lord is the one who extends his mercy from generation to generation, God shows his strength, for He puts down the mighty and raises up the disadvantaged, for He has filled the hungry and taught lessons to the greedy.

"God has helped his servants who worship him, for he remembers his promise to Abraham and all his descendants."

Mary stayed with Betty almost three months and then returned home as the time came for Betty to deliver her baby.

Betty had her son and friends and neighbors arrived, rejoicing greatly, and there was much joy for mother and son were both doing well.

When the boy was 8 days old the time was proper for the ceremony of circumcision, and the friends said, "Let's call him Little Zack[1] after his father."

"Not so," said Betty, "for his name is to be John."

"Why John?" one asked. "You don't have anybody in the family named John."

A couple of the fellows then began to signal Zack and indicate a suggestion from him was in order. Zack signaled for a pen and paper, and wrote "His name is to be John."

Immediately Zack was released from his dumbness and he was able to speak again. The first thing he did was to praise God. This was too much mystery for the neighbors and they hushed up until they were gone from the house, and then they told all about everything everywhere they went.

Many people commented on the whole matter and there was much interest in what would become of this child so clearly marked for God's work.

Zack then, filled with the Holy Spirit, spoke and said, "Blessed is the Lord God of Israel, for he has visited his people and planned for their redemption. For surely God has provided a means of salvation through the line of David, just as the prophets of old foretold.

"The prophets said that we would be saved from our enemies and from the clutches of those that hate us. We will receive the mercy promised our fathers and God is going to make good on his agreement with Abraham. All of this, in order that we might serve the Lord without fear, in holiness and righteousness, all the days of our life."

"Our child, John, shall be a prophet of the Lord, for he shall go as a forerunner, to prepare the way for the Lord. John shall preach of salvation through repentance, because of the tender mercy of God."

"The preaching shall also shed light on how we should live, it will give brightness to those facing death, and it will guide us in the direction of peace."

John grew and developed a very energetic spirit, and spent most of his time in the desert.

Chap.
2

It was about this time that Caesar Augustus decided to tax the whole world.[2] Ole Cy[3] was governor of Syria and everyone who was a native was ordered to report to his home town and pay a tax.

---

[1]Zacharias   [2]His idea really caught on!   [3]Cyrenius

Because of this ruling, Joseph, accompanied by his pregnant wife, went to Bethlehem, his home tax office, and while they were on this trip the time came for Mary to give birth to her child. Because of the shortage of motel accommodations the Holiday Inn Family Complex provided a place for Mary in a covered area out back and gave her a roll-away and a crib for the baby.

In the same general area there were shepherds guarding their sheep at night, and an angel of the Lord appeared to them and the glory of the Lord showed all around them, and they were greatly startled.

The angel said, "Don't be afraid. I bring you good news of great joy for all people everywhere, for the world's benefit there is born this night in Bethlehem a Saviour who is Christ the Lord."

"You will be able to identify him, for he will be a baby wrapped in ordinary clothes, lying in a crib."

Suddenly there appeared with the angel a heavenly choir singing 'Glory to God in the highest, and on earth peace and good will to all men.'

As soon as the angels disappeared one of the shepherds spoke out, "Let's get going at once and go to Bethlehem and see this thing which the Lord has revealed to us."

The shepherds hurried and soon came to Mary, Joseph, and the babe in the manger and when they had seen the child they began to spread the word about their angel experience. People wondered about this strange incident.

Mary kept all of these things in her heart and thought about them a great deal. The shepherds meanwhile returned to their sheep watching, but they praised and glorified God for all things they had learned.

When the child was eight days old it was considered proper to circumcise and name him, and soon he was named Jesus as the angel had instructed.

When the ritual time of purification had been fulfilled, then Jesus was brought to Jerusalem to be presented to the Lord in church.

At this time the parents presented two doves or two young pigeons as the custom was on such an occasion.

There was in Jerusalem at this time a grand ole saint of the church named Simeon, and he was full of the spirit of God, he was a just and devout man, and had been waiting and praying for the restoration of Israel. Simeon had learned in a vision that he would not die until he had seen the Lord's Christ.

This same Simeon was moved by the spirit of God to come to the Temple at the same time that the parents brought Jesus to be presented before the Lord. The old man saw the baby and took him in his arms and blessed God saying, "Lord, now let me die in peace, according to your promise, for I have seen the means of salvation that you have prepared, a light to lead the non-Jews and a means of glory for your people of Israel."

Joseph and Mary marveled at what they heard. Simeon then turned to Mary and said, "This child of yours has a marvelous destiny. He will be responsible for the fall and the rising of many in Israel; he shall be represented by a sign[1] which shall often be denounced, and you will feel the pain in your own heart, but it is all part of the plan of the revelation of God."

An elderly lady then came into the temple, a godly person named Anna, a woman who had been a widow for about 60 years, devoting her life to worship and holy matters and she, on seeing Jesus, gave thanks to the Lord and encouraged all present to seek redemption.

As soon as all the ritual practices had been completed the parents returned with Jesus to Nazareth.

The boy Jesus grew in spirit, filled with wisdom, and the goodness of the Lord was in him.

When Jesus was 12 years old his parents took him with them to Jerusalem at the regular time of the feast occasion. When they had completed their stay, attended church, and paid their taxes, they began the trip home.[2]

At the end of the first day's journey, each parent thinking Jesus was with the other, they were greatly upset to learn that he had not joined either. As a consequence, the parents returned hurriedly to Jerusalem to find the boy.

It took the parents three days of frantic searching to find Jesus, and they found him at the last place they looked, in church. Not only was he in church, but he was involved in an intelligent discussion with the most learned leaders of the church. Everyone was astonished at the great wisdom of Jesus.

When the mother and father saw Jesus the mother immediately said, "Son, why have you done us this way? Your father and I have been looking everywhere, and we have been worried sick."

"Why look for me? Don't you know that I must be about my heavenly Father's business?"

Joseph and Mary didn't understand at all what he meant.

The family group returned to Nazareth and Jesus became again an obedient child, but Mary knew there was something significant about the Jerusalem scene, and she stored all these memories in her heart.

Jesus continued to grow in wisdom, and in physical fitness, and in favor both with God and man.

---

[1] I believe he meant the cross.   [2] They went in groups and often the women travelled in one group and the men in another.

Now about the time Tough Tib[1] was in his fifteenth year as Emperor of Rome, Pontius Pilate was governor of Judea, Herod was the political representative of Tough Tib in the area of Galilee and his brother Phillip was in a similar position in Iowa[2] and Jones[3] was in charge at Abilene. At this time also there were two ruling priests in the church, Audie[4] and Cap,[5] and John was beginning his great preaching career in the wilderness.

The prophet Isaiah had written about this in his book saying, "Expect the voice of one crying in the wilderness, saying prepare for the coming of the Lord, and be ready for him, for every valley will be filled and every mountain brought low for plain seeing, and the crooked matters shall be made straight, the rough edges of life will become smooth, and all people will have the opportunity to see the salvation prepared by God."

John in the wilderness began preaching with great enthusiasm and thundered at those who came seeking baptism and salvation saying, "You bunch of snakes, who warned you that you had better come running to repent and be saved from the wrath of God?

"Put some action into your repentance and begin to do good things. Don't think for a minute that little phrases like "We are descended from Abraham"[6] will save you. If all God wanted was sons of Abraham he could produce them from the stones around you.

"The time is at hand. The Lord will chop down all who do not participate in accomplishing good works. They shall be cut down like a rotten fruit tree and burned in the fire."

"What can we do?" asked some of the people during the question period.

"The place to start is with your greed. If you have two sport coats, give away one to a person who has no coat, and the same goes for food and money. You want to begin by giving."

Some politicians then came forward to be baptized and they said, "What shall we do?"

"Stop taking kick-backs, and collecting more taxes than are needed. No more padding of your accounts," replied John.

A few soldiers then came forward and said, "What about us?"

"Refrain from violence," said John, "quit complaining all the time[7] and be very careful not to make any false accusations."

Some of the people were so excited over the stirring messages of John that they began to wonder if he might be the long-awaited Messiah.

---

[1]Tiberius Caesar   [2]Iturea   [3]Lysanias   [4]Annas
[5]Caiaphas   [6]It is possible that several people left at this point.
[7]Should have said this to the Navy boys also.

John cleared this matter promptly by saying, "I baptize you with water, but the one who comes after me is far mightier than I am, in fact I am not worthy to untie his shoes, and he will baptize you with the Holy Spirit and with a burning devotion. He will come with a broom and clean out, being careful to separate the good from the bad, and seeing that the bad are burned with a never-ending fire."

John preached a whole bunch of other things of a similar nature.

Herod, having been criticized by John for his sin in stealing his brother Phillip's wife,[1] as well as being mentioned by John as being pretty bad in some other ways, decided to hush John by putting him in prison.

Many people were baptized and also Jesus, on which occasion there was a heavenly disturbance, and a voice from on high saying, "This is my beloved son in whom I am well pleased."

At this point in time Jesus was about thirty years old.

Chap.

4

Jesus, full of the Holy Ghost, returned from the baptism in the Jordan and was led by the Holy Spirit into the wilderness. During this period which extended over a month, Jesus was tempted by the devil, and Jesus fasted and prayed, and became very hungry.

"If you are the son of God, as you claim," said the devil, "why don't you show your power and order the stone here to be turned into bread and then you can eat."

"There is much more to life than eating, for this is written in the scripture, for it is more important for a man to be nourished by the word of God," replied Jesus.

The devil then accompanied Christ to the top of a hill and urged Jesus to look out over all the earth, and visualize all the nations, and all the many countries, and then the devil said, "Actually, I have the power and I will give you all the world, and all the glory, if you will defy God and worship me."

"Scram, you no-good devil," said Jesus, "for it is written that a person shall worship the Lord God, and serve no one except the Lord."

Then the devil transported Jesus to the spire of the church in Jerusalem and said to him, "If you are the son of God as you claim, jump and let's see if the angels of the Lord will catch you before you hit the bottom."

"You are foolish, and it is forbidden to tempt the Lord your God," said Jesus.

The devil tossed in the towel and let Jesus alone for an indefinite period.

[1]With her consent.

Jesus returned from the wilderness full of the power of the spirit of God and came to Galilee, and his fame began to spread as he preached and healed throughout the area.

Jesus came to his home town of Nazareth and reported as usual to teach Sunday School, and to speak during the open meeting.

On this Sunday Jesus opened the scriptures to Isaiah and found a particular passage which he read as follows: "The spirit of the Lord is in me, because he has selected me to preach the good news to the poor, he has sent me to heal the broken-hearted, to promise freedom to those whose spirits are in captivity, to restore sight to the blind, to bring ease to the troubled, and to tell about the end of the world."

Jesus closed the book and handed it back to the minister in charge of the service, and the eyes of everyone in the congregation were fixed upon him in wonder.

"I tell you that this day is this prophecy fulfilled in your presence," said Jesus to the complete wonder and astonishment of all.

The people were impressed but also troubled, for some said, "Isn't this Joseph's boy who played here in the streets as a child?"

Again Jesus spoke to the people saying, "No doubt you will pull out some old cliches on me like 'physician, heal yourself' or the like.[1] You will also want me to do some of the same things here that you heard I did in New York. It so happens, though, that a prophet is not recognized in his home town.

"Let me also remind you that in the time of Elijah when there was such a terrible drouth and famine, the prophet was only sent to help one widow and she was in Athens.[2] Furthermore, there were many lepers in the time of Elisha, but he was empowered to heal only Naaman."

This made everybody mad as they felt that Jesus was giving the local yokels the brush-off. In fact, they became so irritated that a few who were prone to violence led Jesus to the edge of a cliff outside the city with the intent of throwing him down the mountain, but Jesus walked away unharmed, and returned to New York to teach again the next Sunday.

There was in the church that day in New York a man who was a psycho, having a vile spirit, and he yelled out to Christ saying, "Let us alone. We don't want to have anything to do with you. I know you are the holy one from God."

Jesus then spoke to the evil spirit within the man and said, "Quiet down, be peaceful, and leave the man."

The malice left the man and he was at peace. The people present marveled at this, and were amazed that Jesus had the authority over evil and that he had the power to heal. Naturally word of this power began to be spread everywhere.

---

[1]Maybe 'if you're so smart why aren't you rich?'   [2]Sidon

After leaving the church Jesus went to the house of Simon and there learned that Simon's mother-in-law was sick in a back room. Jesus went to the lady and seeing that she had high fever, ordered the fever to leave her, and she was immediately well and went scurrying into the kitchen to get the chicken frying.

During the twilight hours people came from every direction seeking help and Jesus healed them, laying his hands on each in his turn.

The devils also were ordered to leave some of those who had come to Christ with their affliction and often one of these would shout, "We know you are Christ, the Son of God."

On each of these occasions Jesus would order them to be silent, even though they knew he was the Christ. The next day Jesus went into a remote rural area, but the people followed him and begged him not to leave.

"It is necessary for me to travel," said Christ, "for the Lord wants me to preach in other cities and reach many people. This is why I have come to the earth."

Jesus continued then preaching in many churches in the area of Galilee.

Chap.

5

On one occasion the people crowed around Jesus so closely at the water's edge near St. Petersburg that Jesus climbed into one of the two nearby boats, for the fishermen who owned the boats were out working on their nets. The one Jesus selected was owned by Simon and so Simon pushed the boat away from shore so that the Master could teach the people using the boat as a floating pulpit.

When Jesus had finished preaching he turned to Simon and said, "Row out a bit into deeper water and lower your nets."

"All right, but only because you request it. We have been fishing here all night and haven't caught even a croaker."

When the men had done as Jesus suggested, however, they were amazed to haul in their nets full and overflowing with fish, to the point that the nets began to tear. Immediately the fishermen called to their partners in the other boat to come to help them and they loaded both boats with fish.

Simon Peter was thoroughly astonished at what had happened, and so he fell down on his knees before Christ and said, "I am not good enough to associate with you."

James and John, the other two fishermen, were also greatly impressed.

"Don't be afraid," said Jesus, "for I will also show you how to catch men." When the men had rowed ashore they secured their gear, gave up their business, and followed Jesus.

Later when Jesus was in another place, a man suffering from leprosy came to him and said, "If you so desire, you can heal me of my leprosy."

Jesus then put out his hand and touched the man saying, "I desire to heal you, be well." Immediately the leprosy departed.

"I would prefer that you not talk about this healing," said Jesus. "It is necessary, of course, for you to go to the health officer and be taken off the quarantine list. You must pay the regular fee at the synagogue as Moses prescribed."

The word of such a miracle began to spread and multitudes of people sought Jesus, wishing to be healed of all their ailments, real and imaginary.

One time while Jesus was teaching there were some church politicians and professor type churchmen sitting around listening, for they had come from various places such as Harvard,[1] Atlanta,[2] and Jerusalem, and the power of God for healing was present on this occasion.

Several fellows had a golfing buddy[3] who had become stricken with some form of a stroke[4] and they could not get their friend near Christ because of the crowd around the house. As a result, the men lifted the stretcher to the roof of the house where Jesus was teaching, removed some tile from the roof,[5] and lowered the helpless man into the presence of Jesus.

The faith of the group impressed Christ quite favorably and he said to the man, "Your sins are forgiven you."

At once the knowledgeable church politicians began to mumble among themselves, questioning the authority of Christ, and stating that only God could forgive sins.

"What are you thinking?" asked Jesus who knew their mumblings. "Which would you consider the easiest thing to do, forgive the sins or tell the man to get up and walk?"

"Well, just so you will know that I have the power to forgive sins, watch me."

Then Jesus turned to the stricken golfer and said, "Get up and go home."

Immediately the man rose, picked up the stretcher and departed to his own house, praising God.[6] The whole occasion was an amazing event, and the people glorified God and realized that they had witnessed a marvelous demonstration of the living Lord.

Sometime after this Jesus was on a short trip and saw a fellow named Levi[7] and the man was sitting at a desk collecting taxes.

"Follow me," Jesus said to the man, and he did.

That evening Levi had a big bar-b-que dinner at his house and

---

[1]Galilee   [2]Judea   [3]The one who usually lost.   [4]They counted it, too.
[5]Maybe the house owner was fishing that day.   [6]While the friends fixed the roof.
[7]His pants were blue.

invited a lot of the local big shots, for he was celebrating giving up bookkeeping.[1]

Some of the more technical churchmen used this occasion to question Jesus and his disciples for lack of discrimination, for the meal was integrated.

Jesus gave a straight answer to their murmurings saying, "The sick people are those who need a doctor; so I am here to teach sinners and bring them into the kingdom, not to just socialize with the righteous."

"Well, what about the observance of the book of church order? The disciples of John followed the book, but your disciples eat between meals and don't always wash their hands."

"Can you make the attendants pass up a good meal when the bridegroom has his bachelor dinner? No. Well, as long as I am here and the disciples are with me they are not restricted. Soon I will be gone, and then will come their time for self-denial and sacrifice."

"For instance," continued Jesus, "No one patches a worn-out pair of pants with new, expensive material, nor does anyone put new wine in old bottles. Just so with new ideas, they must be put in a new framework. In this manner both are preserved, the wine and the bottle. It also needs to be remembered that no person accustomed to old wine is going to like the new."

Chap.
6

On a second Sunday of the month Jesus and his disciples were walking through a corn field and the disciples began to pull an ear of corn or two, rub the grain into their hands, and chew on the kernels.

One of the technical churchmen then asked, "Why do you break the law on Sunday?"

"Haven't you read the scriptures?" asked Christ. "Surely you know David, when he and those with him were hungry, went into the church and ate the communion bread and drank the wine. Supposedly this was only for the priests. There is your scripture.

"Furthermore, you should understand that I am the Lord of the Sabbath."

On another Sunday Jesus came into the church and taught during the open pulpit period and there appeared there a man with a deformed hand.

Some of the church people watched Jesus to see if he would heal the man as they then could accuse him of breaking the blue law.

Jesus knew what they were thinking and he spoke to the afflicted man and said, "Would you please come forward?" The man did as Jesus had asked.

Turning then to the congregation Jesus said, "Let me ask you a question. Is it legal and proper to do good or to do evil on Sunday? Is Sunday a good day to save life or to lose it?"

[1]I've never felt that Matthew (Levi) gave up a whole lot when he quit bookkeeping.

Then Jesus looked at the congregation for a few moments and turned to the man and said, "Put forward your withered hand, please." The man did as Jesus suggested and immediately his hand became completely normal.

Naturally, this infuriated the professional critics as there was nothing they could say and they began to plot against Jesus. Not long after this Jesus went into a mountain area and prayed all night.

At daylight following the night of prayer Jesus called to him his disciples and from them he chose twelve who would be apostles, Simon, or Rocky as they called him, Andy, James, John, Phil, Bart, Matt, Tom, Jimmy, Si, Judas, and Jaybird.[1]

Jesus then came with the twelve to the flat country and there met a great crowd of people who had come from every direction to hear him, or to be healed, or both. There were some troubled with inner demons, and Jesus healed these also. Everyone tried to touch Jesus, for they soon realized that even touching him was effective and that healing and power would come to them in this manner.

Jesus then taught the crowd, saying to them, "Fortunate and happy are those who have very little, for it is easy for you to acquire the kingdom of God; happy are those who are seeking, for you will be filled with what you find, and for those of you who weep at present, the future holds much laughter for you.

"You will be particularly rewarded if because of your belief in me other people will turn against you and disassociate themselves from you, and drop you from their clubs. You are lucky if this happens; rejoice, celebrate, for great is your reward in heaven, for this is exactly what happened to the prophets.

"It is tough to be rich, for you seem to be getting your reward on earth. Or you people who are content, not growing or seeking, when your hunger comes it will be too late. I feel sorry for those who live only for laughs and kicks, for your troubles are all ahead of you.

"It is not good if everybody thinks well of you, for this is the way the false prophets are treated.

"Let me give you some real good advice. Have a loving attitude toward your enemies, do good things for persons who hate you, smile on those that curse you, and pray for those that take unfair advantage of you.[2]

"If a person insults you, let him do it again. If someone takes your top coat let him have your other coat also, if this will prevent an altercation. Be willing to give to anybody, and don't try to recover a gift because you think it is being improperly used.

"As a rule of the thumb, treat other people as you would like to be treated.

"Actually, being very fond of people who are very fond of you isn't any accomplishment. The worst kind of people approve of

[1]Brother of James (Judas)   [2]This has got to be about the toughest,

people who approve of them. What credit is it to do nice things for people who do nice things for you? This is just an exchange.

"The same for lending. If you lend just to receive interest, you are doing no more than any ordinary sinner. The real thing, though, is to actually feel good toward your enemies, lend to people because of their need, then you will have a real reward from the Lord of All, for He is kind even to the ungrateful and to the evil ones.

"Be merciful, for the Lord is full of mercy. Do not judge others, and you won't have others judging you. Don't denounce other people, and you won't be denounced. Forgive people, and then God will surely forgive you.

"Be generous. Give freely and in the long run you will receive even more, a full measure pressed down and running over the sides."

Jesus continued teaching, this time using a parable as a basis. Jesus said, "If a blind man leads a blind man they both fall into a ditch. Certainly the student has no business teaching the teacher, but must strive to reach the point of learning enough to be able to teach.

"Another matter is criticizing. How can you know so much about a speck that is in another person's eye when you have so many blurs in your own vision?

"How then can you say to a person 'let me tell you all things that are wrong with you' when you haven't taken the trouble to remove your own faults or even notice them. You big phoney, first get your own life straight and in order and then you can begin to help someone else.

"In a way, people are like trees. A good tree produces good fruit and you can't expect to get good fruit from a no-good tree. You actually identify a tree by its fruit. No one goes to a cactus and expects to pick peaches, nor does a person go to a rose bush and expect to gather grapes.

"People are the same way. A good person produces good and a bad person causes trouble. A vile talking person is just showing what is on the inside.

"Why do you call me exalted names and say 'Lord, Lord', and yet you do not do what I suggest to you.

"The person, however, that hears what I have to say and follows my advice, such a person is like one who when he built a house dug a good foundation and built his house on a rock, and when the waters arose and beat on the house it was not damaged for it was built on a solid foundation.

"The person, however, who hears what I say and doesn't do anything about it is as foolish as a person who builds a house without a foundation but just flat on the top of the ground, and when the water rises and the stream is swollen the house gets washed away."

After Jesus finished this discourse and came down the hillside, he went to New York. It so happened that the Chief of Police[1] had a highly valued servant who was seriously ill and so when the Chief heard about Jesus he contacted one or two top-notch Jews and asked them to go to Jesus for help. The leaders came to Jesus and said, "The Chief of Police here is very co-operative and he even helped us build our church; so anything you can do in his behalf will be appreciated."

Jesus then headed to the Chief's home to call on the sick servant, but when he was nearing the place messengers came from the Chief saying, "The Chief says that his house is not worthy of entertaining such a person as Christ. In fact, the reason he did not come himself was that he did not feel worthy to speak to the Master in person.

"Actually the chief said to tell you, Jesus, that he understands authority as he has been involved in it all his life, is accustomed to giving orders himself and having them obeyed; so the Chief says that all you need to do is say the word and the servant will be well."

When Jesus heard this he was greatly thrilled and at once Jesus turned to the crowd and said, "Nowhere that I have been have I encountered such faith."

When the messengers returned to the Chief's house they found the servant already restored to good health.

The next day Jesus went to Albany[2] and was followed not only by the disciples but by a large crowd. As the group neared the gate of the city they encountered a funeral procession. There was a fairly good-sized crowd in the processional as the young man being buried was the only son of a very respected widow.

When Jesus saw the mother and her grief he had compassion on her and spoke to her saying, "Do not cry any more."

Jesus then came and touched the open casket in which the young man was being carried, and the pall bearers came to a halt.

"Young man, I order you to arise," said Jesus. The young man who was dead arose and began to speak and Jesus presented him alive to his mother.

This incident caused a great fear to fall on all that were present and many glorified God. Some comments were to the effect that a great prophet had come to visit the earth and others thought that God himself had visited.

Word about this incident and others began to spread around the region and naturally some people told John the Baptist what they were hearing.[3]

John then asked two of his best followers to go to Christ and ask Jesus to reaffirm for John if he were the Messiah, or if perchance John had baptized the wrong person.[4]

[1]Centurion   [2]Noin   [3]John was in prison at this time.
[4]I think John also wondered about his jail status.

When these men came to Christ they said, "John the Baptist is pretty uptight in the jailhouse and he asked us to ask you if you were the Messiah, or are we to look for another?"

Jesus spoke to the men and said, "Go tell John what you see and hear, how the blind are made to see, the lame walk, the lepers cleansed, the deaf made to hear, the dead raised, and the good news of God's care is being preached to the disadvantaged. Tell him also to be satisfied with the way I have chosen to proceed."

After the men had returned to go to John, Jesus spoke to the people saying, "Why did you people go to hear John preach? Just to see a man as mobile as a reed shaking with the wind? Did you expect to see a man clothed in Botany velvet suits? People who dress in such finery are in the King's palace or at a Debutante Ball.

"Did you by any chance go into the wilderness to see a real prophet? Well, you saw one and then some. This John is the one of whom it is written, 'Look, I will send my messenger first, who will prepare the way.'

"I tell you that no one ever born of a woman is greater than John the Baptist. Yet a person who is the least known in the coming kingdom of God is greater than John is in the present world."

This statement pleased the people very much for many of them had been baptized by John and most of them were greatly devoted to John.

Not so with the technical crowd, which naturally included some lawyers. These, of course, had not consented to being baptized by John.

"How can I describe this arrogant crowd?" said Jesus. "They remind me of children in the street playing a game and saying, 'We have turned on the stereo and you don't dance and we have switched to playing the funeral game and you haven't wept.'[1]

"John came observing all the technical laws, neither violating the rules of eating or drinking. You experts at once accused John of being an independent devil.

"Now I, the Son of God, come eating and drinking as an ordinary person and you accuse me of not being strict enough, as well as accusing me of associating with any and everybody. However, the truth finally reveals itself down through the years."

One of the more pious and dignified churchmen then invited Christ to come and have lunch on his patio. While they were eating, a woman who had a shady reputation came to the patio from the street with an alabaster box containing high-grade cosmetic lotion and the woman fell weeping at Christ's feet, pouring the valuable lotion on his feet and drying his feet with the hair of her head.

The host then began to think to himself that Jesus wasn't the prophet type or surely he would have known that this girl was a

---

[1] The two children's games in that time were "weddings" and "funerals."

floozie and sent her scurrying back into the street.

Jesus knew what the fellow was thinking, of course, and so he said to him, "Mr. Clean,[1] I have something to say to you."

"What is it, Master?" replied Mr. Clean.

"There was a certain creditor who had two people owing him money. One owed him $500.00 and the other two bits. When the two appeared and explained that they were both broke, the money lender[2] forgave them and cancelled their debts. Which of the two persons would you think, Mr. Clean, was most appreciative and loved the lender the most?"

"Well, I suppose the person that owed $500.00," replied Mr. Clean.

"You are right," said Jesus.

Then, looking toward the young lady, Jesus said, "Mr. Clean, do you see this young lady? Now think a minute. I came into your house and you didn't wash my feet,[3] but this young lady has used a valuable cosmetic on my feet and dried my feet with her hair, after rinsing them with her tears. You did not give the customary kiss on the cheek, but this girl has been kissing my feet to beat sixty. You didn't bother to ask me if I needed any hair oil and this girl has already put Vitalis on me.

"Take careful note of this. The sins of this girl, which are many, are forgiven, because of her great love. To a person who feels that there is little need for the Lord, such a person shows little love for God.

"Your sins are forgiven," said Jesus to the girl.

The other persons sitting around at lunch began to wonder and talk privately among themselves, saying to each other, "Who is this that forgives sins?"

Turning to the young lady again, Jesus said, "Your faith has saved you. Depart in peace."

Chap.

8

Following this Jesus began to go from one rural place to another, preaching and demonstrating the good news about the availability of the kingdom of God, and the twelve selected disciples went with him.

Accompanying Jesus also were a group of ladies, such as Mary, former Miss Alabama, from whom Christ had driven out seven devils,[4] also Joan[5] and Susie, and several others, all of whom helped sew on buttons and generally care for the needs of Jesus.

---

[1]Simon [2]Not connected with any bank, I'm sure. [3]A servant did it, no doubt.
[4]Which means she was a practicing sinner before her cleansing
[5]Wife of Chuza, Herod's chef.

A fairly large crowd gathered on one occasion coming from several nearby villages and Jesus stopped and began to teach them.

"A farmer went out to sow some seed," said Jesus, "and as he sowed some fell by the wayside and it was either stomped down or the birds picked up the seed, and some of the seed fell on rocks and as soon as it sprouted it was burned by the sun and dried, withering away, and some fell among thorns and the thicket choked it so it couldn't grow. Some of the seed, however, fell on good ground and it grew and multiplied and became very fruitful.

"Think about this now," said Jesus, "for this is important information."

"I'm sorry, Master, but I don't get the meaning," said one of the disciples.

"As you personally associate with me, you will be given an understanding of the kingdom of God, but down through the years most people will learn through such parables as I have just spoken.

"In the parable I have just given, the seed is the word of God. The wayside represents people that hear the word but the devil and selfish motives take away the word and prevent these from being saved.

"The ones represented by the rock are those people who hear the word and get all excited about it, but it is only a temporary and emotional thing with them. They have no depth of belief, and in time fade away. Now the seed that fell among thorns describes those who hear the word but they go out and are choked on their own riches and interests in the pleasures of life and they never take time to put the word into practice.

"Now the seed that fell on good ground portrays the persons who receive the word of God and put it into action, and ponder on the word, and work with patience.

"No sensible person lights a candle and then puts a vase over it, but puts it on a candlestick so that it will give light to the whole room. God does not wish to keep the good news secret, but to let man know and enjoy life.

"Listen carefully, for I tell you that the person that uses the time and ability that God has given to him, such a person shall receive more, but the person who hides the gifts of God shall have even the original gift removed."

After this the mother of Jesus and some of his other kin wanted to talk with him but they couldn't get near because of the crowd.

"Jesus," said a fellow standing near Christ, "I understand your mother wants to see you and also some of your other relatives."

"My mother and my relatives are those that hear the word of God and then put it into practice," replied Christ.[1]

---

[1] I have a feeling that this remark didn't go over very big with the local DAR chapter.

In the next day or so Jesus went aboard a small ship with some of his disciples and Jesus suggested that they cross the lake.

As the ship sailed Jesus went to sleep and there came a storm and a howling wind and the boat began to ship water and seem to be in danger of capsizing.

As a result, the men came to Jesus and awoke him, saying, "Master, Master, we are about to sink and we can't swim."

Jesus then stood up and told the wind to cease and the waves to subside, and they did, so that the lake became calm.

"Where is your faith?" asked Jesus.

The disciples then began to ask among themselves about exactly who was this Jesus, for even the wind and the waves obeyed him. The group then embarked on the coast of Georgia.[1]

As Jesus began walking to the nearest town a man came running to meet him who was a real psycho. The man was a chronic streaker and did not live in a house but spent the night in a cemetery. When the man saw Jesus he shouted saying, "What gives with you, Jesus? I know you are the Son of God. Why do you torment me and let me be crazy?"

Now the man's distress had been eased on occasion, but not for long and the man had broken his chains, and escaped into the wilderness, and there he was subject to the forces of evil.

"What is your name?" asked Jesus calmly.

"Legion. That's because I've got that many things wrong with me," the man replied.

Now the devils in the man did not want to be banished into the sea and they desired Christ to order them into a herd of pigs.[2] As a result, Jesus ordered the devils to leave the man and to enter the pigs, which they did, and as a result the pigs went crazy and ran off a cliff and jumped into the lake.

The pig keepers were terrified as well as scared of getting fired, and they ran into town and attracted enough attention to get a small crowd to come out and see what had happened.

When the people from town arrived they found Jesus sitting and talking with the former crazy, wild man, and they realized that the man was now sane, and they were amazed. There were also a number of witnesses present and they told the people what had happened.

The result of this was that everybody in Georgia was afraid[3] and they pleaded with Jesus to leave the state and he agreed to do so. The man who had been healed wanted to go with Christ, but Jesus told him to remain in Georgia and be a witness for Christ. This is exactly what the man did.

When Jesus returned to the far shore there was a crowd already waiting and in the group was a man named J.J.[4] and he was a local

[1]Land of the Gadarenes   [2]I don't understand this exactly but I believe it. Sorta like television.
[3]A few exceptions, of course.   [4]Jairus

big shot. J. J. bowed down before Jesus and begged him to come to his house for he had a twelve-year-old daughter who was dying.

As Jesus began walking to the man's house there was a crowd jostling along with him and a woman who had had a circulatory problem for about a dozen years and who had about gone broke paying doctors came behind Jesus and touched his coat, and she was immediately healed.

"Who touched me?" asked Jesus.

No one said anything. Then Peter said, "Everybody nearby has touched you for there is a real crowd here with us today."

"No," said Jesus. "This is something special, for I feel a loss of power or goodness has flowed from me."

The lady then stepped forward and said, "I touched you. I have needed healing for so many years and I knew that if only I could touch you I would be well; so I touched you and now I am well."

"Have no worry, lady, for your faith has made you well. Have a nice day. Good-bye," said Jesus.

While all this was going on a messenger came from J. J.'s house and said it was too late for the doctor as the little girl was dead.

When Jesus heard this he said, "Cool it. She shall surely live."

When Jesus arrived at the house he would not allow anyone except Peter, James, John, and the parents to go with him as he entered her room, but he turned to those weeping and wailing and said, "Don't cry so. The girl is only asleep."

Those that heard this snickered, for they had already tested her with a feather under the nose, and they knew she was dead.

After sending all the miscellaneous relatives and friends out, Jesus took the little girl by the hand and said, "Get up."

Immediately the girl came to life, and Jesus suggested that they feed her at once.[1] The parents were astonished and overjoyed and Jesus instructed them not to talk about this miracle.

Chap.

9

Jesus then called the twelve disciples into a special meeting and on this occasion he gave them the power to heal the sick and he also gave them authority over devils. Jesus sent them out to begin their missionary work, preaching the good news of God's care, and healing the sick.

Christ then gave them some instructions for the journeys. "Don't take a big bunch of stuff with you, such as tools for chariot repair or a lot of stationery. One coat is enough, and you don't need to take money or lunch snacks.[2]

"Stay overnight in whatever house you are invited. If the people

---

[1]I love this touch. You always feed a twelve-year-old.
[2]Being a missionary has always been tough.

to whom you minister are rude to you, leave the area and give the place a departing sign of your displeasure." The apostles immediately set forth doing as Jesus had ordered.

Naturally Herod heard about all the activity around Jesus and the missionary movement and he became nervous because he thought maybe John the Baptist had come back to life. Other people told Herod that this new teacher Jesus was Elijah returned and some said that Jesus was just another prophet.

"Well, one thing for sure," said Herod, "I beheaded John the Baptist. Who is this new man, then?" Herod then expressed a desire to see Christ.

The apostles returned from their first missionary trips and came to Jesus at Los Angeles to report on their trips. The people in the area followed them, however, and Jesus then taught the multitude in a deserted area, and he healed many of those who were sick.

After many hours in the desert as Jesus was teaching, the disciples came to him and suggested a lunch break. They urged Jesus to send the people to their homes or the nearest Dairy Queen to get something to eat and then return for more teaching.

"You all feed the people," said Jesus.

"Feed them? We don't have but five pieces of bread and two fish ourselves, and we surely don't have enough money to go and get a caterer to come and do the job. There are about 5,000 people here, did you realize that?"

"Tell the people to sit down in an orderly arrangement," said Jesus. This was done.

Then Jesus took the bread and the fish and looking toward heaven, he pronounced a blessing, then he broke the bread, and began distributing the food. Everyone had plenty to eat and there were twelve litter baskets of scraps and trash remaining.

Jesus then went off to pray and some of the disciples joined him. Since there was a chance for privacy, Jesus spoke to his disciples and said, "What are the present set of rumors about me?"

"Some say you are John the Baptist, risen from the dead. Others say you are Elijah or one of the early prophets," answered the disciples.

"What about you?" asked Christ. "Whom do you say that I am?"

"You are the Christ of God," said Peter.

"All right, but don't blab this all around as yet," said Jesus. "There is a great deal ahead. I must suffer many things, be rejected by the modern church leaders, executed, and then I must rise again on the third day.

"If any of you, or anyone else, decides to follow me, such a person must first have self-control, assume great responsibility, and follow me. Anyone who gives up his own ambitions or desires in order to follow me, will not lose his life, but preserve it eternally.

"On the other hand, anyone who shuns me and ignores my words, that same person will not have me for their advocate when I return in full glory, with the power of God, and accompanied by a host of angels.

"There are some of you standing here who shall live to understand and be involved in the kingdom of God here on this earth," concluded Jesus.

About eight days later Jesus took Peter, James, and John and went aside into the hills to pray. On this occasion as Jesus prayed his appearance seemed to change and his clothing became pure, glistening white. There appeared at this time two men, Moses and Elijah, and they talked of the time approaching for the death of Christ.

Peter and the other two were too sleepy to see everything, but they awoke to the extent of seeing Moses and Elijah. They also saw them disappear.

"It is a great treat," said Peter, "for us to be here. Why don't we at least establish three historical markers, one for you, one for Moses, and one for Elijah."

About this time, a cloud descended and covered their small area and a voice from the cloud spoke, "This is my beloved son, hear him."

When the voice ceased and the cloud disappeared Jesus was alone. Peter, James, and John did not tell of this incident for several years.

The next day, when the group came down the mountain, a man came running forward and called to Jesus saying, "My son, my only son, is sick. He has sudden fits, and I imagine he is epileptic. I took him to your disciples but they were not able to help."

"How difficult it is to teach real faith," said Jesus. "Bring the boy to me."

As the boy approached, he had a seizure and fell on the ground, writhing and foaming. Jesus immediately healed the boy, and everyone standing nearby was amazed.

Jesus then turned aside to his disciples and said, "Try to let this sink into your heads. I must be arrested and fall victim to the devices of men."

The disciples heard this but did not in the least understand, and yet they didn't want to show their ignorance by asking.

Later on there arose a discussion among the disciples as to which one would be the most important in the new kingdom when Jesus established it. Jesus knew they were concerned about this matter.

As a result, Jesus summoned a small child and had the child stand close to Jesus.

"Whoever is kind to a little child like this one," said Jesus, "is being kind to me. Whoever is kind to me is receptive to God. The ones who think to be the greatest usually wind up being the least."

A little while later John spoke to Christ and said, "We saw a fellow today who was casting out devils using your name as his authority. We made him quit because he isn't a member of Disciples, Inc."

"You should not have stopped him, for anyone that is not working against our program is naturally for it," said Christ.

As the time of crisis at the cross drew near, Jesus began to plan for his trip to Jerusalem. In fact, Jesus sent messengers ahead to begin preparation for the most meaningful week in the history of the world.

The nearby towns adjacent to Jerusalem were not friendly, however, for they were jealous of Jesus' intent to go to Jerusalem for Passover Week.

"That is some crazy talk from those little towns," said James and John. "Why don't we order fire from heaven to come down and give them a good burning."

"You have the wrong attitude," said Christ. "My purpose here is to save life, not destroy, and to teach you the same thing."

As they were going along the road a man came to Jesus and said, "I would like to volunteer to be an apostle."

"Let me tell you something, friend," said the Master. "Foxes have holes for themselves and birds have nests, but I have no home and no office."[1]

Another man joined the group and Jesus spoke to him and said, "Follow me."

"Fine, but first let me go to a big funeral we are having in our town," was the reply.

"Let somebody who doesn't have anything else to do attend to the burying. You start now and begin to preach the good news of the new kingdom."

"I would like to be an active disciple of yours," said one fellow, "but first let me go home and kiss my relatives good-bye and enjoy a going-away party or two."

"No one having a tendency to always look back is ready for the kingdom of God. My new kingdom is a going organization."

Chap.
10

After this the Lord Jesus appointed seventy more special missionaries to travel in pairs and to go to places in advance of Christ and help prepare for his arrival.

Speaking to these seventy, Jesus said, "There is an abundant harvest, but the laborers are few. Pray that the Lord above will enable you to inspire more helpers. Actually, you are going on a tough mission and will seem to be lambs among wolves.

[1]This one didn't join. No pension plan.

"Don't carry a lot of baggage, and don't dilly-dally with a lot of friendly visits on your way. When you enter a house present greetings of peace. If you enter with the right attitude you will be received in like manner if you are in a place that is receptive to teaching. Do not be ashamed of accepting the gifts offered to you, for you are worthy.

"If you are well received in a community, eat what is presented to you, heal the sick, and pronounce a blessing on the area, saying to those present, 'The kingdom of God is come near to you.'

"If, however, you enter an area where you are not well received and there is no hospitality, leave, giving them a sign of your displeasure by shaking your foot in their direction, but again tell even these 'The kingdom of God has come near to you.' I tell you, though, that it will be easier for Sodom on Judgment Day than for that place.

"Woe to you Los Angeles,[1] and to you, San Antonio,[2] for if the opportunities for goodness and the great preaching that has come your way had been in Tyre and Sidon they would have repented,and so it will be more tolerable for them in the time of judgment than for you.

"And New York, your city has been exalted to the heavens, but it shall be reduced to hell. Be certain that the people that hear you preach are hearing me, and those that mock you are mocking me, and those that mock me are mocking God who sent me."

When the seventy returned from their first missionary trip they were enthusiastic and reported that even the devils were subject to them through the name of Jesus.

"I saw Satan thrown from heaven," said Jesus. "I give you the power as my disciples to walk safely, without fear of snakes or of stumbling, and you shall have the victory over evil. Be careful, though, that you are not elated simply because of the power that is yours, but rejoice only in the fact that when the roll is called in heaven you'll be there."

This was a great occasion for Jesus and he was elated over the enthusiasm of his missionaries and their feeling of success. Jesus then prayed saying, "Father, I thank you that you have chosen to give these insights of faith to ordinary folks rather than just to the very brilliant, and I know you did this by plan."

Turning then, Jesus said to those around him, "All things are shown to me by the Father. No man really knoweth all about the Son, only the Father, and no man knows all about the Father except the Son, and then those to whom the Son will choose to reveal Him."

Privately Jesus then said to the disciples, "You are fortunate to see those things. Many prophets and rulers have desired to see such

[1]Bethsaida [2]Chorazin

things, and have not seen them and longed to hear the words of truth and have not heard them."

A lawyer, attempting to be a smarty, then said to Jesus, "What shall I do to have eternal life?"

"You're a lawyer," said Jesus, "What does the law say?"

"The law says," replied the lawyer, "that you shall love the Lord your God with all your heart, with all your soul, all your strength, and with all your mind, and then love your neighbor as yourself."

"You are correct exactly. If you do this you will surely live."

The lawyer wanted to shine a bit and be technical so he said, "Who do you mean when you say the word 'neighbor'? Be specific."

"Well, let me tell you a story," said Jesus. "There was a person enroute from Jerusalem to Jericho and he was mugged, robbed, wounded, and left half-dead in a ditch.

"There came along that same way a professional church person but when he saw the man he kept going. Then there also came along a businessman and he saw the man in the ditch, but he also was in a hurry and kept going.

"An ordinary person, a salesman, came along and he saw the man and immediately he became very sorry for the poor fellow. As a result, he went to the man and wrapped some bandages around him, poured a little oil and wine around on the open wounds, put him on his donkey[1] and led him to the nearest motel.

"At the motel, plain old everyday Joe paid the motel keeper to keep the injured man and then he went on the road again."

"Who was the neighbor to the injured man?" asked Christ.

"The one that helped him," replied the lawyer.

"Then go and be a good neighbor yourself," said Christ to the lawyer.

As the small group with Jesus approached one village they were invited into a home by a woman named Martha. Martha had a sister, Mary, and she immediately sat at Jesus' feet and listened intently to his teaching while Martha stirred around in the kitchen.

In a few minutes Martha blew her cool and came to Jesus and said, "Why don't you tell Mary to get in the kitchen and help. She has left all the work to me."

"Martha, Martha," said Jesus, "you are so concerned about many trivial matters, while Mary has chosen to listen to the words of truth, which is far more important than fixing things and maintaining a social status."

**Chap.
11**

A few days later there was an occasion when Jesus had gone aside to pray, and when he had finished and rejoined the disciples one of those present said to him, "Master, teach us to pray, just as John taught his disciples to pray."

[1]The worst ambulance in the district for sure.

"When you pray," said Jesus, "let the following be a guide for prayer, saying 'Our Father, who art in heaven, hallowed be your name, your kingdom come and your will be done on earth exactly as it is in heaven, give daily the bread we need, forgive us our sins even as we are supposed to forgive those indebted to us, protect us from temptation and deliver us from evil.

"Let me illustrate to you how prayer works. Suppose you go to a friend's house in the middle of the night and awake him, and calling through the door say, 'Buddy, there's a hungry man at my house and I need three loaves of bread,[1] and I don't have any. How about letting me have some bread for this fellow?'

" 'Look, Mac, the house is closed, I'm in bed, my children are at last asleep and I don't think I can help.'

"What actually happens," continued Christ, "is that Buddy gets up and gives Mac all the bread he needs, not because of friendship, but because Buddy wants to help a hungry man.

"So ask God. Ask and you shall receive, seek and you will find, knock and the door will be opened.

"If a boy asks for a piece of bread from his father, does the father give him a rock? Or if he asks his father for a piece of fish does the father give him a snake?" Or if he asks for an egg, will he be given a scorpion?

"If mankind, being human, knows how to give good gifts to children, just think how much more capable God is of giving good gifts of his Spirit."

After this Jesus encountered a person who was dumb, and when Jesus ordered the dumb person healed, the man began to speak. This created a great deal of talk and comment among the local citizens.

Some of the sceptics present, however, said, "It takes a devil to cast out a devil, and this healer is simply doing the work of Satan."

Some others, however, stood around hoping that Jesus would put on a show and demonstrate his power over the elements.

Jesus knew what all of them were thinking and so he answered their unspoken questions by saying, "A nation that is divided seriously within itself will collapse and a home that is so divided will also be split, if Satan then is casting out Satan, how shall evil continue?

"If I heal through the power of Satan, on what basis do your own physicians heal? If, however, I use the finger of God to combat evil, then you must recognize that the kingdom of God is very near to you at this very moment.

"When a strong man guards his possessions everything is safe until a stronger one comes, then the stronger removes all the strength and resource of the weaker one.

"There is no middle ground. If you are not in strong support of

[1]Actually, a very hungry man.

the movement of my kingdom you are an enemy, and if you are not growing and learning in the program, you are a wasted one.

"When a person has repented and banished evil from his life he must be careful to replace within himself a strong, aggressive program for good. Otherwise, after repenting and cleaning house, if a person does not get busy, worse evils and temptations will come to him than he previously had."

While he was yet speaking a woman in the congregation said, "Amen, amen. Blessed is your mother who gave you birth."

"You missed the point," said Jesus. "Blessed are the people who hear the word I present, and adhere to it."

In a short time the people gathered again and waited for Jesus to continue with his lectures.

"This is really not a very good generation," said Jesus, "for you want to see a lot of magic tricks. The only sign that will be given to you is the sign of the prophet Jonah, for as Jonah was a sign to the people of Nineveh so I am a sign to all of you.

"You will be justifiably criticized for not paying enough attention to me. Sheba went to all kinds of trouble to come to Jerusalem to listen to Solomon, and yet you have here one far superior to Solomon.

"The people of Nineveh would have cause to turn over in their graves, for they listened to Jonah and repented, and yet you have here a far greater preacher than Jonah.

"No sensible person lights a candle and then puts it under a bushel basket, but puts the candle on a candlestick in order that it might give light to the whole area.

"The light of the body is the eye. If you look at the bad or dark side of everything, then your whole life becomes dark. Be careful then not to let your eye introduce only gloom to you."

"If what you see is good and bright, then your whole life becomes that way."

When the lunch break time arrived one of the church leaders invited Jesus to eat with him.

The church man noticed that Jesus did not wash his hands before eating, as the custom was, and he mentioned this to Christ.

"I'm glad you noticed. I did this on purpose, for you technical church politicians are only concerned with appearances and you clean the outside, while inside is dirt and evil. Did you not know that God made everything, both the inside and the outside? If you are generous to others and thankful to God, then everything about you becomes clean.

"Woe to you pious appearing people, who perform the outward functions of religion, and forget all about true judgment and the love of God. Actually, you should measure up in both areas, for observances are fine if the spirit is fine.

"Another trouble with some of you church leaders is that you enjoy the recognition and like to receive lots of plaques. You really are nothing. You become as forgotten as unmarked graves and men walk over them with no knowledge of the existence of the grave."

"It sounds to me a bit as if you are getting at some of us lawyers also," said one member of the Bar Association.

"You are right. You people lay down heavy and wearisome laws and taxes, and yet you yourselves dodge them.[1] You try to cover up even historical errors and you make great speeches about some of the prophets, and yet it was men like you that persecuted them, and you never have condemned the practice of your fathers in this regard.

"God said that he would send prophets and apostles and that some of them would be killed. The blood of all those dedicated saints must be atoned for in this day and age, beginning with the blood of Abel. Sin must be recompensed.

"You lawyers, many of you, you have not really sought to learn the law for the sake of justice and yet you have prevented others from doing this."

All of this talk, straight from the shoulder stuff, really galled the hypocritical leaders and they began to try to trap Jesus into saying something illegal so as to have grounds for arrest, and they also began to plot against him in many other ways.

Chap.
12

On a later occasion while there was such a crowd gathering that they were stepping all over each other, Jesus turned to those close around him, his disciples, and said to them, "Don't come under the influence of the crusty-like churchmen who are only concerned with appearances and exactness of speech. There is no such thing as covering up mistakes or hiding selfish intentions, for eventually everything comes to light. Even supposedly secret comments will finally get spread around; so a hypocrite never really wins in the long haul.

"Don't be so worried about punishment or mistreatment, or even being killed by some devilish person, but fear only the person who influences you to wrong and thereby kills your soul and dooms you to an eternal hell. You'd better be afraid then of evil companions!

"Yet God cares, and God watches. You can buy five sparrows for 2¢,[2] and yet God keeps track of every sparrow and knows when one is caught by a cat, so just think how much more carefully interested God is in you. The hairs of your head are even numbered.[3] Don't be so shaky, God really cares for you.

"What is more, every person who pronounces a witness for me before his contemporaries, then such a person will I introduce to the

---

[1]There was bound to have been an "Amen" or two inserted here.
[2]Only thing that hasn't gone up in price.
[3]The heavenly account department has been real busy lately.

angels of God, but those who deny me among their friends or associates, the same will I disclaim when the time for presentation to the angels arrives.

"It is possible, of course, for a person to speak against me and then later repent and be forgiven, but a person who resists the urgings of the Holy Spirit has definitely had it.

"When you who are my witnesses are placed on a public platform or have a similar situtation at hand, do not concern yourself that you are not very knowledgeable, for the Holy Spirit will guide you as to your presentation."

About this time one of the great crowd that had gathered said to Jesus, "Master Teacher, I'm having a problem with my older brother, as he will not divide the inheritance with me, and he's the executor of the estate."

"I am not here to rule on civil matters," said Christ.

"Let's get back to the subject, now," continued Jesus. "Be on the look-out for the disease of wanting. A person's life is not to be measured by the amount of things that a person has secured. Let me illustrate.

"The land of a rich man brought forth a huge crop, so much so that he did not have enough storage space for his crop increase. That evening the man came home and announced at dinner saying, 'Tomorrow I plan to pull down all my old barns and build a whole bunch of new and bigger ones and then I can store all my crops and have plenty of money for the rest of my life. I will then eat, drink, and be merry, for I will have complete security.'

"Then God spoke to the man and said, 'You nut, tonight your card will be pulled and in two days you'll be in the Garden of Memories. What then becomes of all your wealth?'

"I tell you people," continued Christ, "don't be so uptight about your life, being anxious about what you will eat, what you will wear, for life is not a matter of food and clothing. What about the not so pretty raven? They don't accummulate stock nor worry about food or clothing and yet God has arranged to care for them. You are a lot more valuable than a bird.

"What does worry do for you anyway? Can you grow taller by sitting around moaning and groaning and shredding Kleenex? If you can't cause yourself to grow why worry about anything else?

"The lilies come out fine, yet they don't go to work or take super-long sewing lessons, yet even Solomon couldn't find a robe that was as attractive looking as a lily. If God clothes the grass which doesn't last but a few months, don't you think he has some plans for you, you collection of people with mini-faiths?

"Don't be fretting all the time about food, and drink, and clothes. Everybody in the world needs and wants these things and God knows about it and is concerned. What you really need to do is to enthusiastically seek the kingdom of God and then these other matters just come along in their properly unimportant place.

"There is no reason to be nervous about all this, for God wants you to be part of his kingdom. Sell the excess of your possessions, give away your money generously, wear out your purse with your spending, and in doing God's work you set aside treasures in his realm where there are no moths, no rust, no thieves. Furthermore, your real interest will always be toward your most valuable treasures; so let them be in the area of the concerns of God.

"Keep your light green and your mind on the 'go' signal. Be busy always with some of God's work so that when the Master returns you will be found active in His business. The Master will give special recognition to those he finds daily at his work, regardless of the hour or whether or not it is a holiday. Keep God's work always on your mind.

"There is no telling when the second coming of Christ will take place. If a person knew exactly when a burglar was going to arrive that person would be armed and ready,[1] but you never know. The same with the second coming. Be ready at any time, for the Son of God is not coming again on a basis of human predictions."

"You are telling this for us privately, or is this information we can pass along?" asked Peter.

"Let me make it even clearer," said Jesus. "What are the responsibilities of the chief servant of a household? He gives the proper food at the proper time, doing his thing in accordance with his duties. Happy is such a person when the master returns from golf and finds the man doing his job well. For such, there is promotion!

"If, however, that chief servant figures the master is going to take an extra hour looking for golf balls and so he goofs off, mistreats the people under him, and generally disregards the wishes of the absent master. What happens? The master returns unexpectedly and severly punishes the bad servant. A servant with a limited understanding would receive a limited punishment. Justice will reign. The person to whom much has been given by God, of such a person much shall be demanded, even as is the case in most human relationships.

"You see, I have come to the earth to start a fire of enthusiasm that must sweep the earth. I will have to suffer in order that this be accomplished and it is difficult to patiently await the time.

"Do you think I have come to make everything sweet and nice and peaceful? You are wrong! I have come with new ideas that will cause divisions in families, and in nations, and between friends.

"You people are always talking about the weather.[2] I hear you say that when you see a cloud rising in the west that you expect rain. When the south wind blows you expect heat. All this occurs. You seem to be able to interpret such relatively minor matters; why don't

---

[1] Or at least asked his brother-in-law to be there.
[2] It has sure been going on a long time.

you take a look at the real values and the important signs to be interpreted?

"Do everything you can to get your life straight as soon as possible. Just like getting a ticket for speeding, first you argue with the officer, then the desk sergeant, next the judge, and finally you pay up or go to jail. Why speed in the first place? In other words, straighten up your life now before one step leads to another and you are finally immersed in multiple difficulties."

Chap.

13

Not long after this some people reported to Christ about an incident involving the slaughter of a protesting group by the soldiers under the rule of Pontius Pilate.

"Do you think that the ones that died were necessarily the worst people in town? Of course not. Yet I strongly urge you to repent before something unforeseen like this happens to you.

"Or what about the 18 people killed when the tower at Yellowstone[1] fell? Do you think these were the worst people on vacation that year? No. Yet I warn you to repent, for fear of such happening to you before you repent.

"Now hear this story. A certain person had a fig tree and the owner came in proper time and found no figs. The owner then spoke to the foreman in charge of the orchard and said, "I've come for three years and I notice that you have a fig tree that doesn't produce any figs. Get rid of it!'

" 'How about sparing the tree another year?' asked the foreman. 'Next year I will dig around it and prune it, and then if it bears fruit, fine, and if not, I will cut it down.' That's the way the Lord works," concluded Jesus.

One Sunday Jesus was teaching the lesson in church and a woman who had been ill for 18 years and was bent over considerably from arthritis was there. When Jesus saw her struggle just to make it to church, he spoke to her and said, "Lady, you are now free of arthritis."

Immediately she was able to stand erect and then she glorified God.

The chairperson in charge of the service was highly indignant over the interruption to the program and this person stated from the pulpit, "There are six days of working and if anyone wants to be healed it must be done then, not on Sunday which is a day of rest."

"What a hypocrite you are," said Christ. "You and your group always take your ox to water on Sunday, why shouldn't this lady be led to a healer?"

This embarrassed the ruling group very much, but greatly pleased the people present.

"You want to know about the kingdom of God?" asked Jesus. "It is like a grain of mustard seed which a person took and threw in

[1]Siloam

the garden and it grew into a large tree and became a haven for the fowls of the air."

"To what is the kingdom of God similar?" continued Jesus. "It is like seasoning which a woman puts in food and it gradually pervades all the food."

Jesus continued his travels, going to cities and villages, teaching and healing enroute, and heading generally for Jerusalem.

"How many people are going to be saved?" asked one of the disciples.

"The way to eternal life is through a narrow and straight gate and more will be hopeful of admission than will get it.

"Once the owner of the heavenly house has shut the door it will be too late. Some will knock and call to be let in, but the owner will act as if he never heard of them.

" 'Well, we have eaten in your presence and seen you around town,' will be the reply of many.

"The owner, however, shall say, 'I never noticed you, for you were busy doing evil things.'

"In the final place there shall be weeping and gnashing of teeth and you will be able to envision Abraham, Isaac, Jacob as well as numbers of the prophets, but you will be outside looking in.

"People from everywhere on the earth shall come together and constitute the kingdom of God. Some that by man have been considered unimportant shall be placed in high positions and some who had high positions on earth shall be demoted."[1]

Later that same day some of the churchmen came to Jesus and urged that he leave the area and they reported that Herod had an APB out on him.

"Well," said Jesus, "go tell that foxy ruler that I am casting out devils and healing people today and tomorrow, but that on the third day I shall become complete in the Lord and in my work.

"Anyhow, I need to hit the road for my time is drawing near and it is not proper for a prophet to perish outside of Jerusalem.

"O Jerusalem, what a shame! You have killed and stoned the prophets sent to you. How often have I wanted to gather the people together as a hen does her brood, but you wouldn't consent, as you wanted to be independent.

"As a result, you really are in bad shape. You will not really acknowledge me or accept me until I return and you can shout 'Blessed is he that comes in the name of the Lord.' "

Chap.

14

After church one Sunday Jesus was invited to eat at the home of one of the elders and the elder had also invited his lawyer and a couple of golfing friends. As they were eating on the patio a man came into their presence who had a circulatory or intestinal disorder.

[1]There go the past moderators!

Jesus sensed the critical observance on the part of the host and others and so Jesus turned to them and asked, "Do you think it is wrong to help a man on Sunday by healing him?"

There were no answers. Jesus healed the man and discharged him.

Then Jesus turned to the small group who were obviously critical and asked, "If one of you has an ox or a donkey that has fallen into a pit do you wait until Monday to pull him out?"

Again there was no answer. Jesus then spoke saying, "I have observed that protocol is quite meaningful to you people. For the most part it is foolishness. It is better for you to seat yourself at a less desirable place and then be invited to a more honorable position, than to be booted out from your chosen high place just to let some Admiral get some recognition.

"In God's kingdom those that exalt themselves will be degraded, and those that humble themselves will be given great acclaim."

Turning them to the elder who was the host Jesus said, "Let me tell you something about inviting people to dinner.[1] Don't invite your friends, or rich neighbors, or even relatives, for they will just feel obligated to invite you in return. When you serve a big dinner ask the lame, the poor, the blind, and this will be a blessing to you for they can't invite you in recompense. You'll get paid back after the resurrection."

One of the persons sitting near Jesus then said, "Happy is the fellow that gets to eat in heaven."

"Let me tell you about a certain person," said Jesus, "who made ready for a big banquet and then sent his servant out with the invitation list. Each of those invited had an excuse, one saying he had to go to look at some property, another said he'd just bought a quarter horse and hadn't seen him do his thing, and another said he was on his honeymoon.[2]

"The master of the house didn't care the least bit about being rejected and so he told the servant to go out into the streets and invite the lame, the poor, and the blind."

A bunch of them came, but the chief steward told the master that there was still room for more.

"Well," said the master to the servant, "get my six iron and go out into the highway and the bushes and force some to come to my big dinner. Then see to it that everything is eaten as I don't want any of the excuse-makers to get a thing."[3]

Jesus then turned to the large crowd that had been gathering while he was lecturing and he spoke to them saying, "If anyone comes to me and still had hate in his heart for anyone, or self-pity,

[1] I think Jesus would say this same thing today to most of us.
[2] I think this is a good excuse. I think he was forgiven.
[3] I still think he saved a doggie bag for the one on his honeymoon.

he cannot make a go of it as a disciple.

"Anyone who is not willing to accept responsibilities is not able to be my disciple. Think a minute about this.

"Which of you intending to build an office or a house doesn't first figure out what it will cost so you will know if you can finish it. You would certainly get the razzberries if you could only build the foundation.

"Or what military leader going out to make war on another military group doesn't try to figure how with 10,000 men he can do any good against the other fellow if he has 20,000. In fact, he might decide that this would be a good occasion for a peace talk.

"So think about the cost. You have got to put me and the good news of God's love that I bring first, or you can't be my disciple.

"Salt is good, but only as long as it has its flavor. If you don't have the spirit and the willingness you are like salt that has lost its taste and is good for nothing. You've got ears, you have heard what I said. Think about it."

Chap.
15

Not long after this a fairly large group of middle and low income people gathered to hear what Christ might have to tell them. The upper crust group immediately criticized Jesus for this as this violated class and status distinctions.

Jesus spoke saying, "Who is there who having 100 sheep and notices that one is missing doesn't immediately begin to search for the lost one? Naturally, when he finds the lost sheep he rejoices, comes home, calls in the neighbors, and serves everybody some beer and pretzels.[1] The rancher was really happy to find the lost one."

"This is the way it is in the kingdom of God," continued Jesus. "There is more real glee in heaven over a sinner saved than a 25 mm slide showing a picture of 300 dedicated Christians reading mimeographed prayers at the church conference.

"Let me give you another illustration. A lady loses a whole book of green stamps. Naturally, she cries and begins to shred Kleenex. She searches, using a broom and a flashlight, even looking in the closet under the stairs. At last she finds it.[2] At once she summons her friends and they have a big celebration.[3] The lady says to her friends, 'Be glad with me. The lost is found.'

"This is the way it is with the angels in heaven when the scoreboard flashes the name of a sinner saved."

"Now here's another," said Jesus. "A certain man had two sons. When the younger son was of draft age, he came to his father and said, 'Father, I want to split. The great world out yonder is calling to me. How about giving me now what I will inherit?'[4]

---

[1]Maybe it was Coca-Cola. [2]Usually in the dirty clothes hamper.
[3]Everybody likes to celebrate. [4]Good tax saving, too.

"The old man agreed and he gave to each son the amount that he figured would come to them. As soon as he could pack and get his traveler's checks the younger son hit the road with abounding joy.

"The young man headed for Las Vegas and blew his money in riotous living.[1] Not long after this he was flat broke and a drought had brought unemployment and he was in bad trouble. At last he got a job feeding hogs.[2] The young fellow was so hungry that he considered eating some of the hog food.

"Lonely, hungry, and meditative, it began to dawn on the young fellow that even the lowest servant in his father's house had a better time of it than he had. He said to himself,[3] 'I will get up and go to my father, apologize, explain that I am no longer worthy to be called a son, and ask for a job as a servant.'

"The youngster did as he planned. Long before the boy reached the big house the father saw him and ran to meet him, embraced him, and welcomed him home."

"The son then said, 'Father, I am no longer qualified to be called your son, for I have sinned against God, and you.'

"The father immediately said, turning to a nearby servant, 'Get a sport coat, a pair of shoes, a family ring, go kill the fattest calf we have, for we are going to celebrate, we will eat and drink and be merry, for my son was lost and is now found.' Then there was great merriment.

"Now the older son was out on the ranch working and when he returned to the big house he heard all the music and the sounds of revelry. Of course, he turned to a nearby worker and asked, 'What gives with the big commotion?'

" 'Your brother is home,' was the reply, 'and your father is exceedingly happy that the boy is safe.'

"This made the older son angry and he wouldn't go in the house for dinner.[4] The father came out and tried to reason with him, but the older son said, 'For all these years I've served you and worked hard, being obedient,[5] and you never had an appreciation dinner for me or gave me a plaque. The minute the young one comes, though, even though he has been in Las Vegas raising hell, for him you stage the big dinner.'

"The father replied, 'Son, you are with me all the time, all the blessings of every day you share with me. Wake up! Your brother is here. He was lost and is found, he was given up as dead, and he is alive. Be joyful with us!'

---

[1] I admit I have a notion that he enjoyed himself for awhile.
[2] This is a sorry job even in Arkansas.   [3] Maybe also to the hogs.
[4] Only a fanatic would have passed up the dinner.   [5] And probably dull.

At a training session with the disciples Jesus spoke to the lay group and said to them, "There was a rich man and he heard that one of his vice-presidents had been wasting money as well as throwing away paper clips. As a result he sent for him.

"The rich man said, 'What's this I hear by the grapevine about your being careless? Bring me your reports and let me check them. Maybe you won't be a vice-president when I've seen the accounts.'

"To himself the vice-president said, 'What in the thunderation am I going to do? If I lose my job I'm a goner. I'm not in shape to do manual labor. I'd be too ashamed to try the tin cup routine. I know what I'll do. I'll go to everybody that owes the company, to those that owe $1,000 I'll agree to settle for $500 and this way I'll collect a batch of money and make a bunch of people happy and maybe get the boss to thinking that at least I'm willing to work when I have to get with it.'

"The plan worked. The boss was pleased. It is really never too late to start to work. There is some merit even in belated energy. It is also good to know something about people, even those who are not very righteous.

"You will find in life that a person who is diligent and careful in doing a little job can certainly be trusted to do a big job, and a person who is careless in small matters will also be careless in major undertakings.

"If you are not willing to work in practical, everyday matters, how can you expect God to trust you to do his work? If you are not dependable in caring for other people's affairs, how do you expect the Lord to give the privilege of handling your own affairs?

"No one can work for two equal bosses. Always a person ends up favoring one or the other. You can't serve God and the devil, either."

The pious advocates of legalism heard his talk and they gave the plan the big pooh-pooh.

"I know you don't agree," Jesus said to them. "You think that the only thing that counts is the appearance. How does it look to other people is your standard. God, however, knows the heart, and it is what is in the heart of a person that really counts.

"For many years the law and the prophets were the whole guide for living, but since John has come and preached repentance we have a new kingdom brought into being and you are urged to be part of it.

"The law is still intact. There is only a new spirit injected into it. It is still basic for a man to establish one family and to strive to keep it intact. No one should attempt to break up a family.

"Listen to this. There was a rich person who lived high on the hog and there was a beggar named Lazybones,[1] who had scurvy, and

[1]Lazarus

so was unemployed. Lazybones had to be content to live on the scraps from the rich man's table, and he even had trouble competing for the scraps with the dogs.

"Then Lazybones died and went to heaven and became friendly with Abraham. The rich man died and was eternally separated from God. The rich man could see Abraham and Lazybones playing checkers and he called out as loud as he could, 'Father Abe, have mercy on me. Send Lazybones down here with a Dr. Pepper, a cold one, and let me have a few sips. The heat here is almost unbearable.'

"Then Abe said, 'Sorry about that, son. Remember that when you were on earth you received all the good things and Lazybones got all the trouble. Now in the new life everything is switched. Unfortunately for you, there is no flight schedule to hell that has a round trip arrangement; so there is no way of anyone going back and forth from either here or there.'

"Then the rich man said, 'That is bad news. At least, Abe, send Lazybones back to earth and tell him to go to my five brothers and tell them as they are all headed to hell and maybe Lazybones can talk them out of it.'

"Abe spoke again to the rich man saying, 'Your brothers have the Bible, they can read of Moses[1] and they can read the prophets.'

"The rich man yelled out, 'That won't cut it. Maybe if they saw someone from the dead they might believe him.'

"At last Abe said, 'No dice, fellow. If they won't listen to the word of the Lord through Moses and the prophets they won't listen and be persuaded even though one was raised from the dead and spoke to them.' "[2]

Chap.
17

Jesus then said to the disciples, "It is not possible for life to be free of errors or for my followers to escape ridicule and difficulty. I just promise you that those who cause my workers trouble or take advantage of the innocent, it would be better for them to have a concrete block tied around their neck and then to be thrown in a deep lake.

"Remember also that if someone insults you or wrongs you, correct such a person nicely, and if he apologized accept the apology graciously. You keep doing this even though you are repeatedly offended by the same person."

"That takes a lot of faith, Jesus, and so you need to increase our faith," said the apostles.

"If you had the faith of a grain of mustard seed you could transplant a sycamore tree by thought process."

"Which one of you," continued Jesus, "who has someone working for him in the field will come to the worker and remind him

[1]Abe was too modest to mention himself.
[2]God so loved the world that He tried this for us also.

that it is time to quit and eat? Do you not rather expect the servant to see to it that you are fed first, and then the servant can eat and drink? Do you thank the servant for doing what he is supposed to do? I doubt it!

"So with you. When you have done all the things that are expected of you there seems to be the feeling that there is no profit. Profit is not the motive for righteousness."

As the group journeyed on Jesus entered a village and there was met by ten persons who were lepers, and who therefore kept their distance.

They called forth, however, saying, "Jesus, Master, have mercy on us!"

When Jesus saw them he instructed them to report to the Board of Health, and as they turned to go they were healed. One of them, as soon as he saw that he was healed, turned back, thanked Jesus, and glorified God.

Jesus said, "Weren't there ten? Where are the nine? Is there only one grateful and willing to glorify God? You may go, good fellow, and be certain that your faith has made you well."

On a later occasion some of the church leaders wanted to know exactly when the kingdom of God was coming.

"The kingdom of God is not to be observed like a parade arriving," said Jesus. "You don't yell out 'there it is, or I see it yonder,' for the kingdom of God is within you."

Then Jesus said to the disciples, "The days will come when you will long to see me again, but I will not be present in person. Some will even suggest that I am here or there, don't go on such wild goose chases. When I return the second time it will be as prominent as lightning shining all the way from the east to the west. There are many things that must occur before this time, however.

"First, I must suffer many indignities during my present visit on earth, and I must be rejected by the people who are alive today. The second coming, however, shall be roughly similar to the days of Noah, when there was much drinking and wife exchanging, and the righteous Noah built an ark and escaped the flood that drowned the wicked. Just as it was when Lot was alive and there was such wickedness.

"Remember how fire came down from heaven on Sodom the day after Lot left. That's the kind of situation that will be existing when I come again and am revealed on a world-wide basis.

"It will be too late then to try to join the church or reform. Looking back with regret will do no more good than it did Lot's wife. I tell you the end of the world will find two men in a dormitory room and one will be saved and the other lost. There will be two women knitting at the health spa and one shall be taken and the other doomed; two persons working side by side in an assembly line and one will be saved and one will be lost."

"Where is all this going to take place?" asked the disciples.
"Where the meat is there do the birds of prey appear."[1]

Christ then began to teach the disciples about prayer and perseverance and he said to them, "Once upon a time there was a judge that feared not God and wasn't afraid of any man.

"There appeared before him a widow who wanted to complain about an injustice done to her. At first the judge wouldn't do anything as he regarded neither God or man, but then he decided later to correct the wrong done the widow simply so that she wouldn't nag him for the next few months.

"Surely God shall be more attentive to the calls of his people than the unjust judge and much more prompt. Even so, when the Lord returns in his glory at the second coming he will not find everyone faithful."

Jesus told this account to a group that was self-righteous and already wearing buttons saying 'I'm saved.' He said to them, "There were two men who went into the chapel to pray. One was a self-righteous, self-made type of person, and the other a very ordinary man.

"The first man prayed saying, 'God, I thank you that I am a good person, not riff-raff, unjust, an adulterer, big-shot gambler, or even like this crummy-looking character praying near me. In fact, for the record, Lord, I tithe and skip dessert twice a week.'

"The other, rather ordinary person, humbly bowing in the corner, prayed saying, 'Lord, be merciful to me, I am a sinner and I need help.'

"I tell you that the second man and his prayer was far more acceptable to God than the first. For sure, everyone that exalts himself shall be taken down a peg or so, and everyone who humbles himself shall be exalted."

Some people began bringing babies and small children to Jesus and some of the disciples began trying to protect Jesus from such inconvenience. Jesus then said to them, "Encourage little children to come to me, don't dare forbid them, for their attitude is the attitude that exists in the kingdom of God. In fact, unless a person seeks the kingdom of God with a motive as pure as a little child's, the kingdom will not be available to such a person."

On a later occasion one of the members of the City Council[2] came to Jesus and asked, "What do I have to do to qualify for eternal life, Good Master?"

"Only God is good, so don't try to flatter me. You are educated, you know the commandments, such as do not commit

---

[1] I have several thoughts on this, but I'm not real sure exactly what Christ meant.
[2] Could have been on the County School Board.

adultery, do not kill, do not steal, do not lie, and respect the family plan of a mother and father."

"I have observed all these commandments from the time I was ten years old," said the person.[1]

Jesus then said, "You are almost qualified for eternal life. All you need to do now is to sell all your possessions, give the proceeds to the poor, building up great treasure in heaven, and follow me."

The person left very sorrowfully for he had a great deal of IBM stock and lots of land.

Jesus commented, "It is really tough to be rich, for it makes entering the kingdom of God more difficult. A rich person entering the kingdom of God must do like a camel that gets down on its knees to crawl through the needle eye on either side of the city gates."

"Who then can be saved?" someone asked.

"Things that seem impossible with men are quite possible with God," replied Jesus.

"What about us, Master?" asked Peter. "We gave up fishing and home life, and followed you."

"I tell you," Jesus said, "that nobody who has left home or made any sacrifice for the sake of the kingdom of God shall fail to receive some blessings on this earth and then everlasting life."

Following this public discourse Jesus took the apostles aside and spoke to them privately. "The time has come," said Jesus, "for us to go to Jerusalem and there shall be fulfilled the things which the prophets said would happen. For they said the Messiah must be mocked, turned over to non-Jews, mistreated, spit upon, beaten and put to death. On the third day, the Saviour will rise from the dead."

The apostles did not understand any of this at the time.

As the group drew near to Mobile[2] a blind man was sitting outside the tunnel entrance to the city. Upon nearing the crowd, the blind man asked what was all the noise. Some of the people told him that Jesus of Nazareth was passing nearby.

As a result, the blind man began to yell at the top of his lungs, "Jesus, Jesus, son of David, help me!"

The people around the blind man attempted to hush him but he yelled all the more.[3]

Jesus then stopped walking and asked that the man be brought to him. When this was done, Jesus spoke to the blind man and said, "What do you want of me?"

"I want you to restore my sight, please," begged the blind man.

"Receive you sight! Your faith has made it possible for me to heal you," said Jesus.

Immediately the man received his sight and followed Jesus, glorifying God. When the people saw this miracle they all praised God and were greatly impressed.

[1]How did such a one get elected?   [2]Jericho
[3]He was a native of Baldwin County.

As Jesus was walking down Water Street in Mobile, there was a man called Short-Stuff,[1] who was rich, and who had made his money by tax rake-offs, and he wanted to get a look at Jesus, about whom he had heard various interesting things. Short-Stuff was not tall enough to see over the heads of the crowds and so he ran ahead a couple of blocks and climbed a sycamore tree.

When Jesus came by the tree he looked up and saw Short-Stuff and said to him, "Shake a leg and come down for I would like to have lunch with you."

This greatly delighted Short-Stuff but it caused murmuring among the people who thought it quite improper for Jesus to eat with such a well known scoundrel.

Following the meal and the conversation, Short-Stuff stood and spoke to Jesus saying, "I repent. I will immediately give away half of all that I have to the poor, and I will return four times the amount to each person that I have cheated."

"You are saved today," said Jesus. "I have come to earth to locate and save those that are lost."

Some of the followers of Jesus heard this remark and for fear of being misunderstood he explained himself in a parable, for Jesus knew that some expected the end of the world to come in a few days.

Jesus said, "There was a certain ruler who went on a long trip in order to acquire new holdings and he called his three vice-presidents to him and gave to each of them $10,000 and told them to stay busy until he returned.

"Now when he left there were many who did not care for him and who did not believe that he would return. However, he did return, and he sent for the vice-presidents who had been left to do his work. The first one came and said to the ruler, 'I have been aggressive and worked hard and increased the $10,000 to $100,000.'

"The ruler then said, 'You have been a good vice-president and I will give you great possessions.'

"The second vice-president then came and said, 'Sir, I have worked hard and made $50,000 from the $10,000 you left with me.'

"The ruler said, 'Fine, you will be give commensurate possessions for yourself.'

"A third vice-president then was summoned and he said, 'Sir, I know you are a careful man, and for fear of making a mistake I didn't do a cotton-picking thing with the $10,000 you left with me.'

"The ruler said, 'Out of your own testimony you condemn yourself. You knew I expected results. At least you could have tried to do something with what you were given.'

"Then the ruler turned to some of his aides and told them to take the $10,000 from the goof-off and give it to the industrious and active vice-president.

"This is the way the kingdom will work. If you do not use the

[1]Zacchaeus

gifts that God has given you, when the judgment comes you will even be deprived of your native talents.

"As for those that did not expect the second coming, they shall perish, for they are enemies."

Following this talk Jesus headed for Jerusalem. When the group was a few miles from Jerusalem, Jesus sent two of the disciples ahead and told them that they would find a young donkey tied to a tree and that it would be one of which no one had ever ridden.

Jesus also told them that if anyone asked why they were untying and taking the young donkey they were to tell those asking that the Lord had a use for the animal.

The two did as they were told and they found the donkey and as they were freeing it the owners appeared and said, "What gives, Mac? You stealing a donkey?"

"No," they said, "The Lord has need of the animal."

They brought the donkey to Jesus and fixed a blanket as a saddle and Jesus rode into Jerusalem on the beast. As he rode, many threw palms and some their coats as a means of expressing their joy. The occasion was one that gave forth a feeling of victory and many were praising God and expressing great happiness in all the things that they had seen and the words that they had heard.

"Blessed is the King that comes in the name of the Lord. Let there be peace, let glory abound!" said the people, shouting in their enthusiasm.

Some of the calmer church people suggested that Jesus might ask the loud ones to cool it a bit, but Jesus said, "If they weren't shouting the stones would cry out."

When Jesus looked at the holy city, Jerusalem, he was saddened and said, "If you only had sense enough to know what is happening today, and the even greater things to come.

"There are some terrible times ahead also for Jerusalem, for the days shall come when the enemies of Israel shall surround the city, they shall level it, killing women and children. This could have been prevented by receiving me now as your true king, but it was not to be this easy."

Then Jesus went to church and found that the sanctuary was being used as a market place and he drove the offenders out saying, "My house is intended to be a house of prayer and you are making it a den of thieves."

Every day after this Jesus taught in the church, but the church and civic leaders didn't like it a bit and began to plan ways of getting rid of Christ. They were puzzled, for the people were attentive and protected Jesus.

Chap.
20

On one of the days when Jesus was teaching at the church, a group of the church and civic leaders came to him and wanted to know on what authority he relied as a teacher, for he did not have a Ph.D. degree.

Jesus said, "Let me ask first a question of you learned men. Was the baptism of John from heaven or was it from men?"

The brain trust group pondered this realizing that if they answered that it was from heaven Jesus would want to know why they didn't believe John. If, however, they said it was of men, the great throng of John's followers would turn against them, and might even give them a physical licking.

As a result their answer was, "No comment."

Jesus then continued with his class and said to the group at the church who were listening, "A certain man had a nice vineyard but since he wanted to go on a golfing tour he leased the vineyard to the Cohen boys.

"Knowing that it was about time for a harvest, for several months had passed, the owner sent a hired messenger to collect the least money. The Cohen boys had a couple of their hatchet men give the messenger a good beating and no money.

"As a result the owner sent another messenger and the Cohens gave him the same type of treatment. The third messenger that the owner sent[1] was also wounded and mistreated."

"The owner then reluctantly decided to send his only son, thinking surely they will respect him.

"When the son arrived the Cohen boys had a meeting and reasoned among themselves that the smart thing to do was to kill the son for then there would be no one left to inherit the ranch and they would never have to pay any lease money. As a result, the Cohen boys killed the son. Now how do you think the owner reacted to that?

"Well, the owner was plenty hot so he came himself in all his power and glory, he completely destroyed the Cohen boys and gave the rich vineyard to others."

"God forbid that this should happen to us," said the people.

Jesus then looked at them and said, "Do you know what is meant by the saying that the stone which the builders rejected has become the most important part of the structure?

"This refers to me. Whoever attempts to destroy my mission will go to pieces, and whoever opposes my work shall be ground to bits."

Before the meeting was over the chief priests were seeking to get their hands on Jesus, but again they were afraid of the people's reaction. The chief priests realized that the story Christ had just told was about them. As a result, they secured the services of a couple of undercover agents whose assignment was to catch Jesus in some indiscretion of words or deed that would enable them to legally arrest Christ.

[1]He found one who hadn't heard about the first two.

One of the undercover agents then spoke to Christ and said, "We know you are a just and honorable teacher and not influenced by bribes or official groups. How about giving us a straight answer to our problem of paying taxes to Caesar, who even lives in a distant land."

Jesus could see through this sham and he said, "Why do you try to entrap me? However, let me see one of your coins."

One of the men produced a coin.

"Whose picture is that on the coin?" asked Jesus.

"It is Caesar's" was the reply.

"Then I would suggest that you give to Caesar what is his, but that you also be careful to give to God the things that are due the Lord."

This great answer floored the agents and made a great impression on the people listening.

There then came to Jesus one of the intellectuals from the Association of University Professors, one of the thinkers that did not believe in the resurrection.

"Teacher," said this person, "Moses instructed us that if a man's brother dies without children, then the brother inherits the wife, and should make an effort to produce children for the dead brother. Now what about the case of the seven brothers, and the eldest took a wife and had no children, then he died, leaving his wife, Sweet Sue, to the next brother. Then the second brother died childless and Sweet Sue was taken to wife by the third. This process continued until all seven brothers were dead.[1] Since you believe in the resurrection, which brother gets Sue in heaven?"[2]

"Marrying is something that takes place in this world," said Jesus. "Those that are worthy of heaven are freed from any and all earthly bonds. They become similar to angels and become the resurrected children of God.

"You are really just questioning the fact of the resurrection. Moses believed in the resurrection. Moses referred to the Lord as the God of Abraham, Isaac, and Jacob, for he is not the God of the dead, but the God of the living. Everyone lives only with the permission of God."

Some of the Sunday School teachers present then said, "You have really given them a good answer." The answer worked, as the big thinker type hushed for a change.

Jesus then said, "Why do some of the modern scholars refer to the Messiah as the son of David? David himself said in one of his psalms that the Lord said to his Lord, sit on my right hand until I make all your enemies as dirt under your feet. If David then calls the Messiah Lord, how then can he be his son?"

[1]Maybe Sweet Sue kept insuring husbands pretty good.
[2]I'd like to know which one wants her!

Then Jesus turned to his disciples, even with the other people listening, and said, "Look out for those that live by the book, who delight in fancy robes, big greetings in public, sitting at the speaker's table, and on the side they take advantage of the poor, cheat widows and cover all this up in long prayers with righteous tones. Hell will be extra hot for them."

As Jesus was standing in the sanctuary he began to observe the poeple as they came forward and made their offerings,[1] particularly noting how showy some of them were with their gifts. While Jesus was watching a poor widow came and quietly slipped her dime into the offering jar.

Jesus turned to the people near him and commented, "This woman has given the most impressive gift. The others have given a minor portion of their abundance, but this lady has given substantially in proportion to her ability."

"Don't you think we have a beautiful church, Jesus? Have you noticed the precious stones and the decor in the Narthex?" mentioned one of the people.

"The building won't last. Nothing made by man is eternal," said Jesus.

"When is the end coming, Master, and what shall it be like?" asked another.

"Try not to be fooled," said Jesus. "There will be a bunch of fakes who come and claim to be me. Don't be suckered into following such. There will be wars and rumors of wars, but don't be uptight, all that is part of life.

"Nation shall rise against nation, there will be earthquakes, famines, the spread of disease, and many UFO's. You present here don't have to worry about these things for as my disciples you will be arrested, you will be put in prison, some will be tried before kings. Let these be opportunities to witness. On such occasions do not worry about what to say as I will provide words and inspirations, and you will well be able to handle difficult circumstances.

"You will find that often you will be rejected because of me by some friends and even members of your family, and some of you will be executed, and others deeply resented. I will see that every bit of you is preserved for the next world; so any harm done to you is temporary. Wrap your soul in patience.

"When Jerusalem is surrounded by armies then you can realize that the period of desolation has started. For those who are alive when this occurs, my suggestion is to run, run, run. Pray that you are not pregnant at this time nor have both legs in casts. There shall be a period of awful violence and blood will flow and man's inhumanity

---

[1]We don't trust 'em, we take the plates to them.

to man shows its worst side. There is a time set aside for this involving primarily the unbelievers.

"There shall be signs in the heavens accompanying these periods. The sun, the moon, and the stars will be affected, the sea will roar as never before, some persons shall have heart failure just from fear, and from being afraid of weird meteors.

"After all these things have happened, then shall there be the coming of the Son again, riding as if on a cloud with great power and great glory. When all the foregoing signs begin to appear look up, be encouraged, expect the second coming.

"Look at a tree. When it begins to show green shoots you know that summer is near; so when you see the signs I have mentioned, then be certain that the kingdom of God is near at hand. In fact, civilization as it is now, this phase of life, shall not cease until all this has happened.

"Heaven and earth may pass away, but the truth as I have told you will always be the same.

"I would suggest that you be careful and not so concerned with your own little affairs of living that the second coming finds you unprepared and busy in selfish undertakings.

"The second coming is going to be a big surprise. Criswell or J. Dixon won't be able to predict it. Watch and pray and earnestly seek to be worthy of deliverance and to stand in my presence when I come."

Jesus continued teaching daily in the church building and spending the evening in meditation on the Mount of Olives. The people arose early to be certain to be each day at the church in time to hear Jesus from the moment he arrived.

Chap.
22

The week for the celebrating of the Passover was near and some of the church and civic leaders among the Jews began to plot various methods by which they might eliminate Christ without getting into trouble with the people.

About this time the devil got into Judas[1] and he went to the leaders and offered to participate in a citizen's arrest. A deal was made, and Judas promised to put the finger on Christ when the people were not around.

When the actual day for the celebrating of the feast of unleavened bread arrived, Jesus sent Peter and John to prepare a place for the Passover meal.

"What place shall we prepare?" Peter asked.

"When you enter Jerusalem you will see a man carrying a pitcher of water. Follow him. When you arrive at the house he enters, talk to the owner and tell him that the Master would like to use his guest facility for the Passover meal with the disciples," answered Jesus.

[1]I've seen it happen in school.

"The man will show you," continued Jesus, "a large upper room and a table and chairs. Make things ready there."

Peter and John went as Christ suggested and found everything to be exactly as Jesus had said.

When the meal time came Jesus arrived and sat down with the twelve.

Jesus then said, "I particularly wanted this Passover meal with just you all, before my time for suffering has come."

Then taking a cup, he gave thanks, and said, "Divide this among you, each taking a sip. I tell you this is the last time I will have wine until the kingdom of God is complete."

Then Jesus took bread and broke it and gave pieces to each of them present saying, "This represents my body which will be sacrificed for you. Do this as a regular memorial."

Then after the meal was finished Jesus took the cup and said, "This cup represents the new affirmation, symbolizing my blood which will be shed for you. I also notice that the hand of a betrayer is with me on the table. It is necessary for me to face what is ahead, but woe to the one who betrays me into it."

This caused the fellows to begin to discuss among themselves who the betrayer might be. Another thing that was discussed was who among them would be the top dogs when the kingdom of God became a reality.

"You fellows don't understand the kingdom of God," said Jesus. "Now the non-religious crowd have all types of organizations, with directors, trustees, privileges, executive keys, but in the kingdom of God the one that will be greatest will be the one who serves the most.

"Normally you think that the person sitting at the table is more important than the one serving, but I have come to earth as a server. You have joined me in my efforts and I turn over the operation of the kingdom to you when I leave, even as my Father turned it over to me. I look forward to eating with you at my table some day in the kingdom to come, and you will all have authority equal to the ruling of one of the twelve tribes."

Then Jesus turned to Peter and said, "Simon, Satan is really after you. I have prayed for your deliverance, and when you are finally victorious, then attempt to strengthen the faith of others."

"Don't worry about me, Master," said Peter, "for I am ready to go to prison, to war, or to death for you."

"Peter," said Jesus, "you will deny me completely three times before the rooster crows in the morning."

Then Jesus turned to the twelve and said, "When I sent you out teaching without luggage or money, did you get along all right?"

"We surely did," they replied.

"The time has now come for action, though. If you have any money use it, if you need some protection buy a baseball bat, for just like the prophets said, 'He was declared a crook and put on the wanted list.'"

"We have two swords already," said one of the disciples.

"That is enough," Jesus said.

Shortly Jesus departed for the Mount of Olives where he normally meditated, and the disciples followed him.

"Pray that you are not tempted too much," said Jesus.

Then Jesus went apart a few paces and prayed saying, "Father, if it is all right with you let's skip this ordeal as planned. Nevertheless, it is your will, not mine, that will be done."

An angel then appeared at the side of Jesus and strengthened him. Jesus then prayed ever more earnestly, even to the point of sweating blood. When he had finished praying, he returned to his disciples and found them asleep.

"Why do you sleep?" asked Jesus. "Get up and pray that you do not fall victim to temptation."

While Jesus was saying this a group led by Judas approached and when Judas came to Jesus he kissed him on the cheek, a pre-arranged signal for identifying Christ to the soldiers.

"You betray me with a kiss, Judas?" asked Christ.

When the disciples saw what was happening one of them said, "Is it time to use our swords?"

Before Christ had time to reply one of the disciples cut an ear off one of the temple guards.

Jesus said, "Now is not the time for violence." Then Jesus touched the wounded man's ear and healed it.

Jesus then turned to the leaders of the group and said, "Have you come out with swords and handcuffs as if I were a criminal? You didn't bother me when I was teaching in the temple. This is your big time, though, and the power of evil will have its brief victory."

The authorities then took Jesus to the bishop's mansion, and Peter followed at quite a distance.

When a fire had been built on the patio and everyone sat down Peter joined them. One of the cuties going around selling coffee, however, spotted Peter and said, "This man was one of the followers."

"You're nuts, sister," said Peter, "I don't know him."

A little later a fellow said, pointing at Peter, "There is an associate of Jesus." "You're dead wrong," said Peter.

About an hour later another man pointed to Peter and said, "I recognize this one for sure. I know he was with Jesus. I recognize his southern drawl, too."

"I don't know what you're talking about," stoutly affirmed Peter.

About this time a rooster began to crow in the distance, and Jesus turned and looked at Peter, and Peter remembered what Jesus had said. Peter left and went apart and wept bitterly.

The men that were guarding Jesus then began to make sport of him, blindfolding him, then hitting him and saying, "Now tell us who hit you?" They continued to abuse Jesus in many ways.

When it was daylight the leaders arrived and led Jesus into the fellowship hall for a phony trial.

"Are you the promised Messiah?" they asked.

"If I told you, you wouldn't believe me. If I asked you a reasonable question, you wouldn't answer, nor would you let me go. The next time, though, you shall see me on the right hand of the power of God."

"Are you the son of God?" spoke Jesus.

"What need do we have of witnesses?" asked one of the council. "Has he not proven himself guilty by his own testimony?"

Chap.

23

The whole crowd then led Jesus to Judge Pilate and there they charged Jesus with misleading the nation, forbidding people to pay their taxes, and claiming himself to be Christ, the king.

Pilate then spoke to Jesus and asked him, "Are you king of the Jews?"

"Yes," said Jesus.

Pilate then turned to the people and said, "I don't see anything wrong with this man."

This just stirred the conspirators all the more and they said, "He is stirring up a revolution, even having influence as far away as Galilee."

"Is he a Galilean?" asked Pilate.

"That he is," was the reply.

Upon hearing this, Pilate reasoned that the trial should be under the jurisdiction of Herod; so he transferred the case to Herod, who was in Jerusalem at the time.

When Herod saw Jesus he was greatly pleased for he had long wanted to meet him and he wanted to witness a miracle. Herod asked Jesus many questions, but Jesus made no reply.

The Jewish church and civic leaders began denouncing Christ in the presence of Herod. Soon the soldiers of Herod began to make fun of Jesus and decked him in kingly robes, and sent him back to Pilate.

In some strange way this exchanging of Jesus back and forth between Pilate and Herod restored their relationship, for they had previously been at odds with each other.

Pilate then called the Jewish leaders together and said to them, "You have brought this man Jesus to me as a rebel and reactionary leader of the people, but I find no fault with him and no basis for your charges. I get the same report from Herod, as I sent Jesus to appear before him. Why don't I just have him flogged for good measure and released."[1]

[1]The Romans didn't like anyone to go completely unpunished.

It was customary to release one prisoner of Jewish descent during Passover week; so Pilate suggested that Jesus be the one released. The enemies of Jesus cried to Pilate to release Batman[1] who was in for murder.

Again Pilate suggested to the group that Jesus be the one released, but they called forth, "Crucify him, crucify him."

"What has he done?" asked Pilate. "I can't find anything wrong. I think I'll just have him beaten and released."

The shouts of the crowd, however, finally swayed Pilate and he ordered that Christ be crucified, and that Batman be released.

As Jesus was led away the soldiers selected a large, husky man named George,[2] who was required to carry the cross of Jesus. There followed Jesus along with the procession many persons, men and women, who moaned and wept over the treatment Jesus was receiving.

"Don't cry for me, ladies of Jerusalem. Cry for your children and for yourselves. Because of what is happening today there shall be times coming of great trouble and distress. During these days women will regret having children and people will pray that the mountains might fall on top of them."

"If the world mistreats one as young and innocent as I am, think what will happen when evil has greater opportunities to develop."

There were two others to be crucified along with Christ, and when they came to Crucifixion Hill one criminal was crucified on each side of Christ.

Jesus then looked upon the soldiers and said, "Father, forgive them, for they know not what they are doing. They are merely following orders."

The soldiers then divided the clothes of Jesus and high diced for them.

The rulers and some of the people witnessed the scene, and some spoke out saying, "He saved others, why can't he save himself? Isn't he the Christ, the chosen of God?"

The soldiers also made fun of Jesus and offered him vinegar as if it were wine saying, "If you be the Christ, the king of Jews, save yourself."

A sign then was printed and placed over Christ saying, "This is the King of the Jews."

One of the criminals spoke to Jesus and said, "If you are Christ, save yourself and us, too."

The other criminal, however, shut him up by saying, "Don't you fear God at all, don't you realize this is the end? We deserve what we are getting, but this man Jesus has done no wrong."

Turning then to Jesus the second criminal said, "Lord,

[1]Barabbas   [2]Simon of Cyrene

remember me when you enter your kingdom."

Jesus then said, "This very day you will be with me in paradise."

At about the sixth hour a great darkness came over the whole earth for about three hours. There were many odd disturbances, for the sun was darkened, the veil of the temple was torn to pieces and then Jesus said, "Father, unto your presence do I commend my spirit." Jesus died.

When the sergeant of the guard saw all that was happening and heard the comments of Jesus he began to glorify God and say, "Surely this was the Son of God."

The people who were present were greatly impressed and returned to Jerusalem with many strange and facinating accounts. The friends of Jesus and the women who had stayed with him through his ministry watched all these things at a distance and were greatly perturbed.

There was a local businessman named Joseph, a good man, and a just man. He was a follower of Christ and had greatly disapproved of the action of the Council of Jewish leaders, and he came to Pilate and asked for the body of Jesus.

Pilate gave the permit to Joseph and he took the body of Christ, wrapped it appropriately in linen and laid it in his family tomb, in a place where no one had ever previously been buried. The women followed Joseph and observed the tomb and noticed the location and how Jesus was buried.

The women returned home and spent the Sabbath day gathering spices and flowers and appropriate momentos for a visit to the cemetery on the first day of the week.

Chap.
24

Early in the morning on the first day of the week the group of ladies came to the cemetery bringing the spices and the flowers which they had been preparing on the Sabbath. When they arrived at the tomb they found the stone rolled away and they entered the tomb and saw that the body of Jesus was not there.

As they stood thunder-struck there suddenly appeared two persons in shining robes, and the ladies in great terror got down on their knees.[1]

One of the persons then asked, "Why are you looking here for one that is living?"

"The one you seek is not here, he is risen. Don't you remember that he told you he would rise from the dead? Didn't he tell you that he must be a victim of sinful men, crucified, and then that he would rise from the dead?"

At once they remembered the words of Jesus. The group split

[1]Pulling out their Kleenexes as they went down.

and went to the eleven apostles and to others and told them of their experience, and in this group who listened to the angels were Mary of Alabama, Joan, Mary the mother of James, and a sprinkling of others.

The men didn't believe what the women told them.[1]

Peter decided to see for himself, however, and he ran to the tomb and he looked in and saw the linen clothes laying in the tomb, but no body, and left wondering what had happened.

Two of the followers of Jesus left that day on a trip to Tyler[2] and as they were walking they were discussing all the strange events and various comments made in connection with all the past few days.

As the two were talking and expounding theories back and forth, Jesus himself joined them, pretty well covered with a robe, and since they were not expecting him they did not recognize him.

"What are you fellows talking about with such interest?" asked Jesus.

One of them, a fellow named Clam,[3] said, "Are you a total stranger in these parts? Haven't you heard about all the goings on at Jerusalem?"

"What things do you mean?" asked Jesus.

"Things concerning Jesus of Nazareth, a mighty prophet in word and deed, full of the power of God and greatly supported by the people, who was arrested by the Jewish authorities, condemned by them, and crucified. We had hoped that he was the Messiah, come to save Israel.

"We are also discussing that this is the third day since the crucifixion and some of the women have been to the tomb and reported that his body is missing. The women also claim to have seen a couple of angels[4] who told them that Jesus was alive. Some very trustworthy men we know went and checked this out and found the tomb empty as reported."

"Aren't you smart enough to believe the prophets? Didn't they say that Christ must suffer such indignities before entering into his glory?"

Then Jesus began to teach the two travelers as they walked, explaining the scriptures, beginning with Moses. As they drew near a village the men decided to have a break and when Christ acted as if he would continue to walk they urged him to join them and to continue teaching.

As they had the evening meal Jesus took the bread and broke it,[5] and asked the blessing, passing the bread to them, and suddenly it dawned on them that they were in the presence of Jesus Christ. As soon as they recognized him, Jesus vanished.

---

[1]You've come a long way since then, babies.   [2]Emmaus   [3]Cleopas
[4]Women seeing angels have always been hard to swallow.
[5]Some say they recognized him then by his hands.

"You know," one of the fellows said to the other, "when he was telling us about the scriptures I felt a deep inspiration, and we should have know that we were with the Christ."

As soon as they had eaten they did not delay in returning to Jerusalem and finding the eleven apostles and telling them at once of their experience, and how they recognized him with the breaking of the bread. The apostles then reported that Jesus had appeared to Peter.

As all this talk was being exchanged, Jesus entered the room.[1] Jesus said to them, "Pax vobiscum."[2]

The men were terrified. They wondered if they were only seeing a spirit.

"Why are you so disturbed and shocked?" asked Jesus. "Look at my hands, touch me, feel my flesh. I am not just a spirit, but I have flesh and bones."

The men were still too overcome to say anything.

Jesus then asked, "Do you have anything to eat?"

At once they produced some fish and honey and gave it to Christ and he demonstrated the fact of the resurrected body by eating while they watched.

"Now is occurring exactly what I told you would happen," said Jesus. "These are the things written by Moses, expounded by the prophets, sung in the psalms."

Jesus then began to teach them and great understanding came to them.

"It was necessary," said Jesus, "that the Christ suffer and rise from the dead on the third day, and it is also necessary that repentance and forgiveness of sin be preached everywhere in all the world, beginning in Jerusalem. You fellows are to be the witnesses.

"I also pass along to you the promise of Almighty God, but you hang around Jerusalem until the power of God descends upon you."

Jesus then led them toward Mobile and blessed them and then Jesus ascended into heaven.

The men worshipped Christ on the spot and glorified God, and then returned to Jerusalem with great and abounding joy, and daily began to teach and preach the risen Lord, the good news.

---

[1] I have often thought this to be one of the most dramatic moments in the history of the world.
[2] Peace be with you all. Jesus knew Latin.

In the very beginning was the Word. God made all things, nothing has ever existed, or will ever exist, except it be made by God.

Within the Word was life and this life became the Light for man. The Light shone, but man, in his ignorance, would not fully understand it.

There then appeared on earth a man named John, who was sent by God to announce the coming of the Light, so that everyone hopefully would believe and follow the Light. John, you understand, was not the Light, but a witness of the fact of the Light.

The true Light, Jesus, was the Light available to everyone ever born. Jesus came into the world, and even though he was with God in the beginning, the world did not even recognize its Creator. To those, however, who did believe in Jesus, to such was given the power to become children of God. This birth then becomes a spiritual birth and is not a birth involving hospitals or midwives, but is the birth of a new spiritual person under God.

The Word then was actually turned into flesh and lived here on earth with us, and some of us were present to behold his glory as is appropriate for the only Son of God. This glory was seen in His grace and truth.

John was the witness for Christ, and on several occasions said, "There is the one about whom I have been preaching. He is the one that is to be preferred above all, and even though He comes after me I know He was also before me, for He is the Eternal One. The law was laid down by Moses, but Jesus Christ has added the dimensions of grace and truth. No man has seen God except Jesus, and God has declared Jesus to be His Son."

The above is the record, the testimony he consistently gave. The Jewish leaders from Jerusalem sent messengers to John and the messengers said to him, "Who are you?"

"I am not the promised Messiah," said John.

"Who are you? Are you Elijah?" one of them asked.

"No," replied John.

"Are you some other returnee?" another asked.

"No," said John.

"Look, fellow," one of the men said, "we are paid by some big shots to come here and find out who you are. Tell us something."

"I am a speaker. I hold forth in the wilderness area. I am telling people to prepare for the Lord, just like Elijah said," affirmed John.

"Why do you baptize people then, if you are not Elijah, nor the Christ, nor some returned prophet?" one asked.

"I just baptize with water," said John. "There is alive today one who baptizes with spirit, who has the power of God. I am not worthy to lace His shoes. This one that comes after me is to be preferred considerably over me."

The very next day John saw Jesus for the first time and immediately knew Him. John said, "Here at last is the Lamb of God, who will take away sin from the world. This man is the one that is to be preferred over me. All I knew about Him was that He was coming. That's why all I could do was baptize with water."

John, the forerunner, testified that the only identification he had was that he saw the Spirit of God descending on Christ's head like a dove. The same Spirit that made this revelation to John also revealed that the baptism which Christ would offer would be the baptism of the Holy Spirit. John saw and believed that Christ was the Son of God.

Again the next day as John was standing talking with two of his disciples Jesus drew near and John said, "There walks the Lamb of God." At once the two disciples left John and joined Jesus.

When Jesus noticed the two following him he turned to them and said, "What do you want?"

"Well, Master," said one of them, "we want to know where your headquarters are."[1]

"Come and see," said Jesus. As a result they stayed with Him all day. One of the two was Andrew, a brother of Simon Peter.

Andrew then went to his brother and said, "We have found the Messiah." Andrew then brought Peter to Christ.

When Jesus saw Simon Peter He said to him, "I know you are Simon, son of Jona, but from now on I'll call you Rocky."[2]

The next day Jesus located Phillip and said to him. "Follow me."

Phil found his friend, Nat, and told him to join them as they had found the Messiah.

"Who is He?" asked Nat.

"He is Jesus, the son of Joseph and a native of Nazareth."

"Can anything good come out of Nazareth?"[3]

"Come and see," said Phil.

As Nat approached Christ, Jesus spoke to him and said, "Here comes an orthodox Jew."

"How did you know?" asked Nat.

"I could see you under the fig tree before Phil ever called to you," replied Christ.

"Then surely you are the Son of God, and the King of Israel." said Nat.

"Just because I saw you under the fig tree? You will see far greater and more impressive things than this. In fact, in the proper time you will see the heavens open and angels going back and forth from me to heaven," concluded Christ.

[1]No doubt they had not been impressed with John's hole in the ground.
[2]Cephas [3]Must have been the poorest town in the district.

A few days later, there was a big wedding in Dallas[1] and the mother of Jesus was in the house party at the reception and Jesus and the disciples were invited. There was a big crowd at the reception and they ran out of wine, so the hostess told Mary and she went to Jesus.

"The wine is gone and the stores are closed," said Mary to Jesus. "Can't you do something?"

"What business is that of mine?" asked Jesus. "It really isn't quite time for me to start my works and signs."[2]

Mary, however, said to the servants, "My son, Jesus, will do something. You just follow his instructions."

There were the usual six water pots handy and Jesus told the servants to fill them with water. When they had done this, Jesus told them to take a cup from one of the waterpots and take it to the man in charge of the catering service.

When he had tasted it, he turned to the bridegroom and said, "What a strange way to do things. Usually the person furnishing the wine serves the best first, as after the people have had a few, they can't tell that the last servings are of poor quality. Now here you are serving the best wine last."

This was the first miracle that Christ performed and it testified to his power and strengthened the disciples' belief.

Following this, the whole group of Jesus' relatives and followers went to Jerusalem to celebrate the feast of the Passover. On arriving, Jesus observed that the church was being used as a place for money changing, card playing and a livestock market.

With great indignation, Jesus secured a whip and drove the violators out of the church, saying, "Get out! My Father's House is to be a house of prayer and not a market place."

This incident reminded the disciples of an old saying about the wrath of God coming down on those who contaminated the church.

"Where is your authority?" asked some of the Jews. "Do you have some sign or permission to control the church?"

"You want a sign?" asked Jesus. "Then tear this church down and I'll build it back in three days."

"Man, it took 46 years to build this building, do you think you can replace it in three days?" spoke one of the leaders.

When Jesus was risen from the dead, the disciples remembered this and realized that He was talking of the church as if it were his body.

Many believed in Jesus during this period in Jerusalem as the miracles that he performed made a profound impression.

Jesus did not permit any of this to develop into some power play and to follow the normal practice of political or social advancement.

---

[1]Cana   [2]Anything short of a positive no most mothers take for granted.

One of the Jewish rulers, a man named Nick,[1] came to Jesus privately in the evening, when he would not be noticed.

"Master," said Nick, "No one can do the things we have witnessed you do unless he comes from God. Any stupe can understand this."

"Unless a person is born again in the complete spiritual sense, it is not possible to understand or accept the Kingdom of God," said Jesus.

"How can a person be born again? Surely you don't mean starting all over within your mother and going through the nine months, teething, kindergarten and that scene?"

"No, a person must be born of the water, a symbol of man, and of the Spirit, a gift of God, only then is the Kingdom available. You see, that which is born of the flesh is flesh, and that which is born of the Spirit is spiritual; so don't be perplexed that I tell you to seek a new birth."

"You know, the wind blows, you hear the sound, but you don't know where it goes or from where it comes![2] This is the way of the Spirit of God, it just is."

"How can it be?" asked Nick.

"Aren't you supposed to be a fairly smart teacher? Can't you understand? You don't even believe the things that I have demonstrated, in changed lives, in answered prayer, in healings. If you won't believe the things you see done on earth, how do you expect me to be able to show you things that are out of this world?

"No one has ever made the trip back and forth to heaven except me. Even as Moses lifted up the snake on the stick in the wilderness; so I must be lifted on a cross, and anyone who looks to me and believes on me shall be saved.

"God so loved the people of the world that He sent his only Son, affirming that whoever believed on Him would not perish, but would have eternal life.

"God sent the Son into the world to save the world, not to condemn the people on it. There is condemnation only for those who do not believe, and who reject the Saviour.

"The situation is this. I have come into the world as the Light of the world. Many will prefer darkness to accepting the Light. The people who encourage evil and enjoy it, live in darkness. These people are afraid to seek the Light for fear that their evil will be made public. Those that truly seek the Light, however, shall find it, and live in light, while the others will always live in darkness."

Later Jesus and his group left Jerusalem and went into an area in which John was preaching and baptizing. Jesus also baptized followers.

---

[1]Nicodemus   [2]Weather-casters prove this every night on T.V.

Naturally a discussion arose between those baptized by John and those baptized by Christ as to which way was the best.[1]

Some of the debaters then came to John and said, "Teacher, the fellow you baptized in the Jordan is in this area and he is baptizing people coming and going, and we don't like it."

"No person can do more than God allows the person to do. Now you birds get this straight, I am not the Christ. I have been sent before Him to announce Him.

"Do you know how to tell the bridegroom? Sure, he's the one with the bride. The friend of the bridegroom stands around and is happy for his friend. Jesus is the bridegroom and I rejoice that I am here to witness to His presence. It means, of course, that he must spread His influence, and mine must fade away.

"The One who comes straight from God is above all, while one of the earth people can only speak of earthly things with firsthand knowledge. Unfortunately, the One who comes from heaven testifies of heavenly or non-earthly things and people find it hard to believe. The One, who God has sent, speaks for God.

"The Father loves the Son and has given to Him all power and complete jurisdiction. Anyone who believes in the Son of God will be saved and will see new insights into life, but anyone who rejects the Son of God will not only be restless and dissatisfied in this life, but the very anger of God will be directed against such a person."

Chap.

4

Some of the trouble-making lip artists in the church began to pass a rumor that Jesus was baptizing more people than John, although actually Jesus didn't baptize, but left this function to the disciples. Anyway, the rumor was irritating to the Lord and so Jesus left the area, traveling on the way to Hilton Head[2] through the land of the Crackers.[3]

As Jesus approached a small village called Macon[4] he became thirsty and stopped by an old well known as Jacob's well. A flussie type woman from Macon also came to the well about this same time to draw water to take into town.

"Would you be kind enough to draw me a cup of water, please?" asked Jesus.[5] At this time Jesus was alone as the disciples had already gone to town to get lunch at MacDonald's.

"You are a Jew, aren't you? Why are you being courteous to me, an off-beat Cracker? Didn't you know that the Jews don't associate with us Crackers?" spoke the woman.

---

[1]I'm afraid to say that one sprinkled and one ducked.   [2]Galilee [3]Samaria
[4]Sychar [5]That was the polite way in that day.

"If you really knew who I was you would have asked me to give you a drink, and it would have been a drink of living water, not H_2O," said Jesus.

"You don't have a cup or a rope, how could you get water, particularly living water, whatever that is?" said the woman. "Are you greater than our famous ancestor Jacob, the one who dug the well?"

"When you drink of this water here," said Jesus, "you will get thirsty again, but if you drink of the water that I give, you will never thirst again. The water I give becomes an artesian well of water, rising up constantly within a person, and brings a person into eternal life."

"Great, give me a slug of this juice you're pushing so I won't have to be always coming to the well," snapped the woman.

"Go get your husband and come back here," said Jesus.

"I don't have a husband," said the woman.

"You spoke the truth that time. In fact, you've had five husbands and the fellow you are living with now isn't even your husband," said Jesus.

"Are you some kind of a mystic or a prophet?" asked the woman. "You must be. Incidentally, our people worship here in the mountains and you birds say no one can worship except in Jerusalem. How about that?"

"Honey, the time will come when people will worship neither in these mountains nor in Jerusalem. You don't know what you worship. At least at Jerusalem the Jews know they are worshipping God. Salvation will eventually be introduced through the Jews.

"In fact, the time has come when the real worshippers shall worship God sincerely, with a true spiritual feeling, for this is what God wants. God is a Spirit and it follows naturally that to worship God properly it must be done in Spirit, with no phoney overtones," concluded Jesus.

"Well, I know there is an old saying that some day a Saviour is coming, who will be called the Christ. When He comes He'll put us straight on all these matters," said the woman.

"I am the Christ," said Jesus.

The disciples arrived at this juncture and were plenty curious about Jesus talking to a cutie, but they were scared to ask Him about it.[1]

The woman hot footed it to town though and immediately started talking to a bunch of men[2] saying, "Come with me. I have found a man who could tell me everything, even things about me. Surely he is the Christ."

A bunch of fellows then came toward the well to see Jesus.

In the meantime, the disciples were trying to get Jesus to eat a

---

[1]They still didn't have complete faith in Jesus. [2]She didn't know many women.

cheeseburger, but Jesus said to them, "I have food about which you don't know or understand."

"What's He talking about, John?" asked Peter.[1] "Did anybody else bring him food?"

Then Jesus said to them, "My meat is to do the job God sent me here to do. Take a look around you. In four months there will be a harvest time. Lift your eyes up on another plain. Don't you see the fields of people ready for the harvest of God? Those who work and bring these people to the Lord shall gather for themselves eternal life and eternal life for those that they bring.

"There is a saying that one sows and another reaps. You reap the harvest from seed that others sowed, and you sow that people coming after you may reap. That is the plan of life."

Many of the Crackers that came that day accepted Christ, largely because of the testimony of the woman. The Crackers then begged Jesus to stick around awhile, and He remained two full days, teaching and helping in many ways.

After Jesus left one of the men said to Maisie,[2] "You know, Maisie, we believed in Christ because you witnessed to us. After listening to Him, however, we were strengthened and we reaffirmed our conviction that truly He is Christ, the Saviour of the world."

From here Jesus went to Hilton Head, not spending any time much around his home town, for Jesus himself had said that it's tough to teach people who think of you as a local yokel.

The people around Hilton Head received Jesus very favorably, for many of them had made trips to Jerusalem and knew a lot about the things Jesus had said and done there.

There was an important man with a home at Sea Island[3] whose son was very sick and the man came to Jesus and asked Him to make a house call.

"That's the way it is," said Jesus, "unless you see a miracle you don't want to believe."

"Just please come with me to the house at Sea Island, please," said the man.

"You can go now. Your son has been healed," said Jesus.[4]

The man believed Jesus and he left rejoicing. As the man was returning to his home, some of his servants came running to meet him and told him that his son was well.

"When did he get well?" asked the man.

"About 3 o'clock yesterday afternoon," said one of the servants.

The father knew that this was the exact time that Jesus had said to him that his son was healed. The father believed then for sure in

---

[1]Peter couldn't understand anybody refusing food.   [2]That was the woman's name.

[3]Capernaum   [4]He didn't have to make house calls.

Jesus and he witnessed to all the people in his home. This was the second miracle that Jesus did near Hilton Head.

After this, Jesus went to Jerusalem to participate in the regular feast time for the Jews. Near Jerusalem there was a spa, with a pool, porches, and a great host of ailing people were waiting to enter the pool when it bubbled, as it periodically did. The saying was that an angel sometimes stirred the water and that at such times the pool had therapeutic values.

There was a fellow there who had been sick for 38 years and Jesus saw him and knew about his long illness.

"Sir," said the man to Jesus, "I really have it tough. Apparently I can never get in the pool on time as I have no one to help me and everybody else beats me to the water."

"Get up. You are now well," said Jesus.

The man did as Jesus said, and he gathered his makeshift hammock and walked away well. This happened on a Sunday.

Some of the Jews immediately raised cain, accusing the man of breaking the Sabbath by carrying his hammock!

"The man who healed me told me to carry off my bed," said the man.

"What man told you?" they asked.

"I don't know. I was so excited I didn't notice carefully and he has now gone," said the fellow.

Later on Jesus saw the man at church and said to him, "You have been healed, but the sins which brought on all your troubles are evil. Sin no more or else worse things will be ahead for you."

The man left then and went and told the church leaders that it had been Jesus who healed him. The Jews then began to criticize Jesus and to cause him as much trouble as possible, and they accused Jesus of violating the Sabbath.

"My Father is at work in the world and so am I," said Jesus.

This irritated the leaders all the more for Jesus not only would not adhere to their nit-picking legalism, but asserted that God was his Father.

"Let me tell you birds something," said Jesus. "The son can do nothing on his own, but does all things in conjunction with the Father. The Father and son work together, for the Father loves the son and has shown him all things. In fact, there are some even more astounding things yet coming, such as the raising of the dead.

"The Father has even entrusted all judgments to the son; therefore, men should honor the son the same as the Father. Now listen carefully. Anyone that hears the Word and believes on me and on Him that sent me, to such are given eternal life, and shall transfer from one life to the next, passing through death without any complication.

"In fact, those who have died previous to my coming, are hearing my word now and it will bring life to those that receive it. As the Father is the Creator of life, so has God passed this creative knowledge to the Son and has given the Son the power to judge. There is a time coming when the dead shall arise, some to eternal life, and those who reject the Son shall arise to eternal separation.

"I actually don't do these things myself. It is all a plan. I judge as I go because my decisions are all just, as I have no selfish gain involved. I am doing only the will of the Father who sent men.

"If I testify of myself, I can't expect people to believe this, but the testimony of John concerning me is true. You asked of him and he told you. I am telling you these things not because I give a hoot about any recognition for myself, but only to help you all be saved.

"You followed John. He was a real sensation and very impressive. Nevertheless, I have a greater function than John, for the Lord has given me a tremendous mission to accomplish in His name. The Father has sent me.

"The Father has made a witness for me through prophets and other ways, but you don't recognize these things. John came and you didn't believe him, although he impressed you.

"Read the Bible. Search through it carefully. The Bible tells of my coming, yet I am not well received or honored by my contemporaries. The trouble is that you do not have the love of God within you.

"I have come in God's name and with His love and you don't accept me. It's weird, really. You will listen to some fellow who comes in his own name, and yet you do not listen to me when I come in God's name. You just can't make it that way!

"I'm not going to be your prosecutor in the day of judgment. I won't bother. Moses will do the job, your own man. You see, if you had really believed Moses you would believe in me, for he wrote of me. If you reject then the writings of Moses, how can you accept me? It'll be something when Moses prosecutes you!"

Chap.
6

After this Jesus crossed the lake and great crowds followed because they were astounded by the miracles and many of them were still seeking to be healed themselves.

It was the time of year shortly before the celebration of the Passover Feast, and when Jesus saw the crowd gathering, even though as always he knew what would happen, he spoke to Phillip and said, "Phil, where can we get some food to feed these people?"

"It would take $2500 just to get a hamburger and shake for everyone."

Then Andrew said, "Master, there is a youngster here who brought his lunch, 5 bread sticks and 2 sardines, and he has offered them, but what can be done with so little?"

"Get the people to sit down. Organize them a bit into sections," said Jesus.

There were about 5,000 present when Jesus took the bread sticks and blessed them and then began to distribute the bread and sardines to the disciples, who, in turn, began to pass the food among the people.

When everyone had eaten Jesus appointed a litter committee to pick up the scraps, and there were scraps in each of the twelve tribal baskets. The comment following this miracle was that surely one of the old time prophets had returned, or the new prophet long expected by the Jews.

Jesus saw this, but the people misunderstood his program and were desirous of appointing him as earthly king, and so he disappeared into the hills.

That night the disciples got into boats and headed for New York, [1] and it was night time and Jesus had not appeared.

A squall came on the lake and in the middle of it the disciples suddenly saw Jesus walking toward them on the water. This scared the willie-nillie out of the disciples.

"Don't panic," said Jesus. "It is I."

They helped Jesus then into one of the boats and it seemed as if at once they were on the other shore where they wanted to be.

The next day the crowd that had seen the disciples leave without Jesus waited for Christ to come out of the hills. Not seeing Jesus, they then crossed the lake and saw Christ with the disciples.

One of the crowd immediately spoke forth saying, "How did you get across the lake?"

"You have been seeking me," said Jesus, "because you think you might get another free meal. You work for the wrong goals. Don't work just to be able to eat well. All such strivings are temporary. Learn to work for eternal values. The food that I will give you is spiritual, God has made this arrangement with me."

"What do we do?[2] How do we know God's work?" they asked.

"The first move toward the work of God is to believe in the Son of God," said Jesus.

"What about a sign? How do we know for sure that you are the Son of God? In the wilderness God sent manna and quail," one of them stated.

"Moses gave you regular sandwich type bread. The bread of God comes from heaven. It is the true bread, and it provides a true life, and is the real heart beat of the world," said Jesus.

"Give it to us then," they said.

"I am the bread of life," said Jesus. "Anyone who sincerely comes to me shall never be hungry or thirsty. Think about this, though. You have seen me and still you are hesitant to believe.

[1]Capernaum [2]Like most church people they expected a mimeographed manual.

"All the promises of God are available through me, and anyone who comes to me has got it made. I didn't come to earth to have a good time, but I came to fulfill the will of God.

"I am here to save all that come to me. It is God's will that all who believe in me and seek to follow me, all of these I will conduct into eternal life, and I will raise all of those who die in my name at the last day," concluded Jesus.

Many of the Jews objected strongly to what Jesus had said about being the bread of life which came down from Heaven.[1]

"Who is this bird?" asked one of the leaders. "Isn't he that little boy born to Joseph and Mary? What does he mean saying he came down from Heaven?"

Jesus knew of their murmurings and he said, "You don't have to murmur. No one can come to me except the Lord be willing. Those that do come will be saved on the last day. The prophets wrote about it all. Everyone somehow will have the opportunity provided by God to accept or reject me.

"No one has seen God except me. Now get this straight again. Any person who believes on me will have eternal life! I am the bread of life. Your fathers ate manna in the wilderness but they are all dead.

"The bread of which I am talking will provide you with eternal life. I am the living bread. Any person who accepts this, receives eternal life.

"The bread I give is represented by my flesh, which will be sacrificed to save all who believe."

"I don't get it," said one of the Jews. "How can we eat his flesh and not be cannibals?"

"Try not to be so limited and earthly," said Jesus. "Unless you eat of my flesh and drink of my blood, you don't have a part in my program. Those that do eat of my flesh and drink of my blood have eternal life. It is all a matter of involvement. You must receive me, share my work, suffer, be a working part of my program, then you are receiving my flesh and my blood as spiritual bread and wine. I am not talking about ordinary bread and wine, but as symbols.

"Believe in me, do my works, and you then are eating my bread and drinking my wine. In this manner I sustain you, and on the last day I will raise you to eternal life."

"This surely is tough to understand," said one of the disciples.

"What bothers you?" asked Jesus. "Suppose you see me ascend up to Heaven. It is the spirit that is eternal. The flesh doesn't really count. I am speaking about your spirit. That is the real life, but you all think almost entirely of the body or the flesh. I also know that there are some who don't believe me."

Jesus knew, of course, that he was to be betrayed from inside his own group.

Again Jesus repeated that even in the matter of coming to

[1]They sold church bread and didn't like this 'for free' talk.

Christ, this was also within the jurisdiction of the will of God. Some will never make it.

After this there were some who quit following Jesus, thinking he was a vague mystic of some kind.

Noticing the conspicuous withdrawal of some of the people, Jesus turned to the twelve and said, "Will you also leave?"

"To whom would we go?" asked Peter. "You are the one with the words of eternal life. We believe. We are certain that you are the Christ, the Son of the Living God."

"Yet even though I have chosen this twelve," said Jesus, "one of you is a devil and will betray me."

Jesus was speaking of Judas, who was the one that later betrayed the Lord.

Chap.

7

After this Jesus spent most of his time around the lake area and avoided the Jewish strongholds, such as Jerusalem, for the leaders there were already plotting to kill him.

Some of the friendly advisors to Jesus encouraged him to seek more prominence and perform more miracles in public places. Some of these people were non-believers themselves and wanted to see more convincing signs before following Christ.

Jesus said to them, "My time has not arrived as yet. Your time is already here. The world won't turn against you all, but it will against me, for I propose that the present system is evil. Go on to the regular feast celebration, but just leave me out of it."

This group then went to the feast celebration and left Jesus in Galilee. Later Jesus followed the disciples, but he did not show himself and went more or less in secrecy.

Some of the Jewish leaders began asking about Jesus at the feast celebration and there was a great difference of opinion. Some said Jesus was truly a good man, while others accused him of misleading the people. No one spoke publicly of Jesus, however.

When the celebration time was about half through, around the middle of the week, Jesus appeared in church and began to teach during the discussion period.

Some of the Jews questioned him, however, asking about what seminary he attended.

Jesus said, "My teaching does not originate with me, but it is provided by God, who sent me here. Anyone who prays and meditates, seeking the will of God, such a person will know that I speak the truth.

"It is not as if I was speaking of myself for my own glory, but I speak for the glory of God, and there is nothing except righteousness in the will of God.

"Didn't Moses give you the law? You don't observe the law, for some of you are already plotting to have me killed!" said Jesus.

"You must be a witch or have a devil in you. How do you know who plans to kill you?" someone said.

"I have performed one miracle that you witnessed and you are all perturbed. Moses expounded on the law of circumcision and you have often circumcized a person on the Sabbath day, to observe the law of Moses. Why do you get offended then if I heal on the Sabbath day? Is it all right to injure with circumcision, but it is wrong to make well, or heal, on the Sabbath day?

"Judgment shouldn't be made on appearances. Judgment is a matter of righteousness."

"Isn't this the man talking that some of the Jews want to kill?" asked one of the observers. "He speaks frankly, and the rulers are afraid to hush him. Do you reckon that the rulers think that surely he might be the Son of God?"

"The trouble with that reasoning," said another, "is that we know this man, but when the Christ comes, nobody is supposed to know about that."

"You know me," said Jesus, "and you know my family. I have not come on my own, but I was sent here by my Father. The Father is the true one, and He sent me. The trouble is, you don't know the Father, I know Him, I have come directly from Him."

After this some of the fellows tried to physically take Jesus, but since his time had not come, they were not able to seize him.

Many of the people believed in Christ and some said, "What more do you want? Do you think another Christ will do more miracles?"

The church leaders heard these remarks and they were all the more aggressive in seeking to find a way to handle Jesus, even sending officers to attempt to take Jesus under custody.

"For a little while I will be here with you," said Jesus. "Then I must return to the Father who sent me."

"Where is he talking about going that we can't find him? Do you reckon he will hide by joining the Gentiles and teaching them? What do you think Jesus means by saying 'You will seek me, but you won't find me, for where I'm going you can't come'?"

On the last day of the feast celebration Jesus stood and preached, saying, "If anybody has a doubt, let such a person come to me for help. A person who believes on me shall have living waters flowing within him."

Jesus was speaking on this occasion of the Holy Spirit, which the believers would receive. At this point in time, the Holy Spirit had not come upon the disciples, for as yet Jesus had not been glorified.

Some people at once said, "This man has got to be some kind of a prophet."

"This man is surely the Christ," some said.

"How can Christ come out of Galilee? Didn't the scripture say that Christ would come from the seed of David, and out of the town of Bethlehem, where David was born?"

As a result, there was considerable controversy and disagreement about the matter. Some persons would have arrested Jesus, or at least beat on him, but no one could.

The officers then returned to the Jewish leaders to report. "Why didn't you seize Jesus and bring him here?" asked the Jews.

"No man ever spoke like this one," said the officers.

"Are you fellows also deceived?" asked the Jewish leader. "Have any of the rulers or important people joined with Jesus? Curses on those who don't know the law."

Then Nick, one of the rulers, spoke up saying, "Does our law judge any man until he has had a fair hearing?"

"Are you one of his followers?" asked another leader. "Look at the Book. It doesn't say anything about a leader rising out of Galilee."

The meeting was then adjourned and no action taken.

Chap.
8

After spending the night on a hillside nearby, Jesus returned the next morning and he began to teach again in the Fellowship Hall portion of the church.

Some of the church leaders, in an effort to embarrass Christ, brought into his presence a woman who had been caught in the act of adultery.[1]

"We have a problem, Master," said one of the more pious type, "for this woman has been caught in the act of adultery and Moses says she should be stoned to death. What do you say?"

Jesus then began to doodle on the ground with his finger as if he had not heard what they said. As a result, they kept asking him.

Then Jesus looked at them and said, "All right, if Moses said so, stone the woman, but let one person among you, who is completely without sin in mind or deed, throw the first stone." Jesus then returned to doodling.

In a few minutes the men began to leave, one at a time, until finally there was no one left except the woman.

Seeing that all were departed, Jesus then turned to the woman and said, "Young lady, where are the ones who accuse you? Are there no prosecutors around anymore?"

"No man, Lord," said the young lady.

"Then certainly I do not condemn you. You may go on your way, but do not sin anymore," said Jesus.

Jesus then turned to the group that he had been teaching and said to them, "I am the Light of the world. Anyone that follows me need no longer walk in darkness and uncertainty or be afraid."

"You can't say that," said one of the church men. "You are just making those things up about yourself."

[1]Her partner apparently escaped.

"You are right. I am testifying of myself, but what I say is true. I know where I originated and where I am going, and you don't know either one of these things. You judge people on an earthly basis, but I don't. When I do judge, my judgment is accurate and final, for I am not alone, but the Father is with me.

"In your law, you say that the testimony of two men is the truth, well, you have my testimony and that of my Father."

"Where is your Father?" asked one of the persons present.

"You don't know me and you don't know the Father. If you had taken the trouble to know me, you would have also known the Father."

No one did anything to Jesus at this time because his time had not come.

"I go my own way," continued Jesus, "and you shall try to find me, but you will only die in your sins. You can't go where I am going."

"Do you think he plans suicide?" asked one of the Jews, for he reasoned that this would enable Jesus to go where they wouldn't follow.

"You are of the earth," said Jesus. "I come from God. I have said that you will die in your sins unless you believe that I am sent from God."

"Who are you?" they asked.

"I have told you all along, but you have been too pigheaded to believe. I have a lot of things yet to teach you, and I tell you only those things which God, who sent me, has told me to tell you," said Jesus.

The listeners did not understand that Jesus spoke of God and his Father as being the one and the same.

"After you have crucified me, then you will begin to understand. Then you will know that I am only doing the will of God, my Father. God is with me. He has not left me alone. I do all things to please God, the Father," concluded Jesus.

At this point there were many present who believed in Jesus.

Jesus then turned to the group that had expressed belief in him and he said to them, "If you continue to follow my instructions then you will grow in your discipleship. You will gradually learn the truth, and the truth will set you free."

"We are Jews, descendants of Abraham, and we have never been slaves. What do you mean, we shall be made free?" asked one of the puzzled listeners.

"Whoever sins becomes a slave of sin," responded Jesus. "Only the Son, who is a permanent resident of the house of God, is able to make you really free. I know you are Jews. I know some of you want to kill me because you don't believe in what I say.

"Yet I only tell you what I have seen in the presence of my Father, even as you do the things you learn from your father."

"Abraham is our father," said one of the group.

"Then why don't you do as Abraham did? Strange that you try to kill me, a person who has told you the truth, which I heard directly from God. Abraham did not hear directly. Anyway, it would be fine if you would do as your father, Abraham, did."

"Well, we really have only one Father, and that Father is God," said another one present.

"If God were your Father, you would love me, for I come here straight from God. I didn't come on my own, I was sent by God. Why don't you understand? You aren't deaf. Your trouble is that you latch on to only the evil desires of your fathers, men of sin. There is evil in many hearts and there is no truth in the speech of evil men.

"I tell you the truth, and you don't believe it. Why don't you believe me? You cannot convict me of not telling the truth. Those who sincerely seek to hear God's word will hear it, but you are deaf to it."

"We are right in saying that you are just a Samaritan possessed by the devil," one spoke from the crowd.

"Wrong again," said Jesus. "I have no devil in me. I honor God, the Father, yet you dishonor me. I don't seek any glory or recognition for myself, for there is only One worthy of glory.

"I tell you again, if a person adheres to my teaching and believes in me, such a person never notices death."

"Now we know you have a devil in you," said one of the Jews. Abraham is dead and so are the prophets. What do you mean that if a man keeps your word, he will not die? Are you greater than Abraham, greater than the prophets?"

"If I give honor to myself it is nothing, but it is the Father who honors me. You claim He is your Father, yet you've never met Him, but I have. Did you know that Abraham rejoiced to see me come to earth and he was delighted?" said Jesus.

"Come off it, man," said one of the mathematicians present. You aren't fifty years old, how could you have seen Abraham?"

"I existed long before Abraham," said Jesus.

Some of those present then took stones to throw at Jesus, but Jesus walked through them untouched and they appeared not to be able to see him.[1]

Chap.

9

As Jesus was walking along he passed a man who had been born blind. One of the disciples said to Jesus, "What caused that fellow to be blind? Did his parents sin or was the man a sinner?"

"No," said Jesus. "This man is not being punished for sin, either his or his parents, but he is fulfilling a plan of God. I have work to

[1]In desperation, they probably threw some stones at a school teacher, rather than put them down.

do. A person must work while it is possible. I am doing now the work of the One who sent me.

"As long as I am in the world, I am the Light of the world." As soon as he had finished speaking, Jesus made a patty of clay and put it on the eyes of the blind man.

"Go to the nearest pool now, fellow, and wash off the clay," said Jesus. The man did as he was told and he left the pool with 20-20 vision.

"Isn't this the man who has always been blind?" asked one of the neighbors.

"It looks like him," some said, "but it couldn't be the same person."

"I am the one," said the man.

"How did you get your sight?" asked one of the people.

"A man named Jesus put some clay on my eyes and sent me to the fish pool in the square and when I had washed away the clay, I was able to see," said the man.

"Where is this man that healed you?" one asked.

"I don't know," the fellow said.

Some people then brought the man to the church to talk to some of the leaders there. This happened on a Sunday and the church leaders questioned the man carefully about what had happened to enable him to be cured of blindness.

"The man Jesus must not be from God, for he has violated the blue law by practicing medicine on Sunday," said one of the sharpies.

"How can a man that is a sinner perform a miracle?" asked another. As a result, a big church argument started.[1]

"Who do you think Jesus is?" said one of the leaders to the man who had been cured.

"He is a prophet," said the man.

There was still a great deal of skepticism about this miracle, and finally the parents of the healed person were called.

"Is this your son?" they were asked.

"Yes, it is. We know it is our son and that he was born blind. That's all we know. We don't know how he was cured, or who gave him his vision," said the parents.

The parents were being cautious because they ran a grocery store and did a lot of business with the Jews. It was also known to them that the Jewish leaders had agreed to ban from the church anyone who claimed to be the Christ.

"Why don't you ask our son?" said the parents. "He is of draft age."

The church leaders then spoke again to the healed man. "Give the credit for your sight to God, and not to this sinner Jesus."

[1]Actually a church argument can start with even less information than this.

"Whether Jesus is a sinner or not, I don't know. All I know is that once I was blind and now I can see," affirmed the man.

"What did he say to you? What did he do? How did he open your eyes?" asked one of the Jews.

"I've told you already and you act as if you were deaf. Why do you want to hear it again? Are you trying to get me to be one of the disciples?"

"Don't be fresh with us! You are one of Jesus's disciples, but we are disciples of Moses. We know God spoke to Moses, but we don't know anything about this fellow Jesus," said another of the leaders.

"You're not a very smart bunch. A man is in town who has given me sight and you never heard of him. Yet we all know that God doesn't cooperate with sinners, but God works with those who worship Him.

"Nobody has any record of a man born blind receiving his sight twenty years later. If Jesus were not of God, then he couldn't have done what he did," concluded the man.

"You were born in sin, fellow, so don't try teaching us good people anything," they said. Then they chased the man out of the church.

When Jesus heard of this and that the man had been embarrassed for His sake, he found him and asked him, "Do you believe in the Son of God?"

"Who is he, Lord, that I might believe on him? I'm not too bright. Tell me who he is."

"You have seen him, for I am the Son of God," said Jesus.

"I believe," said the man.

Jesus then said, "This whole incident is symbolic of the reason that I have come into the world. It is to enable the spiritually blind to see, and to confuse the vision of those who think they know it all."

"Are you saying that we all are blind?" asked one of the Jews.

"It is the assumption that you make that you know everything and see yourself as superior; so you sin. It would be great if you were as humble as the blind."

Chap.
10

"The way to enter a house is through the door," continued Jesus. "Only a thief climbs in a window, or goes down the chimney.[1] The shepherd is the one who comes to the front door, and the doorman knows him and the sheep know his voice, and they follow him. Sheep will not follow a strange voice."

The people who heard this parable didn't have any idea of what Jesus was saying and what he meant.

"I will explain," said Jesus to his disciples. "I am the door for

[1]Santa Claus is an exception.

the sheep. No other voice or name, before or after me, is effective. Only by me are the sheep saved. Phoney   ideologies are destructive and are designed to destroy, but I have come to give life and to save, and to teach that life can be beautiful and enjoyable.

"I am the good shepherd. I will even lay down my life for the sheep. False teachers and erratic leaders will often go chasing off in a world of sin and leave their sheep unprotected. This is because such leaders do not really care for the sheep.

"Not so with me. I love my sheep and they know me, and I know them. I know the Father and the Father knows me. I expect to lay down my life for the sheep.

"There are other sheep of other areas. I must also be their shepherd. These other sheep shall hear my voice and come to me and there will be finally only one great group in Christ.

"My Father loves me because I am willing to die and live again. Nobody really takes my life. I give it. I have the power to keep my life or lose it. This is the promise of my Father. I may lay down my life, and restore it again."

This teaching created another big church argument.

"Why listen to this man?" some asked. "He is screwy, for sure."

"These words are not the words of a nut. They make sense. What's more, can a man of the devil give sight to the blind?"

It was wintertime and Jesus was walking along the porch of Solomon's Temple when he was approached by a group of Jews.

"Why don't you declare yourself?" they asked. "We know that a Christ is to come. If you are the Christ tell us plainly."

"I told you and you didn't believe me. The works I do are at the discretion of my Father. The works themselves testify to my validity. You don't believe because you don't want to believe. You are not willing to humble yourselves and hear my voice and follow me.

"Those that do hear my voice and follow me, to them I give eternal life. They shall never die, and no one will take them away from me.

"My Father, who gave my followers to me, is greater than all, and no one can claim one of my people, for they are safe in the hand of God. My Father and I cooperate and work as a unit," concluded Jesus.

At this point, the Jews decided to get some rocks and stone Jesus.

"For which of my good works are you planning to stone me?" asked Jesus.

"We don't object to your good works, but we stone you for your blasphemy. You are a man claiming to be God."

"Doesn't your own law say 'ye are gods'? If it is written that way, and you respect the scriptures, how then can you be upset when I, whom God has blessed, say to you 'I am the Son of God'? If

I do not do good works of God, then don't believe in me, but if I do good works, such as healing the blind, even though you don't respect me, you are bound to respect the works.

"Really, you should know and believe that I am in the Father and the Father in me." As Jesus finished, he walked away and they were not able to see him.

Jesus then went to a place close to where he had been baptized. People came to Jesus there and many felt that even though John did not perform miracles, his testimony of Jesus was valid and accepted Christ as their Saviour.

There was a man living in Mobile[1] named Lazy Russ[2] and he was the brother of Mary and Martha. In fact, Mary was the long haired girl who had put witch hazel on Jesus's feet and then dried his feet with her hair.

Word came to Jesus, who was on a trip, that Lazy was sick and Mary and Martha were worried about him. When the message was delivered Jesus commented that Lazy was not a terminal case, but that the whole matter was a plan of God, that the Lord might be glorified in his Son. Jesus was devoted to all three in the family.

After hearing about Lazy, Jesus waited two days and then said to his disciples that it was time to go to Mobile. The disciples were worried about the trip for they were afraid that the stone throwers may have become better organized.

Jesus said, "Cool it, boys, it is like walking in the daylight. A man may stumble around in the dark, but in the daylight he can do very well. This is why I say that Lazy is just temporarily in trouble, and is sleeping."

"If Lazy is sleeping, he is doing all right," said one of his disciples. Jesus, of course, had been speaking of Lazy's death, but as was usually the case, the disciples did not look deep enough into Christ's comments.

"Lazy is dead," said Jesus. "I am glad I was not there. The way things will be now will bolster your faith."

"If Lazy is dead then let us go and be dead with him," said Tom.[3]

When Jesus arrived in Mobile, he found that Lazy had been dead four days. Martha, hearing that Jesus was arriving, ran to meet him and said, "Jesus, Lord, if you had been here Lazy would not have died, but I know that even now anything you ask of God will be done for you."

"Your brother will rise again, Martha," said Jesus.

"I know he will rise again in the last day at the resurrection," said Martha.

[1]Bethany [2]Lazarus
[3]Over-expressed sympathy was the order of the day.

Jesus said, "I am the resurrection, and I represent life. Any person that believes in me, though that person be dead in a physical sense, yet such a person lives again, any person who lives, and believes in me, never really dies. Do you believe this?"

"Yes, Lord. I also believe that you are the Christ, the Son of God, for whom the world has been waiting," said Martha. Then Martha went to get her sister, Mary, and told her that Jesus had come and was asking for Mary.

Mary immediately headed for the place where Jesus was, for he had not as yet entered the town. Some of the friends of Mary, who were at the house, presumed that when Mary left hastily, that she was going to the cemetery to do a little more weeping, and they followed her.

When Mary came to Jesus, she said, "Lord, if you had been here, Lazy would not have died."

When Jesus saw how grieved and greatly disturbed Mary was, he suffered in himself.

"Where is the cemetery where Lazy is buried?" asked Jesus.

"Come and see," Mary said. At this point Jesus was moved to tears, which caused the neighbors to realize how much Jesus cared for Lazy.

"It looks to me," said one fellow, "that if Jesus could make a blind man see, he could have prevented Lazy from dying."

Jesus again was hurt by such callous comment. When Jesus arrived at the grave, he found it to be a cave opening with a stone over the opening.

"Take away the stone," said Jesus.

"Master, please, Lazy has been dead for four days and the smell would shock us all again," said Martha.

"Martha, didn't I tell you that if you would believe that you would see a manifestation of the glory of God?"

At once then some of the men present took away the stone and Jesus raised his eyes to the Father and said, "I thanked you, Father, that you have heard my request. I know You always hear, but I wanted to publicly acknowledge this in order that the people here might believe that You have sent me."

Then suddenly Jesus shouted, "Lazy, get up and come out of the tomb!"

Out came Lazy, still bound with grave clothes and the mortician's cloth still over his face.

"Free him from his bounds," said Jesus.

Many believed in Jesus and worshipped God, while others went to report to the rulers and to wonder about there being some trick. The report was so accurate, however, that the rulers could not refute the account.

"What can we do?" asked one of the rulers of the Jews. "This man Jesus does great miracles, and if we let him alone, before long he will have everybody believing in him. Then the Romans will come and eliminate us for letting it happen."

Then the top ruler, a man named Slick Faustus, said, "Don't be stupid. It is simple. For the sake of the nation, Jesus must die." Thus, without knowing it, Slick prophesied that Jesus would die, not only for one nation, but for all men everywhere.

After this, the leaders began to daily plot as to how they would get Jesus killed.

Jesus knew of this, and so he did not unnecessarily expose himself, and withdrew from the neighborhood of Mobile and Jerusalem and went to Horseshoe Bay for a period of rest and refreshment with his disciples.

The time of the celebration of Passover week approached and many people began their regular trip to Jerusalem. People from all over were asking around the church about Jesus and wondering if he would appear for the Passover celebration.

The chief leaders of the Jews had gotten out an APB on Jesus and the word was that any information would be rewarded.

Chap.

12

Six days before the Passover feast Jesus came to Mobile and had dinner with Mary, Martha, and Lazy. On this occasion, Mary took some Chanel #5 and put it on Christ's feet with her hair, and the perfume made the whole house smell good.

Then Judas said, "Why didn't someone take the perfume and sell it for $75 and give the money to the United Fund?" Judas said this, not because he was interested in the United Fund, but because he was the treasurer and a thief and he had been dipping his hand in the till.

"Forget it," said Jesus. "Mary has done this as an act of worship. What is more, there will always be worthy causes, but you will not always have me here."

Word spread that Jesus was in Mobile, but the people came primarily to interview Lazy and ask about his being dead. The next day, however, many people, coming to the Passover feast period, came to see Jesus.

When Jesus entered the gate of the city of Jerusalem the people spread palm branches and yelled, "Hurrah! Hail the King! Blessed is the King of David who comes in the name of the Lord!"

Jesus entered the city riding on a donkey in order that the scripture might be fulfilled, which said, "Fear not, children of God, for the King comes sitting on a donkey."

The disciples of Jesus did not understand all these things while they were happening, but, in retrospect, they could see the meaning. The people, who were present at the raising of Lazy, testified of Christ and were witnesses. Knowledge of the miracles naturally caused the crowds to increase.

The Jewish leaders moaned and groaned, for they could see the people completely supporting Jesus.

There were some Greeks who had come to town for marketing and they asked Phil to take them to meet Jesus. Phil told Andy and Andy told Jesus.

Jesus said, "The time is at hand for the Son of Man to be acknowledged and glorified. You know a little about agriculture. Unless a seed dies it cannot develop into a bush or a plant, or a corn stalk. Anyone who is completely selfish loses his life, but a person who shares and gives of himself or herself, finds a new life.

"If any person wishes to serve me, let such a one follow me, and wherever this person is, I will be there, and my Father will be particularly interested in such a person.

"This is a hard time for me. I would prefer not to go through with it, but it was for this reason that I came to the earth. May all of these things be to the glory of God."

When Jesus said this, a voice from Heaven spoke, saying, "I have already made this a glorified occasion and I will continue the glory." Some people thought they were hearing thunder and some thought the voice to be that of an angel.

"This voice you heard was to help you. It was not for me. The judgment of the world has been set, the leader of the world will be dishonored, but when I am lifted up in apparent pain and disgrace, I will lift all men to me who believe," said Jesus.

Jesus was again foretelling the manner of his death.

"We have always heard that the Christ, when he comes, will live forever. What do you mean by 'the Son of Man must be lifted up? Who is the Son of Man?" one person asked.

"For a little while yet the light is still with you. Enjoy the light while it is present," said Jesus. "While you have the light learn to believe in the light, in order that you might become as children of light yourselves."

Jesus then left and hid from the people.

In spite of the many miracles, there were still many who did not believe. This, too, was a fulfillment of prophesy, specifically the one of Isaiah saying, 'Who has believed our report, and to whom has the revelation of the Lord been clear?'

Isaiah furthermore had said, "Their eyes were blind and their hearts were hardened, nor would any understand, and healing them would be very difficult." Isaiah said these things when the glory of the coming of Christ was revealed to him.

Still there were plenty who believed. Many of the church leaders believed, but were intimidated and hesitated to speak out for fear of being booted out of the church. Many of these enjoyed the praise of men more than they did the praise of God.

Jesus said again, "Anyone who believes in me must also believe on the One who sent me. I have come as a light to the world and to prevent anyone who accepts me from living in darkness.

"I did not come to condemn, but to save. I am not rejecting those who reject me, but the day of judgment will get them. There our word will be against them.

"I have not spoken for myself, but only the things the Father has told me to say. I know that the word of the Father is true and that it leads to life everlasting; so I speak for Him."

Chap.
13

After supper one evening, before the day of the feast of the Passover, Jesus decided to teach the disciples an important truth. At this time Jesus, who loved the people of the world, and who knew that he was shortly to leave them and ascend to the Father, arose from the table, put a towel around his waist, and prepared to wash the disciples' feet.

The devil had, by this time, already infiltrated the heart of Judas and had convinced Judas to betray Jesus.

After pouring water in a basin, Jesus began to wash the disciples' feet and to wipe them with the towel that he had tied around his waist.[1]

When Jesus came to wash Peter's feet, Peter said, "Do you mean you plan to wash my feet?"

"Yes," said Jesus, "but the significance of what I am doing, and the lesson involved, will come to you sometime later."

"You are too important to wash my feet," said Peter. "I can't let you do it."

"If you do not accept me this way then you cannot be part of my operation," said Jesus.

"If that is all there is to Christianity, then give me a whole bath. I want the entire treatment," said Peter.

"It is just a symbol, Peter. All that is needed is to wash the feet, then you are clean entirely. Not all of you, however," said Jesus. Jesus, of course, knew that Judas was to betray him.

After Jesus had washed all the dirty feet, he turned to the disciples and said, "Now, do any of you know what I have done?[2]

"Well, you refer to me as Lord and Master, as King of Kings, and you are correct, for that is why I am here. If I am willing to do the most menial tasks as your Lord and Master, then you are to do likewise. I have done this as an example to you.

"Remember that the servant is not greater than the Master, nor is the one sent greater than the sender. If you understand true humility, then you are indeed most fortunate and bound to be happy.

"I am not speaking of everyone, for in order that the scriptures be fulfilled, there must be a sour apple in the barrel, and we have one

---

[1]This function was normally handled by the lowest ranking slave.
[2]I imagine a bunch of blank looks greeted the question.

with us. I am telling you these things in order that you may look back and realize that I am the true one from God.

"Let me assure you that anyone that receives one of you that I send in my name, receives me, and anyone that receives me, receives the Father that sent me."

Obviously saddened, Jesus said, "I regret that one of you will betray me."

The disciples immediately began to look suspiciously at each other. At this moment one of the disciples, a favorite of Jesus,[1] was close to Christ, and Peter suggested that John ask Jesus who the culprit was.

"Am I the one?" said John.

"It is the one that is dipping his potato chip with me and to whom I will give mine." So saying, Jesus gave it to Judas.

"Do your thing quickly, Judas," said Jesus.

None of those hearing this exchange understood it until months later. In fact, some present thought Jesus was asking Judas, as treasurer, to get some more potato chips, as no one had been able to eat just one. Others thought Jesus was suggesting that Judas make an offering to the benevolent budget.

Judas immediately took his potato chip and dip and went out into the night.

"Now is the Son of Man glorified," said Jesus, after Judas had departed, "and God is glorified in him. Since all things must be to the glory of God, so shall God cause all this to be an occasion of glory. Boys, I'm only to be with you a very little while now. You will look for me, but you cannot go where I am going just yet; so listen to what I have to say to you.

"A new idea I give to you as a basis for living. Love each other as I have loved you, for the basis of a good life is love for one another."

"Back to this trip deal. Where are you going?" asked Rocky.

"You can't follow me, Rocky, at this particular point in time. You will follow me later," said Jesus.

"Why can't I go now? I am willing to die for you, if necessary," affirmed Rocky.

"You mean well, Rocky, but before the rooster crows in the morning, you will have denied me three times," said Jesus.

Chap.
14

"Don't always be in such a turmoil of mind. If you believe in God, you should also believe in me. That's not complicated," said Jesus. "In my Father's place of operations there are many wonderful facilities. If this were not the truth I would not be telling it to you.

"Actually, I go to prepare a place for you. When everything is

[1]This is John's idea of John, not necessarily mine.

set, I will come again and receive you properly, and from then on you may be anywhere that I am. Where I go now you will know and also know the way to follow."

"How can we know the way to go," asked Thomas, "when we don't even know where you are going?"

"I am the way," said Jesus. "In me also is all the truth and life. No one can come to God except through me. If you have become well acquainted with me, you have also become well acquainted with God. In a sense then you have known God and in me you have seen God."

"Just show us one look at God, and we will be satisfied," said Phil.

"All this time, Phil, and you still don't get the point? If you have seen me, you have seen God. So why ask to see God? Don't you realize that I am in the Father and the Father in me? Even the words I speak are the words of God and the deeds I do are the deeds of God.

"Really, Phil, believe that I am in the Father and the Father in me. Or at least believe because of what you have seen happen.

"Anyone who trusts me and supports the works that I do shall have the opportunity of doing works of their own, even greater than the works I have been doing as illustrations.

"I am going to the Father. I'll be right there in the throne room, and the things you ask of God sincerely in my name, I will get it done for the glory of God. There is no limit placed on this prayerful arrangement.

"Remember, though, that if you love me, you will keep my commandments.

"I also expect to ask God to send to you a Comforter and he will be available on earth at all times. The Comforter might also be called the Quest for Truth. Not everyone will recognize the Comforter, but the believers will know.

"I will not leave you forever. In a little while I will depart, and I will live with you only as a Spirit, but then I will come again and you will fully understand my relationship with the Father.

"The persons who love me will keep my commandments and those that do shall be loved by God, as well as by me," concluded Jesus.

"How is it, Lord," asked Ted, "that you will reveal yourself to us and not to others?"

"If a person loves me, such a person will live accordingly, then my Father will love such a person, and I will appear with such a person in the presence of God to live there forever.

"Not so," continued Jesus, "with those who do not obey my commandments. What I am telling you is straight from God and I am using the opportunity of being on earth to tell you.

"When the Comforter comes from God after I have gone, he

will teach you many more things, and will cause you to remember my words.

"The Spirit of Peace, which is my type of peace, I leave this with you. You are not to be troubled or afraid. I told you I was going away, and that I would return. This should be great news for you. Telling you ahead of time will help convince you when you look back and see how true is everything that I have said.

"Most of my talking is done. Worldly cares and temptations will be left with you. In order that everyone may know that I love the Father, and that the Father sent me, I repeat, Love one another, even as I love all of you. O. K. It's time to get up and go," said Jesus, as he got to his feet.

Chap.
15

"You might think of me," Jesus said, "as being the only genuine vine and my Father the person in charge of the vineyard. If any branch of my operation does not bear fruit, the Father cuts it off and thus encourages the multiplication of fruit from the rest.

"Remember also that the fact of receiving the Word directly from me purifies you. Just also as the branch cannot develop unless it is connected with the vine, so you, as my branches, can accomplish nothing unless you are attached to me. You are to be positively progressive and you can accomplish much as long as you are closely connected to me.

"If a person forsakes me, such a person is lost. If you trust me and if you allow my teachings to rule your life, then anything you ask of me, that I will do. This means that you bear fruit, and in this way the Father is glorified.

"As the Father has loved me, so I have loved you. Try to keep it that way, by keeping my commandments. This is the way I will know you are mine. I do this so that you will be happy and full of joy, competent to face life and its problems.

"Work hard to love one another, even as I have loved you. The greatest test of love is the willingness to die for someone.

"As long as you obey my teachings, I consider you my friends. As a consequence, I do not think of you as servants, or employees, who do not know what the owner plans, but I think of you as friends and have told you the plans of the Father.

"You should also bear in mind that you have been selected by me, and charged with a mission. Again, I mention that that arrangement provides for your prayers. Ask and I will get it done, as God has promised. Again, though, you must love people.

"Don't get up tight when you find that a lot of people have no use for you and your mission. Remember that they also hated me. You are particularly hated because you have been chosen. People will think of you as being different.

"Remember what I said about workers and bosses being

essentially equal; so you can expect to be mistreated just as I have been mistreated. On the other hand, some have followed my teachings and there will be those then that follow your teachings.

"The people that mistreat you and do not respect you do so because they do not know God. Before I came, there was some excuse for sins, for man had never seen the truth in the flesh. No longer is this true and so anyone that turns against Jesus, turns against God.

"If I had simply lived a life that was no different from anyone else, then sinners would have some excuse, but now they have had a chance to see me, and to see God. All this is also a fulfillment of the scripture, which says that 'they hated me without any reason for it.'

"When the Comforter comes to earth in my place, coming as the Spirit of Truth, this Comforter will witness for me. You also should bear witness, for you have been with me during my entire ministry."

Chap.

16

"I am telling you all these things," continued Jesus, "so you won't be surprised or upset when you encounter adveristy. You'll have trouble. Some of you will be booted out of the church. In fact, the time will actually come when some think that killing Christians will be a service to God.

"Now when these things occur, remember what I'm telling you now. I wanted to warn you because as long as I was with you, there was no need of alerting you. Now, however, the time has come for me to leave you. There's no need to ask again where I am going as I've made it plain.

"I know this saddens you, but it is absolutely necessary. For one thing, until I leave, the Spirit of Truth, the Comforter, will not be available to you. When this Spirit of Truth comes, then this one will rebuke sin in the world, basically, the sin of rejecting me. The Truth will also attest to the fact of righteousness and the glory, for I ascend to the Father.

"The Spirit of Truth will pronounce judgment, for the people of the world are to be judged, and the instigator of evil denounced.

"There are a bunch of other things I would like to tell you, but you won't even be able to absorb all that I've given you; so I'll stop. The Spirit of Truth will take up where I've left off. Many things will be explained to you and inspired people will be instruments of genuine revelation.

"The Spirit of Truth will be identified as one who worships God and who witnesses for me. Such a one will receive from me, and reveal to you, the truth.

"I will be around for a short spell, then disappear, you'll see me again and then I'll return to the Father," concluded Jesus.

At once, some of the disciples began discussing among themselves the meaning of Jesus saying he would be here a little, then leave, then they would see him again, then he'd leave again. They also wondered what he meant by 'a little while.'

Jesus knew they were curious and he said to them, "Are you mumbling among yourselves about the meaning of 'a little while with you, then leave, then a little while and you see me again'?

"Well, you all will weep while others will rejoice, but your sorrow will then soon be turned into great joy. The situation is comparable to a woman in labor. From great sorrow, she is turned suddenly into great joy, and she forgets all the anguish in the birth of a baby.

"Now then you have sorrow and are uncertain and frustrated, but soon all this will be turned into great joy, and such a joy that no one can deprive you of it. At that point in time you will be fully satisfied. After that, anything you ask the Father for my sake will be given to you.

"All these things are being told to you in future language, but the time will come when you will be able to see and comprehend everything very plainly.

"At a later time you will learn that you can go directly to the Father in my name, for the Father loves you because you have loved me, and have believed that I come from God. I came to the world from the Father and I return from the world to the Father."

"Now that is plain talk," said the disciples. "We can understand that. We know now that you came to us from God."

"Do you now believe?" asked Jesus. "Well, anyway, the time has come when you will be scattered, and you will leave me alone. Of course, I cannot really be alone, for the Father is always with me.

"All the things I have said to you are designed to bring you inner peace through belief in me. In the world, as you know it, you will find great trouble, but be optimistic and cheerful, for I have overcome the world."

Chap.
17

After saying this, Jesus raised his eyes toward the Father in heaven and said, "The time has now come, Father. Make me worthy and capable to overcome, grant that the power given to me over all flesh will be used to your glory, and to enable those that believe to enjoy eternal life with me.

"I have done all that I planned to do on earth. Now is the time for the revelation of Your great power and restore again to me my heavenly status. I have presented the truth to the men You chose to receive it and they have this truth in their hearts. They know that everything I did and said was from You.

"These persons now know that You sent me, that what I have is from God and not from man. They now believe in me as the manifestation of God on earth.

"I pray for these people. I am not praying for the world, but for these people that are mine. Those who are mine are also Yours, and I am Yours. I am no longer really in this world. These people I leave in the world with the charge to witness and preach. I am going home to the Father.

"Keep these people who are mine. Unite them in spirit. While I was in the world I could look out for them and protect them from the devil, just as the Scriptures have said. I am leaving them. I am saying this prayer openly so that these people may know about the arrangements and that the joy of being secure in the love of God may be theirs as it was mine.

"I have, of course, given them the word of truth. This makes them different and really, therefore, causes them to be scorned by many others who do not know about the word of Truth. Protect them, Lord, and secure them in the knowledge of the truth of the love of God. I have gone through the same type of life as they have in order that they might know and understand my security in the truth, and thereby understand theirs.

"I pray also, Father, for those who will receive the good news from those that I leave to teach and preach. Bless all that receive the word down through the years and believe in me.

"Unite all believers in their belief in me. Let this be a testimony to the world that you really sent me. With my spirit instilled in these believers and Your Spirit in me, we all become working in one great cause. This will also show that I have loved them as You have loved me.

"Father, I also ask that You save all those that believe in me, that You arrange for them to be with me in heaven, to actually see my glory, and they will then realize that I have been a part of Your love from the beginning.

"The world has not known You, Father, but I have known You and these believers know that You sent me. I have taught them about You, God, and through my word this teaching will continue in order that the love of God may flow from You to me, from me to them, and then among them as they learn to love one another."

Chap. 18

When Jesus had finished talking, he went with the disciples across Cedar Creek[1] to a garden area. This was a place known to Judas as it was a favorite spot for chatting with the disciples. Judas directed a group of men, consisting of representatives from the chief priests and the church rulers, and this group approached with lanterns, as it was night.

Jesus, who knew all that was happening and all that was to happen, approached them and said, "For whom are you looking?"

[1]Kibron

"Jesus of Nazareth," replied one of the fellows.

"I am he," said Jesus.

Judas was standing with the crowd at this time. The answer of Christ startled the group and they drew back as if not knowing what to do.[1]

Again Jesus said to them, "Whom are you seeking?"

"Jesus of Nazareth," was again the reply.

"Jesus said. I have told you that I am the one. If I'm the only one you want, let my associates be free to go." This was said in order to fulfill the prophecy recorded in scripture saying 'Of those given to me, I did not lose a one.'

Rocky[2] pulled out his fish skinning knife at this point and took a whack at the nearest representative of the priests and cut off his right ear. The man's name was Wings.[3]

"Put your knife away, Rocky," said Christ. "Don't you realize that I have said that it is necessary for me to go through with this ordeal?"

The captain in charge of the group then had Jesus bound and took him to Sully,[4] the father-in-law of Slick Faustus.[5] Slick was the high priest, and he was the one that had suggested that it was preferable for one to die in behalf of the people.

Rocky and another disciple followed Jesus to see what was going to happen. Rocky's companion was on good terms apparently with the church folk and he was allowed to enter the palace where ole Slick held forth, but Rocky had to remain outside the door.

The other disciple then went to the girl at the door and told her to let Rock enter. Turning to Rocky, the girl said, "Aren't you one of the birds that has been following Jesus?"

"I am not," said Rocky.

Now some of the guards, and some of the officers built a fire in the quadrangle to warn themselves, and Rocky joined them around the fire.

Slick then turned to Jesus and asked him about himself and his disciples, what their plans were and the like.

"I have not hidden anything,"said Jesus. "I have taught openly in the church and on the streets, and plenty of Jews have listened to me, so why ask me? Why don't you ask the Jews who listened and hear what they have to say?"

When Jesus said this, one of the officers slapped Jesus and said, "Don't give any smart-alec answers to the high priest."

"If I have spoken anything that is incorrect, tell me, but if I have spoken the truth, why do you slap me?"

---

[1]It has always been customary to run from the cops. [2]Simon Peter
[3]Malchus Other accounts also say that Christ replaced the ear. Most of us, having the power, would have put the ear on backwards.
[4]Annas   [5]Caiaphas

Sully then turned Jesus over to Slick and his crowd with his hands bound.

As Rocky was warming his hands by the fire, one of the fellows present turned to him and said, "Aren't you one of the followers of Jesus?"

"I am not," said Rocky.

Then a cousin of the fellow who had had his ear whacked off, turned to Rocky and said, "Didn't I see you in the garden with Jesus at the time of the arrest?"

Again Rocky denied his relationship. At this point a rooster crowed.

Jesus was then conducted into the main courtroom, but the rulers and the priests did not enter as it would have been a violation of the code regarding the observance of the Passover Feast.

Judge Bean[1] then entered the courtroom and said, "What are the charges against this person?"

"If he wasn't a criminal, we would not have brought him to court," said one of the pop-off officials.

"Take the man then and judge him according to your Jewish laws," said Bean.

"We do not have the right to inflict capital punishment," was the reply. This also was a fulfillment of the prophecy.

The judge then approached Jesus and asked, "Are you the King of the Jews?"

"Is this a question you really are asking, or did someone just suggest that you ask this?" inquired Jesus.

"I'm not a Jew, man. Your own people and your priests brought you here. What have you done?" asked Judge Bean.

"My kingdom is not in this world," said Jesus. "If I had planned to take over this world physically and politically, then my supporters would be around and ready to fight. That is not the way of my kingdom."

"Are you really a King, man?" asked Bean.

"Yes," said Jesus. "I was born to be a King, this is why I came into the world, that I could reveal the Truth. Everyone that recognizes the Truth, recognizes me, and hears my message."

"What is the Truth?" asked Bean. Saying this and not waiting for an answer, Bean went out to where the Jews were gathered and said to them, "I find nothing wrong with the man Jesus. You have a custom, though, that at this time each year, in recognition of the Passover, I release one prisoner. How about my releasing this man Jesus?"

"No, No," they shouted, "release to us Killer Cade."[2] Killer Cade was a well-known robber and criminal.

[1]Pontius Pilate   [2]Barabbas

Then Judge Bean had Jesus beaten as was the custom,[1] and then some of the soldiers made a crown of thorns, and put an old purple robe on Jesus, just as acts of scorn.[2] The soldiers also made smart remarks, slapped Jesus, and generally carried out their ten year old mentality. Bean then presented Jesus, thus arrayed, to the leaders of the Jews and said, "Look at this person! You're afraid of him!"

"Crucify him, crucify him," yelled the rabble rousers.

"All right, take him and crucify him," said Judge Bean, "but I do not find any fault in him."

"That's your law. According to our law, he should die, for he has claimed to be the Son of God," said some of the Jews.

This gave Bean the willies all the more, and he returned to Jesus and asked him privately "Where are you from?"

Jesus just looked Bean in the eye and didn't say a word.

"Why don't you speak to me? Don't you know that I control life or death for you?"

"You have no power at all except what is given to you by God. As a consequence, the group that sent me to you is in worse trouble than you are," said Jesus.

Bean then tried all the more to get the Jews to consent to the releasing of Christ. Finally, one of the Jewish leaders said to Bean, "If you let this man Jesus free, you are no friend of Caesar, for whoever makes himself King is an enemy of Caesar."

After hearing this comment, Bean brought Jesus into the open court, familiar to most people as the Square.[3]

It was about the sixth hour into the Passover preparation and Bean said to the Jews, "Here is your King."

"Crucify him! Execute him!" the Jews continued to yell.

"You have no King by Caesar," was the impudent reply.

Bean then turned Jesus over to the Jewish mob and they led him away. Carrying his own burdensome cross, Jesus was forced to trudge his way to Capitol Hill.[4] There Jesus was crucified, with convicted robbers, one on each side of him.

Bean had arranged for a sign to be placed on top of the cross of Jesus saying, 'Jesus of Nazareth, the King of the Jews.' The sign was written in Hebrew, Greek, and Latin, and many people saw the sign and read it.

The top dog among the Jewish priests tried to get Bean to change the sign to read, 'He said he was King of the Jews.'

"Go jump in the lake," said Bean.[5]

---

[1]The Romans thought this improved their image.

[2]In my opinion, this is when the Roman Empire began to crumble.

[3]Gabbatha   [4]Golgotha

[5]Lots of people have used this saying - another interpretation is 'nuts to you.'

After Jesus was crucified, the soldiers divided his suit into four parts and gave a part to each soldier. The top coat could not be divided as it was made of one piece of material, so they decided to shoot high dice for the coat in order that the prophecy might be fulfilled, which said, 'They parted my rainment among them and for my vesture did they cast lots.' The soldiers did exactly that.

Not far from the cross were some ladies; the mother of Jesus, his aunt, Clem's wife,[1] and Mary of Alabama. When Jesus saw his mother, he turned to John, the only disciple present,[2] and said, "Look out for my mother."

Then turning to his mother, Jesus said, "John will be as a son to you."

From that day forward until her death, the mother of Jesus stayed in John's house, under his care.

Knowing then that all things had now been fulfilled that the Scriptures had mentioned, Jesus said, "I thirst."

One of the soldiers then took a sop of vinegar and touched the lips of Jesus with it. When Jesus had received the vinegar, he said, "It is all over now." Then he bowed his head and died.

Since it was against the Jewish custom that any Jew remain on a cross on Sunday, the Jews requested that the soldiers break[3] the men's legs at once so they could be removed promptly.

The soldiers then came and broke the legs of the two thieves, but when they came to Jesus, they saw that he was dead and limp and there was no danger of stiffening, so they did not break his legs.

One of the soldiers, however, took a spear and struck Jesus in the side and blood and water came forth. These things are absolutely true. I saw it with my own eyes[4]!

After this, Joseph of Arkansas,[5] a believer in Jesus, but also one not intimidated by the Jews, went to Bean secretly and asked for the body of Jesus. Bean gave his approval; so Joseph came and secured the body of Jesus.

Accompanying Joseph was ole Nick, who had come to Jesus privately for instruction, and he brought expensive liquids used as body preservatives.

Together the two took the body of Jesus and bound it in fine linens, mixing up the spices, as was customary in Jewish practice. Near to Capitol Hill was a garden spot in which there was a tomb, which had never been used, and it belonged to Joseph. Jesus was placed in this tomb.

---

[1]Clopha's wife   [2]Presumed to be the only one - not known for sure.
[3]This was a practical device to enable easier handling in case of rigor mortis, etc. Some say the leg breaking was to hurry death. I go for no. 1.
[4]This is John's book, remember.   [5]Joseph of Arimathea

Early in the morning on the first day of the week, Mary of Alabama came to the cemetery plot and saw at once that the stone, which sealed the tomb, had been rolled away. She immediately ran full speed to Rocky and to me and blurted out, "They have taken away the Lord and I don't know where they have put his body."

Rocky and I then went at once to the place where Jesus had been buried. I was faster so I beat Rocky to the tomb. I looked in and saw the grave clothes all in place, but I did not go into the opening.

Rocky, of course, when he arrived entered the tomb itself and saw the grave clothes and the head bindings wrapped and put in a separate place. I then went into the tomb, saw everything as I have described, and immediately believed in the resurrection. At this point, we were not acquainted with the scripture, which talked about the rising on the third day.

We left the cemetery and went home. Mary, who had followed us, stood outside the tomb and when we left she was there, still crying. In a few minutes she stooped down and looked into the tomb's opening and saw two angels, one sitting at the head and the other at the foot of the place where Jesus had been laid.

"Honey, why are you crying?" asked one of them.

"Because someone has taken away the body of my Lord, and I don't know where his body rests," she replied. Mary then turned and Jesus was standing there, but she did not at first recognize him.[1]

"Lady, for whom are you looking?" asked Jesus. "Why do you cry?"

Mary thought Jesus must be one of the cemetery caretakers and she replied, "If you are the one who has taken away his body tell me where you put it and I will get it back so that a proper burial takes place."

"Mary!" said Jesus.

"Master!" said Mary, as she suddenly recognized the Lord.

"Don't touch me as yet, Mary," said Jesus, "for I have not checked back into Heaven. Go tell my disciples that I am ascending to our common Father, to our mutual God."

Mary came straight to the disciples and told them exactly what had happened and what had been said.

That very morning when the disciples were gathered in a room with closed doors, for they feared a raid from the Jews, Jesus suddenly appeared and said, "Peace be with you all."

At this point, Jesus showed them the wounds in his hands and in his side. The disciples were happy beyond description at the appearance of the Lord.

"Peace be with you," said Jesus. "As my Father sent me into the world, so now I send you." Jesus then breathed on his disciples.

[1]How different Jesus appeared is one of the great unknowns.

"Receive the Holy Spirit," said Jesus. "You are now full of the power of forgiveness and judgment."

Now Tommy[1] was not present on this occasion and when the disciples told him about it, he said, "I just can't believe a whopper like that! I would have to feel the nail holes with my finger and examine the wounded side."

About eight days later the disciples were together in a room and Tommy was with them. Again Jesus suddenly appeared, and he said to Tommy, "Put out your finger and probe the nail holes in my hands and take your hand and examine my side, and quit your doubting and believe!"

"My Lord and my God," said Tommy as he bowed his head.

"You have seen me, Tommy, and believed, but exceptionally blessed are those who have not seen me, yet believe."

Jesus did many other things in his resurrected form and appeared to the disciples often, but I have not tried to write down everything.

What I have recorded is designed to convince you that Jesus is the Christ, the Son of God, and that in so believing, you might have a new and eternal life in his name.

Chap.
21

Sometime after all these occurences, Jesus appeared again to the disciples along the edge of Falcon Lake.[2] Present were Rocky, Tommy, Nat, James, John and a couple of others.

Rocky had said to the others, "Conditions look good, I think I'll go fishing."

"We'll go with you," said all the others. That night they fished hard and didn't catch a thing.

In the morning the weary fisherman looked ashore and saw a person on the beach.

"Have you caught any fish?"[3] called out the person.

"No," they yelled.

"Try fishing from the other side of the boat."[4]

At once their nets became so full of fish that they had difficulty handling the nets and stowing the fish.

"Rocky, it's the Lord," said John to Rocky. At once, Rocky took off his shirt and jumped into the water, wading rapidly ashore. The others, fishing in another boat, came ashore and joined them. On arriving, they found a fire going and bread and fish cooking.

"Bring your fish here," said Jesus. There were 153 fish in the net and yet strangely the net had not broken.

---

[1]Thomas   [2]Sea of Tiberias   [3]Fish don't always know about good conditions.
[4]Fishermen will take any suggestion, anytime, from anybody - just in case!

"Come and eat with me," said Jesus. Jesus then served them bread and fish. This made the third time that Jesus had appeared to a large group of the disciples.

After the meal, Jesus turned to Rocky and said, "Rocky, are you committed completely to my cause?"

"Yes, of course, you know I am," said Rocky.

"Then get to work," said Jesus.

A few minutes later, Jesus turned to Rocky again and said, "Do you really love me, Rocky? Are you a committed Christian?"

"Yes, Lord, you know that I love you and that I am committed," said Rocky.

"Get to work," said Jesus.

A third time Jesus said to Rocky, "Are you quite sure, Rocky? Are you completely committed?"

Now Rocky had a short fuse and this insistence upset him, so he spouted out, "You know everything. Certainly you know that I am a dedicated Christian."

"Then get to work," said Jesus. "You know, Rocky, when you were young, you were pretty independent. As the years go by, you will lose this and you will be made to do things and go places against your will."

Jesus was referring, at this time, to the day when Rocky would be put to death for being a Christian.

Jesus then arose and started away, turning to Rocky and saying, "Let's get with the program."

Rocky then saw John following them also, and Rocky said to Jesus, "What about John? Doesn't he have to work also?"

"It is none of your business, Rocky, if it be my will that John stay right here until the second coming. You tend to your own business and follow me."

This statement of Jesus was misunderstood and twisted and caused a rumor to be started that John would never die.

I know all these things that I have written for I was there. There are many other things that Jesus did and said, and if all those things were written down, there wouldn't be room in the books for them, or room enough in the world for all the books.

ACTS

The writer of this book attests to the fact that he made a careful study of all that Jesus did and taught, right up to the time of Christ's ascension. Before ascending, through the use of the Holy Spirit, Jesus gave commandments to the disciples, having already convinced them of the validity of his resurrection by appearing to them on various occasions covering a period of forty days, speaking to them also during this time concerning the kingdom of God.

Jesus instructed the disciples to remain in Jerusalem and await the fulfillment of God's promise. As Jesus put it 'John baptized with water, but you will be baptized with the Holy Spirit.'

On one occasion during this forty day period one of the disciples spoke to Jesus and asked, "Are you about to restore at this very time the kingdom back to Israel?"[1]

"It is not your business as to when the Lord God will do things. You all, however, will receive inspiration and power after the Holy Ghost has come on you and then you are expected to become witnesses for me in Jerusalem, London,[2] Paris,[3] and the fartherest places on the earth."

When Jesus had said these things, even while they were still looking at him, he disappeared, taken up in a cloud. As the stunned disciples gazed toward heaven two men appeared in white robes and said, "Why are you fellows standing there gazing up into heaven? Jesus has been taken up and some day he will return in a very similar manner."

The disciples then returned to nearby Jerusalem and went to a private room for supper together. Present were Rocky, Jimmy, John, Andy, Phil, Tommy, Bart, Matt, Jim, Si, and Judd.[4] Gathered also were a group of the ladies including the mother of Jesus, a few cousins of Jesus, and all together joined in prayer and worship.

The number of dedicated followers of Jesus at this time, who were known to each other, was about 140. Rocky, who assumed a leadership role, spoke to a gathering of this group and said, "Ladies and gentlemen, in order that the scriptures be fulfilled it was necessary, as prophesied by David, that someone, in this case Judas, would be a betrayer of Jesus. As you know, he was one of the twelve.

"To bring you up to date, Judas purchased a deserted piece of acreage with the bribe money and went to the field and committed suicide. Everyone knew about this, and the field is now called Bloody Flats.[5]

---

[1]The Romans owned Israel. It wasn't very funny to the Jews.
[2]Judea [3]Samaria [4]Judas, brother of James [5]Aceldana

171

"The psalms of old said, 'Let his habitation be desolate and let no man live there, and let someone else take his place in life.' I think then that it is in order that we select a replacement for Judas, and that the person be chosen from among those who have been following Jesus and who can witness to the fact of the resurrection."

After some discussion it was agreed that there were two qualified, Joe Boy[1] and Matty.[2]

Instead of voting on which should be chosen, the remaining disciples decided to pray and to ask God to do the choosing. As a result, a coin was flipped with heads for Joe Boy and tails for Matty, and the disciples prayed that the Lord would control the coin. It was tails, and Matty was selected.[3]

Matty was then numbered with the disciples to complete the twelve and he was charged to assume his full share of responsibility in the ministry and witness for Christ.

Chap.
2

When Rally Day[4] finally came all the disciples and dedicated followers of Christ were assembled at a big conference, with one purpose, and meeting in a harmonious and expectant manner. There came then suddenly a sound from heaven like a jet plane coming in to land and the noise filled the entire auditorium. There also appeared twin flames on the head of each Christian, appearing like a split tongue of fire, and they were all filled with the holy spirit, and in the midst of their great emotional experience began to speak in strange dialects according to the inspiration of the holy spirit.

In Jerusalem at this time there were many orthodox Jews who traveled extensively and were sensible men and as word began to spread of this phenomena a great crowd of these men as well as many persons of various interests, including visitors from other areas, all gathered to witness what was happening.

Those coming to the assemblage were amazed to hear someone speaking their language or dialect and they began to talk considerably among themselves.

"Aren't these characters mostly fishermen from Falcon Lake?[5] How is it that they are capable of speaking our language?" asked some present.

Hearing their own language were Mexicans,[6] Swedes,[7] Englishmen,[8] Southerners,[9] some Italians,[10] French,[11] and Spanish,[12]

---

[1]Barabbas [2]Matthias
[3]I've suggested this procedure a few times, but never found a church interested in selecting officers this way. Why not?   [4]Pentecost
[5]Galilee [6]Parthians [7]Medes [8]Elamites [9]Mesopotamians
[10]Romans [11]Ethiopians [12]Arabians

and in their own language they heard of the wonderful and mighty acts of God.

The people were really shook.

"What is the meaning of all of this?" yelled one fellow.

"It's just a bunch of drunks," said one cynical person. "We had the same kind of thing at a fraternity party. Just stupid drunks."

Rocky then stood on the stage and the eleven stood up with him, and Peter began to preach saying "Listen, everyone of you, whether you are local or not. These men are not drunk. In the first place it is just around nine in the morning and they haven't had time to get drunk. What you are seeing today is the fulfillment of the prophecy of Joel.

"Joel said that God told him that during the last phase of this earth's civilization that the Lord would pour out his spirit on some of his people, and the young men and young ladies would prophesy, and see visions, and the more mature people would have meaningful dreams. Also during this last phase there will be seen many wonders, in the heavens[1] and on the earth, there will be eclipses of the sun and the moon will appear to turn red,[2] all of which things will be forerunners of the great Day of the Lord.

"During all of this time, beginning now, anyone who calls on the name of the Lord will be saved.

"Let me tell you the basis now for a sound theology.[3] A man appeared among you, a Jew like most of you, one whose miracles and wonders testified that he had come from God, which you know to be true. God knew that all this was going to happen, but still you are the ones that arrested that man, killed him by crucifying him.

"God raised that person from the dead, because he was not subject to death. David, the prophet you all quote all the time, he said it would be that way. David said he could envision the Lord at his right hand, giving him hope and encouragement, assuring him that his soul would not always be subject to death and separation from God.

"David assured us that the Lord would not allow the Holy One of God to be the victim of corruption and decay, even in death.

"I do not hesitate to speak for David, our own great prophet, dead and buried right here in town, that he died knowing that from his lineage there would arise the Christ, the one to be the great spiritual king of all, and David therefore foresaw the resurrection of Christ, and testified that Christ would not be subject to the separation of his soul from God, nor would his flesh be subject to the corruption and decay known to ordinary men.

"We right here, the twelve of us, and more, are eyewitnesses to this resurrection, and as Jesus promised, the Lord made the Holy

---

[1]UFO's?   [2]Nothing to do with Russia.
[3]We have to assume that some people got up and left at this point.

Spirit available and Jesus has bestowed it on us as the means of directing and searching for the new kingdom.

"You see, David was not talking about ascending himself, but talking about the ascension of Christ; so that the Christ sits on the right hand of God until the Lord God has brought all ·evil under control. Don't you forget one minute that God has made that same Jesus, whom you goofs crucified,[1] has made him both Lord and Christ."

These stirring words made a tremendous impression on a great many of those present and they began to get up and say, "What can we do?"

"Repent and be baptized," said Rocky. "Do this in the name of Jesus Christ, asking his forgiveness for your sins, and then you too will receive the gift of the holy spirit. There is no restriction on this promise. It is good for you, your children, your grandchildren, to all persons everywhere forever, for this promise is available for any who call on the name of the Lord."

Peter had plenty more to preach about and he did on this very occasion.[2]

Those who willingly and gladly received this message and responded came forward and were baptized. The total number so doing was around 3,000.

This one day meeting turned into about a ten day period of teaching, preaching, bearing testimony, praying, discussing doctrine, the fellowship of meals together, and there was great feeling among the whole group, many signs and wonders were observed, and an excitement strange to all those involved.

All of the believers cooperated with each other, shared their possessions, disistributed gifts to the poor in accordance with their needs, and daily joined together happily in fellowship and prayer. There was a great spirit of unbounding joy and love, each person thinking first of others, and the Lord blessed the occasions and there were many more added to the Christian church during this period.

Chap.

3

At the regular temple hour of prayer, a little before noon, Rocky and John went together to the church. There was a beggar, lame from birth, whose spot was at the foot of the steps going up to the Riverside Church, and here again on this day he was begging. Naturally, he tried to put the bite on John and Rocky.[3]

Rocky and John, however, gave the lame man a true blue look in the eye and said to the man, "Look straight at us."

This encouraged the beggar and raised some coin-type expectations.

[1] Poor public relations at this point.
[2] The writer of this book apparently thought what was recorded here was enough.
[3] Like most church people, they were broke.

"Silver and gold I don't have," said Rocky, "but what I do have I will give to you. In the name of Jesus of Nazareth, get up and walk!" Rocky then took the man by the hand and lifted him, and at once strength began to come into the man's legs and ankles. The lame man jumped for joy and entered the church with Rocky and John, praising God and rejoicing.

Everybody who was in the temple saw the well known beggar jumping, walking, and praising God, and they were astounded. The lame man stuck close to Rocky and John and followed them to a patio adjoining the church, and the people gathered around the three in amazement.

"What are you so curious about?" asked Rocky. "Why do you look at us as if we have done something with our own power? Do you want the straight proof? The God of Abe, Issac, and Jacob, the God of our fathers, placed his power in His Son Jesus, the one you arrested and crucified,[1] you wouldn't let Judge Bean release him, you killed the Prince of Peace, the Lord of life, and God raised him from the dead, and we are eyewitnesses to that fact, and it is the name of this one, Jesus, that has restored the lame man.

"I don't doubt but that most of you didn't know what you were doing, even your rulers were not all well posted on the affair, but all these things were predicted by the prophets. It was foretold that Christ would suffer.

"Repent then, be baptized, and seek the forgiveness of sins, and prepare yourselves for the second coming, or for the time when you will face the risen Lord. Jesus is now in heaven, as the prophets said, and is awaiting the time of final judgment and victory.

"Moses said that God would some day send a prophet, born into a Jewish family, and God said you are to listen to everything that he tells you. In fact, every soul that rejects or refuses to listen to that great one shall be eternally separated from God. All the prophets, including Samuel, have all said the same thing in their own way.

"You are descendants in this line of God's chosen people, and all the earth is to be blessed through the life and word of this great prophet, the Son of God. God first sent his Son Jesus to bless you, his chosen people, with the expectation of turning you from your sins."

Chap.
4

This preaching on the patio messed up the services in the church as the people were all listening to Rocky; so some of the preachers, elders, teachers, and a smattering of church officers were upset,

---

[1]Rocky did not know about "How to Win Friends and Influence People."

particularly the group that did not believe in the resurrection of the dead. As a result, the church guards put Rocky and John in one of the storage rooms and locked them up for the night.

The next day all the big shots gathered, Slick Faustus, Dr. Anna, Big Wheel John,[1] and a bunch of cousins and friends of the hierarchy, and they put Rocky and John on the witness stand.

"By what authority, or power, or name did you heal the lame man?"[2]

Rocky, filled with the Holy Spirit, then began to preach saying, "You rulers, big operators, you in control of Israel, if you are asking about the good deed we did for the lame man, wondering how he was healed, then let me give it to you straight. The man was healed by the power of the name of Jesus of Nazareth, the person you crucified, the one God raised from the dead, it is by Jesus that this man is restored to health.

"To quote your own scripture, 'This is the stone which the builders rejected and it now turns out to be the very cornerstone of the building.' There is no other possibility of salvation, for there is no other name under heaven, known to any person anywhere, anytime, whereby a person can be saved."

The boldness and confidence of Rocky and John, knowing that their background provided them with no educational advantages, caused them all to realize that their learning had come from their association with Jesus Christ. Since the lame man was standing there in person there was nothing the rulers could say. As a result, the council dismissed Rocky, John, and the listening audience, and went into executive meeting.

"What are we going to do?" asked one of the council.

"It's a tough problem," said another. "It is obvious that the man has been healed. We can't deny it. Everybody knows it is true."

"I suggest that we threaten Rocky and John and just see if we can't keep things from getting worse," said another. As a result, they brought Rocky and John into the executive session.

"We have decided to let you fellows go," spoke Slick Faustus, "but you are not to speak or teach any more using the name of Jesus. Forget him!"

"To whom should we listen?" asked Rocky and John together. "Should we listen to you or to God? As we see it, we cannot help but tell about the things we have seen and heard."

The council then did a bit more threatening, but having no charge or cause to keep the two, they released them, for many people had been impressed and were glorifying God because of the occasion. The man who was healed had been known to be lame for about 20 years, and his healing was quite sensational.

John and Rocky returned to their own group and reported on all the details of their encounter with the church authorities. Upon hearing this account, the group of dedicated Christians with great

[1]Not the Apostle.
[2]Interesting that none of them questioned the fact of the healing.

unity of spirit praised God, and chanted "Praise the Lord who made the heavens, the earth, the sea, and all that lies within. Praise God who inspired David to say 'Why do the heathen rage and the people imagine weird things?'

"The kings of the earth, all the big shot rulers, stood up and defied the Lord and His Christ. Herod, Judge Bean, a whole lot of Jews, all gathered to try to defeat God and His Christ.

"Take a look at your enemies, Lord, and give us courage to denounce them in public. Stretch out with your power, heal people, show signs and wonders as you did through Christ our Lord. We chant our prayer in Jesus' name, Amen."

When they had finished praying the dwelling in which they were meeting seemed to shake and they were all filled with the Holy Spirit and they were strengthened so as to preach boldly in the name of Jesus.

All present were agreed in their basic concept, and they were willing to share everything, thinking only of others.

The Lord blessed them, and great power came to each of them, and each in his own way went forth as a witness to the resurrection of Jesus.

There was no material need encountered, as each person sold securities and possessions, and everything was turned into the central operation of the church. The central treasurer then disbursed funds as needs arose. One person, a man called Bart,[1] who was a native of Montreal,[2] was pretty well fixed, but he sold all his land[3] and brought the money to the church and dedicated his life to the work of the church.[4]

Chap.
5

There was another fellow, however, named Findly[5] who had a wife named Ruby,[6] and they sold some property and withheld a good part of the money,[7] but brought a portion to the apostles, leaving the impression that they were giving their all.

Rocky said, "Findly, you can't keep a straight face. Satan has induced you to lie, but you can't lie to the Holy Spirit. It was your land, you could have sold it and kept all the money and no man would have blamed you. You crazy nut, you have tried to lie to God."

As soon as Findly heard these words he had a heart attack and dropped dead. A few young fellows standing around with nothing to do carried the body out of the city and buried Findly.

---

[1]Barnabus [2]Cyprus   [3]Including mineral rights.
[4]He's got to be one of the top ranking persons in the next life.
[5]Ananias   [6]Sapphira   [7]Uncle Sam read about this apparently.

About three hours later Ruby showed up, not knowing her husband had croaked.[1]

Rocky then turned to Ruby and said, "Did you all sell your land for the same amount you have contributed to the church?"

"Absolutely. Just like Findly said," replied Ruby.

"Why did the two of you agree to try to deceive God and his Holy Spirit? Do you hear those footsteps approaching? They are the feet of the fellows who have just now buried your husband."

Upon hearing this, Ruby dropped dead.

"Here we go again," said one of the young fellows, and they proceeded to bury Ruby alongside her husband.

Word of this incident spread around and many people in the church were afraid and some even increased their gifts just playing things safe.

Many signs and wonders were shown by the apostles as they conducted informal discussions and did some teaching on the porch of Solomon's temple. People spoke very highly of all that was being spoken and many joined the church. Men and women expressed their belief in Jesus and the sick were brought to the church for healing, hoping even the shadow of someone like Rocky might fall on a needy one.

Many sick in mind or body came from Jerusalem and they were healed by the apostles.

This was too much for the group of church leaders that did not believe in the resurrection and so they had the apostles put in prison.

An angel of the Lord came to the prison, opened the door, and told the apostles, "Go stand and speak in the church and tell them the words of life."

As a result, the Christian preachers and teachers came early to the church and began preaching and teaching.

In the meantime, not quite so early in the morning, however, the high priest sent an orderly to the prison to bring the apostles in order that they might be questioned.

The orderly returned and said to the high priest, "We went to the prison, but they had escaped. We found the cell door locked, however, and the guards standing outside. When we went past the guards to the cell block, however, we found no prisoners there."

The high priest and his advisers gave this account a big pooh-pooh.

In a few minutes, however, a messenger came to the gathered council and reported that the escaped prisoners were teaching at the church. As a result a captain was sent to bring the apostles to the council, being sure that they were nicely handled, as the rulers feared the people.

"Didn't we tell you fellows," bellowed Slick Faustus, "that you

---

[1]Wives usually prefer knowing.

were no longer to teach in the name of Jesus? Instead of that you have been filling the city with this new Christian doctrine and worse still, blaming us for his death."

Then Rocky, speaking for the whole group said, "We feel that we must obey God, rather than men. The God we serve, the God of our fathers, raised Jesus from the dead, after you birds had killed him. God has decreed that Jesus is the Saviour, one to bring repentance to the Jews, and one who can forgive sins.

"We are simply witnesses for Jesus. The Holy Spirit, that God has given to those who believe, also witnesses for Christ."

This really put the council in a rage and they immediately began to plot as to how they could kill the apostles with some legality.

Not all the council felt this way. One man, an educator, Professor George,[1] was a man highly respected for his good sense and knowledge.

"Step forward, please," said the Professor.

Then turning to the remaining members of the council he said, "Be very careful about what you do regarding these men. Do you remember the case of Toto,[2] a fellow who made great boasts and accumulated some good followers, in fact about 400. Well, when Toto died the movement died with him.[3]

"There was another fellow I remember studying. His name was Slinging Sam,[4] and he started a movement to abolish all taxes. Naturally, he had a real good following, but when he died his movement died.

"Now listen to my advice. Free these men. If what they teach is some committee report or is man-made, then it will fade away as the other movements did. If, perhaps, what they are teaching is the truth of God, you had better not buck it, or else you will find yourselves fighting God."

The council agreed to this reasoning, again commanded the apostles to quit talking about Jesus, then had the guards give all the apostles a licking[5] and turned them free.

The apostles left the area greatly pleased that they were privileged to witness and even suffer for Jesus. After that, daily in the church patio, in every house to which they were invited, the apostles never quit teaching and preaching about Jesus Christ.

Chap.

6

As the number of Christians increased there began to develop some flack, particularly from some of the Greek speaking Jews who complained to the orthodox Christian Jews. The complaint was that

[1]Gamaliel [2]Theudas
[3]You can always count on a lecture from a good teacher.[4]Judas of Galilee
[5]In those days you usually got a licking just for appearing in court.

the apostles were having to spend all their time preaching, teaching, healing, and praying at the church and the pastoral care program was going downhill. In fact, there was no one who assumed the duties of feeding the hungry and caring for the widows.

Hearing the mumbling, the disciples gathered and a spokesman for them arose and said, "It just isn't in the cards for us to leave our preaching and start waiting on tables.[1] We suggest that you all select seven honest men and we will appoint them in charge of benevolences, and we will continue preaching and praying."

This sounded like a good idea to everybody and the crowd chose seven men, Steve,[2] Phil,[3] the Old Pro,[4] Nicky,[5] Ty,[6] Pat,[7] and Ned.[8] These men came forward and kneeled while the apostles prayed and placed their hands on the men's heads.

During this period the word of God spread daily and many people became Christians, and even some of the local clergy joined the movement and obeyed God.

Not long after this a hassle arose about Steve, for Steve added to his pastoral work some teaching, and his teaching angered many of the old timers, and many of the routine type of worshippers, and they began to argue with Steve. The trouble was that Steve was smarter and dedicated, and the lukewarm religious groups couldn't successfully argue against him.

As a result, this unfriendly group of church folks decided to frame Steve and they talked some careless fellows into accusing Steve of blasphemy, claiming that Steve didn't believe in either Moses or God. As a result, Steve was brought before the Council of the Church Court. False witnesses had been arranged and they said to the Council, "This man criticizes the church, and the law, and we have heard him say that Jesus of Nazareth will destroy the church and change the laws of Moses." The Council members, however, staring at Steve during this tirade, were impressed with the innocent and angelic look that was on his face.

Chap.

7

Ole Slick, who was Chairperson of the Council, said, "Are these charges true?"

"Listen to me, and then judge for yourselves," said Steve. "God appeared to our good ancestor Abe, long before there was knowledge of Israel,[9] and inspired him to move to the land which God would provide.[10]

---

[1]Did you know this was the beginning of deacons?   [2]Stephen   [3]Philip
[4]Procharus   [5]Nicanor   [6]Timon   [7]Parmsuas   [8]Nicolas
[9]It's always scary when a preacher starts with Abraham — he has the whole
Bible ahead of him.   [10]Known as "The Promised Land" (Canaan).

"Abe didn't inherit the land from his daddy, he moved to it, and God assured him that he would possess it and that his descendents would inhabit the land. Abe didn't even have a child when this was promised. God also through prophets told the people of their living in Egypt under bondage for nearly 400 years, and then the people would be delivered. The Egyptians would be punished by God for this; it was also part of the plan.

"Abe instituted the rite of circumcision and this was handed down from one generation to another as a sign of God's blessing of the development of the people. You recall the story of the brothers selling Joseph and how God blessed Joseph in Egypt and showed him how to corner the grain market and be a successful general manager of Egypt, in great favor with Pharaoh.

"The brothers had to make two trips to Egypt to get grain, and on the second trip Joseph revealed himself to his brothers. Because of the great drouth in the Promised Land the old man, Jacob, came to Egypt with all his family and associates, and there the old man died.

"The Hebrews increased greatly in Egypt, and Joseph and the brothers died and in time there came into power a Pharaoh who had never heard of Joseph. The new breed of pharaoh began to mistreat the Jews and finally the Lord saw that a child was born, Moses was his name, and after a short time as a baby at home he was taken into Pharaoh's household and reared there. Under these conditions Moses received a top-notch education, and became a great and knowledgeable warrior.

"When he was grown to full manhood, Moses visited his people and found one Jew being beaten by an Egyptian; so Moses clobbered the Egyptian. Moses thought the Jews would understand this, but the next day when he separated two of the Hebrews who were fighting they accused him of tending to things that were none of his business. One of the fellows jibed Moses by asking him if he planned to kill one of them as he had killed the Egyptian.[1]

"Moses then decided that he was in great trouble, so he went to the wild area of West Texas,[2] married a beautiful girl whose father had a big ranch, and then had two sons.

"Some time after this the Lord appeared to Moses through an angel posing as a burning bush and when Moses came near to see this strange sight he heard the voice of the Lord saying 'I am the God of Abe, and Ike, and Jacob.' This really shook ole Moses.

"The Lord then said, 'You are on holy ground, son, so take off your boots.[3] I have seen the trouble my people are having in Egypt and I am going to deliver them. You are going to be the delivery boy.'

[1]It's tough sometimes to be a do-gooder.   [2]Midian
[3]So that's how you get a Texan to take off his boots.

"It is interesting that the same person that the Hebrews refused to respect was the one God was sending for deliverance. After going through all types of pressures applied, such as the plagues, Moses finally led the Hebrews out of Egypt.

"Now this same Moses said (remember now Moses was a prophet as well as a leader) 'A prophet shall the Lord raise up among the Jews some day just as He raised me. Listen to that one when he comes.'

"Now that's what Moses said, the same one who provided us with the Ten Commandments, in spite of the short-lived revolution under Arson,[1] which developed while Moses was away working on the Ten Commandments. Those screwy Jews even wanted Arson to make a new god for them. Arson did make a calf and then built a big bonfire for a great party and rally.

"God was really mad about all this, and let the people roam in the wilderness for forty years, frequently worshipping all kinds of strange idols. For this, God decided to eventually see that the Jews were carried into Moscow[2] to suffer for their sins.

"Moses, however, constructed a tabernacle to God in proper fashion, with the ark of the covenant as its central symbol, which lasted until the days of Jesus. The holy symbol was treasured by David who wished to build a temple to house it, but the building was left to his son Solomon. However, this is not particularly important, for God does not just reside in a church built by the hands of man. God has said through his prophets 'Heaven is my throne and the earth is a footstool. Why worry about a house for me? Have I not made everything that ever was?'

"Now let me lower the boom on you, you stiffnecked and closehearted fakers, are you going to act wrongly just like some of your ancestors did? Your ancestors didn't miss a single prophet, but fought every one of them. The prophets who spoke boldly of the coming of Christ you usually had them executed. You received the law from the angels of God and now you are betrayers and murderers."[3]

This speech really upset the court and Ole Slick and his gang began to gnaw on the furniture.

Steve, however, inspired by God, looked toward heaven and he had a vision of the glory of God with Jesus standing on the right hand of God.

"Do you know what I see?" said Steve. "I see the heavens open and the Son of Man standing on the right hand of God."

The leaders then put their hands over their ears so as to hear no more, came in a gang to Steve and threw him out of the city, and began to stone him. A young man named Saul had come out to see

---

[1]Aaron [2]Babylon [3]Tough way to talk to a judge and jury.

what was happening and he kept watch over the coats the men removed to help their throwing.

As Steve was being stoned he spoke aloud saying, "Lord Jesus, receive my soul."

Then kneeling down as the stones pelted him he spoke again saying in a loud voice, "Lord, don't blame these poor dumbos." When he had said this, Steve passed out, and died.

Chap.
8

Now Saul consented to the stoning of Steve and was a major force in the persecution of the Christians. In fact, except for the apostles, most of the Christians had to scatter.

There were plenty of brave men who were Christians and some of these buried Steve and mourned publicly his death.

Saul was a real hellion, though. Actually he went into private homes and arrested Christians, bringing them to the council on all kinds of charges, men and women, and he had many of them imprisoned.

The Christians who had left the area began to teach and preach and spread the word in all the outlying areas.

Now Phil went to Atlanta[1] and preached the good news of Christ there and he was well received. Many were healed in Christ's name and many were relieved of mental difficulties and anxieties, and there was great rejoicing in Atlanta.[2]

There was a fellow in Atlanta known as Mad Cox,[3] who had a great reputation in the city, and often proclaimed himself to be the one great power, and many people followed him. When Mad Cox professed his faith and became a Christian this was a great influence and was instrumental in many people confessing their sins and calling on the name of Jesus.

When word of all this reached the apostles in Jerusalem they decided to send John and Rocky, the big guns of Christianity, to Atlanta as although there were many converts, very few had received the power of the Holy Spirit. Rocky and John then prayed with the new believers and laid their hands on some of them, and as many as they blessed, these received the Holy Spirit.

Now when Mad Cox saw that the spirit was available to believers through the touch of Rocky and John, he offered them money to give him this same power; so that he too could bestow the Holy Spirit on people.

"You and your money are both in trouble now," said Rocky, "for it is awful to think that you can buy the power of God, which is a gift of God. Your heart is not in the right place. You had better repent and seek the forgiveness of God. You apparently are still a

[1]Samaria   [2]Better even than the Falcons winning.   [3]Simon

bitter person and still full of plots to acquire recognition for yourself."

"Pray to the Lord for me," said Mad Cox. "I don't want to die in sin."[1]

Rocky and John then left Atlanta after the week of special services and preached in many of the small towns while en route to Jerusalem.

The angel of the Lord then appeared to Phil and told him to go south and begin preaching in the desert areas around Palm Springs and Phoenix.

Phil did as the angel suggested and while taking a rest at an oasis he saw a man sitting in a chariot reading the scriptures. The man was the Secretary of the Treasury of Ethiopia, and was an exceedingly important person, en route south from Jerusalem.

"I see you are reading from the Book of Isaiah. Do you understand what you read?" asked Phil.

"Not by a long shot," replied the man. "How can I understand it unless someone makes it clear?[2] Why don't you sit here by me in the chariot and explain it all to me."

Now J. Con, the Secretary of the Treasury, was reading the portion of Isaiah that says 'He was led as a sheep to the slaughter; and like a lamb dumb before his shearer, so he opened not his mouth. In his humiliation his judgment was taken away, and who shall declare his generation? His life is taken from the earth.'

"To whom does this refer," asked J. Con. "What prophet? Himself or someone else?"

Then Phil spoke and using the identical scripture as his text he preached a sermon to J. Con,[3] the key message being salvation in Jesus. After this Phil began riding in the chariot with J. Con, and when they came to a water hole, J. Con asked, "Why can't I be baptized?"

"If you believe with all your heart in Jesus Christ, you can be baptized," said Phil.

"I believe that Jesus Christ is the Son of God," said J. Con.

The chariot was stopped and the two men approached the water, and both men went down into the water, and Phil baptized J. Con.[4]

When they left the water, the spirit of God transferred Phil to another area and J. Con went on his way rejoicing.

Phil suddenly found himself in Phoenix and he began moving west, preaching in all the little towns en route to Palm Springs.[5]

---

[1]I presume they prayed for Mad Cox.
[2]Making it clear is what "The Word Made Fresh" is also trying to do.
[3]One on one — good system.
[4]Sounds like immersion, Presbyterians. Sorry about that.   [5]Caesarea

Saul, a determined antagonist of the Christians, went to the high priest and said, "Please give me a license to hunt Christians in Detroit.[1] They are getting real cagey here in Jerusalem. I also want both a buck and doe permit, as the women are just as much Christian as the men. I will bring the ones I catch back to Jerusalem for trial and execution."

With the license in his pocket, Saul headed for Detroit accompanied by a few bounty hunters who had joined his staff.

On the road there suddenly came a bright flash from heaven and Saul fell down as if he had a stroke.

"Saul, Saul, why do you persecute me?" asked a voice from out of nowhere.

"Who are you, Sir?" asked Saul

"I am the Lord Jesus, who you continue to persecute. I know your conscience is bothering you for sure."

"What do you want me to do?" asked Saul.

"Go on to Detroit, and there you will receive further instructions."

The associates of Saul stood flabbergasted as they could hear a voice and yet couldn't see anybody.[2] Saul then got to his feet and when he tried to look around he discovered that the light had blinded him. As a result, the men had to take turns leading Saul all the remaining distance to Detroit.

Saul was blind for three days and refused to eat or drink.

In Detroit there was a man named Ford[3] and God spoke to him in a vision saying, "Listen to me."

"I am listening," said Ford.

"Get dressed and go to Main Street[4] and go to Dr. Mayo's[5] house and ask for a man named Saul, who is no doubt praying. Saul has seen in a vision that there is a Ford in his life and that your touch will restore his sight."

"Lord," said Ford, "I think I could have a better idea, for this Saul has a bad reputation as a Christian capturer. It is also known that he has a license to hunt in Detroit and track down any who profess their faith in Christ."

"Go away," said God. "The man Saul has been selected by me to be a missionary and to present the name of Christ to Gentiles, Jews, and kings. Don't worry, being a missionary will be plenty of punishment for Saul."

Ford did as he was ordered and when he saw Saul he put his hands on him and said, "Brother Saul, the Lord, and I'm talking about Jesus, the one that appeared to you on Interstate 10, has sent

---

[1]Damascus
[2]There were no radios, cassettes, etc., in those days. (The good ole days.)
[3]Ananias   [4]Straight   [5]Judas

me to restore your sight, and to enable you to be filled with the Holy Spirit."

Immediately sight returned to the eyes of Saul and he was baptized at once.[1]

After this Saul began to eat and regain his strength. For a period of time then Saul received instructions from one or more of the local Christian Bible teachers. When this period of training was completed Saul began to preach in the various churches during the open pulpit sessions and he declared Christ to be the Son of God.

This was an amazing thing to the people that heard him for they knew that originally his intention was to arrest Christians, and that he was known as chief Christian-hater in Jerusalem.

Saul grew in strength as he preached and he really bothered the orthodox Jews in Detroit for Saul had switched sides on them. As a result, the Jews began to discuss getting a contract out on Saul.

Learning of the plan to kill Saul, some of the disciples stuffed him in a basket one night and let him down outside the city wall so he could leave for Jerusalem.

When Saul arrived in Jerusalem he attempted to associate himself with the Christians there, but they would have none of this, for they thought he was faking his Christianity in order to get an up to date roll of the Christian church.

Barney,[2] however, took Saul and brought him to the apostles and told them the story of Jesus appearing to Saul on Interstate 10, and then how Saul had preached earnestly and successfully in Detroit. The apostles let Saul join them as they made their rounds.

Saul spoke boldly and made public witness for Christ, and got into some hot arguments, particularly with the Greeks. The Greeks then decided to kill Saul.[3]

The apostles then arranged for Saul to escape to Palm Springs,[4] and from there it was necessary to move him to Quebec.[5] This cooled things off a bit, and all the churches began to be able to operate without a lot of outside interference. The churches grew in number and in spirit.

As Rocky was making the rounds of some of the new churches, he came to Selma,[6] where he was taken to visit a man named Benny[7] who had been laid flat with arthritis for eight years.

Peter said to him, "Get up, you are well in the name of Jesus Christ." The man arose, and this had a profound effect on the people in the area. In fact, a bunch of people joined the church.[8]

---

[1]This gives the sprinkler a talking point.   [2]Barnabas
[3]Saul definitely was the irritating type.
[4]People still try to escape to Palm Springs.   [5]Tarsus [6]Lydda [7]Aeneas
[8]A few of these probably had arthritis.

There was a little town called Greenville[1] and in this town was a wonderful lady named Anne.[2] Anne was always doing good things for many people.

Anne became sick and died, and the family washed her and laid her out in preparation for burial. Now Greenville was close to Selma and knowing that Rocky was at Selma two disciples went and brought him to Greenville. When Rocky entered the home of Anne he found everybody weeping and talking about all the many good things Anne had done during her life.

Rocky then cleared the room and kneeled and prayed. As Rocky finished praying he turned to the body of Anne and said, "Get up."

Anne opened her eyes and when she saw Rocky she sat up on the bed.

Peter (Rocky) gave her his hand and then helped her into a house robe and took her into the next room and presented her to the group there.

This incident also became well known and encouraged many to accept Christ. Rocky returned to Selma and stayed there quite a long time, being a house guest of a man who ran a Western Boot Shop.

Chap.

10

There was a well-to-do businessman in Palm Springs named Corny[3] and he was President of the Italian Club there. Corny was a good man, he believed in God, and he was generous to the church and people in need.

On one occasion he had a dream and there appeared in his dream an angel of God who said, "Hi there, Corny."

"What is it, Sir?" asked Corny, who was plenty scared.

"Your prayers and your gifts have been well received by the Lord in heaven. Send to Greenville and request that Rocky, who is staying at the seaside home of the owner of the Western Boot Company, and he will answer your questions about God."

Corny then dispatched two servants and a bodyguard and sent them to Greenville to locate Rocky. The next day Rocky was on the upstairs balcony and he became very hungry.[4] On this occasion he fainted waiting for lunch to be ready.[5]

While he was passed out, Rocky saw in a vision a huge sheet coming down from heaven, which looked to him like a tablecloth. On the sheet were all kinds of God's creatures. Rocky then heard a voice saying, "Get up and kill whichever of these you wish and eat."

"I can't do that, Lord," replied Rocky in his dream, "for I have never eaten ham, or anything that is not kosher."

[1]Joppa [2]Tabitha [3]Cornelius
[4]Peter was hungry a great many times [5]He may have smelled the ham.

"Forget such talk," said the Lord, "for I have never created anything that is unclean."

This dream was repeated three times while Peter was in his faint.

As Peter revived he began to meditate on the dream that he had and to wonder as to its meaning. While Peter was thus thinking the three men arrived from Corny, knocked on the door downstairs, and then asked for Rocky, whose name was also Peter.

The spirit of God then told Peter to go downstairs and to listen to the men who were there as they had been sent by God to talk with him.

Peter went to the front door and spoke to the men saying, "I am the fellow you seek. What do you want?"

"Corny, a centurion, a good, God-fearing man, who is well thought of in all circles, including the Jews, was inspired by God to ask that you come to him and speak to him as a witness."

Rocky invited the men in and arranged for them to remain overnight. The next day Rocky and a few of his friends went with the three men to Palm Springs.

When they arrived in Palm Springs they learned that Corny had prepared a big bar-b-que and invited a bunch of his friends to all gather and meet Rocky and hear what he had to say.

When Rocky arrived Corny bowed down to him as if Rocky were God himself.

"Get up, fellow. I am just a man like you are," said Rocky.

As they began to move toward the dining area Rocky spoke again to Corny and said, "You know that it is not considered proper for a Jew to associate with anyone of any other race, but God has shown me that it is not proper to consider any person common or unclean. As a result, I have come to you promptly at your request. What do you want me to do?"

"Four days ago," said Corny, "while I was having my meditation period an angel appeared in my presence, in shining clothes and told me that my prayers were answered, that my gifts were favorably noted by God, and that I should send for you.

"I have done as the angel suggested. You have come. I have gathered a good crowd of people and we are all here to hear you tell of the things God has commanded you to teach."

Peter then adjusted the mike to his own height and spoke, "One thing for sure, I fully understand at least that God is not choosey when it comes to people. One person is just as meaningful to God as another. In any nation, anywhere, a person who respects God and works for righteousness is automatically in good standing with the Lord.

"The specific word which God sent the Jewish nation was to seek peace in Jesus Christ, for Christ is the Lord of all. This word has been spoken throughout all the area.

"God, you see, anointed Jesus, filled him with the Holy Spirit, and with all power so that he could heal the bodies and souls of men. We are witnesses of these very actions. We saw Jesus while he was doing these good things, and we also saw him crucified.

"The great news is that we saw him raised by God on the third day. In his resurrected body Jesus appeared to many, not to everybody, but to witnesses chosen by God. Some of us are those witnesses. We ate and drank and talked with him after he was raised from the dead.

"We have been commanded to tell these things, to witness to the fact of the resurrection, and to inform everyone everywhere that Jesus is to be the judge of the living and the dead.

"The prophets of old all testified to this, assuring everyone that accepts Christ as Lord that in their belief there is forgiveness for their sins."

As Peter preached these words the holy spirit filled the room, and the Gentiles present were also filled with holy spirit, and this was particularly startling to the Jews who were present. Some of those present began to speak with tongues and to glorify God.

"Can anyone say that these people should not be received into the church and properly baptized?"

Rocky then commanded that those who believed should be baptized, whether Gentile or Jew.

Chap.
11

Word of this overt act of desegregation reached the church supporters in some of the other areas, particularly around Jerusalem, and so when Rocky returned to Jerusalem some of the influential early Christians jumped Rocky about the matter.

Peter very carefully explained the entire circumstance saying, "I was in Greenville praying and I saw a vision, and in the vision I saw a container resembling a great white sheet being lowered from heaven into my presence.

"As I began to see clearly, I could discern all types of four-footed beasts, many varieties of birds, and some wild game, and I heard a voice from heaven saying, 'Rocky, kill and eat.'

"Naturally I explained that I did not eat unclean or non-kosher food. Then a voice from heaven said, 'Don't call anything that God has made unclean.' This whole thing was repeated three times so the idea could really soak in.

"Almost at once three men appeared who had just arrived from Palm Springs and the spirit of God moved me to accompany them at their request. I took six members of my traveling staff with me.

"After we entered the man's house in Palm Springs who had invited us to dinner we heard him explain how he had seen an angel and the angel had directed him to me, Peter, called Rocky. The angel had told the man that I would explain the plan of salvation to him and to his guests.

"When I began speaking the Holy Spirit filled all of us and I recalled how Jesus had said that John baptized with water but that we would have the baptism of the Holy Spirit.

"Now be reasonable. If God granted to the non-Jews there the same gift that was given to us who originally believed in Jesus Christ, who was I to withstand God?"

When Rocky finished the objectors were quiet and began to reason among themselves that God's plan was to offer repentance and salvation to non-Jews as well as Jews.

The missionary group that had departed from Jerusalem after the stoning of Stephen had already been to places like Tokyo,[1] San Diego,[2] and Richmond,[3] and had even been preaching Christ to the Greeks at Athens. God blessed the work of these people and many were added to the kingdom through this work.

When word of these things had been received by the mother church in Jerusalem they sent Barney to Richmond to lend a hand. After Barney arrived he perceived that the grace of the Lord was very active and he encouraged the people in their new faith. Barney was a real good man, full of the Holy Spirit, a man of great faith, and he led many people to Christ.

Barney left Richmond after awhile though and went to find Saul, looking first at Cape Cod.[4] When Barney had located Saul he brought him to Richmond and there Saul and Barney worked for Christ for a whole year. It was here at Richmond that the name 'Christian' came into use.

Some prophets came to Richmond from Jerusalem and told of a great drouth which was just beginning, which history records as being in the days of Claudius Caesar, and so the Christians, or followers of Christ, made gifts for relief and sent the gifts to Jerusalem with Barney and Saul.[5]

Chap.

12

Not long after this ole Herod the king began to get sore at the churches, or at least at some of the outspoken Christians. One of the first things that he did was to have James, the brother of John, executed. A lot of Jews applauded this high-handed action, and Herod was so encouraged that he had the guards seize Rocky.

Herod had Rocky put under close guard in prison as he planned to produce him after Easter. Church people everywhere began to pray earnestly for ole Rocky.

The night before Rocky was to be brought to trial, as he was sleeping between two soldiers, and bound also with chains, the angel of the Lord appeared and a light shone in the prison.

[1]Cyprus   [2]Cyrene   [3]Antioch   [4]Tarsus
[5]They raised a large sum without a brochure. Amazing!

The angel touched Rocky and said, "Get up quickly." Rocky arose, and as he did the chains fell from him.

"Get dressed quickly and put on your shoes," said the angel to Rocky.

"Put on your coat and follow me," continued the angel.

Rocky went out groggy with sleep and he was not even really conscious of all that had happened, but thought he might even be dreaming.

The angel and Rocky went through two cell sections and when they came to the well-secured main gate it opened on its own. When Rocky was outside and free the gate closed and the angel disappeared.

When Rocky was fully awake, of course, he realized that the Lord had sent an angel to deliver him from Herod and from the trial by the jury of orthodox Jews.

After sizing up the situation, Rocky went to the home of John Mark where there was a good-sized supper group meeting for prayer. When Rocky reached the locked door he knocked upon it and a girl named Rhoda came to the door.

When Rhoda heard Rocky's voice she was so excited that in her joy she forgot to unlock the door. When she told the group that Rocky was at the door they all made fun of her.

"Maybe it's Rocky's ghost," suggested one. Rocky continued knocking and when they unlocked the door and saw him they were all astonished.[1]

As soon as quiet was secured, Rocky explained how the Lord had delivered him from the prison. Rocky asked them to go and tell Big James and the other church leaders, and then Rocky went on about his own business.

At daylight there was pandemonium at the prison. Herod was in a rage and ordered all the jailers killed, figuring the matter was definitely an inside job. In fact, Herod was so hot that he went to Palm Springs to cool it.

At this particular time, Herod was real sore also at the cities of Minneapolis and St. Paul, but since these places had a friend who was an advisor to Herod, Herod agreed to listen to their pleas.

Herod appointed a time and place for the meeting and when all the representatives were present, Herod appeared in his fanciest robes and made a big speech.

When he had finished the people began to shout that Herod spoke more like a god than a man.

At this juncture, the on duty angel of the Lord could stand the hokum no longer and whacked Herod with a stroke, and he soon died.

---

[1]People still seem surprised at answered prayer. Why?

The word of the Lord increased, and Saul and Barney returned from their ministry in Jerusalem and brought with them John Mark.

Chap.

13

In Richmond at this time there was a gathering of, church leaders, including Barney, Saul, Dr. Thompson,[1] Ben Rose,[2] and others discussing plans for the progress of the church. As they prayed and fasted, the Holy Spirit was present and inspired them to determine to sponsor Barney and Saul on a missionary journey to the remote areas.

Barney and Saul began in West Virginia and then moved into the Ohio Valley with John joining them on one or two special occasions.

When they came to Cleveland[3] they encountered some competition in the form of a phony showman named Milton.[4] Now Milton was primarily supported by Meany,[5] a very careful man, and Meany asked Barney and Paul to call on him as he was interested in the learning of the truth, wherever it might be found, or anything that might show a profit.

Milton, of course, was on hand to argue against Barney and Saul. Then Saul, who was now often called Paul, being inspired by the spirit of God, looked straight at Meany and began to preach saying, "You are being misled. You must immediately quit all the devious ways in which you operate.

"Because of your actions you are being struck blind by God and for one year you will not be able to see."

At once Meany became blind and had to ask someone to lead him by the hand. Milton immediately joined the church.

Paul and his group then left Cleveland and came to Philadelphia[6] and John[7] went then back to Jerusalem. After leaving Philadelphia the evangelistic team then went to Boston[8] and on Sunday went to church and sat down in the front row.

After the period of the reading of the law and the scriptures, the man conducting the services asked if there was anything that Paul or his group would care to say.[9]

Paul immediately stood up and said, "Fellows, and others who acknowledge God, wake up and listen. God chose our people of Israel, God blessed the Jews when they were living as captives in Egypt, and God delivered the people out of the bondage of Egypt.

"For training purposes, and to learn the facts of responsible living, the Lord let the people wander in the wilderness for forty

[1]Lucius of Cyrene (Ernest Trice Thompson, historian) [2]Manaen (Ben Rose, noted preacher) [3]Paphos [4]Barjesus [5]Sergius Paulus
[6]Perga   [7]This was John Mark   [8]Antioch in Pisidia
[9]We quit doing this so we would be sure and get home in time to watch the ball game

years. When finally the people of God moved into Canaan the Lord divided the land for them and they were ruled by judges for four hundred and fifty years, until Samuel, the first of the prophets, took charge of all the tribes, more or less.

"The people then howled for a king and God gave them Saul as a king for forty years,[1] then he was replaced by David. God really endorsed David and said of him, 'I have provided David, the son of Jesse, a man after my own heart, and he will be an instrument for working my plan.'

"It is from the line of descent of David that God has fulfilled his promise to provide a saviour, Jesus Christ. John the Baptist preached about the coming of Christ and called on the people to repent in preparation. Do you remember what John said? He said, 'Who do you think I am? I am not the Saviour. There comes one after me that I am not even worthy of untying his shoelaces.'

"Now listen, you Jews. Any of you that acknowledge God, be certain that to you is this special word being sent. The crowd of Jews at Jerusalem were the ones that condemned Jesus. Even though they could not make a case against him, yet they turned Jesus in for the Roman governor Judge Bean to have him killed. The prophets foretold this, and also that they would take him down after the crucifixion and place him in a tomb.

"Then God raised him from the dead and he was seen many times by many people who are true witnesses. We, therefore, declare to you the good news that the promise made to your ancestors has been fulfilled in Jesus Christ. As the Psalmist has said, speaking for God, 'You are my son, and in this day and age I have placed you on the earth.'

"God raised Jesus from the dead, no more to return to live as a human being, as the prophet said 'You shall not allow your holy one to return to corruption.' David, of course, being a person like us, when he died he decayed as a human does, but Jesus never went through the process of corruption.

"Be certain then that in the name of Jesus we preach forgiveness of sins. By believing on Jesus, you are able to correct all errors of life, which can't be done by just trying to stick to the laws of Moses.

"The prophets have also said that there will be people who won't believe what is being preached, but you'd better be careful and not fall into that category."

After church was over and the Jews were all gone home a lot of the non-Jews, who were not allowed to come to church with the Jews, asked that they too be given an opportunity to hear the preaching of the evangelist Paul.

---

[1]Paul never cared much for exactness of time.

Some of the Jews who were impressed with what Paul and Barney had to say urged them to stay in Boston a week and preach to everybody the next Sunday. The next Sunday almost everybody in town came to church.[1]

When some of the Jews saw what a great crowd had gathered they were envious and irritated and spoke strongly against Paul and Barney and their preaching.

This type of opposition just made Paul and Barney all the more eager to preach and they said, "It was necessary that the good news should be first announced to the Jews, but since you don't seem to want to hear it and are not interested in eternal life, then we will preach the good news to the non-Jews.

"The Lord has revealed to us that we are to be a light to those who will believe regardless of race or geographical restrictions, for we have the good news for the whole world."

When the general mass of people heard this they were jubilant and many professed their faith in Christ at once. The word of the Lord began to spread throughout the entire area.

The Jewish leaders were very influential, however, and they got behind the City Council and working through other political channels had Barney and Paul kicked out of town.

As a result, Paul and Barney thumbed their noses at Boston and went to Naples,[2] and they were full of great joy and blessed by the Holy Spirit.

Chap.
14

In Naples Paul and Barney held very successful services and many people, Jews, Greeks, and otherwise professed their faith in Christ. Some of the Jews, however, who didn't care for the Christian movement, began to stir up trouble, using some of the minority groups as fronts for protest.

The evangelists stayed quite awhile in Naples, speaking boldly for God, and showing many signs and wonders, with the result that the place was split into two groups, those that believed and those that supported the orthodox Jewish stand.

It wasn't long before Barney and Paul learned that again the influential Jewish leaders were getting set to run the evangelists out of town; so they left on their own so they would have time to pack. The two, along with their staff,[3] decided next to preach in Monroe,[4] and West Monroe,[5] two places divided only by a river.

There was a crippled man at Monroe who was born lame and unable to walk without assistance. Some friends brought him to the

---

[1]Definitely before TV. [2]Iconium
[3]There never was a church group without a staff. [4]Lystra [5]Derbe

services and Paul noticed him, and realized that the man fully believed that Paul could heal him. Paul then looked intently at the man and said to him, "Get up. Stand on your feet."

The man obeyed and stood on his feet and then leaped for joy when he realized he was healed. When the people saw this they were amazed and some said that surely the gods were come to Monroe in the form of Barney and Paul and they began to call Barney the god Jupiter and to refer to Paul as the god Mercury.

The priest in town who represented the god Jupiter wanted to get into the act and so he brought a care package to Barney. When Barney and Paul realized what was happening, they began to shred Kleenex and give similar signs of great distress.

At once they called an assembly and spoke saying, "What in the thunderation are you goofs doing? Don't you know that we are persons just like you folks? We want you to be better that we are, we want you to begin to give up worldly things, we want you to worship the living God. Granted that the one God has given you great freedom of choice, but he also had left many signs of his power and wisdom, such as rain from heaven, fruitful harvests, and some real happy times for people."

Even with all their reasoning they had a tough time keeping the Monroe crowd from giving them all kinds of fruits and vegetables as well as other more expensive gifts and sacrifices.

The good times didn't last, however, as some of the really mad groups from Boston[1] and Naples came to town and stoned Paul until he was unconscious, and left him outside the city, thinking him to be dead.

When the disciples came to get Paul, however, he managed to get to his feet and came back into the city. The next day, however, Paul, Barney, and staff left the Monroe side and crossed the river into West Monroe. After preaching here a few days they traveled again and returned for some family night supper meetings in Monroe, Naples, and Cleveland. On these occasions Paul and Barney encouraged the Christians to stick to their faith, assuring them that the road into the great kingdom was tough traveling, but worth all the suffering and effort.

On these occasions the evangelists also ordained elders in every church and prayed with them, and commended them to the Lord in whom they believed.

From here they went various places, preaching in Canton,[2] Adamsville,[3] Albany,[4] and Jersey City.[5] Finally they returned to Cleveland where their work was prospering and which was also their home office.

---

[1]Tea party types. [2]Pisidia [3]Pamphylia [4]Perga [5]Attalia

When they returned, Paul and Barney reported to all the members of the home church about their experiences and told how the Lord was opening the way for the word of God and the good news to be spread among the non-Jews. The evangelists stayed home then for quite a spell.

There was a strict group of church people from Sea Island, Georgia, who came to town and began to tell the Christians that in spite of the promises of Paul, Barney, and the others, they could not be saved unless they both believed in Jesus and were circumcised. They used Moses as their authority.

This created a major church dispute and many different voices were raised for one side or the other. Finally, it was agreed that Paul and Barney would go to Jerusalem and convene a general assembly of the top church leaders and present the matter for their consideration and action.

Since the trip was at church expense, and since Paul and Barney were missionary minded anyway, they stopped at places like Providence[1] and Silver Springs[2] and preached to the people there, bringing great joy with the good news which they declared.

When Barney and Paul finally arrived in Jerusalem they gave a full report concerning all their experiences and they also reported on the big dispute about circumcision being essential to salvation.[3] A big church meeting was convened.

After a great deal of disputing, Peter, called Rocky, got to his feet and said, "All of you know that God has revealed through me that salvation from God is available for everybody, and the gospel is to be preached to everyone. God permitted non-Jews to receive the baptism of the Holy Spirit just as we did, and there was no distinction made between them and us.

"Now why try to start an argument with God? We believe that we will be saved through the grace and goodness of the Lord Jesus Christ and the same goes for all believers."

No one said anything as arguing against Peter and God was too much even for the hard-headed. Then Paul and Barney each took a turn relating all the wonders and miracles that God had made possible through them in behalf of the non-Jews as well as the Jews. Everyone was quiet for a brief spell.[4]

Then James, the moderator of the church, spoke, "Listen to me for a few minutes. Rocky has explained how the Lord first showed an interest in the non-Jew and all this is in accordance with the prophets, one of them saying, 'After this I will return and rebuild the

---

[1]Phenice   [2]Samaria
[3]I wonder what they figured the women had to do to qualify.
[4]I wonder where the Baptists, Methodists and Presbyterians were?

church that David started, and I will repair the ruins in order that the remnant of the Jews and all the non-Jews that worship me may be part of the church.' Now that is God speaking.

"God knows all things from the very beginning. Now I am saying don't disturb the non-Jew who has turned to God. Why don't we write them a letter and tell them not to worship idols, to refrain from running around with wild women, and from eating the meat of an animal that has choked to death?

"This is giving them the old-time religion, without imposing on them customs that might merely be our own."

This idea made a big hit. As a result the church decided to send Joe Boy[1] and Silas along with Barney and Paul who were to take the letters, since the mail service was not reliable.[2]

The letter which they sent was as follows:

Dear Friends in Christ:

We send greetings to you from all of us Christians at Jerusalem.

It has come to our attention that some of the spokesmen for Christ have troubled you by telling you that you must be circumcised in order to be saved, as well as observe the laws of God. That is not the case. We unanimously approved sending this letter, which will also be verbally strengthened through Barney, Paul, and others who daily risk their lives in the cause of Christ, two of these being Joe Boy and Silas.

It seemed like a good idea to us as well as to the Holy Spirit that there be no greater burden placed upon you than was necessary.

You know, of course, that you are not to worship idols, nor to chase women, nor to eat contaminated meat. That is being good enough.

Yours truly,

The Elders of the Church

When the crowd had gathered at Cleveland the letter was publicly read, there was great rejoicing. Joe Boy and Silas, being good preachers, used this opportunity to preach to the assemblage and many were added to the church.

Sometime later they were told they were free to go as the special services were ended, but Silas stayed on anyway.

Barney and Paul continued preaching and teaching in various parts of the city.

Sometime after this Paul said to Barney, "Let's hit the trail again. I think we should re-visit every church we started."

"That's not a bad idea. I would also like to take John Mark along," said Barney.

"No way," said Paul. "Don't you remember that John Mark pulled out on us on one of our trips because his feet hurt?"

[1]Judas Barrabas   [2]See how modern the Bible is?

"I still want to take him," said Barney.

"OK. You take him and go one way and I'll take Silas and go another," said Paul.[1] As a result, Barney and John went to Hawaii[2] and Paul and Silas went to Turkey.[3]

Paul finally worked his way back to Monroe and West Monroe and there learned about a young man named Tim[4] whose mother was Jewish but whose father was a Greek. Paul decided that this young Christian was just right for a missionary trip companion. Tim even consented to being circumcised to avoid any possible criticism from the extreme right wing of the church.

Paul and Silas carried with them official documents from the headquarters in Jerusalem, which documents were to be used to begin each new church in the faith and to allow each church to have its own charter. In this manner were many churches started and attendance steadily increased.

Paul and Silas considered going into Indochina, but the Holy Spirit influenced them to go in another direction and so they went to Tel Aviv[5] and although they wanted to try east again, thinking of going to Viet Nam,[6] the spirit led them to Troy.[7]

While in Troy, Paul had a vision and there seemingly appeared to him a European[8] who kept saying, "Come over to Europe and help us."

Paul and Silas concluded that this was a sign from God indicating that the missionary thrust should first move toward Europe. As a consequence, the very next day the pair headed for the Greek mainland and made their first major stop at Philadelphia.[9]

After hanging around town for a few days, Silas and Paul chose Sunday afternoon to visit the beach area where the women came to pray and take sun baths.[10] A very prominent person, Lady Lil,[11] who was a fashion designer and clothes merchant, came to see Paul and Silas, for this lady was a god-fearing person and greatly interested in hearing Paul preach. Lady Lil was taught about Christ, and baptized by Paul, following which occasion she set Silas and Paul up in her guest house, encouraging them to stay as long as they desired.

A few days after this as Paul and Silas were on the way to the chapel for a prayer service, a young lady who was possessed by the devil and had an affinity for picking winners at the chariot races[12] stopped the two men. The young lady made a lot of money for the syndicate.

---

[1]Some churches still use this plan. [2]Cyprus [3]Cilicia [4]Timothy [5]Mysia
[6]Bithynia [7]Troas [8]Macedonia [9]Philippi
[10]Paul was not a girl watcher, though. [11]Lydia [12]Some form of ESP.

As Silas and Paul were walking along the young lady began to yell and point saying, "These men are servants of God and they know the true way to salvation." She kept this up several days running and attracted a great deal of attention.

Paul finally got fed up with the young lady and turned to her and said, "I order the devils that are tormenting you and us to leave — in the name and power of Jesus Christ."

Instantly the young lady was purified and lost her ability to pick the winners or at least was no longer willing to let the racketeers use her for gain.

As soon as the men who had been running the gambling saw that their prime source of income was gone they became furious with Tim and Paul and brought them to the City Council.

Turning to the rulers one of the crooks said, "These fellows are Jews and they are here ruining a good bunch of Greeks, not to mention contaminating a whole lot of us Romans, and they teach new ways of doing things and have introduced some new and troublesome ideas in our area."

The City Council put on a big act of indignation, acting as if they were tearing their clothes in anguish, and ordered Paul and Silas to be given a good beating.[1]

After this Silas and Paul were tossed in the jug and the jailer, who became entirely responsible for them, placed them in the very back of the prison.[2] As a further precaution the jailer tied their feet to the bars.

In the middle of the night Paul and Silas began to have a two-man church meeting, with hymn singing and the works, and all the prisoners could hear them.[3]

Suddenly there occurred an earthquake which shook the very foundations of the prison and in the process opened all the cell doors and snapped all the chains.

The jailer awoke and saw that all the cell doors were open and pulled his sword with suicide in mind.[4]

"Wait a minute there, Bub," said Paul. "We haven't left yet."

Trembling the jailer came with a light and said to Paul, "What in the world can I do to be saved?"

"Believe on Jesus Christ. You and all your family."

As a result the jailer put witch hazel on the wounds that the whips had made on Paul and Silas and then had them baptize everyone in his family. The jailer took Paul and Silas to dinner and the whole evening was a great occasion.

---

[1]A good beating is always one somebody else gets.
[2]In those days if a prisoner escaped the jailer had to take his place.
[3]Some rattled their cups on the bars.
[4]He knew he couldn't take all their places.

The next day, however, word came from the City Council to the jailer to free Paul and Silas.[1]

The jailer came to Paul and Silas and said, "You are free. The City Council is sorry for all the trouble."

"Not so fast there," said Paul. "We are Romans, we have been beaten, and humiliated. We are going to sue the Council, or something. You tell the Council to come here and free us themselves."

The jailer reported all this to the City Council, and the news scared the willie-nillie out of the fellows; so they came to the jail to apologize.

The members of the Council then released Paul and Silas and cordially invited them to leave town.

As a result, Paul and Silas left the prison, went to kiss Lady Lil goodbye and get their toothbrushes, left a few instructions with some of the church leaders, and left town.

Chap.
17

Paul and Silas then headed for Decatur,[2] passing through Milltown[3] and Lexington[4] on the way, for there was a church full of Jews at Decatur. Paul tore into them for three straight Sundays, straight from the shoulder, reasoning with them from the scriptures.

"It was absolutely necessary," said Paul, "that Jesus had to suffer and to be raised from the dead, and this is the Christ that I present to you."

A lot of people believed what was said and responded to the preaching including some prominent females, and a lot of Greeks.

As usual, the fellows who didn't accept the new doctrine began to raise sand, even organizing a rabble group, buying them some black leather jackets and getting them to pull a protest in front of the house where Paul and Silas were staying. Paul and Silas were not there at the time, but Solemn Jed,[5] who owned the house, was seized and taken to the city court where he was accused of harboring fellows who were trying to tilt the world their way.

The rabble leaders went on to say that Paul and Silas were opposing Caesar and claiming that Christ was the new ruler. This created no small stir and a few fist fights. Finally, they let Solemn Jed out on bond along with a few friends who had come with him.

That night Jed and friends slipped Paul and Silas out of town and the two went to Bloomington[6] and started preaching there. The people in Bloomington were more receptive and they really listened and studied the scriptures. Again a number were added to the church, including some very fine women.

[1]The Council had learned they were Romans and had not had their rights explained.   [2]Thessalonica [3]Amphipolis [4]Apollonia   [5]Jason [6]Berea

The Jews, however, in Decatur heard of this and they decided to come to Bloomington and create more problems for Paul and Silas.[1]

This time Paul was put on a ship and eased out of town, but Tim and Silas stayed.[2] Not long after this, however, Tim and Silas heard from Paul in Athens and he badly needed his assistants.[3]

While Paul was waiting in Athens for his assistants, he became greatly troubled over the prevalence of idol worship that consumed the city. As a result, Paul began preaching, teaching, debating, arguing and haranguing everywhere, to the point that some of the local college faculty members began to mutter such things as, "What is the guy babbling about?"

"He preaches of a strange god," said one, "whose name is Jesus. In fact, he says Jesus rose from the dead."

After this he was invited to the Chamber of Commerce banquet in North Athens and asked to speak on the new doctrine he advocated. The program committee thought Paul would give them something new to think about. Actually, the main form of entertainment in Athens was arguing.

Paul then stood at a Mars Hill Country Club dinner and spoke to the assembled guests saying, "As I was strolling about the city I noticed a monument 'to the unknown God.' I want to tell you all about him, for you worship him and yet know nothing about him.

"The Lord, who made everything that is and ever was, the one who doesn't live in a church or a house, is certainly not to be worshipped just with gestures or gifts, for certainly God doesn't need anything for himself. Don't you realize that he gave everyone life and breath, and all things?

"God made all mankind of one blood, he planned everything about the development of the earth, and God set all the limitations of man as well as the physical world. Man was made to seek after God, to find Him, even though He is readily available any time.

"In God we live and move and have our whole operation, for your own poets have written that we are descended from God.

"Since we are descended from God we should not put such undue emphasis on gold or silver or statues. God has put up with this jazz long enough and God calls for repentance.

"Actually, God has set a day when He will judge everybody in accordance with their acceptance of Jesus, and God has given man hope in that God raised Jesus from the dead."

When some of them heard Paul talk of people being raised from the dead, some of the fellows began to boo and hiss. Many others, however, wanted a few days to think these things over a bit.[4]

---

[1]The taxpayers footed the bill, as usual.
[2]Paul was always the one that irritated people.
[3]No one to cook and wash for him. [4]Standard procedure from the Greek Manual.

Paul pulled out of Athens, but not before he had converted a number of people such as Long John,[1] Maud,[2] and a number of others.

After this meeting Paul left Athens and went to Corinth and located there a fellow named John Alden[3] who had a wife named Priscilla. This was a Jewish couple who had been run out of Rome during the purge of the Jews there. Actually, Paul became acquainted with them because they were tent makers, and Paul, likewise a tent maker by trade, needed a job to tide him along.[4]

On Sunday, however, Paul taught at the church school and won a number of Jews and Greeks to Christ. While Tim and Silas came from Philadelphia to join Paul, Paul became bolder and testified strongly to the Jews that Jesus was the Christ.

The Jews argued against Paul heatedly and denounced Christ, which put Paul in a real dither, to such an extent that he tore the pockets off his Levis and said to the Jews, "Your blood can rest on your head. I know I am right. From now on I'll preach to the non-Jews and leave you pig heads alone."[5]

Paul stormed out of the church and went next door to the home of Richard Ray,[6] a good man who served the Lord.

Some time later one of the top ranking ministers announced his acceptance of Jesus and this influenced many and so many others became Christians.

During the night one time following the rip-off Paul had at the church, the Lord spoke to Paul and encouraged him, telling him not to be afraid, for not only was the Lord with Paul, but there were more Christians around than Paul thought.

As a result Paul remained in Corinth a year and a half and continued to teach and preach in behalf of Christ.

The next year was an election year and there was put in the office of Sheriff a fellow named U. Grant and at the instigation of the Jews he put Paul under arrest and brought him to court. The charge was that Paul was encouraging people to worship in a manner contrary to the law.

Before Paul had time to testify, however, U. Grant said, "If this charge was a matter of being drunk or stealing or the like I'd go along with you, but the charge of a religious difference is out of my realm and I am releasing this man under his own cognizance. Case dismissed."

---

[1]Dionysius   [2]Damaris   [3]Aquila
[4]Missionaries still need to moonlight — get with it, Christians!
[5]Paul was really peeved at this point.   [6]Justus

The Greeks then went to Soapy,[1] who was Chairman of the Board of the church, and gave Soapy a good beating.[2] Sheriff Grant didn't do anything about this, either. Paul hung around the area quite awhile after this.

Next Paul took a trip to Australia[3] and Priscilla and John Alden went with him. John had gotten his head shaved because of some promise or pledge of a religious nature. On arriving at Sydney[4] Paul left Priscilla and John at the motel and he went to the church and started preaching. Paul reasoned with the Jews and they even asked him to remain in town for further discussions, but he refused.

From Sydney Paul went to Palm Springs where he spoke at a family night supper and then proceeded to Cleveland. After spending time in Cleveland, he went into the surrounding area, preaching and teaching.

In the meantime, back at Sydney, there came to town a fellow named Frank Blair,[5] a gifted speaker, and a man very savvy about the scriptures.

Blair knew the laws of God, he was an enthusiastic speaker, but he was acquainted only up to the time of the baptism of John. Blair began to speak to large crowds at the church.

John Alden and Priscilla came to him and privately began to tell him of Jesus and the resurrection. After this Blair went to New Zealand[6] and was well received for the Christians in Sydney had written favorably about Blair.

Blair was a great help in New Zealand and he convinced many Jews, through the use of the scriptures, that Jesus was the Christ, and some made their public confession.

Chap.
19

Frank Blair took his crusade to Corinth while Paul journeyed to Sydney, Australia and there he called together a handful of professing Christians to discuss the local situation.

"Have each of you received the Holy Spirit?" asked Paul.

"We never heard of the Holy Spirit. What are you talking about?" they asked.

"Under what name were you then baptized?" asked Paul.

"We were baptized under the plan of John the Baptist, or so we were told," said one of the persons.

"Well, let me give you the straight poop," said Paul. "John baptized with the baptism of repentance, telling each one that this was done in the name of a saviour yet to come, Jesus Christ. Jesus has come.

"Let me baptize you again, this time in the name of Jesus

---

[1]Sosthenes
[2]I think Soapy was the program chairman who invited Paul to preach.
[3]Syria [4]Ephesus [5]Apollos [6]Achaia

Christ," said Paul. There were about a dozen people involved and they all consented.

As a result Paul placed his hands on their heads and the Holy Spirit came upon them, and each began to speak in tongues and make prophetic utterances.[1]

After this Paul remained speaking regularly at the open church meetings, participating in debates, and testifying for Christ. Paul continued this for about three months. Then some of the hard core group opposing Paul's viewpoint became very vocal. Paul asked the Christians to refrain from going to the open church meetings and to begin to meet together in a school house, where actually they would meet every day for prayer or discussion.

This lasted about two years and reasonable progress was made; so that the word of the Lord Jesus began to be spread all through Australia, both to the Jews, the Greeks, and the outlanders.

During this time the Lord granted special powers to Paul even to the point that he could heal some ailments and relieve some mental problems by simply sending one of his handkerchiefs or socks to a person and they would be healed, if they believed.

Now there were some Jewish exorcists who made a living through crackpot psychiatry who decided to cash in a bit themselves on the program. The plan was to demand that the evil spirits depart from a person saying, "Depart in the name of the Lord Jesus, the one about whom Paul preaches!"

There was one group of seven brothers, the Smith Brothers,[2] sons of one of the local priests, and they brought in their first case to try, who happened to be a fellow named Ali.

When they tried their flim-flam on Ali he cried out, "I know Jesus, and I know Paul, but I don't know you bums."

As a result Ali jumped on them and began to beat them so that finally all seven ran out of the trailer they used as an office, wounded and half naked.

This incident was widely known in the area and was a real help to the Christian movement. Many who had previously hestitated began to come forward after this and make public profession.

Many of the local quacks who were exorcists or fakers of some kind came and brought their weird books and had them burned in front of the Christian church and confessed themselves to be phonies. Over $250,000 worth of various material was thus consumed.

With the word of God doing so well in Sydney, Paul began to plan to take another trip, thinking that he would go through part of New Zealand, then eastern Europe and check back to the home office in Jerusalem. Paul said to one of his buddies, "After doing this

[1]This is known as glossalalia. [2]Sceva

trip I am going to Rome, somehow. I just have to see Rome."

What actually happened was that Paul decided to leave Tim and Rastus[1] in Eastern Europe and not remain there himself; so Paul went to Asia Minor on his planned return to Jerusalem.

A great controversy arose in the Greek islands and throughout that area. It all started at the big Arts and Crafts Fair held in West Virginia, where the Arts and Crafts Association held their annual convention and banquet. This year the President of the Association was a man named Tiffany,[2] a prominent silversmith.

When Tiffany arose to speak at the big banquet he said, "Ladies and gentlemen, you know that all of us here make our living selling art forms, mostly statues or jewelry of a religious nature. Now there is a fellow named Paul who is trying to put us out of business. Paul is telling everybody that there are no gods made with hands. This not only puts our Association in great danger, but even the temple of Diana, our favorite goddess. Everybody likes or worships Diana, and we make oodles of jewelry with her likeness or symbols on it."

"Down with Paul! Hurrah for Diana of the Ephesians!" shouted those at the banquet.

The whole city and area then began to break forth into a mighty hubbub. A great crowd caught two of Paul's companions and brought them to the city auditorium and hundreds of members of the Association gathered along with a lot of indignant local citizens.[3] Paul's two friends were Bart Starr[4] and Bobby Orr.[5]

When Paul wanted to go to help them he was restrained by some other Christians, and also some of the local officials strongly suggested that Paul stay clear of the auditorium.

The assembly in the auditorium was a mad house. There was no one in charge, a few fist fights, some people shouting one thing and some another. Some of the crowd did not even know why they were there, having just joined the crowd to see what was happening.

Finally someone got a man named Alex,[6] a prominent and highly respected businessman, and put him on the platform. Alex got everybody quiet for a few minutes and then someone yelled, "Alex is a Jew!"

This brought on a two hour shouting session with the main cry emanating from the Arts and Crafts group yelling, "Great is Diana of the Ephesians!"

At last the Chief of Police took charge, and he was a cool, knowledgeable character.

The Chief took the mike and spoke to the crowd saying, "Now just cool it, people, and listen to a little reason. Everybody knows

---

[1]Erastus   [2]Demetrius   [3]There is still a good supply of these.
[4]Gaius   [5]Aristardus   [6]Alexander

that in this city and area the great name is Diana of the Ephesians, and also everybody here knows about the statue that fell down from the god Jupiter. Nobody can speak against such facts, so what are you howling about? Don't do some rash thing when there is no need.

"You have two men here. These men are not robbers, they have not damaged or touched your statues. Now if your Arts and Crafts Association has some legal charge against these fellows then file your charges and I'll arrest them.

"If you simply want to discuss something or have a religious debate then you must get a license to use the auditorium. This thing you've done today is dangerous and will hurt the tourist trade and people will be afraid to come to the Fair. Now all of you quietly leave and tend to your own business and in the future do things legally."

The assembly then quietly dispersed.[1]

Chap.
20

After all the furor had subsided Paul decided to take another trip to eastern Europe and so there was a farewell dinner for him. Paul returned to Greece after covering a number of the churches in the eastern Europe area.

After staying about three months in Greece, preaching and teaching regularly, some of the Jews decided that they had had enough of Paul and they set up an ambush at the pass. Paul heard about it and so left by the back route to go to parts of Asia. On the trip, Paul took quite a bundle of converts with him, including such men as the well-known John Templeton,[2] Bobby Orr who was still with the Christian group, Bart Starr, Tim, Oral Roberts,[3] and Julia Child.[4] For security reasons these disciples went ahead and waited for Paul and Silas at Troy.[5]

Paul and Silas arrived about five days later and remained in Troy for a week. On Sunday, the day before Paul was scheduled to leave Troy, he appeared at the Sunday night supper the Christian group had arranged and Paul preached to them until midnight.[6] Torches were, of course, lighted while the evening meeting was in process and there was a young fellow named Dusty[7] who had propped himself on a rafter near the top of the ceiling, as there were no seats available and the church was crowded.

The preaching was so long that Dusty went to sleep and fell from the rafter nearly thirty feet to the floor. Paul momentarily quit

[1]I can't help but think that somebody set off a firecracker before it was over.
[2]Sopater (John Templeton, religious journalist) [3]Tychicus [4]Trophimus [5]Troas
[6]Proving that Paul was not a Presbyterian. [7]Eutychus

preaching and went to the young man who had already been pronounced dead by those close to where he fell.

Paul embraced the young fellow and told the people not to worry, that the young man would live. The accident occurred about midnight and so Paul called for a brief recess for a little eating and drinking and then resumed teaching until daylight.[1]

The people were greatly cheered, however, over the miraculous recovery of Dusty.

Silas and one or two others took a ship to Augusta[2] while Paul had decided to walk or hitch hike, going the long way. After Paul arrived in Augusta the whole group took ship to Tampa[3] and from there sailed to Pensacola.[4] From there he went to Havana,[5] and then on to Trinidad,[6] and the next day sailed for Cairo.[7] Paul also wanted to go by Sydney and did not want to waste a lot of time in Viet Nam for he was insistent on getting to Jerusalem for the day of Pentecost.

Paul sent for some of the leaders from Sydney and talked to them saying, "You are the Christian leaders in Sydney and throughout Australia. You know about me, about my diligence, regardless of weather, that I have really served the Lord, sometimes suffering, often trying to dodge presecution from the Jews. Yet I have told you everything, and did not guard my words simply to protect myself from being attacked. You know that I have witnessed for Christ to Jews, Greeks, and other non-Jews, teaching repentance to God and faith in the Lord Jesus Christ.

"Now I am leaving for Jerusalem, completely committed to the cause of Christ, not knowing what may happen to me, except that the Holy Spirit is everywhere and will always be with us.

"None of the dangers scare me; in fact I consider my life not even to be my own, but I feel that it is a great joy to be full of a great purpose. I am happy to have received the call to minister for the Lord Jesus Christ, and so I can testify to the gospel of kindness and the grace of God.

"None of you, to whom I have preached so much, shall ever see me again. I want you to know that I am under no obligation to tell you anything except the truth, and I re-affirm to you the goodness of God.

"Be careful with yourselves and with all the Christians of your denomination, for the Holy Spirit has put you in charge of a great group. You are to nourish the church of the Lord Jesus, for he shed his own blood for this church.

"I know that after I've gone there will be trouble. Some weird characters will join the denomination and insert some strange doctrines, and I also know that some of you are apt to get contentious and draw some of the folk after you to form a new

---

[1]We have no record of a pulpit committee calling on Paul.
[2]Asos   [3]Mitylene   [4]Chios   [5]Samos   [6]Trogyllium   [7]Miletus

church or another denomination.

"Nevertheless, I commend you to God's care, to the word of God in the Bible. These things will encourage you, and give you a sense of security and a feeling of being at home among those who follow Christ.

"I want you to know that I have never begrudged other people being rich and having Cadillacs, jewelry, and solid silver putters. You know that I have always had to look out for myself and have helped to care for the staff of folks who made trips with me.

"I have showed you in order that you might learn from me how to support the helpless and the disadvantaged and to remember that Jesus himself said, 'It is far better to give than to receive.'"

When Paul had finished he kneeled down and led the group in prayer.

There was great sadness and yet great joy as they warmly shook hands. The sadness was because they knew they would never see him again and the great joy was because of the encouraging words and the great assurance of the common bond in Jesus Christ. The whole crowd went to the dock to wave good-bye to Paul as he sailed.

Chap.
21

Paul and his staff then sailed and stopped at several small ports en route, finally docking at Tyre where the cargo was unloaded.

At Tyre there were a number of Christians who encouraged Paul and his group to remain for a week. During this time several of the Tyre Christians told Paul that they were inspired by the Spirit to warn him against going to Jerusalem. Paul was not impressed with the warning. All of the Christian group with their wives and children came to the beach for prayer service and farewells before Paul and the staff sailed away to Palm Springs.

In Palm Springs Paul and Silas stayed in the home of a local evangelist called Phil, the Lip. Phil was one of the very honored ministers, being in the Big Seven Club. Phil had four daughters, all virgins and all prophets.

While staying with Phil there came to town a prophet named Redhead[1] who naturally came to visit with Paul.

Redhead took Paul's belt and simulated binding his own hands and feet and then said, "The Holy Spirit has revealed that this is what will happen to Paul if he goes to Jerusalem."

After this several of the staff members tried to discourage Paul from going to Jerusalem,[2] but to no avail.

"What are you all moaning about? Don't you know that I am prepared to go to jail and be killed in Jerusalem for the sake of Christ?"

---

[1]Agabus   [2]The staff was usually thrown in jail also.

After this statement the staff just said, "God's will be done."

From Palm Springs, Paul and his staff went overland to Jerusalem, accompanied by a few joiners and one fine elder named Howell Cocke[1] who agreed to pay for all the motel stops.

The group was well received in Jerusalem and the next day after arriving visited James, who was the titular head of the entire Christian Church. All the church leaders gathered to hear Paul's report on his missionary journey.

Paul reported that God had blessed his trip and that the Lord had worked miracles in winning the non-Jews to the cause of Christ. The whole assembly was greatly impressed.

"Now, Paul," said James. "There are thousands of Jews who are now Christians, and yet they are very particular about all the old Jewish laws. These Jews have been told that you are teaching some of the Jews in foreign countries that live shoulder to shoulder with non-Jews that it is not necessary for sons to be circumcised nor to follow the old Jewish laws.

"What are we to do? The local Jews here will know that you have come and they will want to hear from you directly. Now we know you are all right, but we have a suggestion in the public interest.

"We have a communicants class of four young men who are about to go through the acts of purification. You go through the ceremony with them as their leader, and authorize the shaving of their heads. Then everyone will know that the wild rumors about you are not true and that you yourself keep the Jewish law perfectly.

"As far as the non-Jew is concerned we have granted them special exception from the law, requiring them only to refrain from bar-b-que that has been offered as a sacrifice to an idol, or from eating the meat of animals that died from disease, and from chasing bad women or running slow when chased by bad women."

As a consequence, the next day Paul took the young persons and after purifying himself liturgically entered the temple and fulfilled all the obligations of the ceremony.

About the time the seven days of the process were complete, the Jews who had been coming to the temple became fed up with seeing Paul there, whom they thought was an extreme liberal. As a result, they organized a big crowd of rabble rousers and grabbed Paul while he was in church.

One of the big lips then jumped up in the pulpit and shouted saying, "Men of Israel, we need help. This is the man here who has been causing all the trouble, teaching things contrary to our law, even bringing a bunch of greasy Greeks into the church, and he has polluted our holy temple."

---

[1]Mnason (Outstanding Presbyterian layman)

Actually it was reported that Paul had been seen in association with Jimmy the Greek[1] and they thought this was Paul's doing.

Everybody got all excited and in a froth and dragged Paul out of the church. The intent was to take him outside the city walls and kill him.

The Chief of Police of Jerusalem heard about the big disturbance and ordered several squad chariots to the place and put a stop to the beating of Paul, which had already started.

The Chief of Police had Paul put in chains and then he turned to the crowd and asked, "What has this fellow done?"

"He slugged the priest," yelled one fellow.

"Naw, he went dancing with a Greek girl in Athens," yelled another.

The chief easily recognized there was no answer from the mob and so he escorted Paul to the Police Station. Actually Paul had to be carried by the cops for his own protection as the people were still howling, "Get rid of Paul! Kill him!"

As Paul was entering the Police Station he said to the Chief, using Greek, the native tongue of the Chief, "May I talk with you?"

"Say, you can speak Greek real good," said the Chief. "Are you the Egyptian that started the big Watts riot in which 4,000 were killed?"

"No," said Paul, "I am a Jew, a native of Florence,[2] Italy,[3] a citizen of a very respectable city. Give me a chance to reason with the people."

As a result, the chief made the people quiet down. When this was done Paul arose and began to speak to them in Hebrew.

Chap.
22

The fact that Paul spoke in Hebrew was helpful in keeping the crowd quiet and he said, "Ladies and gentlemen, I am a Jew, born in Florence, Italy, and yet I was essentially reared here in Jerusalem under the great teacher, Professor George, and I was taught strictly according to the law and was as dedicated toward God as any of you. In fact, I persecuted and caused to be put to death anyone who varied from the strict teaching of the law, whether a person was a man or a woman.

"There is a complete record and proof of this in the temple here and also in other places where I carried out the punitive work of the high priest. I even went to Detroit to capture Christians there. It was while I was on my trip to Detroit that I was blinded by a light from heaven and I heard a voice saying, 'Saul, Saul, why do you persecute me?'

" 'Who are you?" I called.

---

[1]Trophimus [2]Tarsus [3]Cilicia

" 'I am Jesus of Nazareth. I am the one you are persecuting,' came the reply.

"The fellows with me saw the light, but they did not hear the voice. I then said, 'What shall I do, Lord?'

"The Lord said, 'Get up and go to Detroit and there you will be told what you are supposed to do.'

"I was so blinded by the light that I had to be led by the hand the rest of the way to Detroit and there a good, law-abiding man named Ford came to me and said, 'Saul, you may now receive your sight.'

"The same hour I was able to see enough to look at Mr. Ford. Then Mr. Ford spoke to me and said to me, 'Saul, the God of our Fathers has selected you to know his will, to have seen his son Jesus, and heard his voice. You are to be a witness throughout the world for Jesus, reporting what you have seen and heard.

'Don't delay. Get up. Be baptized, repent and have your sins washed away, calling on the mercy of God.'

"It happened that when I finally returned to Jerusalem I was praying in the First Church and fell in some type of trance so that I saw Jesus and heard him say, 'Hurry, leave Jerusalem, for the people here are not ready to hear you yet as a witness.'

"Then I said to Jesus, 'Lord, everybody in town knows how I have been having the Christians beaten, put in prison, and some executed. I was even standing there while Steve was stoned to death, and held the coats for the stone throwers.'

"Nevertheless, Jesus said to me, 'I am sending you as a missionary to the non-Jews.'"

The last tore it. The crowd went wild and some shouted, "Kill the buzzard. He is not fit to live!"

The Chief of Police then rescued him from the angry mob and took him to the interrogation room.

The Chief turned to the desk sergeant and said, "Get this fellow Paul tied to the wall and we'll beat the facts out of him."

As they were about to start whipping him, Paul turned to the captain in charge of the beaters and said, "I am a Roman citizen, born in Florence, Italy, do you think you can whip me without a trial and deprive me of my right?"

The captain stopped everything then and went to the Chief of Police and said, "That bird Paul is a Roman citizen, we'd better be careful what we do."

The Chief then came to Paul and said, "Are you a genuine Roman citizen?"

"Yes," said Paul.

"It cost me $10,000 to buy my freedom as a Roman citizen," said the Chief.

"I was born free," said Paul.

There was no more talk of whip interrogation as the authorities

were not about to tamper with a real Roman citizen. The Chief was
scared already for he had tied Paul's hands.

The next morning the Chief delivered Paul with his hands free
into the presence of the Jewish leaders for a hearing.

Paul, who did not need to be introduced, stood on the platform
and spoke to the group saying, "Ladies and gentlemen, I have lived as
good as I know how, conscientiously living in the presence of God."

At this point the Program Chairman asked the sergeant-at-arms
to bust Paul in the mouth, which he did.

"God will get you for that," said Paul to the Program Chairman.
"You big stuffed shirt, you are planning to judge me according to the
law and then you have me socked one, which is against the law."

"Are you bold enough to criticize our top dog, the high priest
and Program Chairman?"

"I didn't know this character was the high priest or I wouldn't
have said what I did for I know we are told not to criticize the ruler
of the people," said Paul.

Now Paul was a good thinker, and he began to see that the
crowd consisted of both Democrats[1] and Republicans.[2] Paul then
turned to the assembly and said, "I am a Democrat and the son of a
Democrat, yet you have questioned my belief in the hope and
resurrection of the dead."

Immediately a great controversy arose between the Democrats
and the Republicans, for the Republicans did not believe in angels,
spirits, or the resurrection, while the Democrats believed in all three.

As a result the Democrats immediately arose in defense of Paul
saying, "We don't see anything wrong with this fellow. If an angel
has given him some inside poop we don't want to buck this and
suddenly find ourselves opposing God."

Such a shouting and fist shaking began to develop that the Chief
of Police sent a detachment from the Riot Squad to rescue Paul and
bring him safely back to prison.

That night the word of the Lord came to Paul indicating that
even as he had witnessed and testified for Christ in Jerusalem so also
must he do in Rome.

The next day a splinter group known as the Watergate Plumbers
organized and took an oath that none of the forty of them would eat
or drink until one of them had killed Paul.[3]

The leader of this group then went to the big chief and told him
of the plan to kill Paul and suggested that the big chief ask the police
to bring Paul the next day for some private questioning. The Number
One Plumber then told the chief that they would ambush Paul and

[1]Pharisees [2]Sadducees [3]This has always been a dumb approach.

kill him as he came to the meeting.

Paul's sister had a 12-year-old son who was selling popcorn outside the church and he heard the men plotting and so he went to the jail and told Paul. Paul then asked one of the jailers to get the Chief of Police and let the boy tell his story.

As a result the jailer went to the Chief of Police and said, "Paul, the fellow in cell 2 sent for me and told me to bring this boy to you for you to hear what he has to say."

The Chief of Police then in a kindly fashion took the boy's hand and led him aside in private and said, "What is it that you should tell me, son?"

"Some of the Jews from a particular group have decided to ask you to bring Paul to them for a private interview, but I hope you won't agree. The plan is that another militant group plans to ambush Paul and kill him. This group has sworn that they will neither eat nor drink until Paul is dead."

"Thank you, son," said the Chief. "Now you run along home and don't tell anybody about your coming to see me."

The Chief of Police then called the local head of the National Guard and told him to get 200 soldiers ready for special escort duty as they were to take a prisoner to Palm Springs, leaving in the dead of night, in fact about 3 a. m.

The Chief also suggested that Paul be provided a jeep or some leisurely way of transportation. The orders were to deliver the prisoner to Felix.

The Chief wrote a note to Felix saying:

Dear Governor:

Hope you are having a nice day. I am transferring a prisoner to you. This man was arrested by the Jews and if I had not intervened they would have killed him. I had to use a whole riot squad to get him, but since the man is a Roman citizen I felt that such extreme tactics were necessary.

When I tried to discover what the charges were that the Jews had against the fellow it turned out that he had done nothing against civil laws or criminal laws, but was merely being questioned on religious differences.

Shortly after this I learned of a plot to kill the man; so I am transferring him to you and have told his accusers to notify you of the charges that they wish to file.

Sincerely yours,

Hardnose Hogan[1]

The soldiers then took Paul as they had been ordered and went as far as Tucson[2] where they stayed in the Holiday Inn. The next day the foot soldiers returned to Jerusalem while the cavalry section

[1]Claudius Lysius [2]Antipatris

escorted Paul to Palm Springs and presented him to the Governor along with the explanatory letter.

The Governor asked, "In what country is your citizenship registered?"

"In Italy," said Paul.

"Well, I will hear your case when the prosecution is ready. In the meantime you can stay in the jail area back of Herod's palace."[1]

Chap.
24

About five days later the high priest, Rabbi Wise,[2] accompanied by his staff and a professional orator named B. Cerf,[3] came to Felix and asked for a hearing.

When everyone had been seated, B. Cerf arose and said, "We are indeed most fortunate, Governor Felix, to have you in charge of our area. You are a great blessing to our nation.[4] We are really grateful for your just and kind leadership.

"In order to save time and not to bore you with a lot of details, let me tell you that we have found this fellow Paul to be the biggest pest since the days of the plagues. He has caused all kinds of dissension and division, and he is a ringleader of the James Gang.[5] This group has violated the church and its program. We would have handled the matter under our own religious laws if Hardnose Hogan, the Chief of Police, had not butted in and taken Paul to jail. The Chief used police brutality in his actions, too.

"The Chief even forced us to go to all this trouble and bother you with this matter."

The Jews who were present all nodded their heads in support of his declaration.

The Governor then called on Paul, who spoke forth saying, "I know you are a fine judge with a great reputation for justice, and so I do not hesitate to speak frankly.[6] Well, I went to Jerusalem twelve days ago to worship God. I did not enter any arguments, I did not stage debates in the church, nor in the city, and these loud mouths cannot prove anything else.

"I tell you this, though, that these fellows make it sound wrong to worship God. I do serve the God of my fathers, believing everything that is written in the law and in the prophets, looking to God for the resurrection of the dead, both of the just and the unjust.

"I further proclaim that I have no animosity toward God or man. Feeling this way, I returned to Jerusalem after many years to bring my offerings and my gifts to the church.

"One of the things I did was to participate in the purifying

---

[1]Judges and lawyers always postpone cases, with or without reason. [2]Ananias [3]Tertullus [4]The old soft-soap routine. [5]Nazarenes [6]Paul had a little soap, too.

process of worship and meditation, making no big to-do about it. I don't see any of those fellows here to accuse me. If any of these characters here have anything to say against my presentation in Jerusalem I'd like to hear some specific testimony. I admit that I stated that I believed in the resurrection of the dead. Is that objectionable?"

When Felix heard all this he postponed the case, for Felix was already informed on the Christian movement. As a result he said, "When Hardnose Hogan comes to town, I'll get the real poop from him."

Felix then asked one of the local National Guard officers to let Paul stay in his guest room and see that he was free to come and go and to have visitors.

A few days later Felix came with his wife Johnnie Mae[1] to visit Paul and to listen to him tell about Jesus Christ.

Felix was greatly moved by Paul's teaching as he explained the matters of goodness, temperance, and final judgment. When Felix left, he said to Paul, "You may go about your business. When I have a convenient time I will send for you and we'll have a trial."

Felix also indicated that if Paul would come forth with a reasonable bribe[2] that Paul would be freed. In the meantime, Felix visited Paul often.

About two years later, C. Darrow, a prosecutor for the Jews, prevailed on Felix to confine Paul and treat him as a prisoner.

Chap.

25

Not long after this Darrow came from Palm Springs to Jerusalem and immediately the group plotting against Paul talked with him and urged him to send for Paul so that they could kill him en route.[3]

Darrow wouldn't cooperate, but he did invite anybody that so desired to go with him to Palm Springs and accuse Paul there. About ten days later Darrow departed for Palm Springs, and when he arrived he set up a trial and ordered Paul to appear.[4]

On this occasion the Jews who had come from Jerusalem accused Paul of all kinds of things but could produce no proof of anything.

Paul testified saying, "I have not spoken against the law, or against the church, or against Caesar."

"Will you go to Jerusalem and stand trial there?" asked Darrow, for he was anxious to please the voting Jews.

---

[1]Drusilla   [2]This practice still exists in some places.
[3]The oath not to eat or drink had no doubt gone down the drain.
[4]Lawyers have always delayed trials for two years.

"I demand a change of venue to Caesar's court, not the prejudiced outfit in Jerusalem. I surely have done nothing wrong to any Jew; so if there is a point of law it must be Roman. If I have committed some crime worthy of death then I'm willing to die. If there are none of these charges against me filed by the Jews, I then appeal to Caesar."

Darrow then called a brief recess while he could confer with his staff. On returning he spoke to Paul saying, "Do you appeal to Caesar?"

"Yes," said Paul.

"Then to Caesar you will go," said Darrow.

A few days after this King Paul Harvey[1] and his wife Bernice came to visit C. Darrow and after they had visited a few days Darrow told them about the prisoner Paul.

"The Jews at Jerusalem were really hot after this fellow and tried to get me to lower the boom on him. I told them that the Romans didn't use capital punishment without a cause and invited them to appear and accuse Paul to his face.

"When I brought Paul into the court the Jews didn't have anything specific at all of which to accuse him. The whole argument was an internal affair concerning a man named Jesus whom the Jews said was dead and Paul said he was alive.

"I then asked Paul if he would consent to a trial in Jerusalem and Paul would not, but insisted on appearing before Augustus Caesar."

Then Paul Harvey said to Darrow, "I would really like to hear this fellow Paul."

"Fine. I'll get him here tomorrow," said Darrow.

The next morning Paul Harvey and Bernice came to the large board room, dressed fit to kill, and also present were all the local dignitaries. Paul was, of course, brought into the room.

"Paul Harvey, Bernice, friends and guests, you see this man Paul here before you," said Darrow. "Now the Jews, mainly the group in Jerusalem, have been bugging me to have this man executed. I have not found, however, anything that he has done that is criminal. Furthermore, the man as a Roman citizen has exercised his right to appeal to Caesar. I have decided to send him to Caesar for trial.

"The trouble is, I don't know what to write on the notice of appeal. It bothers me to send a man to Rome and not to have any charges to go with the case. The Emperor will call me a nut.

"Anyhow, I have brought Paul before this wise group, particularly Paul Harvey, and I hope after you have listened to Paul you will be able to give me something to send to Rome. I admit that it seems stupid to send a fellow to Rome without being able to file any kind of charges."

[1] Agrippa

Then King Harvey turned to Paul and said, "You may now speak for yourself."

Then Paul, using impressive gestures, began to speak saying, "I am delighted at the opportunity to defend myself against the false charges brought against me by the Jews. I am particularly pleased to be able to speak in your presence because I know how well acquainted you are with the customs and the controversies among the Jews.

"Everyone, including even my Jewish enemies, know that I was reared very strictly as a pure Democrat, schooled under the famous Professor George, and I continue to testify to the hope which God promised to our forefathers. All the tribes of Israel look for the fulfillment of this hope, and yet it is at this point that I am being accused.

"Why should anyone who believes in the total power of God think that it is not possible for God to raise someone from the dead?

"I admit that when I was younger I worked diligently against the teaching about Jesus, I persecuted believers, put them in prison, and even voted to have some of them executed. I was angry and tough with these believers and pursued them in many small towns as well as Jerusalem.

"On a special trip to Detroit where I was headed to further persecute the followers of Jesus, a light came down from heaven, brighter than the sun, and shone all around me and my staff. All of us kneeled on the ground. Then I heard a voice from heaven speaking to me in Hebrew saying, 'Saul, Saul, why do you persecute me? I know it bothers your inner conscience.'

" 'Who are you, Lord?' I asked.

" 'I am Jesus, the one you are really persecuting,' was the answer. 'Get up now, Saul, for I have appeared to you for a purpose. I want you to be a witness for me, to testify of what you are now seeing, and also of other things which I will reveal to you.

" 'I want you to go not mainly to the Jews, but to the non-Jews, open their minds, turn them from darkness to light, from ignorance to knowledge, and deliver them from the power of evil as represented by Satan and turn them to the one true God. In this manner then they may receive forgiveness for their sins and they may become part of the active kingdom of God.'

"I was obedient to this vision, King Harvey. At first I witnessed in Detroit, then Jerusalem, and then to places all over the world, urging the non-Jews to repent, to turn to God, and to begin living the Christian life.

"Because of these actions the Jews have tried to kill me. With the help of God I am continuing my mission, testifying only to those things which the prophets and Moses said would come to pass. For these writers in the Old Testament said that Christ would come, that he would suffer, be killed, rise from the dead, and be the saviour for the world."

"Paul, you have got to be nutty. You've been reading too much," said Darrow, rudely interrupting.[1]

"I am not crazy," said Paul. "I speak the truth and what I say makes good sense. The King, Paul Harvey, knows about these things. He is well informed and none of these things have been kept a secret.

"Paul Harvey, don't you believe the prophets? I am sure that you do."

"Paul, you are about to persuade me to be a Christian," said Harvey.

"I wish I could persuade you, and not just you, but all that hear me. I wish everyone felt like I feel, believed as I believe, but not handcuffed as I am."[2]

When the meeting adjourned King Harvey, Darrow, and Bernice had a coffee break and talked among themselves.

"This man has certainly not done anything to warrant capital punishment," said Darrow.

"In fact," said Harvey, "if he had not foolishly appealed to Caesar we would dismiss all charges and let him go free, but we can't withdraw an appeal to Caesar."

Chap.
27

When arrangements had been made for Paul to be transferred to Rome, Paul was placed along with some other prisoners under the care of J. Edgar,[3] a security chief for the emperor. Luke arranged to travel as a passenger as well as a couple of other members of Paul's staff.

Bart Starr was also along as a passenger and they sailed on a Lykes Bros.[4] ship. J. Edgar was very considerate of Paul and let him roam around the ship and visit his aides and the other passengers.

Because of poor sailing conditions it was necessary to stop at several ports and finally Paul, J. Edgar, and the various aides and passengers were transferred to another ship.

This ship also found sailing conditions erratic and the ship got so far off course that it went by Crete and then sailed and drifted into a doldrum area under Greece.

Paul offered the opinion to the captain of the ship that the way he was sailing would bring only trouble and maybe cause the loss of life and cargo. The captain disagreed and J. Edgar figured the captain knew more about the sea than Paul.[5]

The idea was to find a place where the ship might lay in a safe harbor for the winter; so the captain ordered a course change and headed toward Crete. A gentle wind encouraged the captain and he

---

[1]Forgive him, he was a lawyer. [2]Paul was real sharp. [3]Julius [4]Adramyttium
[5]Anyway, nobody ever tells a ship captain anything.

thought all was well.

Not long after this, however, there arose a small typhoon[1] and the ship could not stand into the wind and so had to come about and run with the gale. The storm blew the ship into the treacherous area around Hatteras[2] and orders were published to batten down the hatches and secure all loose deck attachments.

The second day of the storm the captain ordered some of the cargo to be thrown over the side and on the third day everyone was ordered to throw everything overboard that could be spared, even pulleys and similar gear.

The storm continued and in a few days it was considered impossible for the ship and personnel to be saved.

Finally Paul stood on a hatch cover and shouted, "I told you so.[3] You should have listened to what I advised and docked at Crete. However, cheer up, for though the ship will be destroyed there will be no lives lost.

"There appeared to me in the night an angel of God, the God that I serve, and said that I was not to be afraid for it was God's will that I appear before Caesar. The angel said that in the saving of me it was arranged that all who were with me would be saved, so cheer up. I certainly believe God and that everything will work out exactly as God desires.

"Nevertheless, we will be washed ashore on an island."

After about two weeks of this terribly rough weather some of the sailors decided the end was in sight for their depth indicator kept going down and they were sure that the ship was being blown onto rocks in the night.

As a result, the sailors put four anchors in the stern and then all the sailors made ready the lifeboat as if to put an anchor off the bow, but they intended to desert the ship.

Paul said, "If those men are allowed to go on their own, J. Edgar, the rest of you cannot be saved."

As a result, J. Edgar had one of the undercover agents cut the life boat ropes and let it drop into the sea.

The next day Paul said, "Everyone eat a good meal. Today makes two weeks and the fast effort was senseless anyway. The food will make you feel better and you are all going to be saved."

Paul then took bread, and after he had pronounced the blessing, and given thanks to God, he began to eat. Everybody then began to eat and became very cheerful. There were 276 people all told in the ship, and after they had eaten they threw most of the remaining food over the side.

When daylight came they could see a narrow creek as a break in the shore line and although they did not know where they were[4] it

[1]Euroclydon [2]Clauda [3]Thank you, Paul.
[4]Navigator lost his sextant.

was determined to try to get the ship into the saftey of the creek.

The captain then ordered the sea anchors to be hoisted, sail spread, and the ship headed for the creek. Cross currents, however, caught the ship and it was run aground. The waves tore off the stern of the ship.

The soldiers then recommended killing all the prisoners so they could say that they were killed trying to escape.[1] J. Edgar, interested primarily in saving Paul, would not let them do this.

"All of you who can swim," shouted J. Edgar, "jump overboard and make it to shore. The rest of you get boards, life jackets, or something and kick your way ashore."

The result was that every person safely reached the shore.

Chap.
28

After they were safely ashore they realized that they were on Long Island.[2] The natives, even though they had a bad reputation, were good to the shipwreck victims, building some fires and offering shelter from the pelting rain.

When Paul was helping by gathering sticks for the fire a rattlesnake bit him and hung on his arm.[3]

One of the superstitious Long Islanders immediately blurted out, "That man must be a real criminal and since the sea didn't get him the gods are working on him with a snake."

The snake did not harm Paul and when the natives saw that he did not begin to shake and quiver and then fall down dead they decided that he must be some type of god himself.

Paul, Luke, and a couple of aids were the house guests of J. P. Morgan[4] and in the same house was Morgan's father, who had high fever and a small hemorrhage. Paul called on the elder Morgan, placed his hands upon him, prayed to God, and the man was healed.

As soon as word of this was spread around other people came with various illnesses, mostly arthritis, and they were healed.

The people of Long Island gave the refugees many gifts and three months later when another ship came to get the crowd, they all left with many new possessions. The ship that finally took all the refugees was the Mayflower[5] and after several stops and a little more faulty navigation the Mayflower landed in Italy and Paul and his group started overland to Rome.

Word had gone ahead about Paul coming to Rome and so some of the Christians came to meet him on the outskirts of Rome. The Christians met Paul at Sardi's Restaurant[6] and Paul was greatly encouraged by their presence.

---

[1]The soldiers were responsible for seeing that the prisoners were tried.
[2]Melita [3]I think Paul shook him off pretty fast, though. [4]Publius
[5]Castor & Pollux [6]The Three Taverns

On arriving in downtown Rome, J. Edgar delivered all the prisoners to the jail except Paul. Paul was given special permission to live in a private apartment accompanied by one soldier.

About three days later, Paul called a meeting of the Jewish leaders and when they had gathered he spoke to them saying, "Ladies and gentlemen, I want you to know that I have not violated the customs or the traditions of our people; nevertheless I am a prisoner, being delivered from Jerusalem to Rome.

"My trial in the lower court went well and I was found innocent, but because of the big stink some of the Jews made I felt it wise to appeal to Caesar. I certainly don't care to criticize my own race, the Jews. That's why I have called you to hear me. I want you to know that I am a prisoner because of my faith and not because of my lack of it."

"We never heard anything about any of this," said the spokesman for the group. "Nobody wrote us about your difficulties, and nobody who has come from your area has been complaining about you. We do want to hear what you have to say, though, as we have heard strange things about Christians and their beliefs."

Not long after this an arrangement was made to have Paul speak and he taught a large group off and on for a full day, testifying about the kingdom of God and telling them of Jesus, the Christ.

Some of the hearers believed and some did not. Paul's final statement to them that day was that Isaiah the prophet had said, "When you go to the Jewish people you'll find they will hear but not understand, they will see visible manifestations and yet not understand. The hearts of the Jews are hardened, their eyes are closed, their hearing gone, and they will resist conversion and salvation."

Paul then assured them that the salvation of God and the good news of the gospel was going to the non-Jews, and that they would accept it.

The Jews then left and began to argue and discuss these matters among themselves.

Paul remained in his private apartment for two years[1] and visited with many people and did a great deal of teaching. Paul preached the kingdom of God and taught the people about the Lord Jesus Christ, teaching openly and positively, and no one stopped him.

[1]New lawyers; so two more years before a trial.

Dear Romans:

As you no doubt have heard, I was called of God to be an apostle, to witness for Jesus Christ, about whom the prophets wrote. This is the same Jesus to whom was given all power, and holiness, who being raised from the dead himself is a symbol of the resurrection for all believers, in whose name any person may believe, accept in faith and be saved.

You are, of course, included in this group. Blessings on you all, may the grace of God be abundant for you, and may you receive peace from God our Father, the Father also of our Lord Jesus Christ.

First, let me thank God through Christ for all of you. Your faith has created a wonderful impression on many people. As God is my witness, I promise you that I pray for you every day of my life. Included in my prayers is the request that the Lord will work things in such fashion that I will come to Rome to visit you. I'm really anxious to get to preach to you, and to know you all, and to associate in such a manner that we might strengthen each other's faith.

Don't think I haven't tried to come to Rome, but every time something happens to mess up my plans. I know I would learn a great deal from you all.

Actually I am always learning things, from the Greeks, the college sophomores,[1] the wise and the foolish. As a result, I am ready to preach in Rome. I am not ashamed of the good news that I have to preach about Jesus, for in the good news is the very power of God revealed, a power capable of providing salvation to everyone that will believe. The Jews had first shot at this truth, but it is also available to Greeks and anybody else.

The fact that God makes no distinction between races or peoples is a great testimony to the righteousness of God. This is why the scriptures say 'The just shall live by faith.'

The angry disapproval of God is reserved for ungodly deeds, injustices, particularly when such things are perpetrated by persons who know better. God knows they know better!

There is no excuse for not knowing God. Any dunce can just look around at nature and know that God is great, and the Creator. Some persons have foolishly puffed themselves up as if they were very smart and were not thankful to God, but indicated that they knew everything themselves.

As a result these foolish persons tried to fashion their own god,

[1]The Barbarians

some making idols like birds and some like dangerous beasts. As a consequence, God let their evil thought bring on their own degeneracy, and they worshipped money, or power or other false gods and forgot the Creator, the Lord God.

Naturally, these opponents of God went from bad to worse, and the Lord allowed their own evil to destroy their natural inclinations, so that many became homosexuals and other forms of perversion became commonplace with them.

The minds of these evil persons were always directed toward lusts of the flesh, gambling, cheating, murder, gossip, causing young people to be disobedient to their parents, unmerciful people, shameless. The strange thing about these corrupt people is that they continue their evil ways even though they know that the end is death. They even praise others who are evil.

Chap.
2

Actually, there is no excuse for anybody to judge anyone else. Only God is perfect and only God can judge. Why are people always criticizing others when they do the same things themselves or other things just as bad? The long and arduous effort to be good eventually is rewarded in forgiveness, while the hard-headed, hard-hearted, unrelenting, unforgiving attitude toward another person just builds up for the day of God's punishment when God exercises his judgment.

God is planning to balance every person's books in accordance with the deeds on this earth. For those who patiently, firmly, and with real dedication seek to lead an honorable life, for them the Lord has prepared eternal life.

For the person, however, who is contentious, disobeying God's laws, avoiding the truth, for such, whether that person is a Jew or a Greek or from Ohio, there will be provided anguish and punishment. For the person who searches for righteousness, for a better understanding of God, for such persons there will be glory, honor and peace. The Jew has first shot at this, but the non-Jews have in their time the same happy provision.

God does not make distinctions based on race, color, athletic ability, or brain power. Persons who have had a fine opportunity to learn God's law will be judged by that very law, while those who never heard of the law will be judged by God in some other manner, based possibly on a system of handling life without knowledge of God's law.[1]

When a person who does not know the law of God lives a good life, such a person provides his own law, showing that such a person is good-hearted, having an effective conscience, and becomes a witness for justice and mercy without even knowing that such is of God.

[1]I don't think Paul is very clear on this.

As I have it figured, when God begins making decisions on Judgment Day and all the hidden thoughts and deeds of man are revealed by Christ, it goes like this: A full-fledged churchman, who knows the laws of God, supports worthy causes and backs the doctrines of the church, being absolutely sure that he knows what it's all about, constantly teaching the word, preaching, laying down the law—well, such had better be mighty sure that he obeys the law himself.

If you are going to tell others not to steal or cheat, then don't do these things yourself. What about chasing women? If you are going to denounce this then you'd better not chase any yourself. You no doubt rant about the worship of idols, but be careful that you don't worship money or some other form of idol worship. You reflect on God if you teach one thing and practice another.[1]

Sometimes some of you strictly orthodox Jews create real doctrinal problems for the non-Jew. Just like circumcision. If you are circumcised and obey the laws of God this is fine, but if you are circumcised and do not follow God's teachings then you leave the impression that the rite of circumcision is of no use.

This would make one reasonably assume that if a person were not circumcised but obeyed the laws of God, then circumcision would not be necessary for such a person. Legalism is definitely not the answer.

A person is not a Jew simply because he has a big nose, but he is a Jew if he is inside a believing Jew, circumcision or no circumcision of the flesh, for it is the heart of a person, his spirit that makes a person what he is, it is not the outward appearance, the liturgical performances, nor the letter of the law. It is not for the praise of man that a person must live, but for the praise of God.

Chap.

3

This naturally brings up the question of whether or not it is an advantage to be a Jew, circumcised, and knowing about the laws of God. Of course, it must be admitted that God chose the Jewish race as the first to receive his revelation. What if some of the Jews did not accept the revelation, this certainly has no effect on the truth of God. If a person differs with God, the person is automatically wrong. The fact that God is the final judge means that God is always right.

Certainly we are not to do something that is wrong simply to accomplish a good result. God has not empowered us to do his judging and dispense his punishment.

If I tell a lie just to produce a good result, I am still a liar and a sinner. The end does not justify the means. We, as Jews, are no better than anyone else simply because we first received the revelation. There is no one completely righteous, Jew or non-Jew, we are all

[1]It's easier to preach than to practice, but that's no excuse, I guess.

sinners in some manner.

Human beings are troublemakers. Often people are malicious with their talk, destructive, seeking personal gain, their mouths are full of bitterness, they gripe a lot, they are quick to be violent, and they do not seek peace. Often human beings act as if they have no respect for God, his creation, or his laws.

The law puts in plain language what man is to do, and since no person completely adheres to the law, everyone is a sinner. No one then can justify himself, claiming to have lived perfectly according to the law.

Now an understanding of God is available to people who are not reared under the Jewish law. Faith in Jesus Christ unlocks the knowledge about God to all who believe in Christ and are led to an understanding about God. Yet everyone has sinned, whether a person knows the law or not, and everyone has fallen short of measuring up to the glory of God. The justification then comes through the goodness of God and is bestowed on those who seek redemption in Jesus Christ.

God allowed Christ to pay the penalty for the sins of mankind, paying with his own blood, and thereby redeeming mankind from all past sins. Jesus was completely just and fair, and he therefore justifies before God all those that accept him and believe in him.

How can a man possibly boast about being good? Can he judge himself? Certainly he can't win quality points with God by doing good deeds. We must necessarily then conclude that a person does not work his or her way into salvation, but it is a gift of God and based on faith, not deeds only.

God is the God of the Jew and the non-Jew alike. God supports those who arrive at their faith through doctrinal conformance and God also justifies those who arrive at their faith through belief. This doesn't do away with the law, it makes the law a guide, a signpost, an established indicator.

Chap.

4

What about Abraham, thinking of him as a man on this earth? Abraham was not saved by works, for the scriptures say he was saved because of his belief in God. If a person felt that by doing good deeds such a person would have earned the right for salvation, then there is no explanation for the necessity of the grace of the Lord. Good deeds then are a result, or a supplement, but it is faith that produces salvation, and belief that brings one under the grace of God.

David even wrote about the Lord blessing some people who had done no great deeds, but to whom God made revelations because those persons believed the scriptures, saying that indeed fortunate are those who had their errors washed away and their sins forgiven.

Particularly happy is the person who has been forgiven and has no sin left as far as God is concerned. This happens, for God forgives.

It is stupid, however, to think that it only happens to Baptists, or Presbyterians. It is a matter of faith, not alignment. Was Abraham considered no good before he was circumcised and joined the church and then righteous only afterwards? Abraham was circumcised as a symbol, that he might be considered the father of all that believe, whether all the believers were circumcised or not.

Understanding God and drawing near to him is available for those who have been circumcised as well as those who have not been. The promise that Abraham was to be the father of the faithful did not mean just the Jew or any one particular group, for the promise was based on belief in God, not biological production.

If following some set code or observance is the only way to become sons of God and heirs of the kingdom, then there is no place for faith, and the promise then is no good. Yet there must also be law or else there would be no violation of law and no error, but there must be faith in order that there be a way of the grace of God being available. In this way, the goodness of god is made abundant for the Jew who in the procedural line of Abraham studies and is under the law, and yet this same goodness is equally abundant to those who are descendants of the faith of Abraham, but who are not under the ritual concept of the law.

God said of Abraham, 'I have made you a father of many nations.' Abraham held strongly that God was the creator of all life and made all things out of nothing. Even when it seemed to be impossible, Abraham believed that God could do anything, and so Abe hoped for things that did not seem at all reasonable. Abe never gave up and he did not think of his vitality as being gone, in spite of his age, nor did he think it impossible for his wife Sarah to have a son. It didn't rock old Abe back on his heels when God told him that he would have a son in his old age. Believing made it so!

This belief was the great mark of righteousness. This classic picture of hope was not just for old Abe, but a great lesson to all of us. The same mark of righteousness is for us also if we believe that Jesus Christ was raised from the dead by God, that Jesus was killed for our sins, and that he lived again that our existence might be justified, and that we might live again in him.

Chap.

5

Complete faith in Jesus Christ then brings with it peace, for we receive the grace of the Lord and we are presented the hope which is the glory of God for us.

We can even then be able to understand trouble for it teaches us to learn patience, and patience is a real experience to absorb, and this leads us right back to hope. There is no reason to be ashamed of being optimistic, for the love of God is spread everywhere by those of us who have received it from the Holy Ghost.

When everything in the world seemed to be in a hopeless mess, then Jesus died for us and also for the ungodly. This is a tremendous thing, for a person might give his life for a good friend or even maybe for a very good individual, but God showed his extreme love for us by permitting his son Jesus to die for us when we were all bad, all sinners. All the more reason for us to testify to salvation in the name of Jesus.

Certainly if we were given the chance of reconciliation with God while we were his enemies, you know that now that we are in Christ we will be saved by his life. We just can't help but celebrate about this good news, there being atonement for all of us in Jesus Christ.

As sin entered the world through the first person, death became the result of sin, so that all persons must die for all are sinners. Of course, until there was law there was no way of telling when sin occurred or when the law was violated. Yet there has always been death, since Adam blew the whole scene. Just as Adam was responsible for death for all persons, so is Christ responsible for life for all those who seek him. This arrangement is a free gift, it is not earned nor inherited.

Death might be considered by some to be in control of life, but the grace and goodness of God have made available a gift, a gift initiated by the willingness of one Jesus to give his life for people.

Granted that in original sin Adam made all mankind sinners; so Christ made all persons become righteous. The law, of course, appeared and made sin a more obvious circumstance, but the goodness of God outshone the darkness of sin. Sin can be in control only until death, but the grace of the Lord is capable of overcoming death and bringing believers into eternal life through Jesus Christ our Lord.

Chap

6

What about all this reasoning? Should we sin up a storm just so we can receive forgiveness? No way! If we are Christ's we are committed to try to avoid sin. If we are thoroughly in Christ we are conscious of being baptized with him, of dying with him, of arising to a new life in him. If we were with Christ before his death we are surely with him after his death. It is in a sense the old life, the conformance to the written law, this is the life that is gone, and the new life has freed us from death, we have defeated sin. This again means that if we really feel that we died with Christ, we shall then certainly live with him.

Death now has no longer any place for Christ, for he has died, and the allowance is still that you die once; so there is no more death for Christ. Christ died because of sin in the world, but he lives because of the will of God. That's the plan. You persons should feel the same way, that sin is dead and gone and that you live for God, through your belief in Jesus Christ as Lord.

Don't let sin get the best of you, even though your personal desires may be hard to overcome. Don't let other people use you for wrong purposes, but respond only to the will of God. Try to let everything you think and do be done for the sake of the Lord's work. You can readily lick sin, for you are not under the law, but under the grace of God.

Watch there though, boy, don't let not being under the law make you a victim of permissiveness. If you have yielded yourself to be a servant of God then you have fully agreed to do whatever he wants you to do. God has made it plain that sin leads to death, while obedience leads to understanding.

Even though a lot of you have been victim of sin, you have continually known in your heart that the real truth is in the love of God.

Freed then from sin, you are automatically servants, searching for the truth of God. I know all about sin. I know how I have followed the calls of the flesh and so have you, and just as you joyously committed yourselves to evil things, so now must you joyously commit yourselves to things of God.

Nobody has ever acquired anything through sin that was worth keeping. The refreshing joy of your kindness and goodness in the name of Christ is a treasure that you can save and that you can take with you into everlasting life. In short, the pay-off of sin is death, but the gift of God is eternal life in Jesus Christ our Lord.

Chap.
7

You persons who have been pretty well exposed to the church, you know the rules. If you know the rules you know you are not free, but must live under the knowledge of the rules.

Take marriage, for instance, where a woman is bound by the law to her husband.[1] If the husband dies the woman is free.[2] If the husband doesn't die and the wife runs around on him, she is then committing adultery. If the husband dies[3] then the woman can marry again and she is in the clear.[4]

Symbolically speaking then, the death of Christ freed believers from the rules committee and all persons in Christ may seek and obtain a new life. This is to enable believers to be productive for Christ and his kingdom. The lesson is that we now can live afresh with a new spirit and not be under a routine conformance to rules.

Does this mean we pooh-pooh the rules? Definitely not. The rules are a good guide, for sin is made known by its variance with the rules. Just as in my case, I did not know I was being sinful until I came to Christ and became aware of the law and the spirit of the law.

---

[1]And vice versa, Paul.   [2]Some widows really blossom, too.
[3]Like he is supposed to do.
[4]Unmarried fellows as Paul always seem to know a lot about marriage.

It really hurt when I realized I was a selfish sinner and not just a carefree, independent person. When I realized what the rules signified, I then realized how sin was killing my soul.

The true law is spiritual while sin is earthly and involves the desires of the flesh. It is therefore always the spirit at war with the flesh.

Often I find that those things that I know deep down that I shouldn't do, those things I do, and then I naturally don't do some of the things that I know I should do.[1]

It is not the real me that does things that are wrong, but at times the desires of the flesh win out over the feelings of the spirit. It is easy to say "The devil made me do it," when I am looking to excuse myself. I know about the love of the Lord and his rules. It is a constant battle and like everyone I need to be delivered from the war between good and evil that rages within. I serve God with my mind, and the devil with my body, but I know that deliverance and help comes from the Lord Jesus Christ.

Chap.
8

Everything works for persons who live so completely in Christ that the devil can't get a foothold. The rules themselves were not impressive enough to do the job, and so Christ came that in him victory could be assured, and people could change from living by the rules and losing, to living by the spirit and winning. The more a person thinks and dwells on spiritual matters, the less chance there is for thinking of devilish things.

The more a person thinks about selfish, carnal desires, the closer one draws to death, while the more one thinks of spiritual matters, the closer such a person draws to life. This means that those who live to fulfill their own desires fight against God. This is not the case of those who live seeking and learning in the name of Christ. This is the road to victory.

If the spirit of Christ is in you, then also is the spirit of God there and since it was the spirit of God that raised Christ from the dead so it will be that the spirit of God will raise you from the dead.

We are not then to be so grateful for the body and its desires, but grateful that the spirit of God is available, for as many as accept the spirit of God become the children of God. God adopts those who receive his spirit.

The spirit then declares us to be children of God, if children, then heirs, and thereby joint heirs with Christ. We must be willing to suffer for this, though, as nothing comes easy.[2]

The good news is that the bad news of the present time is nothing in comparison with the abounding joy and the glory that is

[1]Paul definitely was a golfer.
[2]You can say that again — and of course Paul does.

ahead.

It seems kind of natural to be greedy, lustful, success-oriented, but when we become more and more children of God we become less and less addicted to worldly matters. Sometimes it seems as if help will never come, and righteousness will never be an easy way, but we are saved by hope.

This is not something that you see, for if you could see it hope wouldn't be necessary, but we must learn to wait with patience.

There is also great help in prayer. The spirit joins us in this and often intercedes in our behalf. The Lord knows of our problems and our hang-ups and he listens to the requests of the spirit in behalf of the believers.

It is a sure thing that matters all finally work out to be good for those who love God, and who respond to God's call for their lives. God knows everything, the past, the present, and the future and God made plans from the first persons created, and God considered his creation successful, and God prepared everything for final victory.

If God then is for us, who can win but God's people? God even was willing to loan his own son to all of us. If God was willing to give us his son, surely God will give all things finally to those who accept the gift of Christ.

Who is going to successfully challenge the believers? For Christ, who died for us and was raised for us, he is the one who stands by our sides.

Who could possibly separate us from this love of Christ? Arthritis? National problems, earache, hard times, loneliness, war? Shall any of these things come between us? Certainly not! Even if we are killed like cattle at the slaughter house, we are saved by the love of Christ.

I am absolutely sure that neither death, nor life, nor angels, nor presidents, nor the IRS, nor daily news, nor future predictions; whether we are flying high or in the depths, nothing can possibly separate us from the love of God which we can find in Christ Jesus, our Lord.

Chap.

9

I promise you people, on a stack of Bibles, that I deeply sorrow and moan over the fact that my Jewish brothers, to whom first came the promises of God, the revelation of his glory, the presentation of his commandments, that these brothers have not accepted Christ. Not all of them, thank goodness, but there are far too few who have come to Christ.

The scripture does not specify that only the biological seed of Abraham are the chosen of God, but all the children who accept and receive the promise of God. There is no reason then to brag about being a Jew or any other race.

God has worked some strange and interesting things. Remember Rebecca, who had twins? Do you remember that it was told her by God that the older or first born twin would serve the younger? This was not a natural procedure in that day, but God had said that he would sponsor Jacob for a purpose but that Mike[1] wouldn't turn out very well.

Does this mean that God has favorites? Not at all. God told Moses, saying, 'I will have mercy on those I choose.' It is not a choice of man but a choice of God, and God has compassion on his own choosing.

The scripture even says that God raised Pharaoh to be a hard-headed terror in order that Pharaoh might be used as an instrument of God. God uses some people one way and some another.

This raises an interesting question as to whether or not a man has any choice. The answer seems to be that you don't argue with God about his ways.[2] A person has no basis for griping about how God made him, short, tall, or what not. This would be the same as the vase complaining to the potter.

Maybe to get his point across, God has sponsored some suffering and destruction. Perhaps God creates problems sometimes so that people may grow in compassion and the mercy of God may be revealed in the acts of his people.

Just like God is as much God for the non-Jew as the Jew. God will call any people his people who respond to his call and turn to him, whether they be in Jerusalem, Cairo, or New York City.

Isaiah said that Israel might suffer great losses, but always there would be some saved, always there will be some few people of God to do his work and accomplish his purpose. If it had been left to man the world would be burned like cities flattened to nothing.

The non-Jew who has attained understanding has done so primarily by faith, for he has not known the rules nor has been reared in the liturgy. The Jew, however, who tried to be righteous by observing the rules and living not in faith but attempting to save himself, such found the rules a stumbling block. In Christ, however, is found the confirmation of the faith of the non-Jew and the power to see the rules and guides and to live in the spirit of Christ.

Chap.
10

I certainly want you Jews to know that I really yearn for all of you to be saved. There are many Jews who have a willingness to be under God, but they have no direction, and seek to establish their own rules and follow them rather than submitting themselves to God. Christ is the goal; the Jews, as well as all others, must seek to find Christ.

[1]Esau [2]Good suggestion.

Moses told all about the law and explained that those who had only the law would have to live under the law, but this does not apply to those whose faith leads them under the inspiration of the Spirit.

The plea is not a question of calling on heaven to send Christ down or calling for the resurrection of the dead, but the plea is really to make the spirit of God a part of a person now. The inspiration is available. If a person believes in Christ as the Lord of Life and believes that God has raised Christ from the dead, then such a person is saved, law or no law. The heart of a person, his own desire, then leads such a person to righteousness.

There is no distinction of persons either, and it matters not whether one be a Jew or a Greek or a Canadian, for whoever truly seeks the Lord will be saved.

Of course, this raises some questions. How can a person believe on someone of whom they have never heard, or have not seen? They can't hear unless someone preaches. Somebody then must always do the preaching. How great it is that there are those beautiful people who preach the good news of Jesus, and bring fresh hopes of peace.

Not everybody listens, unfortunately.[1] Isaiah said there would be people who wouldn't listen. The word, however, will be preached throughout all the earth.

The Jews know about this for Moses said it would be, and that some of the Jews would be upset because other non-Jew types would receive the word. Isaiah said that often he just made people listen,[2] even some that didn't want to hear. Isaiah also complained right bitterly about the Jews who would not come to hear him preach.

Chap.
11

God, of course, has not decided to completely abandon the Jews. I'm a Jew, and therefore a descendant of Abraham, and I'm very much a member of God's team.

Do you remember when the prophet Elijah was so disgusted? Actually, Elijah prayed to God for death, claiming all the good Jews were dead and God told him that there were still 7,000 good ones left in his own country.

The same thing holds true today. There are plenty of good Jews alive and active under God, and subject to his goodness. This is not at all based on their good deeds or what they deserve, but based on the love of God.

Israel had a chance to be the big force for Christianity and they muffed it, and others chosen and inspired by God have come along to do the job, and a lot of Jews are just asleep at the switch. As David used to say, they trap themselves in their own rules.

[1]I've seen them not listening!   [2]That means compulsory chapel.

This doesn't mean their cause is lost, not by a long shot. Actually, it has all turned into a blessing as the non-Jew is thereby immediately assuming an important part in the Christian movement. It is reasonable to think that if good thereby comes of Jews ignoring God, think of how much good will come about when the Jews become Christian.

Admittedly, I spoke very straightforward to the non-Jew and I have hopes then not only of reaching the non-Jew but of stirring up some of the Jews and getting them involved in the cause of Christ.

Listen to a little logic.[1] If the fruit is holy then the tree must be holy, so must be the root of the branches. If some outside piece is grafted and grows into the tree, it becomes a valid part of the tree.

Those Jews who reject Christ represent the cast off branches, and they were removed because of unbelief. A lot of you non-Jews were added because of your faith. Don't be too self-satisfied, though, for if God was willing to throw away some of the natural branches, don't think he'll hesitate to throw you away.

Now you see both the compassion and the strictness of God. Separation is prepared for the ungodly and inclusion is prepared for the believers.

Don't be misled by all of this, or become full of yourself, for all things are under God's plan. The Jews will eventually begin to see and understand their initial error.

Salvation shall come to the Jews. A leader will come who will influence the Jews onto the right path, and God will forgive them. The present Jew may seem to be an enemy, but he is being used to implement the will of God.

The mercy of the Lord is steadily pouring down on all, and the non-Jew may help the Jew by praying for him. No one is perfect, and God made things this way in order that his mercy might be needed and might show itself.

Understanding God is impossible, and there is no way of explaining or anticipating his mercy. Nobody knows or understands the mind of God, and certainly God does not ask for advice from strangers. What's more, nobody makes deals with God.

All things are God's, and to God goes all the glory.

Chap.
12

My suggestion and urgent plea to you is to give yourself to God. The best thing you can do is devote your life to his cause. This means, of course, that you do not do things simply on a basis of the fact that others are doing it.

Be willing to change your way of life and your attitudes, so that you might reflect in your life the will and the glory of God.

First off, don't get too high an opinion of yourself, but take an

[1]Paul really wanted a lot of logic.

honest look. Comparing yourself with other people is not the way to do either, for we are all different. The human body makes a good analogy on this point. We have many different parts of our bodies, and no two have the exact same function; so are all of us members of one body in Christ.

All of us have different abilities. The main thing is to use the ability that you have for a good cause. If you have the gift of prophecy, then prophesy. If you are inclined to the ministry, go to Seminary[1] and become a minister, or if you have teaching talent, begin to teach, while if you are a tent-type evangelist, get your tent up.

People with money should give this freely and without strings being attached.

People with leadership ability, who hold posts as rulers, should show great enthusiasm for their work. When the occasion arises to show mercy do so cheerfully and omit the 'I told you so.'

Don't be a phony, resist evil and stick close with goodness, be friendly and concerned with others, not pushy. Work hard, and show enthusiasm for God and his work.

Sing out when things look good, and wait it out when things look bad. Always be prayerful and in close touch with God. Be concerned with the welfare of others even if they are obnoxious people or persons that don't like you.

Be very generous and look for ways of being nice to other people. Sympathize with people who are sad and celebrate with those who are celebrating.

Try to feel good about everybody, and don't let it make any difference if people are wealthy or poor, smart or stupid.

The old idea of getting even with people is silly kid stuff. If it is at all possible, live peacefully with everybody.

Forget revenge. It will get you nowhere. Just cool it. God has promised that he will tend to all punishments, and do it his way. If you then learn of some local stinker who is thirsty, get him a drink, or if such a one is hungry, treat him to the Pizza Hut.

This often is a good way of teaching a fellow something and it will certainly prick his conscience. Don't let wrong thinking or wrong acting get the best of you, but rise to the occasion and overcome evil with good.

Chap.
13

The only real authority is God and all authority should be related to God. If a person bucks the ways and orders of God then such a person bucks God, and is put on the list for eternal separation.

Rulers who operate under God encourage good deeds, and then good deeds receive good recognition. If a person insists on doing evil then this person should be afraid to face one of God's ministers, for as a representative of God such a person can denounce evil and disturb a conscience.

[1]There are some short cuts, though not recommended.

In general, the same thing applies to a citizen. A citizen should pay his taxes, respect duly constituted authority, and recognize the working of the system.

Don't be a dead beat. Develop a feeling of loving concern for all people. This is the backbone of the law, and a person who is really considerate of others will not steal, commit adultery, lie, covet or anything else mentioned in the Ten Commandments, for concern for one's neighbor would in itself prohibit violation of any of the commandments. Love is all good, and so cannot be against the law.

Get with it! The time is ripe to announce salvation, the new day is close at hand. Let everyone walk openly with no secret or hidden arrangements that are evil, let there be no rioting, or drunkenness, or chasing wild women, let there be no plotting or struggle for power, but try to be similar to Christ, and not concerning yourself all the time with your own human desires.

Chap.

14

There are some persons who are not strong in the faith, just borderline interested. Well, include them when you meet, but don't have big church arguments when they are present as they will misunderstand. Some people have different beliefs about what to eat, what to wear, or the like. Be understanding. If a person doesn't want to eat, don't insist and if another person wants three helpings, let such a one have three helpings, with no smart remarks.

Anyway, who has the right to say what is good and proper anyway. People don't have to all think alike. Some people want Wednesday afternoon off, and others Thursday.[1] So what?

The main thing is to realize that every day is God's day and everything that a person does should be done with the thought of pleasing God.

There is no such thing as living and dying all alone, for we are God's, and if we live we are under God's regime or if we die we are under his regime. This is the reason that Christ died and rose from the dead, in order that it might be recognized that he is the Lord of the living as well as Lord of the dead.

Why then do people feel free to criticise other people? We are all going to face final judgment, that's when the truth comes forth!

The Lord has said, 'The day shall come when every knee shall bow and every tongue confess to God'; so we are all going to be judged. There should be no preliminary judging, for only the last one counts.

If you want to think about something though, think about being certain that you are not a cause for trouble for anyone else.

I know of a fact, I learned this through my experience with Jesus Christ, that there is nothing unclean among all things created

[1]Some want more than this.

by God. We can make some things unclean by our use of them or outlook on some things.

If you are doing something that is causing great problems for another person, the answer is to quit doing what you're doing, don't just get rid of the other person.

Food and drink actually have nothing to do with the kingdom of God,[1] but understanding, peace, and joy are the meat and drink of the kingdom of God. The person who operates under this philosophy serves Christ and is therefore approved by God and usually even by other persons.

The sensible thing then is to pursue the matters that make for peace, and for the increase in understanding.

All things are actually clean, but if a person is reared thinking it is bad to eat ham and he really thinks this, then let him skip the ham when it is served.

It is not good to eat anything or drink anything that will offend another person or influence them to do wrong. A person should not feel that everyone should do or believe in every particular exactly as they do. If a person is in doubt about eating something the person should skip it. Good faith is accompanied by a good feeling, not worries and debates.

Chap.
15

Some of us who are tough and experienced should always be willing to help and encourage those who are weak and problem prone. Try to be a good neighbor and do not always please yourself. Christ didn't even always do what he wanted to do. Christ had to put up with a lot of static that had nothing to do with him.

The Old Testament was written for our better understanding, to teach us patience and to give comfort. I certainly hope God will encourage you to be fair-minded in dealing with others for the sake of Christ, whom you represent. It is helpful to be united in love for one another as well as in your common love for Christ and in this spirit worship and praise the Lord.

Now the way I look at it is that Jesus Christ was a minister, primarily in the framework of the established synagogue, to reform it, of course, and to reassure the Jews about the promises of God. Jesus, however, stated that his mercy and his truth was also for the non-Jew and there are many references telling the non-Jew to rejoice.

Isaiah, in telling about the coming of Christ in the Old Testament, said that there would be a descendant of Jesse who would rule over the non-Jew and that the non-Jew would put complete trust in him.

May the God of hope then fill you with joy and peace as you accept this truth, and then you may live in hope because of the

---

[1]Except church people really like to eat.

power of the Holy Spirit.

I am convinced that you people to whom I am writing are a great outfit, full of goodness and knowledge, and even able to disagree without being disagreeable.

Because of the grace of the Lord that is within me I have felt free to write a bit more openly to you than would normally be wise. The reason primarily is that I feel called of God to minister for Jesus Christ to the non-Jew, in order that I might teach the non-Jew to make acceptable offerings to God, and that all these things might be to the glory of God through Jesus Christ.

I wouldn't dare make up anything, but I speak only the things that I have been told by experience in Christ that I may say convincingly.

The idea, of course, is to make the non-Jew obedient in word and deed and so I testify to the signs and wonders of the power of the Spirit of God which I have seen in action as I have traveled everywhere preaching the good news of Jesus Christ.

Also I have preached the good news in places where the name of Jesus had never been uttered, and so I have not been building on another man's work.[1] This also fulfills the Old Testament prophesy that says 'they shall understand who have never seen or heard of the Messiah.'

Actually, all these missionary trips and family night suppers have kept me from coming to Rome. I'm planning to come at last. First, I have to go to Jerusalem, then I'll head for Spain, stopping by Rome. I'm sure you'll help get me to Spain after I've been around awhile.

Interestingly enough, I have some benevolent money to take to Jerusalem from some of the churches of New England and the Deep South.

These gifts were given gladly as the non-Jews in these areas felt a great appreciation and were interested in helping the poor in Jerusalem. As soon as I have delivered the money and gotten a receipt I will come to see you on my way to Spain. I know Christ will be blessing my visit with you all.

Pray for me, please. Particularly pray for my deliverance from the unbelievers around Jerusalem, and pray that the church in Jerusalem will be pleased and not insulted by the benevolent money. Pray also that circumstances will enable me to come to Rome in a joyous way, and that my visit will refresh you and will work to fulfill the will of God. Blessings on you all, and may God's peace be with you always.

---

[1]There is nothing wrong with building on another's work, though, Paul. (Just for the record.)

Let me add a few personal notes to this letter as I don't have time to write people individually.[1] Tell Jeanette,[2] God's servant at the little town of Kerrville,[3] that I said 'hello.' Be sure and treat her well and help her in any way she asks, as she has done many very fine things and is busy in the Lord's work.

Tell Priscilla and John Alden 'hi' for me, for this couple has risked every kind of danger for me as well as for the protestant churches everywhere. My blessings also go to the little group that uses the Alden home as a church.

Give my greeting to ole Pappy[4] who was the first to step forward for Christ in New Zealand. My best to Mary, who was so helpful to me.

My best regards to June and Andy, two who were in the pen with me, and who actually were Christians before I was.

Tell Laurie[5] I love her,[6] for she is devoted to Christ. Give my best also to Ben Rose,[7] Al,[8] and Clayton.[9] Remember me to the entire Gordon family,[10] and also to Little John.[11] Greetings also to the entire Page[12] family.

Don't forget to say 'hello' for me to the Powells[13] as well as Bob Smith.[14]

Tell my mother I'm looking forward to seeing her, and the same goes for Rufus and his mother. My regards also to Raymond,[15] Lon,[16] Felix,[17] Marcus,[18] Orian,[19] and all the group on the Divide.

Greetings also to Phil,[20] Julia, Ned,[21] and his sister, as well as Oliver[22] and the Christian group that is with them.

Do all this greeting with a holy kiss.[23]

Another afterthought which I should have put in the main body of the letter is to be careful about contentious and argument prone people. Avoid them. These loud mouths are only interested in themselves and in attracting attention.

You people have established a real good reputation for yourselves and I am greatly pleased. I would encourage you again to be greatly interested in everything that is good and just move away or look dumb when evil occasions arise.

---

[1]Thank you, Paul, thank you. It's true today, too. [2]Phoebe
[3]Cenchreae [4]Epaenetus [5]Ampliatus [6]They finally made a song of it.
[7]Urban [8]Strachys [9]Apelles [10]Aristobulus [11]Herodion [12]Narcissus
[13]Tryphena and Tryphosa [14]Persis [15]Asyncritus [16]Phlegon
[17]Hermes [18]Patrobas [19]Hermas [20]Philologus [21]Nereus [22]Olympas
[23]So Paul got all this "kiss on the cheek" going.

1st LETTER TO THE CORINTHIANS

Christian Friends
Church of God
Corinth, Greece

Dear Believers in Christ:

This letter is from Paul, an apostle of Jesus Christ, and I know you remember me. There are about four fellows actually writing this letter, but as usual I'm telling them what to say.

Blessings on each of you, grace be to you, and peace from God our Father and from our Lord Jesus Christ. I often thank God for you and the love he has given you in Christ. I'm sure that every area of your life has been enriched since you professed your faith in Christ. About the only real blessing left for you is the second coming of Jesus, who will at that time seal you and mark you pure, so that you will be saved on judgment day. God has faithfully promised that this will be the case.

Let me urge you all not to get into church arguments. Disagreeing will get you nowhere. I have heard rumors, however, from the Martha Mitchell[1] family that there is dissension in your church.

It is reported that there are some factions who claim to follow Paul, others who follow Frank Blair,[2] still others who follow Peale,[3] and some who simply follow Christ.

How goofy can you get? Was Paul crucified? Were you baptized in the name of Paul? You can't divide Christ. I'm glad I didn't baptize but two of you and I hope they understand that I baptized in the name of Christ.

In the first place, Christ did not commission me to do a lot of baptizing, but to preach, and even in preaching not to rely on the cuteness of phraseology, lest the story of the cross lose some of its meaning. Preaching about the cross seems foolish to the agnostic, but it is the power of God to those who believe.

The Old Testament states that God will bring to nothing the so-called wisdom of the sharpies. Where are all the great thinkers and disputers? These worldly minded people never could come to a conclusion about God, and so God decided to reveal his truth through preaching.

The Jews always want some type of magic sign and the Greeks want some deep reasoning, but we simply teach Jesus, crucified. This really stumps the Jews and seems silly to the Greeks.

This is not true for those Jews and Greeks chosen by God to receive his power. God is ten times smarter than any man even on

[1]Chloe   [2]Apollos   [3]Cephas

God's off-day and God at his weakest is stronger than any man could ever be at his peak.

Just look around you. You don't see many of the top dogs, big thinkers, big money politicians, this type; not many of these are called by God. God has chosen the apparently small and unimportant matters to be eventually the most important, and some of the trivial things God has chosen to be the most lasting and impressive. This is done so that man will not be able to glory in himself and his own accomplishments.

Any time you wish to recognize greatness and extend glory, do it to God, for you are believers in Christ, and God has made Christ the revealer to us of wisdom, understanding, goodness, and finally redemption. Glory then, not in man, but in God.

Chap.

2

When I preached in your church I did not give any fancy, polished sermons, with all kinds of complicated reasoning. I merely preached to you Jesus Christ, crucified and risen from the dead.[1] I didn't use snappy language either, for I did not want to win you with words, but to win you with the spirit of God. Your faith then should not be rooted in the word of men, but in the power and spirit of God.

Our Christian preaching testifies to the mysterious wisdom of God. It is not known or understood by most of the big shot leaders, for if the rulers had known what we know, then they would not have crucified Christ.

It is promised, however, to all of us believers that no one has ever seen nor has anyone ever heard of, nor has man ever imagined the things which the Lord has prepared for all those that love him. Now God has revealed a good inkling of these things to some of us through his spirit.

Even as no one knows what is in another man's mind, so much more is the case of our not knowing what is in the mind of God.

We have actually received the spirit of God now rather than the selfish spirit of the world, and these things that are God's will.

Inspired by the Holy Ghost, we then present things that are spiritual and these things are to be received as spiritual instruction, and not worldly arrangements.

Most people think all such talk is foolishness, as they believe only in a practical existence, living without the knowledge or inspiration of the spirit of God.

A purely spiritual person does not worry about worldly matters, and even though no one knows the mind of God, those of us who follow Christ at least have a revelation in the mind of Christ.

---

[1]It's still the best preaching.

When I preached to you in Corinth I could not speak essentially in spiritual terms as this was beyond your grasp. Naturally, I treated you as babies in the spiritual area and I fed you milk more than meat. Now it's different. You have grown spiritually and I can lay it on the line.

Of course, you obviously are not yet very spiritual, but quite worldly, for you have dissension and strife among you. This business of bragging about who baptized you is for the birds. Whether it is Paul, or Frank Blair, or Peale, what does it matter? All of us work for Christ. Maybe I sowed the seed and Blair watered it, but the growth is always dependent on God. It doesn't matter who plants or who waters, the whole thing depends on God.

We are all workers, pulling together in a common cause. You are the result, the building, so to speak. By the grace of God I have laid the foundation and another has added a floor or two. It is permissible to add to the building as long as the foundation is Jesus Christ. This foundation must remain intact.

A person may put all kinds of things on top of the foundation of belief in Christ, but all these things are perishable, only the foundation is eternal. If a person adds creditably to the building then the person will be rewarded. If a person's work perishes, let it perish, for as long as a person's life is based on belief in Jesus that person shall be saved.

Actually, each of you is really a little church of God. It is very understandable then that God takes a dim view of anyone mistreating their body, for it is God's little temple.

Another thing about which I warn you is getting to be too smart. This causes a person to begin to think more of a man's wisdom than of God's; so remember how little you really know, and praise God.

God knows about pompous smartheads, how vain they are, and God doesn't care for this. Don't get all steamed up about how wonderful mankind is.

Actually, you are plenty fortunate, for all things are yours, you who believe in Christ. It doesn't matter whether you were baptized by Paul, Blair, or Peal, don't worry either about the world, or life or death, or the sad state of affairs today, or the bad days ahead, don't worry for you are Christ's, and Christ is God's.

Please consider us ministers of Christ, and persons responsible for attending to godly matters. Of course, we have to be faithful to be stewards for the Lord.

It really doesn't matter to me what others may think about me as I am only trying to please God. You all should quit judging people anyway, as there is only one real judgment that counts and that is God's on judgment day.

It seemed a good idea for me to use myself and Frank Blair as examples; so that you would know not to listen to judgments of men, and not therefore to get icky with each other. You are all different because God made you different. What's more, any talent or attribute that you have God gave you, it was not earned; so don't boast.

It seems to me at times that God has fixed things so that those of us who are apostles are always in the greatest difficulty. You stand before the world as successful people, with honor, while we are despised, kicked around, underfed, no place to sleep, no clothes at all, working our fingers to the bone,[1] yet we extend blessings, accept punishment, and see ourselves treated like dirty dogs. I'm really not trying to shame you, but to warn you of some of the dangers on the Christian highway.

There are plenty of instructors and know-it-alls teaching you, but there is only one Christ; I have preached to you of this Christ and I urge you to follow me in this matter of being Christian.

As a result, I have sent Tim to you, one I count as a son, faithful to the Lord, and he will refresh you in the Pauline doctrines.

There may be some who don't care for my not coming myself, but I will come as soon as I can. When I do come I will preach with power and not rely on tricky words. The kingdom of God is not found in words but in power.

How do you want me to come to you, as a school man with a switch, or in love and kindness?

Chap.

5

Word has reached me that the sexual promiscuity of many of you is at an advanced state. It is even reported that one fellow has had relations with his stepmother. Apparently, you have done nothing about this.

Although I am absent in the body, I am in Corinth in spirit and I tell you to drum that person out of the church. You must do this to preserve the spirit that is with you. In fact, if you're not careful, everybody will get in the act, just as a bad smell spreads across a room.

Once before I wrote you not to fool around with women chasers, but of course you have to have some association with such or you wouldn't get to associate with anybody much. It is a difficult problem, but I am now convinced that you need to separate yourselves from bad company, such as drunkards, loud mouths, money grabbers, women chasers, or extortioners.

A wicked person like the one who brought on all this discourse should be kicked out of your crowd. God will judge him, just keep away from him.

[1]Paul gets a little carried away here.

Don't try to duck the issue by saying that it is a matter of law and if there is a legal wrong let the court try him. No. You do something. Eventually, the believers will rule the world anyway; so just exercise a little leadership.

Didn't you know that we, as believers, will be called upon to judge angels?[1] Haven't you one person in your church that is capable of making a decision? There is no point in taking a church matter before a criminal court.

Don't take people to court who are Christian. Act Christian and settle things peacefully among yourselves. Don't you know that the unrighteous are going to be socked plenty by the Lord?

Don't be fooled. The mean, promiscuous, conniving, drunkard types will never make it the kingdom of God. Some of you were just this kind before you were converted, but now you are cleaned in the name of Christ.

Because of my attitude of love, anything is lawful for me, but not everything is proper. I am not going to be a victim of my excesses. The good steaks are meant for the belly and the belly made to accommodate good steaks, but God is not keeping these things permanently.

Remember that your bodies are the churches of our Lord and they are not to be misused and taken into whore houses. If a man joins with a prostitute the two, though temporarily, become one body. Is that a place for the church of Christ? God forbid.

Stay clear of prostitutes. Most sins are outside the body, but joining with a prostitute is within the body and is a definite no-no. Remember, your body is like a temple for God, keep it clean and fresh. You have been bought with a price, therefore glory God in your body as well as in your spirit.

Some of you have written me asking some difficult questions on behavior. I'll tell you bluntly what I think, as I am always direct.

You have asked about sexual relations and my opinion is that it is preferable for a man never to touch a woman.[2] Since this doesn't seem feasible with most of you, I recommend marriage.[3]

The husband and the wife should be kind to each other. The wife should remember that in consenting to marriage she surrenders her body to the husband, and vice the versa.[4]

It is understandable that there will be periods of separation for missions, sickness, prayer vigils. These are acceptable and then you should be together again.

If you just can't stand being single or a widow, then get

---

[1]I didn't know it. [2]Paul's opinion. Very few agree with Paul.
[3]Marriage is first choice, not second. Two strikes on Paul.
[4]A hit! No double standard for Paul.

married. It is better   to marry than to burn.[1] God has said that a
marriage is supposed to work, and the two involved are to work at
making it work.

Now back to my own opinion. If one of the marriage partners is
a Christian and the other not one, let the Christian be capable of
being good enough for two, and then the children will be as holy as
any other kids.

If a non-Christian husband or wife leave the other, let that one
go. Good riddance. Forget it! If one person is a Christian and married
to a non-Christian, then the Christian should try to convert the
other. Let everyone do his own thing as God has made him. This is
what I teach in the church.

When a person feels the call of God and turns to Christ let that
person come just as he or she is. It is not necessary to be circumcised,
or to wear particular robes, etc. Also a person called to work for the
Lord doesn't have to quit his business as God encourages a person to
work for the Lord wherever that person is, and to use the skills given
by God.

Even if you are a servant, you don't have to rebel, if you are
God's you are free in the Lord. If you are free of bondage, that is
fine, remain free, but continue in the Lord's work.

As for the matter of virginity, the Lord has not yet revealed
anything to me in this regard.[2] I'll tell you my own opinion, though.
I think it is good for a man to be a virgin. Nevertheless, if a fellow
has a wife he should stick to her. If a man's wife has died or just run
away with a camel driver, don't get married again. If you do marry
again though, it is all right.

Nobody has much time on this earth anyway so there is no
reason to worry too much about details of marrying, weeping and
sadness, hilarity and great joy, big business deals for all these things
soon pass away.

One more time, now, let me tell you that a person that never
marries can spend more time thinking about the Lord, for a married
person must spend a lot of time trying to please a husband or a wife.
In summary, I think everybody would be happier single.[3]

Chap.
8

There is a big discussion about whether or not to buy barbecue
on Monday that was offered to an idol on Sunday. Well, we know
that idols are nothing and so it makes no difference whatsoever.
There is but one God as far as we are concerned and one Lord and
Savior, Jesus Christ.

Not everybody understands this; so I recommend that you be

[1]Some cutie must have really bounced Paul hard.
[2]Thank you, Paul, for admitting it.
[3]No wonder Paul was often run out of town.

careful not to mislead people. If it seems improper for you to eat pagan pig, don't eat it. If you think it might create the wrong impression on others, don't eat it.

Don't do anything to cause the weak to stumble, for you then offend the Christ that you serve. If eating meat misleads a friend, don't eat it.

Chap.
9

Although I may not be considered an apostle to everybody, I surely am one to you folks at Corinth. If it weren't for me you all wouldn't even know about the Lord Jesus, the same Lord Jesus that I have actually seen.

I am saying this because some may say 'Who does this bird think he is, writing us a bunch of instructions?' I exercise merely the same right that a man who plants a vineyard has. Surely he can enjoy the grapes. Can't a rancher eat one of his steers?

This is not just my own reasoning, but the scriptures say the same thing, such as 'Thou shalt not muzzle the mouth of the ox that treadeth the corn.' Just like a man plowing, surely he does this in the hope of planting and then enjoying the produce.

We have taught you all spiritual things and we expect spiritual results. We must all share the blessings and joys of the Lord, no matter on what side of the altar we stand. Nevertheless, the Lord has made it plain that we are to practice what we preach.

Don't think I'm bragging about my position. I take none of the credit, for God has actually forced me into this. I have to preach the gospel! If a person preaches the gospel willingly and easily there is real reward in this, but if you're jerked out of the saddle as I was and forced to preach, then special powers and pressures are given to you.

In one way, I am completely free in that I am my own boss, and yet I am dedicated to be a servant to all mankind.

I actually try to get the job done with everybody. When I teach the Jews, I teach from my Jewish background, to the legalists I am sensitive to their training, and to those who know no law I deal with them accordingly.

When preaching to the disadvantaged I do not speak patronizingly but as one of them, for I am always seeking to save the lost.

Life is something like a track event. Everyone runs like mad to win and receive the prize. In track it is just a trophy or a medal, but in life the pay-off is in the effort and the striving. As for me, I really work at it. I don't beat the air with my fists, but I exercise self-control, and I desperately strive to practice what I preach.

Chap.
10

Let me clear up a few things about your forefathers. I know you enjoy telling of them being guided by day with a cloud and a pillar of fire by night, that the miracle of the Red Sea was for their benefit, and that all of them lived under the Ten Commandments. Well, they weren't all good by a long shot.

In fact, the record states that 'they sat down to eat and drink and rose up to play.' This play mainly referred to chasing wild women. Some of them were punished with death in the wilderness. You don't want to be like they were. A lot of those old timers griped about the journey and complained about God. Don't let any of that get started among you. These early incidents are recorded as examples or lessons for us.

Another thing, don't get over-confident about your goodness as it is easy to fall, particularly if you think you've got life licked.

Temptations are part of life. They exist for everyone, but God sees to it that either you are not tempted beyond your ability to overcome, or else God provides some other way out.

Please don't take to worshipping idols, money, or fun and games. Our whole religion is quite simple when we realize that the wine we drink is a sign of Christ, and the bread we eat is also testimony to Christ, and we are therefore really all one body in Christ.

The Jews have their way of doing things and the non-Jews have their way. Some of the giving of the non-Jews is to the devil. You can't drink with the devil and the Lord also. Why do some of you try to make God mad?

Use a little common sense. Since my whole life is devoted to the Lord I do not have to operate under the law, but I observe the law frequently for the sake of expediency. Since my motives are pure I can actually do anything I wish to do, but not everything is good or helpful; so I use a little common sense.

Don't be concerned with how much money you make either, but you can be concerned with helping someone else make money.

If you are invited to some type of pagan feast or Chamber of Commerce banquet and you decide to go, don't worry about whether or not the food is kosher or well cooked. It won't hurt you, unless it creates a bad impression on someone else, then skip it.

The big point is attitude. Everything you do or say should be to the glory of God, and should not be offensive to anyone.

I please everybody in everything because I am unselfish and I seek only to save souls.[1]

Chap.
11

I am greatly delighted to get a report that you all remember some of my sermons and that you are following me even as I follow Christ.

___

[1]Great! Why did some people kick you out of town, though?

In principle, the chain of command goes like this; God is in charge of Christ, Christ is in charge of man, and man is in charge of woman.[1]

A man should always take off his hat in church.[2] Every woman should wear a hat in church.[3] If she doesn't she should have her head shaved. These differences are because woman was made from man and not vice versa, and also the woman was created for the man. Nevertheless, the man and the woman both complement each other, and both are made by God; so this evens things up.

Be sensible. Shouldn't a woman cover her long hair before praying? As for man, he shouldn't have long hair, it isn't natural. Long hair is a glory to a woman, however, as it is a sign of her need for covering. There is no reason for a big argument about this, however, as we have no church rules on it.

The hair business is of no great consequence, but the report of divisions in the church is quite disturbing. Also I am told that you are having big banquets and getting drunk in the Fellowship Hall. You should just stick to communion together and do your eating and drinking at home.

I told you exactly how things were to be done in communion, instructions that I received directly from the Lord. I remind you that on the same night on which the Lord Jesus was betrayed he took bread, and when he had asked the blessing, he broke the bread and said, "Take, eat this, it represents my body broken for you, do this as a memorial service for me."

In the same manner also Jesus took the cup, and when he had taken a sip, he handed it to them and said, "This cup is a new arrangement symbolizing my blood. Every time you drink this, do so as a memorial service to me. As often as you eat this bread and drink this cup you remind yourself and others of my death. This will continue until I come again.

"If anyone participates in this service who does not profess faith in me, such a one is as guilty as those who put me to death."

Take a good look at yourself then before taking communion. Be certain that you come to communion as a memorial service for Christ. If you are hungry or thirsty, eat and drink at home. There are some other details but I will attend to them when I come in person.[4]

Chap.

12

Now let me unload on you a bit about spiritual gifts. In the first place, no one can sincerely testify that Jesus is Lord unless such a person is full of the Holy Spirit; so anybody that denounces Jesus is not speaking with the blessing of God.

[1]That's our Paul, fellows. Strike one on Paul again.
[2]Except in West Texas? [3]Paul really had a bunch of his own opinions.
[4]You gave them enough, Paul, for a few hundred years.

There are all types of abilities and gifts, but there is only one
Lord. There are all types of leaders and systems of church
government, but only one Lord.

Some believers are blessed with good horse sense, some have
great book knowledge, others have a great faith, some have the
power to heal, or to work miracles, some can prophesy, while others
speak in strange tongues. All these varied attributes are traced back
to the Holy Spirit.

A good analogy is the human body, which has all types of
different parts, yet together the parts make one body. All those who
accept Christ are baptized into one body, Jews and non-Jews, slave
or free, and all are bound together in Christ.

Just like the human body. It is not one member, but many.
Nobody thinks the foot is not part of the body simply because it is
not the hand. The ear doesn't complain to the eye that it is not of
the body because it isn't the eye. If the whole body was the eye then
there'd be no hearing. If the whole body was an ear, how could we
smell? God put all the members together, each to its own function,
yet all together to form the body.

As a consequence, no part of the body can lord over any other
part. Certainly the eye couldn't tell the hand it has no use for it.
Strangely enough, the more fragile the part of the body seems to be
the more necessary it seems to be.

Some parts of the body that seem less attractive are really the
most necessary for functioning. God wisely made the less usual parts
more attractive, for a sense of balance.

There should be no division in the body. All the parts of the
body should cooperate with each other, and if one part hurts then
every part feels the pain.

Now bear in mind that you are the body of Christ and each
member a distinct part of the body of Christ. God planned that some
would be apostles, some prophets, then teachers, workers of
miracles, healers, church politicians, those who speak in tongues. Can
everybody be an apostle? Everybody a teacher, or can everybody
work miracles, perform healings, or speak in tongues? Of course not,
thank goodness.

The thing to do is to develop the best talent that you have, and
yet I can tell you about a shortcut to the goal.   Chap.
                                                                    13

This shortcut is love toward all of God's creations. For if you
have a gift of beautiful speech and yet do not have love in your heart
you will be no more effective than tumbling tin cans, and though
you have prophetic vision and great understanding, if you have such
faith that you can move mountains or create corporations, and you
do not operate with love, you are nothing.

Even if you are generous, giving to the poor regularly, or risking
your life for a cause, and do not have love in your heart, it is all

wasted.

Love puts up with anything, is kind, is not envious, is not egocentric, doesn't act outlandishly, is not selfish, nor is love easily provoked.

Love does not look for what is wrong, but for what is right, does not admire evil but admires good. Love believes what it hears, is always hopeful, endures all abuses. Love never fails. Prophecies fail, tongues stop wagging, knowledge disappears and changes.

Actually, on this earth we only know in part anyway; so we only prophesy in part. When the day of perfection comes then all the part knowledge is a goner.

When a person is a child, the person speaks as a child and has a child's understanding, but when one becomes an adult childish things are put away,[1] for we see in this world as if through dark glasses, but eventually we will see clearly. Now we know in part, but finally we will know everything about ourselves, even as we are known by God.

In summary, there are three basic truths, faith, hope, love, these are the three, but the most important of these is love.

Chap.
14

Develop love. There is nothing wrong with speaking in tongues, but it doesn't do people much good as no one much understands and apparently the speaker is talking only to God. An evangelist, however, speaks to men, encouraging them and leading them to Christ. A person that speaks in an unknown tongue may be teaching himself, but the evangelist is building up the church.

If it were left up to me there would be no speaking in tongues, but only evangelists. I must insist that preaching to be understood is far better than speaking and not being understood.

What good would it do for me to come to you speaking in tongues? How would you learn anything? Even a violin or a trumpet does not make music unless it can be interpreted in a beat or understandable notes. If the guy with the trumpet gives an unfamiliar toot the army doesn't know whether to charge or retreat.[2]

It's the same thing. Unless you speak so as to be understood there is no point in it. If I speak and you don't understand me, what's the point? I might as well be a duck quacking. If you really seek a spiritual gift, seek one that is productive.

If you find yourself speaking in an unknown tongue, start praying that an interpretation may come to you, for a spiritual experience must bear fruit or it ceases to be a spiritual experience. If you are asked to lead in prayer and you break out in an unknown tongue, how will people know when the prayer is óver or the choir to start the sevenfold Amen? You have no doubt given a fine prayer, but it hasn't helped the church.

[1] I know an exception to the case
[2] And don't ever give an army a choice!

I admit that sometimes I speak in tongues, yet I would prefer to speak five words in church that are understood than 10,000 words in an unknown tongue. If you insist on being mysterious be so about mischief, not good things or clear understanding.

In the old law book it is recorded "for the benefit of impressing people who are generally ignorant will I speak in tongues they do not understand, saith the Lord."

Speaking in tongues are for a sign, not to the unbelievers, but to the believers. Good preaching is the thing that helps unbelievers.

Suppose everybody in church spoke in tongues. There would be bedlam. If one unbeliever accidentally then came to church he'd think everybody had blown their top. If this same person, however, had accidentally come to church and there heard good preaching, he might be converted and praise God.

When you get together at church, some for singing, some for theological discussion, some for a tongue chance, some seeking a revelation, bear in mind that everything must be for the good of the church.

If the tongue speaking thing does start in a church, let it be done in the presence of only two people, at the most three, and let one of them try to interpret. If there is no one to interpret, then hush. If the evangelist starts speaking, let the two or three nearest him decide if he's got anything worth the others hearing. In this way take turns, so that not everybody at church is speaking at the same time.

God is the originator of order, not confusion, and of peace, not bedlam.

As for women, let them keep absolutely quiet in church. Don't say a word.[1] What's more, if they want to learn something, let them ask their husbands, and wait to get home to do this.[2] I tell you it is a shame for a woman to speak in the church.

If any one of you men think you are an evangelist or truly spiritual, you will know then that what I have to say is good stuff. If you want to be stupid, that's OK by me. Stay that way.

In summary then, yearn to be an evangelist, don't forbid anyone to speak in tongues, but let all things be done decently and in order.

Chap.

15

Let me remind you about what I preached to you when I was in Corinth. I was only telling you what I knew directly, that Jesus died for our sins, just as the Old Testament said, that he was buried and rose again from the dead on the third day. Believe on this and you are saved.

---

[1] Strike two on Paul.
[2] Suppose the husband doesn't go to church?

Certainly you should believe for he was seen by N. Peale, then all the twelve apostles, and plus them about 500 others, most of whom are alive today and testify to this fact.

James, the present leader of the home church in Jerusalem, saw the risen Christ and finally he appeared to me, though I saw him as one who was lifted out of time for a moment.

I really don't think of myself as an apostle, if so certainly the least important one, for I persecuted the church before I saw the risen Lord. It is the grace and goodness of God that has put me in action for Christ, so that I have been able to do more than anyone else. This is God's doing, though, and not my own.[1]

Whether you were influenced by me or someone else, nevertheless you now believe.

Let's reason a bit. We preach that Christ rose from the dead. Why do some of your people question the fact of the resurrection?

If there is no resurrection, then Christ didn't rise, then if Christ didn't rise we are not preaching but blowing hot air, and there is no point in faith. In fact, if Christ isn't risen from the dead then we are liars, because we have affirmed that God raised him and that we saw him. If there is no resurrection, then this isn't true.

If Christ isn't risen then our preaching is wasted and those who have previously died are total goners. Being Christian is a bunch of painful foolishness and a poor way to live if Christ is not risen.

The truth is, however, that Christ is risen, and is the first great blessing to those who have already died. Just as death came into the world through man, so is death conquered by a person; for as in Adam all death originated, so in Christ may all become alive in a new life.

There will come a time when Christ will take over the world, with full power and authority, and he will present the world to God. Christ must rule on earth until all opposition to him and his teaching has been squelched. The last enemy to go will be death.

When Christ has put all things on earth under his control, then Christ will turn everything over to God. This is why we know the dead in Christ shall live.

What do we have to fear in life? Nothing. I wasn't afraid of the wild beasts or the facing of death because I knew there was a resurrection in Christ.

Adopt a decent philosophy then. Don't buy that old slogan 'eat, drink and be merry for tomorrow we die.' This is based on the false idea that death is the end. Not so.

Pursue righteousness, speak friendly, also drive friendly, and declare the truth of God to those who have not heard of him.

Some people naturally wonder how the dead are raised and with what body. All I know is that it must be like a seed. Unless the seed

[1]It's Paul's evaluation though.

dies it cannot become a new plant. What we really are then is not just the body, but an individual seed, some one kind, some another, just as there is wheat, corn, or barley. God gives to each seed a distinct body in accordance with God's will.

There are all types of bodies. Just as there are fish bodies, beast bodies, and bird bodies, so there are earthly bodies and heavenly bodies.[1] The attributes of the earthly bodies are different from the heavenly ones. Each body has its own glory just as each star its own glory, the moon has its, the sun has its glory, too.

The resurrection then means that the seed, which is a man, dies usually old and decayed, and then is raised without blemish. The natural or earthly body dies and the heavenly body arises. Mankind, as represented by Adam, started out as a living soul, but ends up as a living spirit.

Mankind, as an earthly creature, responded to the environment and was a natural person, but after the resurrection we will respond to the heavenly environment and the spiritual will replace the natural.

Flesh and blood, sore feet, tired eyes, and aching backs have no place in heaven, as there is no mixture of bad and good in the resurrected life. Strangely enough, not everybody will die, for there will be some alive at the end of the world.

The end will be sudden, almost as if signaled by the sound of a trumpet. The dead shall rise in their spiritual form and those of us left alive will be transformed on the spot.[2] When this happens, when all corruption disappears, death is defeated.

So death doesn't have a sting and the grave is just a station break. Thanks be to God who gives us this marvelous victory through our Lord Jesus Christ.

Because of this wonderful news I urge you people to be steady in the boat, busy doing the work of the Lord, for you are not wasting your time a bit when you work for God.

Chap.
16

Now let me talk to you a bit about money. I don't want to have to scrounge and carry on about the offerings to the church when I come. The plan is simple. The first of every week each one of you set aside a generous gift for the church so that the offering will already have been taken when I get there.[3]

When I come to Corinth you can tell me who you have selected to take the benevolent gifts to Jerusalem. I may even go with them.

I will visit you when I come to eastern Europe. I might even spend the winter with you. I do expect to spend a little time at Sydney, Australia, for I have a cordial invitation to preach there and

[1]Now and then somebody has a sample.
[2]Paul thought he would live to see it.   [3]Great plan!

it is a great challenge.

If Tim travels your way look out for him as he is a fine Christian. Don't mistreat that young fellow as I think a great deal of him. As for Frank Blair, he will come sometime in the future but at present he is busily engaged elsewhere.

Act like good, stout, decent citizens. Be strong in the faith. Everything you do please do with a loving spirit. Listen to your sound leaders. I am glad that you have with you Pat Boone,[1] Anita Bryant,[2] and Alvin Dark.[3] All of these are true Christians, and they have been an inspiration to me.

The churches here in the east send their greetings. Priscilla and John Alden send their regards, along with the little church group that meets in their home.

Kiss each other on the cheek for me. My own best regards to you and I am even going to sign this letter myself.

If there is any person who does not love the Lord Jesus Christ I hope he ends up with an Edsel franchise and the mumps.

The grace of the Lord Jesus Christ be with you and my love is with you in Christ the Lord.

Sincerely yours,

Paul

---

[1]Stephanas   [2]Fortunatas   [3]Achaicus

2nd LETTER TO THE CORINTHIANS

Dear Christian Corinthians:

My name is Paul, and by the will of God I am an apostle of the Lord Jesus, and Tim, our brother in Christ, joins me along with all the Christians in New Zealand to write to you all at Corinth.

Praise the Lord, for he is the Father of Mercies, the God of Comfort, the Father of our Lord Jesus Christ, and God is the one that calms us and teaches us so that we in his name may be of comfort to others. There is a strange balance, for as much as we suffer because of our Christian witness, we are all the more abundantly blessed by Christ. Even suffering, affliction, arthritis, and sore muscles, all these things will be amply rewarded for all that you are having to endure.

We don't want you to think that you are the only ones with troubles.[1]

We have really caught it over here in the Asia area.[2] Often we even thought we would all be killed, but we trusted in God. God delivered us when we didn't see how we could get out alive. Your prayers for us were also helpful.

It is exhilarating to realize that our change from the old, worldly way of life was brought into being not through courses in graduate schools or even transactional analysis, but by the grace of the Lord. The main thing we have to tell you is just really the same old story of the good news and the great hope in the coming of the day of the Lord.

Every time that I preached to you I did so with real confidence and assurance, not only when I was headed to eastern Europe but when I was on my way back to Jerusalem.

Let me re-affirm that my preaching was the real McCoy, it was positive, not argumentive. Tim, Sibyl,[3] and I were not trying to make an impression on you in our behalf, but we preached Jesus Christ, the son of God. We also stated that all of the promises of God are in Jesus Christ. God is the one responsible for bringing all of us together. I didn't come to Corinth to be the great preacher and control your belief or clarify your doctrine, I simply came to establish ourselves together in Christ, working with great joy, and all together under God in Christ.

After doing a good bit of criticism of you in my first letter, I am determined not to be so oppressive in this letter, for my real goal is to bring you joy, even as I have received joy. I know I complained

---

[1]Everybody, including Paul, likes to get their own moanings mentioned.
[2]With no help from Kissinger, either. [3]Silvanus

about some of you and some of the things that I said were harsh, but the intent was to heal, not damage.

Anyone that you have decided to forgive for wrongdoing, then I also forgive, just as Christ has forgiven me. We all must be forgiving, for if we don't ease up on each other Satan will take advantage of our dissension, for surely this is one of his weapons.

The Lord made it possible for me to go to Berlin[1] and to preach the gospel there. I kept thinking that I would run into Titus, but I couldn't find him. This was very disappointing.[2] I left Berlin and went again into eastern Europe. Thank God for the power that Christ gives us, and we affect a place like a good smell. People can tell that we are of Christ and that we have good news. Our message says that death is defeated and this is really good news. We preach sincerely about God in the name and the power of Jesus Christ.

Chap.
3

Actually, I am greatly proud of you all at Corinth. If I wanted a letter of recommendation sometime I would just tell them about you all, for you all are a living letter of recommendation for me. The reason for this is that your lives are letters in reflection of Christ, of whom we taught, and though the letters are not in ink they are written in the spirit of God, not on tablets of stone but in the hearts of people. We who teach Christ are not much in ourselves, but your witness for Jesus makes us great.

It is not a matter of the observance of the letter of the law, for this is a deadly practice, but it is a matter of the spirit, for the spirit refreshes life.

When Moses appeared with the Ten Commandments the glory of the Lord shown so brightly on him that people could not see his face. If the glory of God is then manifested this way in the cold presentation of law, think how much more glorious is the manifestation of the spirit of God in a life that is free in Christ.

It just stands to reason that the information about law and punishment should not be as glorious as the information about freedom and salvation.

Another difference occurs in that we preach in this modern day in plain language, in simple terms, and do not use the oriental, flowery touch, full of complications, as was the custom in Moses' day. As Moses placed a veil over his face in presenting the Ten Commandments, people since then have been hiding from the truth of the Old Testament. Not so with us, for in Christ we turn to the Old Testament as a point of departure. When a person turns to Christ, then a new understanding of the Old Testament is available, and the veil is lifted.

[1]Troas   [2]I suspect Titus of hiding.

The Lord is the spirit of liberty. When we begin to see ourselves in the image of God we see a new glory, and the richness of our lives is increased through the spirit of the Lord.

It is God's mercy that enables us to endure and this mercy is given to us because we serve the Lord. This means, of course, that we must speak the truth of God, that we must give up sly and ungodly ways, and we must be good examples.

Some people just seem never to see the light of the truth of the gospel. If we are preaching to people to just follow us I would understand, but we are telling people to follow Jesus Christ, our Lord and Saviour, and we are just servants in his name.

God has provided the light of his spirit for our lives, a light which comes from knowing Jesus and accepting his rule. This valuable gift is in our earthly body as a manifestation of God's concern and love for mankind.

As a result, the true believer may be greatly troubled, but not completely in despair, such a person may be tormented but never forsaken, embarrassed and defeated, but never hopeless. This is all possible because the believer carries within a knowledge of following Jesus, that Jesus went through the same things for our sake. We will always continually re-live his experiences ourselves.

As we believe, so we testify. This means that we conquer death by life, and all this because of our knowledge of Jesus Christ. It stands to reason, and it is a promise, that the Lord of All who raised Jesus from the dead will also raise us who follow him.

Everything in life points to the glory of God, and our receiving the abundant grace of the Lord is another way of showing the working of the glory of God. This keeps us humping. Our physical body may ache and deteriorate, but our spirit thrives. The troubles of this world are brief and soon depart and we exchange them for the multiple glories of the life to come.

This certainly means that we must anticipate things we have never seen or imagined, for the things we see and feel are earthly matters, but the things which are eternal we have not seen nor can we even imagine.

We really have a lot going for us, for we know that when our present body wears out[1] we have a special replacement prepared by God, waiting for us in heaven. We moan and groan a great deal in this life, sometimes even wishing we could have the new body now, to try it for size. God knows this, and has therefore supplied his spirit to take us through these times.

---

[1]You can easily tell when this begins.

As long as we are in our earthly bodies we are not in heaven, and we must live by faith, not by actually seeing the next life, being mindful of the fact that we are not yet living in God's eternal home. We must work then to please God, for we are all going to appear before the judgment seat of Christ, at which time there will be an awards banquet, good things for the good and bad things for the bad.[1]

It is our duty then to warn people and tell them of the punishment of God. Again let me remind you that we are not trying to sell ourselves as a bunch of good preachers. We are not interested in appearances, and anything we do, even if it seems glamorous, it is done for God, and when we reason with you it is for your sake and God's glory, not ours.

It is the love for Christ that keeps us humping. Since Christ died for everyone, then there is certainly an obligation for everyone to live for Christ, for he died and rose again for all of us.

Now we think of Christ as risen, the son of God, and therefore in Christ we can become new people. No longer pragmatists, glorying in man, but new persons with new spirits.

Our new basic theology reassures us that God is sovereign, that we are back in good with God through Jesus Christ, for Christ has been given the job of getting mankind back to God. It is for this that God was in Christ, the personal factor for reclaiming man, paying for mankind's sin himself.

Our place is similar to that of an ambassador, for we are ambassadors for Christ to you, just as if God was coming straight to you using us as the instruments. We implore you then to turn to Christ and be restored to God. In order that we might again understand the ways of the Lord, Christ, who was himself sinless, assumed all our sins, in order that we might meet the Lord with a clean slate.

Chap.

6

This business of turning to Christ is not a thing to be postponed, for every day is a day of salvation for those who turn to Christ.

Those of us who teach and preach Jesus Christ have to be pretty careful, for certainly we should not offend or embarrass anyone, and we ourselves have to be very patient and capable of enduring hardships of all kinds, such as being tossed in the jug, missing a bunch of meals, being bored at long meetings. We also need to be exceedingly kind, very tolerant and understanding, learning to accept graciously the good and the bad. We also need to be content to be poor ourselves, money-wise, and yet be willing to help others get rich, being sure that we remember that although we may have no

[1]Marshall Dillon gives a preview on Gunsmoke.

earthly possessions we have all things by the grace of God.

You Corinthians are to me as if you were my own children. I am concerned that you follow my directions rather than your own. For one thing, you can't constantly associate with riff-raff, for if you lie down with dogs you'll get up with fleas. You won't see Christ and the Devil going on a trip together.

You can't mix worship of God and the worship of idols. You really are yourselves the temple of God, for God has said that he would live and walk in people, and God cares for people. Get yourselves cleaned up for Christ's sake, and then be ready to meet the Lord. The Lord has said that on this basis you all will be sons and daughters of the Lord.

Chap.

7

In short, people, it is worth it to clean up your lives when you think of the ultimate benefits, not to mention the need of standing in awe of God.

Obviously some of your general group has been complaining somewhat about some of us. That's weird! We have not misled anyone, we haven't stretched the truth. I'm not trying to criticize you all, though, for all of you are really dear to me. It is because I care so much that I speak so frankly.

There have been some tough times with us, particularly in Eastern Europe. A lot of hassling went on all around us and we were shaky inside, but the Lord was with us, and Titus showed up, and he is good, tough help.

Titus also brought us good news about you all, your messages of concern. I realize I irritated you with my last letter[1] but I had to write it. Sometimes I wish I hadn't, but I realize now that it was a good thing for me to stir you all a bit.

As a result, your irritation turned to repentance, and that is great! Good, healthy irritation that results in improvement is a fine godly matter, for it is the irritation that turns into violence that brings death and that is not good at all.

You have really cleaned your slates now and all is well, for I didn't write to point out all your errors, but to bring you to repentance. This is because I earnestly want you to belong to the Lord, and now I know you do.

Let me assure you that we are celebrating, for Titus is happy with you all and I am rejoicing at all the good news. My confidence in you was not misplaced and Titus had a great ministry with you which he enjoyed tremendously.

[1] I know he irritated the Women of the Church.

Let me tell you about some of the churches in Eastern Europe, for they have done a fine thing, setting a wonderful example. We didn't put the heat on them, either, but they decided, although they really are what you would call poor churches,[1] to make a fine benevolent gift for us to use in the missionary and the disadvantaged programs.

We were so impressed that we decided to send Titus to you all to try to teach you the same kind of thing. We know you are measuring up well in faith, regular church meetings, hard work, and adequate mimeograph material, and now we want to see how you take to benevolences. I am simply passing along the example of some fine churches. This is not a financial campaign run by Paul.

You know the Christian story, or you certainly should, how Jesus became poor for all of us so that we might become rich in grace. I know you have been talking about a benevolent, free will offering for missionaries, but you've been talking about it for a year. Get with it!

A willing mind and a generous spirit is the first requirement, but unless this is transferred into action nothing is gained. You will not be giving to some dude who will quit work and try to live on welfare. Your giving will help the needy and the giving will be also a blessing to you.

Thank God for Titus and his great interest in you all, and his willingness to come to you and preach. Be good stewards, give generously to Titus and the associate ministers who are with him. Don't worry about what will happen to your money. The fellows with Titus are dedicated completely as is Titus, who of course is closely associated with me. Introduce Titus and his staff to all the churches in your area and be assured that Titus fully represents me everywhere he goes. I have complete confidence in Titus and also in you all, and I am certain that everything will work out together well, for the preachers I am sending are messengers of the churches of Christ.

9

Actually, I am stressing the matter of your stewardship for several reasons, one being that I know you wish to know all the necessary workings of the Christian way. I have sent the messengers of Christ with this letter to help encourage you for we have all talked big about your generosity and thoughtfulness and I certainly wouldn't want you to be embarrassed or not prepared to make a fine offering to the mission work.

Let me remind you of an old saying, 'He that sows sparingly reaps sparingly, and he that sows bountifully, reaps bountifully.'

Every person should give as his heart dictates, not grudgingly or because of pressure, for the Lord delights in a cheerful giver. God is

---

[1]All churches consider themselves poor churches.

able and willing to supply everything for everybody, the Christian simply has the chance to be part of the program.

One of the old Hebrew writings has indicated that the giver is blessed in giving even as the sower reaps the harvest of his planting. The harvest in the case of giving to God is a bountiful understanding and peace in the Lord.

Giving to the visiting ministers not only supplies their needs, but acts as a means of expressing your thanks to God. God is glorified by your generosity in proportion to your giving. The ministers will also continue to pray for you, to ask God to bless you and increase his kindness toward you. Thanks be to God for such fantastic gifts.

**Chap.
10**

It is generally said about me that my letters are strong, deep, powerful letters, but that when I am present I'm not too hot a preacher. I guess that this is true, but you should simply let this be another lesson, for outward appearances aren't everything. The real thing is a matter of inner commitment to Christ.

Although I go around like my fellow ministers in a human body, I am not at war with other humans and I naturally try to get along peacefully. I promise you for sure though that whatever I put in my letters, that is exactly what I aim to do and to teach when I am with you in person.

Our group of missionaries doesn't try to outshine each other, either. There are no rankings among us.[1] Non-Christians are foolish to always be ranking each other and striving to be more acceptable than others. We simply try to do all that we can, each within the confines of personal ability, and we do this as representatives of Jesus Christ.

There is no point in a person commending himself, for the commendation of God is the only thing that counts. If a person likes glory, let such a one glory in the Lord. Our missionaries are not interested in claiming the success of others, but we hope that your growth in Christ will commend our work to the Lord.

**Chap.
11**

My concern for your people at Corinth is almost fanatical. I am afraid that the devil might get you, though I have claimed you for Christ. There is great simplicity in the good news about Jesus Christ, and it scares me to think that some slick tongue smoothey might come by and talk you into another belief and into following some strange god.

Frankly, I feel that I am about the number one apostle, full of clear knowledge of Christ, even though I am a poor speaker.

[1]Except Paul was #1.

Certainly I was doing the right thing in coming to you and telling you the story of Jesus. A number of churches pitched in travel money for me, and when I was staying with you I paid my own bills. The brothers from Eastern Europe furnished expenses and enough of an honorarium for me to get along in Corinth. I haven't cost you birds a dime and I don't expect to get anything. Why shouldn't I praise the people of New Zealand and other places that make my missionary trips possible?

Be on the look-out for fellows who don't operate as I do, they put the bite on you for their own use, they are false apostles, phony workers, claiming to be Christ's when actually they belong to the devil. The devil is real, and even sometimes poses as an angel.[1] No wonder some of his cohorts get in a pulpit now and then.

Let me tell you something on my own. God hasn't told me to tell you this, but I'm tired of hearing about how great you all think some of the phonies are.

Let's compare. I am a Hebrew, so what if one of them is also? I am an Israelite, descended from Abraham, also a life member of the 4-H Clubs. I am a minister for Christ, having been in prison, beaten, and almost killed. Five different times I received 39 lashes. You can multiply that for yourselves. Three times I have been beaten with a rod, once I was stoned, 3 times I was shipwrecked, I spent the day and a night in the ocean. I have had to travel a great deal, endangered by robbers, in difficulty with my own countrymen, in trouble with foreigners, alone in the wilderness, cleaned by a bunch of con men, hungry, cold, naked, tired, and hurt.[2]

All that is on the outside. Inside I hurt every time a church suffers, or a saint is lost, or another missionary persecuted. If I ever needed to brag a little I surely could brag about my problems.[3]

God knows that I am telling the truth about all my hardships. I remember when the C.I.A.[4] was after me and I was saved by being lowered over the wall in a basket like a bunch of bananas.

Chap.

12

It isn't a good thing for me to carry on too much about myself. I guess I could tell about the man I was, selected by the Lord, caught up momentarily into heaven, told things I dare not tell, and I am proud that this happened. I do not want to attract your attention through my direct contact in heaven. This would be foolish and you probably wouldn't believe me.[5] I would also be pushing myself instead of Christ.

To remind me to be humble, the Lord has chosen to give me an affliction, and although I've earnestly prayed to have it removed, the

---

[1]I think I know two.   [2]Definitely ready for Queen for a Day.
[3]Granted. You deserve a few verses for bragging.
[4]Aretas and his men.   [5]You're probably right.

Lord has decided to let me learn to live with it.[1] The Lord has furnished me the necessary grace to live with my infirmity.

For some reason, I consider my sufferings as a means of recognition, for these punishments are testimony of my love for Christ. When things get tough, I seem to like it.

It's a shame I have to present myself like this to you all, but I needed to answer the gossip and mumblings that have come to me from you all. It doesn't mean anything to me, but I am about the #1 apostle. Certainly you saw the signs of an apostle when I was with you, exhibiting patience, understanding, doing wonders, and healing people. What irked you? Are you miffed because I didn't let you pay me?

Well, I'm coming to see you again, and it will be my third time.

Again I will be no burden to you. Since I feel that you are my children I will provide for you rather than vice the versa. It is strange, though, that the more that I seem to care for you all the less you seem to care for me:[2]

Naturally, I have kept up with you all. I sent Titus and his staff. You really liked him. Well, we both think alike, we testify to Christ. Why have you got a beef with me? Everything any of us has said has been for your own good.

What worries me now is that when I come to see you we won't get along as well as we should. You'll be concerned that I might be displeased with you and I'll be concerned about how you feel about me. I certainly hope that when I come to preach there won't be debates, envy symptoms, gossiping, hurt feelings, and a lot of disagreement.

It also occurs to me that I might come and blow my cool and lash out at some of you who have fallen into sin and not repented. Naming names, and that type of thing.[3]

Chap.
13

Let me remind you, I am coming to visit. I plan to be careful in what I say. Since there are no tapes available, I'll speak always in the presence of two or three reliable witnesses.

I want to warn you, that those who have been misrepresenting Christ will get called by name when I come. My outspoken manner will be a witness for Christ.

Christ was crucified, which seemed an inadequacy, but then he rose from the dead, which exhibited the power of God. We will come to you then as if we too are risen with the power of God, for in Christ we are.

---

[1]Lots of theories. I think it was poor eyesight. Clue — he wouldn't write his own letters.   [2]Life is that way sometimes, Paul.
[3]A sure way to start trouble in a church.

Take a careful look at yourselves. Examine yourselves in the name of Christ. It would be a pleasure to learn that you all are even stronger in the cause of Christ than we are, for we would like for you to be perfect.

I am writing all these things to you all frankly in the hope that I won't have to preach this way.

It is time now to conclude this letter. Strive for perfection, be confident, not argumentative, live in peace, and God, who is the Lord of peace and love, will be with you.

Greet each other with a holy kiss. All the believers here send their regards.

May the grace of the Lord Jesus Christ, and the love of God, and the inspiration of the Holy Spirit, be with all of you. Amen.

Sincerely yours,

Paul

P.S. Titus and Lucas did the writing for me this time. P.

LETTER TO THE GALATIANS

Church Friends
Galatian Church of Christ

Chap.
1

Dear Christians:

This is your friend Paul writing to you. As you may know, I am an apostle of the Lord Jesus Christ, not by a vote of a church court, but by a direct act of God, who arranged this through his son Jesus Christ. The church people here join me in this letter to you. All together we send you greetings in the name of God the Father, with the grace of the Lord Jesus Christ. This is the same Christ who forfeited his own well being for ours, and so to him we give eternal glory.

Word has reached me that you are experiencing some wandering from the true faith, even though it has not been long since I was with you. The word is that an occasional, talented preacher has caused some of you to stray from the basic truth of Christ which we preached to you. All I can say is curses on anyone who attempts to adjust or change the good news. I would say the same to one of us if we wandered from the basic truth of God. In short, curses on anyone that preaches anything contrary to the fundamentals which we gave you.

Do you think that we preach to entertain people or to establish ourselves as being important? I am absolutely a servant of Christ and I preach his true gospel as was given to me by the Lord himself.

You know you have heard of my past record and how I persecuted those who taught in the name of Christ and I actually became known as the #1 opponent to Christianity. It was God's will, however, that the grace of the Lord came to me, and Christ was revealed to me in order that I might be a missionary to the non-jews all over the world. I didn't go to seminary or even take the special 90 day wonder course established in Jerusalem, but I preach directly from inspiration and revelation.[1]

There were lots of places I visited and I preached in plenty of churches before finally going to Jerusalem. In fact it was three years before I went to Jerusalem and there I spent two weeks getting acquainted with Rocky. The only other apostle I saw at that time was James, the brother of Jesus. I am flat telling you people the straight truth.[2]

From Jerusalem I began traveling again as a missionary, preaching to people who had heard of me but never met me. Most of

---

[1]Such preaching won the West for Christ. [2]I, for one, believe you, Paul.

them thought it was a great asset that I had formerly persecuted Christians and that now I was all out for Christ.

It was fourteen years before I returned to Jerusalem, and Barney and Titus were both with me then. As you no doubt have heard, I was a missionary to the non-Jew, directly appointed by God in Jesus Christ, and the revelation to me was to the effect that the non-Jew was free in Christ, as we all are, and not bound by the Jewish law, such as the one requiring circumcision.

My place was to meet first in Jerusalem with a very select group with whom I could discuss my views without fear of creating trouble, for I was as committed to the doctrine of permissive circumcision as Rocky was committed to the view of compulsory circumcision.

Unfortunately, there was a blabbermouth present[1] who insisted on making an issue of the matter. I felt that Rocky had as much right to his view as I to mine, for we were serving one Lord and the intent of God was to inspire each of us to minister in a specific area.

James, Peale, and John, who were apparently real pillars in the church, could easily see that I was sincere and each of them gave me the right hand of fellowship, and encouraged me to continue to preach to the non-Jews while they would continue their endeavors with the Jews.

When I saw Rocky later in Cleveland I asked him bluntly about the matter, for actually he was responsible for the whole trouble. My gripe with Rocky was that after he had the revelation that enabled him to eat with non-Jews, and to note that God was no respecter of persons, he then backed off his position when he was meeting with the orthodox Jews. Rocky did this to stay out of trouble with the circumcision pushers, and what's more Rocky influenced Barney to do the same.

Being the non-diplomatic type, I spoke up publicly and said to Rocky in front of everybody, "If you, who are a Jew, follow the rules of a non-Jew, why do you try to get the non-Jew to follow the rules of the Jews?"[2]

Now you Galatians listen carefully, if all that were needed in life was to obey the rules of the Jewish program, then there would be no need for Christ, but people must be just fed by faith, not by works. The faith must be in Jesus Christ, and even though we are sinners, Christ is not a sinner, but stands ready to forgive our sins.

Completeness of life cannot be attained by works or by observance of the law, or else Christ would have died in vain. The thought of Christ being crucified by Jews, such as me, really kills me, and yet I am alive and active, for now Christ lives within me. I live

[1]We still have them. [2]At this point, Paul's public relations counsel must have had a stroke.

strictly by the faith of the son of God, for he loved me, and he gave his life for me, and for you also. In a sense then, I am indifferent to the law in order that I might be even more enthusiastic in the work of the Lord.

You nutty Galatians,[1] you mean that you let some legalistic, technical-minded preacher sway you from the simple faith in Jesus Christ? Now tell me this—did you receive the spirit of Christ from the law or from inspiration? Don't you have any sense? You found Christ through the spirit, do you think now that you'll turn to legalism?

The spirit of God which works among you, and changes so many lives, do you think this is done by technical observances of the law or by faith?

God foresaw all these things. In the very early days with Abraham, God said that in Abe all nations would be blessed. You don't forsake Abraham by following the route of faith in Christ.

If all a person knew to observe was the law, then following the law is a must, but the law is not the faith, though it may lead one to the faith. Christ, you see, redeemed us from the necessity of the minute observance of the law. Christ became accursed for our sake in order that we might avoid the curse of the law.

This was done in order that the promise of the spirit might come to the non-Jew, as a blessing initiated through Abraham, and fulfilled in Christ.

Let me be practical with you. A contract is a contract, one person to another, and is not legally subject to change. Now God made a contract that through Abraham would come salvation, as it did in Christ. You can't change or ignore this.

If this arrangement is a legal contract it is earthly, but it is a promise of God, above legality, and it is eternal.

Why have the law at all? Well, it was necessary because of the general meanness of the people and it was to provide help until the mediator would come. If it had been possible to provide salvation simply by law, the Lord would not have sent a mediator, The Christ.

All men are sinners, and so Christ came as the fulfillment of God's promise. Before Christ came all people were necessarily under the law and in a sense the law became the teacher to prepare us for Christ and the promise of God, which was justification by faith. Now that the promise has been fulfilled, we are no longer under the law, but we are all able to become children of God by faith in Jesus Christ.

If you have been baptized in the name of Christ, you are

---

[1]Paul had no tact. This confirms it.

Christ's. There is no distinction. Anyone who believes in Christ is a Christian; it makes no difference whether a person be male or female, rich or poor, Jew, Greek, or French, dumb or smart, all are one in Jesus Christ.

If you are Christ's, then you are of the seed of Abe and you automatically come under the promise of God.

Chap.
4

The situation in general, as I see it, is like a child, who is under tutors, rules, regulations and the like, until the child becomes an adult and is free, accepting responsibilities. Just so people were before Christ, operating under rules, commandments, and law, not free, and then Christ came and we became sons of God, free in Christ. No longer then were we enslaved by the law as children, but we were the adopted sons of Christ, and heirs of God through Christ.

Now that you know God and are known by God, how in the thunderation can you return to the weak and silly concept of mechanical observance of some technical laws?

It scares me to think that I might have wasted my ministry on you. You suddenly have become so particular about what you do on what day, and a whole lot of little picky things. I want you to be as I am. You haven't hurt me, I surely would not want to teach you something that wasn't good.

When I was preaching to you all, you were kind and listened and didn't make fun of me or call me Blind Paul, but received me as a representative of Christ. You seemed to be so taken with my preaching that I felt that any one of you would have given me their right eye if I had asked.

As your friend, I simply tell you the truth. It is good to be moved or impressed by a person who preaches, but you shouldn't forget all about it when the person has gone.

Actually, I long to be with you right now. I feel that you are somewhat my children. I think that if I were with you, I'd feel better about things and not so doubtful about how you all stand on fundamental issues.

To those of you who want back under the technical law, what do you say to this regarding the law? It is recorded that Abe had two sons, one by a bonded woman and another by a free woman. This is a picture of the two different covenants. One represents the arrangement highlighted by the commandments at Sinai, centralized in Jerusalem, and we, just as I so was, are children of the promise of God.

The children of flesh, represented as children of the bonded woman, are people concerned only with worldly cares, and they are always trying to cause the rest of us trouble. Even as it was illustrated in the case of the two sons of Abe; so it is now. Don't pay any attention to the worldly minded, legalistic folks; reject them and their views, for we are free under the promise of God.

Don't get bogged down with church law, but stand fast in your freedom in Christ. Again I say it doesn't matter about circumcision. If you have been circumcised, you are obligated to fulfill your vows, but that does not bring you salvation or justification. The pay-off comes through faith in Christ, with or without circumcision, but faith operated in love, that is the pay-off.

It doesn't take much of a bad influence to create a big smell. I have confidence in you all, though, and I don't think you'll get snowed. Whoever is causing you all to stumble will get his from God.

If I am accused of being legalistic, then why doesn't someone work me over? It is obvious that someone is poisoning you all toward me.

I sometimes wish that it would be proper to just kick such folks out of the church.

You have been invited by Christ to be free in love, but be careful not to use this freedom as a license to do anything you want to do. Let your love be shown in service. The whole fulfillment of one law is found in the simple statement, "love your neighbor as yourself."

If you are going to argue, growl and snap at each other you will just eat up the whole church. If you live fully in the spirit of God you don't have to worry about the law for you'll automatically obey it.

Life is a constant battle between the desires of the flesh and the feelings of the spirit. Let me refresh your mind on the evils of the flesh. They are readily seen in the worship of money, not bathing, chasing wild women, rioting, loud arguing, murder, drunkeness, and violent strife or fighting.[1] The people who do the above listed things will never make it into the kingdom of God.

The results of a person whose spirit is free in Christ is found in the exhibiting of love, joy, peace, gentleness, patience, kindness, faith, temperance, and the like, against which you'll never find a law.

If we are going to live in the spirit then let us walk in the spirit, not seeking any self glory, or envying other people, or provoking other people.

Now for some common sense, spiritual advice, let me advise you not to hold a person's errors against him for you are apt to make a few mistakes yourself. Help people with their problems, for this is Christ's way.

A person that begins to think pretty highly of himself, when actually he is very ordinary, is only fooling himself. Do exceedingly

---

[1]This is where the TV writers get their ideas.

well in your work and the work will testify for you. If you don't work hard you'll have to watch the success of others and have none for yourself.

Try to carry your own load.

If somebody teaches you something good then teach the same thing to someone else who will also teach it, and in this way goodness is spread.

You can't fool God. God made life in such a manner that you will reap what you sow. If all that interests you is the fulfillment of bodily desires you'll reap aches, pains, decay, and eternal separation from God, but if you are concerned with good spiritual matters you will reap eternal life.

Don't get pooped out doing good things, as you will finally be rewarded. It may be tough going, but stick with it. Everytime you have a chance to do a nice thing for someone, do it, especially if that someone is a Christian.

This surely is a big, long letter I've written to you all, and with my own hand.[1]

Let me take one more crack at the preachers that are misleading you.

They make a big thing out of getting you to agree to circumcision, just so they can brag about their influence. They don't keep the law perfectly themselves, but they want you circumcised for their own glory.

Not so with me, for I glory only in the cross of Jesus Christ. As far as I am concerned the cross represented the end of worldly pursuits for me and the beginning of a new life. In the new life circumcision doesn't mean a thing one way or another.

God bless everybody, with mercy and peace, and also the church of God. From now on tell anybody that denounces me that I bear on my body the marks of the Lord Jesus Christ.

The grace of the Lord Jesus, his kindness, and his peace go with you.

Amen,

Paul

---

[1]Paul usually had a staff member write.

LETTER TO THE EPHESIANS

Dear Australians:

My name is Paul and I am an apostle of the Lord Jesus Christ. Most of you have heard me preach. My theme is the same although I am in jail,[1] I continue to urge you to praise the Lord, the Father of Jesus Christ, the one who planned for the spread of the gospel through believers such as you and me. To some of us, God has revealed a portion of the inside information on his will, and all of us who believe in Jesus have become adopted children of God in Christ.

All such things, including our involvement, were planned by God to get the job done. I am greatly thankful that many of you have professed your faith in Christ and are thereby sealed within the sure promises of God. Your faith makes me love you, and my concern causes me to pray for you. I chiefly pray that the Lord will give you wisdom and some common sense to go with it, so that you may grasp the significance of the promises to you and value of the type of riches that such brings.

Surely you will see the greatness of the power of God as God works through his people. The most impressive example of the power of God is the raising of Jesus from the grave and the placing of him on the right hand of God.

God has exalted Christ above every name in heaven and on earth. God has put all creation under the power of Christ, and Christ has been made the head of the church, which church is charged with the preaching and teaching of his good news.

Chap.
2

God has really also brought a bunch of you all to life. You were actually dead in your sins and ensnared with the life of worldly matters, as if bewitched by the devil himself.

Most of you were really a bunch of supreme hell raisers, but God cared for all of us, even when we were sinning at full speed. History will testify to the restoring of our lives and activities by inspiration of Jesus Christ.

Actually, we are saved by the kindness of God, for salvation cannot be earned. If a person could be saved by doing good he would get the idea that salvation could be earned, and then somebody could brag about how important and self-satisfying people are, independent of God.

We are created to be workers for Christ and made for the purpose of doing his good works.

[1]Though he had the cell keys and could come and go.

As people look at things, you all were non-Jews, not circumcised, which is a man made distinction, and you were without hope for you were not aware of the promises of God through Jesus Christ, but now that you know Christ you are brought close to the family of God.

Jesus Christ mended all these torn pieces of life by being two, human and divine, dying on the cross, and thereby killing all man made distinctions between people, for he died for all. As a result, everyone everywhere has access to God through the united Spirit of Christ.

As a result, you are no longer strangers, outcasts, disadvantaged people, but you are as much in the household of God as anybody. This whole concept, which is a new church concept, is built on the testimony of the apostles and the words of the prophets, with Jesus Christ being the cornerstone and head of the entire church universal, and all of you who believe are part of this great church of God through the Spirit.

Chap.

3

Now I am the minister dedicated to teaching Christ to you non-Jews, for I was selected by God for a clear revelation of the truth of Christ, even though I was one of the worst fellows anywhere.

Christ was a mystery in older days when all that was known was the words of the prophets, but now I am chosen to preach unsearchable riches of Christ to you non-Jews.

It is my intent to try to make all men see and understand that which was in olden days a mystery stored in the heavens with God, but now this knowledge is released and is to be spread abroad by the church of Christ.

Don't get fed up that I worry so about you all. Be pleased. It is for this very purpose of showing you new life in Christ that I myself bow my knees to the Father of our Lord, for whom all the family of God are called, all being Christians. I pray that you will be greatly strengthened in your faith. I further pray that Christ may be deeply rooted in you, and that your faith is founded on love.

Surely you will learn of the love of Christ, how it may cover all places and all conditions, and in this way you may become full of the Spirit of God.

I send this letter in the name of Christ, who is able to do all that we ask and more so, and may glory be to Christ in his church, world without end, Amen.

Yours in Christ,

Paul

Dear Australians:

Since I didn't get the first letter ready for the messenger, let me write some more.

Try to do a real good job of anything you undertake, being considerate of others, and being willing gladly to do more than your share.

Why shouldn't we be able to live peacefully with one another? We are all under the same Spirit; there is only one great church in Christ, one hope, one faith, one baptism,[1] one God and Father of us all.

We are all given a measure of the grace of the Lord. Christ said that these gifts varied and we were all free to pursue our particular gift. What if Christ did descend first,[2] he certainly ascended, the same Christ.

This is the Christ, empowered to do so by God, who gave some people a knack for prophecy, some apostles, some evangelists, some teachers, some pastors, all given to improve the believers and to help them, showing to them the ways of the Lord.

The goal of this is to lead everyone to ultimate perfection even as Christ was, and that we become sure and stable, so that we won't be tossed around by every new wrinkle or winsome philosophy that blows our way.

It is to be hoped that we learn to speak the truth in a loving way, promoting Christ pleasantly, and all of us working together as the coordinated body of a natural athlete.

This means that you must give up many of the things that you are accustomed to doing. There are some among you who are hardened to a stupid, selfish way of life, greedy people, indulging themselves in all manners of sins.

If you have taken Christ seriously you will put away all your evil habits, become new persons, seeking understanding and holiness. As for lying, just quit it; tell the truth. Don't get emotionally upset and then resort to sin, and if you do blow your cool be sure and quiet down by the time the sun sets.

Stealing is strictly no good. If that's the way you make a living, quit it and go to work, and maybe you can earn enough money to help some poor, underprivileged fellow. Cussing, also, will get you nowhere, and God won't like it either.

In fact, let all bitterness and anger and complaining be thrown aside, along with all hate, and be kind one to another, tenderhearted, forgiving one another even as God, for Christ's sake, has forgiven you.

---

[1]The sprinkling vs. immersion argument hadn't started at this time.
[2]Whatever that means.

You should live with love and understanding, even as Christ loved and understood us, and then you should act as children of God. If you are a true follower of Christ you do not live an uncontrolled sex life, nor are you foul mouthed or dirty, nor do you try to grab everything you see that you like. You shouldn't waste time in idle chatter, and again I say that no fellow that runs from one woman to another, who despises God, shall ever enter the kingdom of heaven.

Don't let someone tell you there is an escape hatch for the wicked, for God will enforce his wrath on the disobedient people who defy him. Stay away from evil people and you yourselves walk in the light, for you should really be lights yourselves since the result of the Spirit of God is kindness and thoughtfulness to others.

You need to get with it, for we live in a time of evil[1] and the righteous need to shed their light, to show the power of being new persons in the risen Lord, and use common sense along with all that you do.

Be uplifted and joyful because of the spirit of God and not because of too much wine. You should do a lot of singing for there are plenty of happy, helpful songs and hymns. Sing in thanksgiving to the Lord in the name of Jesus, being considerate to each other out of respect to God.

Wives should submit themselves to their husbands just as they do to the Lord, for the husband is head of the wife even as Christ is head of the church.[2]

Husbands, you should love your wives even as Christ loved the church, and Christ blessed the church so that it might be pure and wholesome. A man should care for his wife as he cares for his own body.[3]

It is for the purpose of a new relationship and the establishing of a new family that a man shall leave from under the care of his parents and shall get married, and the man and wife shall become one unit. There is a lot about all this that I do not understand.[4] I really am trying, though, to tell you more about the church than I am about marriage, but I still say that every woman should reverence her husband and every man should love his wife as much as he loves himself.

Children, if your parents served the Lord, then you listen to your parents and obey them. Respect the family plan, for this is basic to the understanding of life.

Now you fathers, don't tease or aggravate your children, nor take advantage of them, but bring them up in the knowledge and love of God.

[1]Everybody is always saying this.
[2]Paul, I'd like to ask a question: What if the husband is drinking, two-faced, scoundrel and yet an elder in the church?
[3]Some mistreat both.   [4]You better believe it.

Employees or servants should do as ordered by the person for whom they work, not faking work, but doing work conscientously as if for Christ. Anybody who works hard and does good things will be recompensed by God in the finals.

Executives, you be careful in dealing with the people who work for you. They may be under you, but you are under the Lord and Master, and Christ thinks no more of one person than another.

You can be strong because of your faith in God, and the knowledge of his power. You can wear the whole protective suit furnished by God to help withstand the devil. We strive in this world against more than weight and muscle, but against designs of evil, against spiritual wickedness in high offices, therefore wear all the protection God furnishes.

This means put on bullet proof shorts, representing the truth, have understanding as a chest protector, and wear as shoes a thorough knowledge of the New Testament gospels. Get behind a wind shield of faith, wear a head gear of salvation, and carry the Old Testament in one holster and the New Testament in another. Be constantly in touch with the Lord through prayer.

You might also pray for my preaching, that I may become bolder and more affluant in presenting the mystery of the good news of Jesus.

Ty Cobb[1] is writing this letter as I dictate it and he will enjoy bringing the letter to you. Ty is a great one, and you will enjoy him. Ty will also bring you up to date on all the church affairs and he will be a source of great encouragement.

May peace be with you all, also love with faith, from God the Father and the Lord Jesus Christ, and may grace abound with all who believe in Jesus Christ. Amen.

Sincerely yours,

Paul

---

[1]Tychicus

Dear Philadelphians:

This is your preacher Paul, joined by Tim, who writes to you, even though I actually dictate to Delli,[1] and Tim and I wish for all of you believers, bishops, deacons, or what not, that the grace of the Lord Jesus Christ, from God the Father, may be with you abundantly.

I am always praying about you all, sometimes just thanking God for you and sometimes asking God's blessing on you. I am confident that the Spirit of Christ will grow in all of you.

In a way, I feel that you all join me in my prison condition, as I await trial and as I confirm everywhere the word of Christ. I really would enjoy seeing you all but I content myself to pray that you grow in love and knowledge. I hope that you pursue good things and that you will be faithful to Christ right up to the time that you will face him.

The things which have happened here to me, being a prisoner, even though somewhat on the loose, although bad for me has been good for the cause of Christ; so I really have no complaint.

Everybody asks about my prison status and word of my situation goes everywhere, even in the Emperor's palace, and thereby word of Christ goes also. Since I am not brought to a hasty trial and there is so much attention given to me, many others have been bolder in preaching about Christ.

Admittedly, some of the preaching has been lousy, but some has been very good and sincere. The preachers all know that I am preparing to defend the gospel before the Emperor. Anyway you cut it, though, Christ is being preached. I am certain that you are praying for my deliverance, which encourages me.

I am really excited to be preparing to confront the Emperor's court with the gospel of Jesus. It really no longer matters to me whether I live or die, am freed or executed, for me to live is Christ, and to die is simply to gain a new sublime life.

It is strange. Given a choice, I would not know what to choose, for although on one hand I would like to live and continue preaching and to come and see you all, yet on the other hand if I die, I am with Christ eternally.

At least I will continue to think of you people in Philadelphia and to look forward to visiting with you if conditions warrant.

Make sure that I hear good things of brotherly love from you all. Work together for the furtherance of the gospel. Don't let the

[1]Epaphroditus

enemies of Christianity bluff you, for you have chosen the real salvation.

Not only are you to believe on Jesus Christ, but you are to suffer in his cause if the necessity arises. You should reason just as I do, being happy to live or die.

There is a great comfort and happy fellowship in the sharing of the love of Christ and this means that Christians working together should not bicker or be contentious with each other. The key to this is to assume that every other Christian is better than you are.[1] Don't be totally concerned with your own opinion or ideas, but consider the thoughts of others. Try to have the same attitude that Christ had.

Christ, even though he had come straight from God, was very humble and not pushy. Christ even accepted death, which was really an option with him. Because of this, God has exalted the name of Christ above every name that ever was or will be, and God has further ordered that at the name of Jesus every knee should bow, both in heaven and on earth, and that eventually every tongue must testify to the fact that Jesus is Lord, to the glory of God the Father.

Work at the job of being Christian! You should really be scared not to do so, for God works in you and through you, and you are his instruments. Lay off the mumbling and complaining.[2] You live in a city that has a lot of wicked people on the loose and you must be a light shining in such darnkess. If you do this I will feel that my ministry with you has been a great success. I hope you are glad that I came and that I try to let my light shine for Christ's sake.

The Lord willing and the creeks don't rise, Tim will be coming your way and he can bring me an on the scene report about you all. Tim is the best one that I know and the only dependable one that I have available at present. Tim has been as a son to me, as well as a great bearer of the gospel.

Naturally, I would enjoy coming to visit you all, but the trial judge hasn't ruled on my case yet.

My plans also are to send Delli[3] to you for he has miraculously recovered from severe illness and he wants you all to see how complete has been his recovery. Delli is a real worker, one of the troops that get the jobs done, and I'll feel better knowing he also is coming your way. Be real good to Delli, for he has come close to dying in the work of our Lord, and he deserves every consideration.

It is a great risk I take writing to you, encouraging you to rejoice in the Lord, but fortunately there is no danger to you in

---

[1] Quite often this is a correct assumption.
[2] That means even when your water gets cut off.   [3] Epaphroditus

receiving my letters. Let me warn you about trouble makers and legalistic minded leaders. These technical minded ones harp on the rite of circumcision, but your circumcision is the Spirit of God.

It is foolish to trust in your own human ability. If anybody is inclined that way it is me, and I have a reason to feel that I have obeyed the law scrupulously, for I was circumcised the eighth day, a child of Israel, of the tribe of Benjamin, an outright Hebrew, and as careful about the law as a congressman on election day.

It was with real enthusiasm and vigor that I persecuted Christians and I was blameless as far as liturgical observances were concerned.

I have given up everything to pursue the cause of Christ, and it has been the best thing that ever happened to me.

The righteousness and understanding that I have found was not found in the law or the observance of the niceties of the Jewish religion, but what I found was in the Lord Jesus Christ, an understanding that has come from God, not from books or from liturgy.

The Spirit of God has come to me in order that I may know Jesus, the power of his resurrection, and so then I could sympathize with the sufferings of Jesus. These things enable me to strive for my own resurrection in Jesus, not that I have arrived and am perfect, but at least I now know what is right, for sure.

Certainly I don't understand everything, but I know that looking back will get you nowhere; so I dismiss past errors from my mind and I stretch forward eagerly toward the future, and I am aiming for the grand prize of eternal life with Jesus.

We should all think this way, but if you don't think this way now I'm sure God will lead you to this understanding in due time.

We should all seek the better life together and you can use me and some of my staff as examples. Be careful in choosing your model, for some that look and act pious, fold up when the going gets tough.

Some persons only live to eat and I really pity people who can see no more to living than eating, drinking, and abusing their bodies with careless living. This is a sure way to a bad end.

Those of us who accept Christ can look forward to a new and heavenly body, fashioned in the image of Christ, the same Lord who is able to control all things.

Chap.

4

Hold the fort, good people, I really care for you all and I urge you to stand steady in the faith.

I urge the Gabor Sisters[1] to quit squabbling. Be especially good to the women of the church, for some of them were of tremendous

[1]Euodia and Syntyche

tremendous help to me. Their names are in the Book of Life, and that's for sure.

Rejoice in being a Christian and let your good habits show. Don't go around worrying, but when you have a problem take it to the Lord in prayer. As a result, you will find that the peace of God exists, that it is not the result of reasoning, but it comes from keeping your minds and interests on the affairs of Christ.

Spend your time talking and thinking about good things, things that are true, and lovely, things that reflect honesty and purity, good stories about good people. Think positively and about the nice things of life. If you follow my example, God will bless you.[1]

It is really good to learn that your concern for me is genuine, and I greatly appreciate your gifts to me. It is not that I needed the gifts; it was the thought, for you no doubt realize that I have learned how to be poor[2] and how to be rich, I know what it is like to be hungry and I know how it feels to have tucked away a big meal, for I have finally learned to take anything, good or bad, for Christ furnishes me the strength. Still, many thanks for the chocolate chip cookies.

You Philadelphians have always warmed my heart, for you were the first church to send me gifts, and although I don't need the gifts, I like to testify to your kindness.

Delli brought me money from you all and also some after shave lotion. May God provide you fine people with whatever you need.

All the believers here send their greetings and particularly those who are actually working in Caesar's palace. May all things be to the glory of God and may the grace of the Lord Jesus Christ be with you always. Amen.

Sincerely yours,

Paul

---

[1]Paul, you were so dedicated that I'm refraining from any comment here,
[2]Easy to learn.

LETTER TO THE COLOSSIANS
Written in
Rome, Italy

Dear Colorado Friends[1]:

As you know, my name is Paul, and Tim joins me in this letter which I am dictating in sections, some being typed by Delli and some by Vickie.[2]

In accordance with God's will I am an apostle of the Lord Jesus and it is a pleasure to write and send the blessing of God through the grace of Jesus Christ to you believers in Colorado, for you are a great group and I pray for you every day.

It is wonderful that you know the hope that is born of the good news, and we are told that you all are growing in spirit, as might be expected. Our information comes from Glenn Murray,[3] a faithful minister and servant of Christ who has told us of your good spirit. We have all prayed all the more earnestly for you since we heard this, praying that you may grow in wisdom and in understanding about spiritual matters, and that you might accomplish a great deal with good works.

You certainly should find strength in the power of God, which should enable you to develop patience and remain joyful in the face of difficulty.

All of us should thank God that he has enabled us to be enlightened about life and given us the bright hope that takes us out of depressive times and feelings. Now that we believe in Christ we know we have redemption in him, and that Christ forgives our sins.

Christ is in charge of all the earth; all creation is given to him by God the Father, and Christ is the head of the church, and through the suffering of Christ and his death we are all eligible for forgiveness and for a new life, eternally in the presence of Christ.

Some of you who were really about as bad as they come, are now restored in Christ, and through the sacrifice of Christ you can now be presented, holy and blameless before the throne of grace.

Actually, I have been specifically called to proclaim the good news, which has been kept secret in all the past years, but now can be told. The news is so good that I even rejoice in the sufferings that came my way in the performance of my missionary work.

God wants everyone now to know about the gospel, that it is available to non-Jews as well as Jews. We preach and teach forcefully that Christ is in you and that such is the hope of glory. We warn everyone of pit falls and we teach as wisely as we can for we want everyone to become perfect in the love of Jesus.

---

[1]Colossae inhabitants   [2]Epaphras   [3](Former missionary in Africa) Gnesimus

I really wish you could comprehend how much I worry about you all, the many fine people in Colorado, as well as some in Wyoming.[1] I am so anxious for you to know the comfort that comes with great faith, being also concerned that you might grow in love for one another and in the knowledge of the great mystery of God being in Christ.

Although I can't be with you in person, my thoughts are with you and I am delighted that you all are keeping the faith. Don't let some lip artist or con man mislead you. There is only one way, and that is to walk in the faith made clear by Jesus Christ. Watch out for vague philosophy talk, trying to shake your faith with deceitful matters, pushing some talk as "you've got to be practical."

All you need is found in the Lord Jesus, for he is the chief over everything and everybody. The only circumcision you need is belief in Christ and faith in the Lord's operation of the world. Christ forgives your sins when you turn to him.

Christ has already shown that he is victorious over so called world leaders who attempted to thwart his plans. Don't let any church critics bug you into pious observance of a bunch of specific holy days and traditional rites. You serve Christ.

Don't let anybody confuse you by making light of your satisfaction in the Lord, puffing himself up with phoney humility and claims about controlling angels.

Observe rules and follow instructions that are helpful to your body's well being, not punitive. Common sense in looking out for yourself and complete faith in the Lord Jesus is all you need for a great start.

Since you believe in Christ, you will rise from death as Christ did, for Christ even now sits on the right hand of God in the heavens. You should then show concern primarily for spiritual matters for these will stay with you while worldly goods will be left behind when you ascend.[2]

When you die your life is set aside by Christ, and when Christ appears for the second coming you will join him in the day of glory.

Dump all your evil tendencies, such as chasing wild women, wanting things that belong to other people, worshipping money, or the things money buys, for these are the things that make God angry.

Just get rid of temper tantrums, dirty jokes and cussing, mean talk about others, lying, then you may become a new person, patterned after Jesus Christ. For Christ had no prejudice; he made no distinction between jew and non-jew, white and colored, male or female, rebel or yankee, for Christ was for all people.

---

[1]Laodicea   [2]Nobody ever sees a hearse pulling a U-Haul-It.

If you become a new person in Christ, as you should, you will develop the attributes of mercy, humility, tolerance, and patience. You will also cease to be contentious, forgiving others as Christ has forgiven you.[1]

Become a loving type of person, full of God's peace, and thankful that you know about it. Use songs, poems, stories and friendly talk as a means of winning others to Christ. Remember to always act in the name of Christ, and give thanks to God for making Christ available.

Personally, I think wives should submit to their husbands.[2] Husbands should love their wives and not bless them out much. Children should obey their parents.[3]

My advice to fathers is not to provoke the children but to encourage children and help them.

Employees should do what they are told, whether they like it or not. Do this because God expects a person to work, and if you are working you should do the job well, feeling that you are working for the Lord, not for some fellow person.

Certainly you know that if you follow Christ you will receive the reward as promised, and the person that misbehaves shall be punished accordingly.

Chap.
4

If you are a boss you should deal fairly and kindly with those who work for you, remembering that you are under the one big boss yourself.

Pray regularly, and include us in your prayers, remembering that I am in jail.

Be very wise in dealing with those who don't know Christ, so that you may soon find a way of properly introducing a person to Jesus.

I am sending Delli to preach to you. Delli will give you a full report on me and I will learn from him all about you all.

All the bunch here who are christians send their greetings, such people as Naylor,[4] Dick Ryan,[5] Bill Logan,[6] Luke, the beloved doctor, and others. Pass this letter along also to the churches in Wyoming. If you see Van[7] tell him it is close to the time for him to begin his ministry; he's learned enough already.

Grace be to all of you. Amen.

Paul

P.S. Don't forget I'm in jail.

[1] I know, but it's tough to do it!   [4] Aristarchus   [5] Marcus
[2] How about just 'co-operate' instead of 'submit'?   [6] Epaphras   [7] Archippus
[3] Parents have to tell them something first.

1st LETTER TO THE THESSALONIANS
Athens, Greece

Dear Oakies[1]:

Tim, Sully,[2] and I (Paul) are always being thankful for your people, and we pray for you regularly. We know of your faith, your love for God, and your patient hope in the Lord Jesus Christ, for surely you are chosen of God.[3]

The good news which we preached to you came not just in words, but you put action into it and the power of God was added. It wasn't easy for you to accept what we said, but you did, and you followed us, but more important you turned to the Lord.

The great thing is that you became examples to people in Eastern Europe and New Zealand.[4] We have met some of the people that you influenced and they have told us how you turned from worshipping oil and blowing dust to worshipping God, and that as true believers, you were waiting for the second coming.

Chap.
2

As you may remember, we did not try to flatter you when we first came to you, even though we were fresh from a really rough time in Philadelphia.

In spite of this, we didn't use the old forked tongue, but spoke straight to you and we urged you to try to please God rather than people. We gave you the gospel as it is, in spite of some difficulties which we encountered.

We didn't ask for any recognition or help from you all, as we did not wish to be a burden, even though as an apostle of Christ we were due some hospitality. We tried to deal with you as a nurse deals with children. Our concern was such that we were very frank with you all and we held nothing back; we preached night and day and we gave you the straight gospel message.

We put the heat to you as a father lays down the law for his children, urging you to live as worthy followers of Christ. It was a great experience for us to have you all receive the word of God as if it were direct from the Lord, and not as some committee report.

We are delighted that you became followers of Jesus and we know you were criticized by some of your contemporaries. You had trouble just like some of the Israeli churches had trouble, theirs coming from Jews, the very ones who crucified Christ and then persecuted us. Those very Jews forbid us to preach to the non-Jews.

Wish we could come to see you again. I planned to come, but

---

[1]People of Thessalonica   [2]Silvanus
[3]Every now and then you find an Oakie that thinks that, too.
[4]Oakies really travel a lot.

282

the devil stopped me.[1]

The good news is that we can really rejoice and be pleased that we will all be together at the second coming of our Lord. We are really very proud of you all.

Chap.
3

It has been comforting to get the good word about you from Tim. We are stuck in Athens and we have been worrying that maybe the devil has been working overtime in your area and that you all were in trouble. Tim reports that you are strong in the faith and so our ministry has not been in vain. This is really great news! Keep this up and the knowledge of that will keep us going.

Actually we cannot thank God enough for you all, and we still pray and hope that we might have another preaching mission with you and add to your Christian growth. I hope the Lord will lead us your way.

May the Lord bless you people and let your love grow toward God and toward each other and then surely the Lord Jesus will present you blameless before God the Father at the time of the coming of Jesus again.

Chap.
4

No doubt you remember what we told you to do when we were with you, for it is the intention of God that you live properly, avoiding improper sex relations, stay away from prostitutes, and that you should not take advantage of anyone in a business deal. As for revenge, the Lord will handle that, for God has told us to seek holiness and understanding, not contention.

If a person begins to despise another person, he despises God, who made both of them. I don't need to harp on brotherly love, for you know all about that requirement. You actually do a good job of it in your area, but you need to be more considerate of the Texans, your neighbors.

Another thing that I advise is to tend to your own business.[2] Be very considerate of people who are poor and who do not have a business to which to tend.

Now let me wise you up a bit about people dying. It is natural to show sorrow when a loved one dies, but your sorrow should be brief, for those who die in Christ will rise again and be with Jesus when he comes. The resurrection is not just for those who are still alive at the second coming. When Christ comes again he will come with a bang.

There shall sound the trumpets of the angels and the dead in Christ shall rise first, then those who are still alive shall be caught up to meet the Lord in the air and all of the saved shall be forever

[1]Energy crisis again.   [2]Great, terrific advice.

thereafter in the presence of Jesus. These are really comforting truths, so repeat them to each other down through the years.

Don't ask me when the end of the world will come. We are told that it will be like a thief in the night. It will be unexpected, that's for sure! The bad people have no idea when judgment will come, and it will hit some of them just exactly when they think they have it made.

You know better. All of us are children of light, not darkness, and so we should be always ready, constantly busy at the Lord's work.

People who don't know Christ are like people living in darkness or like a drunk passed out, but those of us who love Christ stay prepared. We look on the bright side, and using the symbols of a football player we put on the shoulder pads of faith and love, the helmet of salvation, and we are ready, really ready!

God has provided for us salvation in Jesus, who died for us, and who will bring us to him whether we are still alive or previously dead; so pass the word.

Be good to your preachers for they are doing the best they can to help you. Keep the peace.

Now for a little final group of tidbits of advice, very sound.

Stay away from the trouble makers.

Help the retarded, be tolerant to everyone, don't swap evil for evil, but try to be good to everyone. Be happy. Pray regularly. Be constantly thankful to God, for God expects this of all Christians.

Don't throw cold water on christian enthusiasm, at least listen to prophesy; don't go off half cocked, get the whole story, and hold on tightly to good habits.

Avoid even the appearance of evil. If you try hard on all these the Lord will bless you.

I pray that God will help you be free of sin and ready for Christ when he comes, for the word of the Lord is absolutely true.

Please pray for us. Give each other the usual peck on the cheek.

I insist that you read this letter aloud in church.

The grace of our Lord Jesus Christ be with you. Amen.

Paul

2nd LETTER TO THE THESSALONIANS
Athens, Greece

Dear Oakies[1]:

Chap. 1

Tim, Sully, and Paul (that's me) are writing to you all again, that is to those who believe in Christ and are associated with the church. May all the goodness of God the Father and the Lord Jesus Christ come your way, for you are a wonderful people and we thank the Lord for you. It is reported that your faith is increasing and that you are getting along with each other in the spirit of love and understanding.

We are very proud of you, how you are developing in spite of difficulties, and you can be sure that the Lord will punish the people who give you trouble. We will all get a big break when Jesus comes with all the angels and at that time Christ will fix the wicked, but good! For the wicked shall be doomed to eternal separation from God, and this will be done at the time Christ comes in glory, to be acclaimed by all who believe on him.

Our prayers are that you remain faithful, that you continue to do the work of Christ and then your good works will be a glory to the name of Jesus, and you will all draw closer to Christ.

Chap. 2

Don't let our writing to you this way make you apprehensive about the second coming nor should you get the impression that it will happen any day now. There are lots of things yet to happen before Christ comes again.

One thing, there will be a great loss of interest in spiritual matters. There must also arise a great man of sin, a real meany, and he will try to convince people that he is above God, having his own church and his own system. This man of the devil has yet to come, but when he does, remember that we warned you.

It seems strange that the Lord allows evil to exist, but that's God's business. God will stop evil when the time is ripe. At this time, the Lord will reveal the wicked one and shall squash him with the full power and brightness of God.

At this time also there shall be the destruction of the evil one, the #1 Bad Man, and God will allow many to follow this big blow hard and this will mean that those who reject the truth of Christ will follow Satan to destruction.

It is great that you all have been designated by God for salvation for you are believers, having responded to the good news of

[1]People of Thessalonica

285

the gospel and thereby attaining glory in the Lord Jesus Christ.

Be tough and faithful. Hold on to the basic truths that we taught you. I am certain that God the Father, who loves all of us, and who has given us hope through his kindness will continue to bless you and comfort you and will also support the work you are doing in the church and will strengthen your teaching program.

Chap.

3

Good friends, pray for us, pray that we may successfully testify to others as we did with you all. Pray also that we may be protected from some sorry and unreasonable people, for there are plenty of them who have no real religious depth at all.

We are confident that the Lord will bless you and protect you from evil and lead you even more surely in the love of God, being willing to be patient as you expect the second coming.

We order you to quit all unnecessary associations with disorderly folks. We set you a pretty good example when we were with you, for we paid our bills, and we worked hard, even though we didn't have to do either, but we wanted to set a good example for you.

You may remember when we were with you that we had a staff slogan which said "if you don't work, you don't eat."

We are told that there are some religious phonies operating in your area who don't work, but are just busy bodies, sticking their noses in other people's business and never picking up a check, even at the Dairy Queen.

Never tire of doing good work. If any of the people in the church don't follow the above instructions, begin to leave such persons alone. Don't consider such enemies, but when one of them wonders why you are not as interested in him as you had been, tell him and try to win him to a better understanding of Christ.

May the Lord be always with you. I will make my mark at the end of the letter so you'll know that is from me.

The grace of our Lord Jesus Christ be with you all. Amen.

Sincerely,

Paul

EDITOR'S NOTE

Paul wrote to Timothy letters of advice when Timothy was elected a bishop. Although Paul himself had never been a bishop, he felt in a position to advise Tim[1], as the letters indicate. Paul did have specific ideas about the church and how it should be run.

1st LETTER TO TIMOTHY
Wyoming Territory[2]

Dear Tim:

Continually I think of you as my own son, and you are my son in the faith. I remember instructing you to straighten out a few teachers and preachers in Sydney and also to tell the people not to get sucked in or influenced by fancy fables. Another thing to warn the people about is discussion groups whose sole purpose is to raise disturbing questions. You be sure and just present the faith, straight and unadorned.

Teach the people to show love emanating from a pure heart and a good conscience. Some of the church people have turned from the basics and are enjoying developing a lot of side issues. There are some others who are merely church legalists or people who have learned a number of high sounding phrases and theological expressions and don't know the meaning of them when they say them.

The law is fine if it is properly used. The law is not designed for the good man, but the law is set up because of murderers, thieves, whore house regulars, women who entice men, liars, perjurers and other matters completely contrary to the teaching of the gospel of Jesus Christ.

God has really been good to me for I was a blasphemer and a persecutor of Christians, but since I did not know any better, God showed mercy on me, and the Lord placed me in the ministry a new person with a new mission.

Jesus came into the world to save sinners, and when he saved me he saved the worst sinner of them all. I was changed and made an apostle in order that I might teach and preach the good news, and be an example.

I am therefore exceedingly grateful to the King Eternal, immortal, invisible, the only completely wise God, and so to Him I give honor and glory forever and forever. Amen.

I charge you then, Tim, to wage a mighty war on the wicked, keeping your faith and your conscience. Some Christians have wrecked their lives by thinking that they can get by without a

[1]We still have bachelors teaching programs or courses on marriage and family life. [2]Laodicea

conscience. I know two by name,[1] Hoot[2] and Alex[3] and I have pronounced a curse on them so the devil can have a big time with them. That will teach them to make fun of God.

Chap.
2

Let me give you some good instructions. Pray for all people, give thanks to God regularly, pray for those in authority that they may rule fairly and wisely, for God would prefer that all men be saved.

There is one God, and there is only one Christ, who is the mediator between mankind and God, and who gave himself as a ransom paid for the release of man.

I promise you for sure, Tim, that I am an ordained minister, a full-fledged apostle, and I teach people to pray without anger and with complete faith.

Here are a few suggestions that I make. Tell the women to dress modestly, not to wear pearls and expensive jewelry, not to tint their hair, and tell the ladies to learn with their lips zipped, in full humility, and tell them not to teach or to talk, but to listen.[4]

My reasoning is that Adam came before Eve and so had more experience.[5] Since the women produce the children, though, they will be forgiven the apple trick as long as they live in faith, and love, and sobriety.

Chap.
3

It is absolutely true that it is good to desire a prominent church office. If a man is to be a bishop, though, he must have only one wife, he must be industrious, well behaved, serious minded, not inclined to do much drinking, not greedy, nor a loud-mouthed brawler. A bishop should rule well his own house and have the respect of his children. It stands to reason that if a fellow can't administer his own house, he won't do much of a job of administering the house of God.

A bishop shouldn't be too young, but should be experienced and should have a good local reputation.

Deacons in the church should be serious minded, dedicated, and they should not be two-faced. Deacons shouldn't be much on drinking; they should be generous people, and strong in their faith. The above attributes should be proven before a person is elected a deacon.

The deacon's wives must be on the up and up also, not gossip types, but dedicated and faithful. The deacon should be able to rule his own house. A good deacon stands very high with God.

---

[1]I know four   [2]Hymenaeus   [3]Alexander
[4]It could be that Tim wrote back and said, 'Paul, you tell them.'
[5]But no experience with women.

I am writing all these things in case my plans to come to see you shortly don't materialize. I am anxious for you to know how to behave in church, which is the church of the living God, and the basis of truth.

I admit it all sounds mysterious, but God revealed himself in the flesh, was proven in the spirit, seen of the angels, all of which has been preached to the non-Jews. Jesus was believed by many and then taken into glory.

**Chap.
4**

The spirit has made it very clear that as the time for the end of the world approaches, there shall be a loss of influence on the part of the church, and people shall be influenced by mediums, horoscopes, and doctrines of the devil. There shall be people telling big lies, hypocrites pronouncing all types of strange rulings such as prohibiting marriage, giving up eating meat, although God says we are to thank him for giving us meat to eat.

A good minister points these things out to his congregation. Don't be sucked in by quaint old remedies and long winded old wives tales. Taking a lot of bodily exercise doesn't help you, but spend more time working on the things of the Lord. The things of God, such as peace and good will, are good for this world and the next. You can't beat that deal!

All the work we do and all the miseries we endure are signs that we trust in the Lord. Preach this way.

Don't let the people give you a hard time because you're young. You be a wonderful example in spirit, in purity, in love, in conversation. Until I can come and give you more personal instruction, read a lot and preach a lot.

Don't neglect your talents, nor the inspiration that came to you when you were ordained and had the laying on the hands. Spend time in meditation.

Keep close tab on yourself, stay fresh in your belief, and you will help yourself as well as the people to whom you preach.

**Chap.
5**

There is no use in you smarting off at an older person, young as you are. Be gentle and persuasive. Treat younger men as friends and elderly women as mothers while you must treat the young ladies as sisters.

Be very considerate of widows, if they are genuine ones and not phonies.

Tell the children to learn to behave at home before they come to church.[1]

A good widow is one who prays, behaves herself, does church

---

[1] I think you better tell them more than once.

work, and is respected while a wild widow is already dead and doesn't know it.

A fellow that doesn't provide for his family is a real bad one.

Try to convince a widow that is over 60 years of age to concentrate on church work, to live a life of service, to be a busy and helpful person in the community. As for the young widows, it is better for them to remarry and raise another family, or else they may just become hell raisers, idle persons, gossip carriers.

If a man is able to support the widows in his own family, such as a brother's wife, let him do it and let the church be responsible only for those who have no family connection.

Give extra recognition to elders who rule well and who work well in the church. It has been said that you shouldn't muzzle the ox that treads the corn, or that a laborer is worthy of his hire.

If an elder is charged with doing wrong let it be a matter presented by at least two or three witnesses. If the elder is guilty, then publicly rebuke him as an example.[1]

I seriously charge you, Tim, before God the Father and our Lord Jesus Christ, that you follow my instructions, that you do so without showing any partiality or preference in dealing with people.

Don't ordain anybody in a hurry, and don't fall into sin just to be with the fellows.

You should quit drinking water as it is polluted and you should use a modest amount of wine. The wine will help a little with your bad knee.

Some people's sins are obvious and some won't be known until judgment day, and the same goes for the good news, as some persons good deeds show very readily and others will be acclaimed on the final day.

Chap.

6

Employees should show respect for their employers, because this is the system that God devised. Employees should show even more respect to an employer who believes in Christ. Teach your congregation these things.

Anybody in church who resents hearing this type of preaching is too proud, and stupid to boot. Fellows like that want to waste most of their time in aimless disputes, trying to corrupt minds, and mislead the innocent.

Look out for the fellow that thinks that if you're good enough you'll get rich. Nuts to that!

A godly man has peace, which is worth more than money. We didn't bring anything into this world and we aren't going to get to take anything out of it. If you've got food and clothes, that's enough.

[1]This also usually means you lose an elder.

It is very difficult to be rich, for there are many temptations and snares, for the love of money is the source of all evil. Don't just sit around wishing for money.

The things to seek are righteousness, faith, love, patience, humility, and understanding. Fight the good fight of faith, hold on tightly to the concept of life eternal. You have chosen the highest calling, Tim, that of the ministry, and so rejoice.

I remind you in the name of Christ, who was condemned by Judge Bean, that you follow my instructions until Christ comes again. Christ is coming; he is King of Kings, Lord of Lords; he is immortal, the great source of all light, and in this state, he cannot be seen, but to him is all power and all honor.

Preach to the rich and tell them not to be snooty, nor to trust too much in their riches, but to trust in the living God who has given to mankind all the riches of the world.

Encourage the rich to do good so that they may be rich in good deeds, ready to give generously, willing to listen to other's ideas, and thereby set aside for themselves a store that will stand them in good when the day comes for final judgment.

Tim, keep the faith. I've entrusted it to you. Avoid cussing and useless popping off at the mouth, and don't concern yourself with silly bits of unproven science that may seem to oppose your faith.

Grace be with you. I am Paul, of course, an apostle of Jesus Christ by commandment of God.

Paul

2nd LETTER TO TIMOTHY
In jail,
Rome, Italy.

Dear Tim:

It would be a tremendous treat to see you, for actually I think of you as a son. May the grace of God be with you abundantly. I am, as you know, Paul, an apostle of the Lord Jesus Christ by the will and plan of God.

It was a great day when I put my hands on you and you dedicated your life to Christ, the holy spirit surely came to you, with power and love and clear thinking. A lot of good things come to you naturally through your mother Eunice and your grandmother Lois.

Never be ashamed to affirm your faith in Christ, and don't be ashamed of me either. Bear in mind that we are called of God to holy pursuits, nor because we are something ourselves, but because God chose to make us his instruments. Such things are in accordance with the plans of God, which plans have been in existence since the beginning.

Part of the plan involved the coming of a Saviour, Jesus Christ, who conquered death and who brought a new life and a bright immortality through the good news of the gospel. As for me, my part is to be a teacher and a preacher of all these things to the non-jew.

I know exactly in whom I believe, and I am positive that everything I do for Christ will be recorded favorably for me and mentioned in the final judgment.

Stick carefully, Tim, to the basics that I taught you. I guess you know that there are some who object considerably to me, such as Bonnie[1] and Clyde.[2]

May the Lord bless the home of Bob Trull[3] for he helped refresh me when I needed him and he didn't mind my being a jailbird. In fact, he often looked me up, and I pray that the Lord will look very favorably on him at judgment day, for he is a real good man, and was good to me.

Chap.
2

Tim, you have to be pretty tough in the preaching business, if you are true to Christ. Tell others the things that I have taught you, for this is the mission of the church. Don't get too involved in business matters and pursuits that are entirely earthly, for your goal is to please Christ.

If a person seeks to excel in anything this is fine as long as it is legal and a good cause. The hard working man has the right to benefit from his work. I hope the Lord will give you further understanding in everything.

[1]Phygelus [2]Hermogenes   [3]Onesiphorus

As you know, I am in jail, but the gospel of Jesus is not restricted and the essence of that gospel is that Jesus rose from the dead. I am able to adjust to all my problems because I am working hard to present the means of salvation in Christ to everybody that I can reach.

It is true that if we die as christians we shall be resurrected as Christ's people. If we suffer because of Christ we will be all the more honored when he comes again, while if we deny him, then when Christ comes again he will deny us. Christ is sure, certain, and true, whether anyone believes or not.

Tell the people all these things. Don't mince words. Study hard yourself, work at improving under God, and you need not be ashamed of what you're doing. Skip most of the big bull sessions as a monumental waste of time, as well as possibly being a bad influence and irritating to boot. Tom[1] and Joe[2] are good examples.[3] These fellows poo-pooh the resurrection and think death is the end.

The Lord knows who are his. God has marked them. Everyone then that professes faith in Christ should at once cease to do evil. Every community is full of good people and bad people, some help a place and some ruin it. Try hard to be one of the good ones, and convince others of this.

This means doing away with young man's antics and pursuing faith, love, peace, and understanding, talking and thinking often of these things.

Avoid foolish arguments over unimportant matters, and remember that a true servant of the Lord learns to be gentle and understanding, patient and willing to teach. Inform people of opposite views in a calm and helpful manner and you may lead them to repent their ways, turn to the Lord, and escape the clutches of the devil who has had them all along.

Chap.

3

As the end of the world approaches things are going to get mighty dangerous on this earth. People will be selfish, loud mouth boasters, proud, disobedient to their parents, truce breakers, ungrateful, violent types, against Christians, high falooting braggarts, and more concerned about their own pleasures than about God.

Turn away from these people, for they have no power from God. Some of these people are rapists and others are notorious procurers and drug pushers, always seeming to learn something bright and new and yet never learning the truth of life. There were some people like this that defied Moses and they were eliminated in time and so these modern agnostics will be mowed down in the grind of life.

You know all the difficulties that I have endured, persecutions,

---

[1]Hymenaeus   [2]Philetus   [3]You can supply your own local names.

beatings, cussings, ship wrecked, well I came out all right for the
Lord was with me. If you live properly under Christ you will get to
suffer, but it will be even worse for the evil types, for they shall lead
a life of deceit, deceiving some people and being deceived by others.

You just keep following the basics that I taught you, Tim. You
have also known the word of God from the time you were a baby
and you have been brought under the plan of salvation in Jesus
Christ.

All of the scripture is the result of inspiration by the Lord and
should be used for doctrine, as a means of pointing out people's
errors, for instruction in the right way of life with the result that a
true man of God moves toward perfection, full of good works.

Chap.

4

Finally, Tim, in the name of Jesus our Lord, I charge you to
preach the word, winter and summer; encourage those that need
stimulation and help those that need correction.

The time will come in the church when many leaders will get
bored with teaching sound doctrine[1] and will develop all kinds of
strange tangents, and people will seek odd characters as leaders who
will scratch their itching ears with fables and false comforts.

You're an evangelist. Work like me!

As for me, I'm about to have my second trial under Nero, and I
think it's going to be the last of ole Paul. I have fought a good fight; I
have kept the faith; and I know there is set aside for me a crown, so
to speak, of real understanding which has my name on it, and which
the Lord will give me on Judgment Day. I won't be by myself, for all
who have died in Christ will also be crowned.

Try to come to see me, Tim. Ole Slim,[2] who just loved to glory
and frolic too much, has gone to the land of the Oakies. In fact,
everybody on my staff has gone except Luke.

When you come bring Mark with you. He'll be a help now. Ty
Cobb has gone on the Family Night Supper Tour in Sydney.

I left my good winter coat at the Hilton so bring it when you
come, also my books and all my parchments.[3]

Alexander, the penny-pinching tightwad, did me wrong and I
have asked the Lord to reward him according to his works.[4] Watch
that Alexander; he's pigheaded to boot.

My support here has dwindled away since I made the Emperor
angry. The Lord is with me though, and the Lord gave me the
strength to preach so that the word is out in Rome, and the non-Jews
now know that Christ is for them also.

The Lord will help me keep the faith, having gotten me through

---

[1]It's come a time or two already.   [2]Demas
[3]Tim decided not to come.   [4]High level sacking.

with my first session with Nero without getting fed to the lions. The Lord will preserve me for his heavenly kingdom, and to the Lord may there by glory forever. Amen.

My love to Priscilla and John Alden and to Mrs. Childs and her household.

Try to get here before winter, Tim. Several around here send their best regards.

The Lord Jesus Christ be with you and keep your spirits in high gear.

Grace be to you,

Your friend,

Paul

Dear Titus:

I consider myself a servant of God, an apostle of the Lord Jesus Christ, living in the hope of life eternal, a thing which God, who never lies, has promised. God has also committed me to preach his word.

You are in a sense my own son because of our common faith, and may the grace, mercy, and peace of God the Father and our Lord Jesus be with you.

Your purpose in Crete, where I left you, is to set things in order, to ordain elders in every city. Select men who are as blameless as possible, the husband of one wife, and with well behaved children, for a Christian leader must act as a steward of God. Actually he should not be selfish, nor hot tempered, nor given to a lot of drinking, nor should he be quick to slug anybody, and not greedy, but a friend of cordiality, a man who engages in wholesome fellowship, sober, just, temperate. Each leader should be strong in following the word of God, for he must be able to exhort and persuade people.

There are many unruly people, big talkers, real phonies, especially among the Christian Jews. These men mislead whole households and they must be hushed for they are only interested in money.

One of their own natives has accused some of these Cretans of being liars, evil doers, and bums. I agree with this evaluation. Do what you can to straighten up this crowd. Be careful not to get trapped by clever sayings which simply originate with men.

All things are apt to look good to the pure in heart but to the vile, or two-faced person, nothing is pure and everyone is suspect. These people profess to know God but their deeds disprove this, and they actually are unscrupulous reprobates who oppose everything that is truly good.

When you teach, Titus, teach good, sound stuff; tell the older men to be sober, temperate, strong in their faith, full of love and patience and tell the older women to excerise integrity, to hit the wine very lightly, and not to be falsely accusing people for they need to teach the young women to be sober, to love their husbands and their children. They also need to be taught to be discreet, faithful and primarily homebodies, and obedient to their husbands.

Young men should also be sober minded. You, Titus, must set a good example. You need to be careful about what you say and what you do so that there will be no grounds on which others may disapprove of you.

You should counsel servants to be obedient to their masters, and to give no smart aleck back-talk. These servants thereby glorify the teaching of our Lord, which teachings assures us that the grace of God is available for the salvation of all men.

We are all taught to live soberly and properly, giving up ungodliness and worldly lusts in the sure hope of the glorious appearance of the great God and our Saviour Jesus Christ. For it was Christ who gave himself for us to redeem us. These things speak forth boldly and with authority and do not put up with any denouncers.

Chap.

3

Instruct the Cretans to be law-abiding and respect authority, and to be ready to do any good work. They should be taught to speak evil of no one, to desist from brawling, but to develop gentleness and understanding toward all men.

You and I both, Titus, have sometimes been foolish, disobedient, pursuing worldly lusts, doing malicious thinking, hating people, but you know what happened to us when the love of Christ came into our lives. For he saved us by his love, not through some good deeds we may have done or will do, but the refreshment of his Holy Spirit. We have been justified by his grace and made heirs of life eternal.

It is true that they who have believed in God should be careful to continue to do good works. Good works are profitable to mankind. In the process, however, avoid foolish questions, bragging about ancestors, arguing about the law, for these things merely waste time.

After you've tried twice to teach a man about Christ and he still won't listen, forget him.

My present plans are to send either Art[1] or maybe Ty Cobb[2] to you, then you can leave the work with them and join me in Miami, for I am determined to winter there. Give my lawyer Zeke[3] and friend Abe[4] help on their journey, and don't forget yourself. See that our people look out for you properly.

Everyone around here sends greetings to you and to those of the faith that are with you.

Sincerely yours,

Paul

[1] Artemus
[2] Tychicus
[3] Zenas
[4] Apollos

LETTER TO PHILEMON

Dear Philemon:

Timothy and I are writing this together, though the words are mine. Show this letter also to Alvin[1] and to Art[2] and to the little church group that meets in your house.

First, to all of you let me say 'peace' and grace to you from God the Father and our Lord Jesus Christ. I often thank God for you because I hear of your love for Christ, your faith, and your fine attitude to those believers around you. I hope you will be increasingly effective in your witness. We are delighted that you are even now so helpful and refreshing to the saints.

I have a request to make. I could make the plea as an old man, completely devoted to Christ, but I make my plea on a basis of love, and my plea is in behalf of Osa.[3] I know he has been a loss in running away from you, but I think all this can be made a good thing for both of us.

I could, of course, keep Osa with me, as a son, but he is technically your slave, and I suggest that you take him back, without punishment, and that you receive him not as a slave but as a brother. For he is a brother to me, and to you, both in the flesh and in the Lord. If you think of me as an equal, think of him as one also.

If Osa has cost you, or if he owes you any money, simply bill it to me and I will pay you. I will do this even though you actually owe me your very life.

But, Phil, let me have occasion to greatly rejoice in you, and be refreshed that you too are working for God's cause, as I am sure you are. I am so certain of your adhering to my request that I feel you will do even more than I ask.

You might also expect me to visit you and I hope that you want me to come.

'Say 'hello' for me to Ed,[4] closely bound to Christ, and to Mark,[5] Artie,[6] Don,[7] and Lupe,[8] all fellow laborers.

Now may the grace of our Lord Jesus Christ be with your spirit.

Paul

[1] Apphia
[2] Archippus
[3] Onesimus
[4] Epaphras

[5] Marcus
[6] Aristarchus
[7] Demas
[8] Lucas

LETTER TO THE HEBREWS
Italy

Dear Hebrews:

In times past God communicated with mankind by having prophets who would speak to the people for God, but in modern times, God has chosen to speak to all of us through Jesus Christ, to whom God has given all power. Christ, being in the image of God, used the power of the word, and this same Christ is the one who purged us from sin and now sits on the right of God in glory.

Jesus has been given a higher place than any of the angels, or else the Lord would have assigned the role of redeemer to some angel. Did any prophet or anyone hear of God saying about an angel "I'll make of him a son?" Furthermore, God said that he wanted all the angels to worship Jesus.

Certainly God gave certain powers and areas of operation to the angels, but to the Son, Jesus Christ, God has said, "Take charge; it is yours." Because Jesus chose righteousness over all other available gifts, the Lord has added many other gifts. The earth will in time perish, but not Jesus. In fact, Jesus will fold the earth up as you would a coat or slip, but Christ is eternal.

Did God ever ask one of the angels to sit on his right hand? The angels are at work for Christ ministering to believers all over the world.[1]

Chap.
2

We need to make a real effort to grasp the things that have been told us, for it is easy to forget. We would be real goofy to miss the great opportunity of salvation simply by being diverted with worldly things. The angels have passed the word to us[2] and in addition we have seen signs and wonders, miracles, the demonstration of gifts of the Holy Spirit, and all those things testify to the plan of God.

The angels have a big function in the operation of the world to come while mankind has a big chance here on earth. Didn't the Psalmist raise the question, "What is man that Thou art mindful of him, or the son of man that you associated with him?" God made persons only a little lower than angels, gave mankind power and glory, and put all earthly things under his feet, subject to his control. Some things, such as pollution, have not as yet fully come under man's control.

Jesus, who was necessarily made lower than the angels on a temporary basis, suffered death for the sake of every person, in order that all people may have the chance of salvation in Christ. Jesus is not ashamed to think of believers as brothers and sisters.

[1]There are bound to be a few lazy angels.
[2]I'm not certain how this is done.

Jesus actually put the ax to the devil when he consented to die and was raised triumphant from the grave so that all people could in him overcome death. It was for this reason that Jesus came to earth as a person rather than an angel. Jesus was made man so that he could be the one to completely reconcile man to God.

It is proper to think of Jesus Christ as the top High Priest and Apostle of christianity, for Jesus was solid true to God as Moses was, and then some. Christ is to be more honored than Moses as you naturally honor the builder of a house more than the house itself.

Moses was a great one for his job and with his authority, but Christ is over the whole church and is the real hope that all people have.

The Holy Spirit reminds us to hear the words of Jesus and not to harden our hearts as the early Jews did during the 40 years in the wilderness. The Lord really got fed up with that bunch. Be careful that you don't get like some of these folks and resist the word of the Lord. Not all the people were pig headed; some were faithful and God delivered them, but most of the hard-heads died in the wilderness. Those that died in the wilderness were simply not being allowed to enter the promised land because they didn't believe in the power of God.

All of us should learn from this and be careful not to lose the opportunity of eternal life because we didn't believe.

The good news has been preached to us as it was to the early Jews; but they had no faith. Those of us today who believe have it made, and not by works, for the works of the world were planned long ago by God.

God said that after creating everything he entered a period of rest, known as the era of the seventh day, and we have the chance to enter this era with God. Jesus explained that God has promised mankind a period of rest, set aside for those who believe and obey.

The basic thrust of work must then be to reach the place of rest in God, rather than work to accomplish earthly advancements. The word of God is impressive, it is sharp like a double edge razor, and creates all kinds of inner conflicts. There are no secrets or devious matters hidden from God.

We have an exalted high priest, ascended already into heaven, and so let us be faithful Christians. Our high priest is very understanding of our problems, for he was tempted in all points just as we are, and yet he never sinned or faltered. We need then to present ourselves to Christ and seek forgiveness and call on his mercy.

Priests or ministers that conduct services in the churches are ordained by men and these persons offer public prayer and seek forgiveness for the people as well as 'for themselves. Ministers or priests should be called of God and not persons seeking something for themselves.

Christ did not make a big noise about himself, but the Lord God who said of Christ "Thou art my Son" also said that Christ was made the head of all churches, and that Christ had direct access to God himself. Jesus Christ was perfect and completely obedient to God.

There are a lot of things about theology and religion that you need to know, but you people are really slower learners in this area. I had hoped that by now you would be teaching, but instead of that you are still in the learning process. In a way, you are like youngsters still on a milk diet and I am anxious for you to mature enough so that we can start giving you some real theological meat to chew on and digest.

So much for that. Now as to the matter of reaching to perfection, let's consider a few things. Baptism, the laying on of the hands, and the resurrection of the dead; all these things are basic and points of beginning.

Once a person has repented and truly turned to Christ, such a person should never forsake the basic truths. If a person, once having given over to Christ, turns bad again and rejects Christ, then it is as if that person crucifies Christ again. This is a real bad scene and usually means that the person burns like thorns and weeds in the hot summer.

Don't get me wrong, I don't expect any such disaster for any of you all. We really plead with you to work hard in the cause of Christ, and be completely hopeful that all things will eventually turn to be good.

Just like old Abraham; God promised Abraham a son and ole Abe obeyed God, remained faithful, was patient, and in his advanced years was given a son.

Since men seem to be impressed by high sounding affirmations and promises, God made his promises as an oath or vow so that mankind would understand that God meant business.

Our real hope then is like a strong anchor, for we have Jesus Christ, our high priest and holy leader, and we can turn to him with all our troubles and in him see all our hopes being fulfilled.

The first front line priest that we know anything about was Big Poppa,[1] and somehow he just happened to be. There is no record of

[1]Melchisedec

who were his father and mother, all we know is that he was a priest of God and he was so all fired important that Abraham, our big chief leader, paid him a tithe and did so gladly. It is hard to imagine a person so important that Abraham voluntarily gave him large sums of money.

Now the descendants of Levi, who have all gone to seminary and definitely appointed priests, these persons all received tithes because that's the way the Book of Church Order set things to be. The ministers and priests who receive the tithes from the people are also required to pay tithes themselves.

If the system of priests or ministers on the order of Levi[1] operating under the law had been a perfect system then there would have been no need for a new high priest, one mysteriously born like Big Poppa, who was created not just as a temporary person, but the introducer of life eternal.

The system of law did not make for perfection, but the new hope in Jesus did make perfect our opportunity with God. God simply said to Christ, "You are a priest forever."

The normal, everyday minister is subject to death just as is everyone else but not so with Jesus Christ, who is a minister forever. Jesus is therefore able to save those who come to him, as he intercedes with God in behalf of the believers.

The one super high priest, Jesus Christ, is holy, completely separate from sin and sinners, and does not need to perform daily rites or have his sins forgiven, for he is sinless.

The law and the liturgy may make a person a minister, even though such continue to be very human, but the word of God makes an eternal minister of the Lord Jesus Christ.

Chap.
8

In short, we have a leader sitting in heaven, he is in charge of all functions, and he doesn't need to be on earth now as we have ministers representing him and priests. Christ, the head of the church and of all things, has arranged a new agreement with God. If the first agreement had worked we wouldn't need the new arrangement, but it didn't work.

In fact, the Lord said in the Old Testament, "The day shall come when I will make a new agreement, different from the arrangement that I had with the early Hebrews, leading them out of Egypt. This deal didn't work because the early Hebrews blew their chance."

The new arrangement which the Lord promised is an arrangement where the Lord puts the desire to be good in the hearts and on the minds of the people. Eventually it will not be necessary to preach or teach, for everyone from the smallest to the greatest

[1]Nothing to do with pants.

shall believe in God.

God also announced that a plan was devised for the forgiveness of sin and that the new agreement meant that the old agreement was a goner.

Before Christ, the eternal high priest, came to earth there was a formal and legalistic arrangement made between man and God relative to worship. The tabernacle was considered the place of worship and the first section of the tabernacle was usually referred to as the sanctuary. In the sanctuary was always a candlestick, a table, and bread. There was a curtain separating this area from the second section, which was called the Holy of Holies. No person was allowed to go into the Holy of Holies except the high priest, and the high priest only went once a year. In this area was the golden incense pot, the ark of the covenant, and on the ark of the covenant was manna, Aaron's rod, and the written covenant which God made to the people through Moses.

Although regular worship services were conducted in the tabernacle, once a year the high priest, carrying a blood offering, went into the second area and sought forgiveness for the sins of the people.

The sacrifices made during these services were not always helpful to a person's conscience, as all the meats, the blood of the calves and goats, the ashes of a heifer, were too obviously worldly to be completely helpful.

Now when the blood of Christ was shed for mankind, this made the whole picture different. It is easy to reason that if the blood of bulls and goats was helpful in an arrangement with God how much more helpful was the blood of Christ.

It is then understandable how Christ exists as the mediator of the new arrangement between mankind and God. The new arrangement is in the form of a will, which means that it comes into operation only after the death of the originator; so after Christ died and rose from the grave the new covenant became effective.

Moses initiated the first covenant by taking the blood of calves and goats, scarlet wools, and hyssop, and sprinkled the blood on the book as well as the people. Moses also sprinkled the tabernacle with blood as the people all felt that nothing was sanctified or cleansed without a blood offering.

The sacrifices of calves and goats was acceptable for handling earthly affairs, but heavenly affairs needed a heavenly sacrifice. Christ then was not brought as a sacrifice into the church, but was taken to heaven and to appear before God in our behalf.

It is also to be noted that Christ did not need to be sacrificed each year and brought into the church, but only one time was it necessary for Christ to die for our sins.

And so it is with all mankind, that we die only once. Christ has offered the one time to bear the sins of man and so persons die only once and may look to the second coming and resurrection of those persons who have accepted Christ, for he will claim all such to be his.

The old way was good, but inadequate, for it was a year by year, and it was a earthly matter. Not only that, it is reasonable to figure that the blood of bulls and goats couldn't completely cleanse a person of sin.

The Lord had already said that he had no pleasure in burnt offerings, or the sacrifice of animals, the liturgical approach. When Christ came, though, to do the will of God, then we were really able to be purified in the sacrifice of the body of Jesus Christ.

Christ offered himself, was one great sacrifice one time, then ascended and sits on the right hand of God as a mediator for mankind. This I can believe and furthermore it makes sense. The Holy Spirit is a further witness to this fact.

It was to this time that God referred when he said that he would write his new agreement on the hearts and in the minds of mankind.

There is then no longer a second section in the church into which we cannot enter for we have a new system and a new high priest, who is Christ. Let us then face life with fresh vigor and a new faith.

This means that we should think in terms of love for our fellow man, and we should grow in faith and practice as we get older and nearer to the end which will mean judgment for us.

Once we know about Christ and accept him we do not need to sacrifice bulls and goats. Yet it is a very dangerous thing to run the risk of defying or making angry the living God, for with two or three witnesses an early Hebrew could be convicted and executed by Moses, but that was only earthly death. To violate the new arrangement with God brings eternal punishment, for God has said "Vengence is mine."

There are no doubt some persecutions and afflications, and people often will give you the poo-pooh as a Christian, but wait it out, for Christ is coming again, you'll meet him, and Jesus will subdue all enemies, putting all of them in their place, and he will honor the believers.

I urge you to live by this faith, and I have no use for a backslider. We don't advocate slipping back into a lost condition, but we offer salvation in Christ.

Faith is made up of things which we hope will be, and these things are not things that can be seen, or felt, or smelled. Faith teaches us that the world was created by God, even though we weren't eye witnesses. Faith testifies to the word making all things from nothing.

By faith Abel offered a more acceptable sacrifice than Cain because he had a good attitude about it. Even though the result was the early death of Abel his goodness and his generosity lived as a memorial to him.

Bill Slater[1] was such a good man and so close to God that he didn't die but just walked off one day with God.

There is no way of pleasing God without faith. A person must truly and sincerely believe in God and also believe that God rewards those who earnestly search for him.

Noah is a good example of faith for he built a big ship where there was no water and he took a lot of flack from his neighbors,[2] but his faith saved him and his family.

By faith Abe went at God's call to an unknown land, without even a map. Abe lived in a new land and reared his children in the faith for he was counting on eventually living in a place built by God for believers.

Abe's wife Sarah had a child in her later years because of belief in the absolute power of God and from the son which she had there came a nation plus nations, many thousands of people who lived and died in complete faith in the power of God. Many of these died without having received many benefits in this life, but they knew they were just short time strangers on this earth and were looking to the fulfillment of God's promises in a world to come.

God is delighted to be the God of such people and God has prepared a special place for them.

Abe was the one who was willing to offer his only son, Ike, to be sacrificed being confident that God could raise Ike from the dead. Ike in his time passed the blessing of God on down through Jacob and J.P.[3]

Joseph in his time passed the blessing of God to his sons, mentioning the eventual departure of the children of Israel from Egypt and even arranged to make sure that his bones made the trip.

How about Moses? It was all a matter of faith, the being hidden in the duck blind, defying Pharoah, for he thought more of the greater riches forthcoming in Christ. Moses kept the faith, led the people through the Red Sea and watched a whole bunch of Egyptians drown trying to catch him.

It was faith that destroyed the walls of Jericho and saved Virginia Slim[4] and her group. Do you want to hear more?

[1]Enoch [2]His wife also wanted him to clean out the attic.
[3]Esau   [4]Rahab

I could go on telling about Gideon, Samson, David, Samuel and a bunch of others, who knew the promises of God and in faith they subdued kingdoms, closed the mouths of lions, put out fires, escaped from the sword, were heroes in battle, and some even worked their way through college.

Women were persons of faith also.

Some accepted torture, lived on when loved ones died, suffered imprisonment, beatings, and stoning. Many persons of faith were forced from their homes, wandered in the wilderness, were broke, sick, poorly dressed, forced to live in caves and these stuck it out in faith, receiving no reward on this earth, but still believing the fulfillment of the promises of God in the world to come. God has, of course, provided a better place for all such than even they could imagine.

Chap.
12

When we consider such a tremendous host of witnesses to the faith, surely we are inspired to set aside our petty gripes, resist temptation, and move forward faithfully in life, constantly working and improving.

We are fortunate, for we can look to Jesus who wrote the first as well as the last chapter in the book of life. This same Jesus, because he considered it a pleasure to serve, endured the cross, accepted the taunts and mortification of his trial, and he is now at the right hand of God. Think of all that Christ did and don't worry about the little inconveniences and set backs that come your way.

You have been told as children not to take lightly the sufferings of Christ, nor to fold up when you have to suffer, for whom the Lord loves he causes to suffer. After you have shown that you can take it a bit God will receive you as a son. Even an earthly father has to correct or paddle his son, and then he rejoices in him. If you never suffer then you are not a son and that leaves you entirely out of the family.

Reason this way, maybe. We have received correction from our earthly father and we still loved and respected him, certainly we should even more show love and respect for our heavenly Father.

I agree that nobody really likes to suffer or ache or be mistreated, but enduring such builds character and makes a person more understanding.

Get with the program! Walk a straight path, plan to be peaceful, and seek to be holy, or else you'll never see God.

Watch for bitterness as it will defile you, beware of being a money grabber and one who seeks only riches, or you'll be like J. P. and be willing to sell anything anytime. You are not living on Sinai with God and petrified with fear, but you are living in the kingdom of God, a place controlled by love; you are going to the city of God, into an association with hundreds of angels. You will be joining the one great eternal church in Christ, with others, many great persons, all purified by Christ. You will be in the presence of Jesus, the mediator, it is his blood that shall be sprinkled as a part of the worship. Accept Christ. Don't dare refuse him.

Those that refused Christ when he was present are doomed, so what chance do you think you'll have if you refuse him as he speaks to you today through his preachers? Christ, you know is ascended, and runs the world from heaven.

God is a great consumming fire; let us serve him, let us accept the kingdom that is his and that is unshakeable, let us receive the kindness and grace of God and then serve God reverently and with great respect.

Chap.

13

Please grow in your concern for each other and be thoughtful and helpful to strangers, for sometimes without knowing it you might have cared for an angel.

Be very sympathetic with those who are in jail or who have arthritis.

Marriage is a fine arrangement, but persons who frequent houses of prostitution and who are adulterers will be judged by God.

Be satisfied with what you have and don't always be wanting things because other people have them.[1] Don't be always talking about things you'll never get, remember that you have the Lord with you, and God will never forsake you.

You shouldn't ever be afraid of what man will do to you for you have God as your helper. Listen carefully to your preacher and follow the teaching which he gives you from the Bible. Jesus Christ never changes; he is the same yesterday, today, and forever; so don't get swayed by some new wrinkle that some bird teaches or some new twist that makes the rounds.

Have your heart established in peace and love, and your belief in Christ. Christ allowed himself to be tortured outside the city as a symbol of the liturgical practice of doing away with the bodies of the beasts whose blood was brought into the tabernacle as a sacrifice.

Let us go to Christ where he is, out in the world, looking for a city that is to come, praising God and giving thanks continually in his name.

To do good deeds and to teach about Jesus are the sacrifices that please God under the new arrangement.

Respect authority. Pray for us, for we are trying in good conscience to do a good job. Maybe you might pray that I get to visit with you all soon.

May the peace of God that brought Jesus Christ from the dead, the one great shepherd of the sheep, in the shedding of his blood,

[1]Ouch!

help you grow toward perfection, doing good works according to the will of God. May all that you do please God as you do things in the name of Jesus Christ, to whom be glory forever and ever. Amen.

This is a short letter, but you pay attention to everything in it.

Tim has been released from jail and is headed your way. Give your church leaders and all your associates in Christ my best regards. The people here in Italy send their best.

> Sincerely yours,
> Peter, Paul or the like
> (I think it was Paul)

JAMES

Dear Members of the Twelve Tribes:

You are, of course, scattered widely, but do not worry, not even about unfamiliar temptations in strange places, for actually encountering these things in faith strengthens you, and you develop patience, knowing that eventually this works to perfection.

If some of you feel that you just aren't smart enough to cope with modern conditions, simply ask God and He will come to your assistance. However, you must ask fully believing, not just to see if asking works, for if you just trifle with prayer you are no more effective than the top of a wind-tossed wave. You must ask unselfishly, too, and not with ulterior motives, or you will receive nothing. There is no security in self-purpose.

It doesn't matter really whether the disadvantaged is exalted or the affluent is brought low, as long as it is God's doing, for man's days are as grass, it withers under the sun and the flower falls. So shall the self-seeking worldly-minded be.

Full of life, however, is the man that overcomes temptation, for when he is victorious he receives the wholesome joy of living as well as the eternal crown promised of God.

Now don't blame temptation on God. Since God cannot be tempted, he does not tempt anyone, but a man is tempted when he responds to his own base desires. It is from these very desires that man involves himself in sin, and the final end of uncontrolled and unchecked sin is death.

Go as straight as you can, Brothers.

You should note that all good gifts come from God, direct to man, for we are his prized creation, and we should be the outstanding product above all his creatures.

Let me urge you to be ready to listen, slow to speak, and even slower to become angry, for anger in a man never works for the good of God.

You should lay aside all filthiness, and worldly naughtiness, and receive directly the word of God. When you hear the word of God, do not just listen, but put the word into action.

For if all you do is know what is right and don't do it, it is no more effective than seeing yourself in the mirror when you shave and going on about your business without so much as contemplating truly what kind of person you are.

The person of you, however, who does something as a consequence of belief and finds oneself under the true law of liberty, the time is happy in the deeds that are done.

If you are a person that poses as one who is deeply religious, and yet you exercise no control over your tongue, you are a phony. The religion of the true believer has results, such as visiting the fatherless and widows who are in trouble, and watching carefully to practice what one preaches.

Develop also, my friends, a faith like that of Jesus, the Lord of Glory, regarding people. Do not deal preferentially to an important person and ignore the ordinary one. It is not for you to judge who is deserving and who isn't. God has often chosen the unimportant of the world to be rich in faith and important in His kingdom. I accuse you, friends, of ignoring the common person, although you know it is the influential people that do most of the oppressing and that brings you yourselves to trial, often even making light of the cause of Christ.

If you, however, observe the royal law of 'love thy neighbor as thyself,' you are to be commended, but if you discriminate, you sin and violate the law of God. You cannot violate one part of the law without violating the whole idea of the law of God.

For God, who said, 'do not commit adultery,' also said 'do not kill'; so it is not much help to say 'I have not committed adultery' if you have killed.

The unmerciful are not apt to receive mercy, but the merciful can rejoice in hope, even more so if they both speak and live within the law of the liberty of God.

Be responsible, friends, for what good is it for one man to believe, but not to practice one's beliefs. Can people expect belief alone to save them?

For instance, if a man or a lady be without clothes or food and you say unto them "Blessings on you, I hope you will some day be warm and well fed." What is the good of this unless you get to work and provide some food and clothes?

So belief, if that is all by itself, is as if it were dead. The man who has only belief has no testimony, but real belief in Christ is shown by the works of a believer.

It is no great credit to believe in one God, even the devil does this. Belief must be put to work!

Abraham was honored by God in that he was willing even to sacrifice his son if this action would show his faith. The two are really complementary. A person must do good works, but must do these good things because of belief. Just like Abraham, he believed in God, and his integrity was tested, and he was found to be a friend of God. A person therefore is justified not just by faith, but by faith which results in works.

Do you remember about Rahab, the operator of a boarding house, how she was justified by the works she did for God's representatives? It is just like the body and the spirit, to really live it takes the two together; so with faith and works.

Now, friends, don't all of you try to be teachers and leaders. Only a completely perfect person, of whom there are none among you, could go without a slip of the tongue; so let the most skilled teach. A horse is turned easily by the bit in his mouth and a mighty ship driven by great winds is turned by a small rudder; so is the power of the tongue. The tongue is potentially a great fire and great influence, and can cause a terrific amount of trouble and evil.

Mankind has managed fairly well to tame most of the animals, but has had a hard time controlling the tongue, which is often unruly and poisonous. It is strange how blessings and cursings can come from the same mouth. It should not be this way any more than a fountain spilling forth good and bad water. Certainly you wouldn't expect a fig tree to bring forth olives! A wise person and a good person should let conversation and works represent their integrity.

Envy and strife bring about confusion and this is a concoction of mankind, it is earthly and devilish, so remove envy and strife from your heart and accept the wisdom of God, as His gift, and you will find yourself becoming gentle, peace loving, merciful, living without partiality, doing kindly deeds, devoid of hyprocrisy, and you will find an association with peaceful people, born of the fruit of a life of integrity.

Friends, have you ever thought about the real source of wars and fighting? It all starts within you. You begin by wanting something that you do not have; so you fight for it one way or another. Some pray for what they selfishly want and then wonder why they don't get it.

You crummy people, don't you know seeking wordly benefits for yourself lines you up against God? Envy is a terrible thing. God is always making adjustments because of this, resisting you proud ones and blessing the humble. Just turn yourself over to God. Give the devil a good fight and he'll flee. Move toward God and He will move toward you. Do everything you can think of to repent, wash your hands, purify your hearts, mourn, and weep, and seriously repent, present yourself humbly to God and He will lift you to unbelievable heights.

Another thing, friends, quit criticizing each other. If you judge other people you actually place yourself as a judge of the law of God, and only God is the judge. Who are you to be judging?

I understand also that a lot of you are great planners, saying I am going to do thus and so, and go to this place or that, and buy this parcel and sell that, and you don't even know if there is going to be a tomorrow. The least you can do is say, 'If the Lord is willing, I will do thus and so.'

You might also remember that you are responsible for what you know, and if you knowing what is right do not do it, you inevitably sin.

Chap.

5

Let me warn a lot of you very influential people that if you have prospered through corruption, you will in time suffer; your gold, your silver, your family shall all work against you. If you have not been fair in dealing with your workers, the Lord will hear about it even if the government doesn't. You may have it pretty easy in this life, which is short, but the judgement day of God is coming. You good people have patience, the day of the Lord is coming!

You don't need to anticipate the day of judgement of pre-judging or by being mad at the inequities of life. God is coming! Think of the prophets and all they endured, and it didn't seem long to them, or to Job. Remember God is merciful and he loves you greatly.

One of the most important things I want to say, friends, is to beware of big-mouth stuff, making big promises and threats, and swearing by heaven or earth, neither of which is yours. Simple speech is sufficient.

Adjust to your circumstances. If you feel offended, pray; if you are happy, sing; if any are sick, let the elders pray for them, and attend them, and let all seek the forgiveness of sins. I even suggest confessing to one another and praying in behalf of each other, for this brings healing. The fervent prayer of a man of integrity is very effective.

There are plenty of examples of this. Eligah was a man like anybody else, and he developed great integrity and one time asked God to cause the rain to stop and it quit for 3½ years, and then he prayed again and God caused the heavens to give forth rain again and the earth began to grow things again in that area.

A final word, friends, if any of you convert another from error and sin and bring him to Christ, that person builds up a credit for himself with God which will make up for a lot of shortcomings.

1 PETER

Dear Friends:

My name is Peter and I am an apostle of the Lord Jesus. I am writing this letter and I hope that it will be read and shown around among people everywhere, regardless of race or creed.

Thanks be to God, the father of our Lord Christ, for providing for us the great fulfillment of hope through the resurrection of Jesus Christ. In Jesus then we have the opportunity of a pure and spotless life in a world to come, a provision possible only through the power of God, all of which we will realize when the final day arrives.

We should rejoice in this assurance, although we may presently be facing many problems, even encumbered by grief and hardship. The difficulties are temporary and simply participate in the purifying process. All these things, too, will merely accentuate the glory and joy of the second coming of Christ.

There are many who have not seen Christ, yet they love him, believe on him, and are filled with the unspeakable joy of their faith.

The prophets have related the general fact of these things, telling us of the grace that would some day arrive in the flesh. It was the spirit of Christ in the prophets that enabled them to foresee the suffering and the glory of our Saviour.

So get with it! Think about it. You must realize that hope has now been fulfilled in Christ, so be obedient to the word of God, for you must seek to be holy as Christ who called you is holy.

You cannot possibly be saved by donations to worthy causes, good as such endeavors may be, but you are saved by the death and resurrection of Christ. God had planned all this, but it did not happen until our own day and age.

God raised Christ from the dead so that you might see his power and so that your faith and hope in God might be confirmed.

If you follow this reasoning then, you will develop a loving attitude toward all men, you will find yourself to be a new person, remade through the word of God, which cannot be corrupted. Flesh perishes like grass, but the word of God endures forever. This is known as preaching the gospel.

Being a new person in Christ is not easy. You must set aside all forms of hate, or prejudice, you must quit criticizing other people, and you must take the word of God like a baby to milk.

What really makes a church is the gathering together of people in Christ, who are willing to make spiritual sacrifices to the Lord, and to recognize that Jesus is the foundation stone upon which the church is built.

As Christians then you become a new group, a holy priesthood, a people who are different, you are then to become the people of God, you are called forth from darkness into light, and you are to receive the full mercy of God.

Let me suggest to you, as you become new persons, that you give up all forms of evil, that you speak fairly with all kinds of people, and that you live in such a way that the ungodly may see your good behavior and through you begin to see the glory of God.

Obey the law, for God expects this of you. Your good conduct in itself will do more to enlighten the ignorant, for you are free in Christ, but this freedom must not be misused.

Be considerate of all men, love particularly all Christians, fear the Lord, and respect authority. Deal respectfully with persons for whom you work, whether they deserve it or not, for you are enduring these hardships for God's sake.

Acutally, if you get kicked in the tail for making a mistake there is nothing to this, but to accept the kick graciously when you have not made a mistake, now that is getting close to God. You see, that is really what Christ did for us.

Christ was sinless, there was no bitterness in him, yet for our sake he accepted the suffering and the judgments against him. Christ bore in his own body our sins so that we might live in righteousness. It is by his punishment that we are healed, and instead of sheep gone astray, we are returned to the fold in Christ.

Chap.

3

Wives, I suggest that you respect your husbands if they obey the word, but if they don't, you set such a sure and stable example to them that they may see the goodness of the Word in you.

Don't concentrate on your outward appearance, worrying whether or not you need a shampoo and set, or a new piece of costume jewelry, but concern yourselves primarily with inner beauty of gracious and gentle spirit.

In the good old days, the really holy women so concerned themselves and they showed respect to their husbands. You ought to be as Sarah, who obeyed Abraham.[1]

You husbands, you should be considerate of your wives and recognize that they are weaker than you are.[2]

The best way is for husbands and wives to be of one mind, showing compassion for each other, not returning evil for evil, nor smart remark for smart remark. If you want to enjoy life you must learn to hold your tongue.

Seek peace and really pursue it. The Lord will bless the righteous and listen to their prayers, and the Lord protects his own in many different ways.

[1] Thanks, Peter, but I think your program has had it.

[2] You said it again, Peter.

Even if you suffer, and you do it for Christ's sake, you haven't lost but gained. Seek God, and be ready to answer any man in such a way that you will lead him to see real hope.

Actually, those that criticize you unjustly suffer in their own conscience, and it is better for you to suffer under criticism than to participate in evil doings.

Christ suffered, and even died, and he did it for us. It was the spirit of Christ that preached to those in prison, that was even in existence in the days of Noah and converted eight souls in the ark, who were baptized with water.[1] It is the same spirit that we expect to have transferred when we baptize, for it is the spirit of the risen Lord, who has gone to heaven and sits on the right hand of God and has charge of all the angels.

Chap.

4

For as Christ suffered for us in the flesh so must some of us suffer also, for through this we obtain a new purity and are no longer among those who drink excessively, pursue shameless women, and worship false gods.

Naturally, some of your friends will gripe about your changing, but they can tell it to the judge at the end of time.

This is why an arrangement was made for the good news of Christ to be preached to the dead.[2]

The end is near.[3] Be sober and prayerful, be generous, for this will cover a multitude of sins. Be friendly,[4] and use your talents for good. Whether you are a teacher or a minister or whatever, do your thing because it is a gift from God, that God may be glorified in the witness you make for Christ, to whom is dominion and praise forever.

Don't be upset by your hardships. Rejoice, for you are suffering with Christ, and when the revelation of his glory comes so then shall yours. If you are criticized for being Christian, feel that you have been complimented.

Don't permit youself to be a murderer or a thief or a busybody, but if you suffer, suffer as a Christian.

The time of judgment will come, with the church people being judged first and if some of them just barely make the grade in a photo finish, you can imagine what it will be for the ungodly.

Chap.

5

A word to the elders in the church, and I am one myself. Tend to the people under your care, and do so joyfully, and not with the idea of making it profitable.

You are not rulers, but examples. You will get your crown at the second coming.

[1]There was plenty of water for immersion or sprinkling. [2]A real mystery. [3]Certainly within 70 years to everybody. [4]Also drive friendly.

You young folks, listen to the experienced elders in the church. Do not be proud or vain or know-it-alls, but seek the true knowledge of God. You'll get recognition when the time is right. Depend on God. Be diligent and watchful. Your enemy is the devil and he is like a roaring lion, walking everywhere, devouring any young innocent he can find.

But the God of all grace who has called us to eternal glory in the Lord Jesus, after you have suffered a bit, will make you all well, and he will strenghten and stabilize you. To him be glory and dominion forever and ever.

I am sending this letter by hand through Sid, who I suppose is a good friend to you all. The church at Babylon sends greetings, my companion Mark says to tell you "hello," gather yourselves together regularly, greet each other with a holy kiss, and peace be with you all in Jesus Christ.

Sincerely yours,

Simon Peter

2 PETER

Dear Fellow Church Members:

Blessings on you. All of us have available the power which he gave to us, as well as other promises, all of which make it possible for us to overcome the temptations of the world.

Let me advise you never to stop growing in your faith. For your faith must produce virtue, and virtue will produce knowledge, and knowledge will lead to temperance, and temperance to patience, and patience to godliness, which then leads to brotherly love, which leads finally to the full love of Christ for all mankind.

If you grow this way, you've got it made, and you will be helpful to the cause of Christ.

A person who lacks the spiritual growth as outlined above has missed the boat, while those who do grow in Christ will eventually be living in the everlasting kingdom of our Lord and Saviour.

I know you know these things, but I expect to keep reminding you. In fact, every time I get the chance I will mention your duties to Christ, for I don't expect I will be allowed to live much longer, so I speak when I can.

The things to which I testify are not fables, for I was an eyewitness to the majesty and power of Christ.

I heard with my own ears the voice of God coming from heaven and saying, "This is my beloved son in whom I am well pleased."

Several of us heard this same voice when we were on the mount of transfiguration.

We also have the sure word of prophecy, which is as a light shining in the darkness of ignorance. Take careful note of the prophecies, for these are not the idle sayings of persons, but words spoken by holy men inspired by the Holy Spirit.

Let me warn you about phony teachers. There have always been some of this nature and they will always be present, denouncing the mysteries of God, and trying to make significant religious matters a means of making money.

God will surely punish. Didn't God even throw out the angels that smart-talked to him? Didn't God wipe out the evil people on the earth with a flood and spared only Noah, a righteous man?

Look what God did to the wicked cities of Sodom and Gomer. God did that as an example!

[1]Silvanus

Lot was delivered because he was a righteous man.[1] The Lord knows how to deliver the righteous and how to store up the wicked for the day of judgment.

People that don't believe in any type of restriction or control, are presumptuous, do as they please persons, these birds are really in for it.

Some of these persons do worse than the fallen angels and speak out big-mouth about things in regard to which they have very little information.

These people go in for rioting in the daytime and committing adultery at night. They are evil people, seeking only selfish gain, like the prophet, who being misled, had to be corrected by a donkey.

Such big-mouth operators are wells without water or like clouds blown away in a tempest. These people lure others with honey words and false promises. They offer liberty and then entrap the people at the same time.

It is terrible to follow Christ and then be influenced away by false teachers. It would be better to have never heard of Christ than to accept him and then later reject him. The case of such is like the sow getting washed and then returning to the mud.

Yours truly,

Simon Peter

Chap.
3

The next year:

Dear Fellow Church Members:

First let me remind you again of the prophecies and the commandments.

Let me warn you against scoffers that will come and they will begin to taunt you, saying, "When is Christ coming again? Maybe he missed the plane? Everything seems the same as usual, history repeats itself, and life goes on."

How stupid they are. God made the whole of existence ages and ages ago, and a thousand years are but like a day to the Lord. The Lord is coming when he gets ready, giving as much time as possible for people to repent. When the end does come, however, it will be as the thief in the night, and the whole earth and the heavens shall vanish in a big explosion.

Knowing all this, isn't it obvious what type of person you should be? For we look for a new heaven and a new earth as God has promised. Some of the things in the letters of Paul are difficult to understand and some people argue greatly about the meaning. These same people argue about the meaning of the early scriptures also, and they are headed for trouble.

[1] Also he was Abraham's nephew.

Since you know all this, be careful, do not vary from your righteous path, but grow in grace and in the knowledge of our Lord and Saviour Jesus Christ, and to him be glory both now and forever. Amen.

Yours truly,

Simon Peter

1 JOHN

Dear Folks:

Some of us were fortunate enough to actually see the Word of God in the flesh, and we tell you of these things in order that you might share with us our association with Jesus Christ. We have learned that eternal life is available and we have knowledge of God the Father and his Son Jesus that we wish to share with you.

The message is essentially that God is light and there is no darkness or depression in his presence. It is not possible to say that we believe and follow Christ and then go around like a gloom-buggy. If we walk joyfully and hopefully and have a happy relationship with our fellow believers then we will be cleansed by the blood of Jesus. Everybody sins and stands in need of cleansing, but if we confess our sins to Jesus he is willing and able to forgive us. Anybody who says he doesn't have any wrong thoughts and never does anything the least questionable is telling a big whopper, and that's a sin in itself.

Chap. 2

The reason I am writing these things to you is to encourage you not to sin, for a sure sign of following Jesus is observing his commandments. Jesus came for everybody and he has accepted the burden of the sin of the world.

Anyone who follows Christ and works at the job is always improving. You know all the old commandments and so I won't repeat them, but they are to be observed.

I have for you a new commandment in Christ, and that its that you love one another. No one can claim to be a real Christian, joyful, walking in the light, who hates another person. A person who loves people lives in the light and so isn't always stumbling over things.

A person who hates other people is really in the dark and falls over other things and has no direction in life, for such a one is in darkness.

To the beginners in Christ I say to you, "your sins are forgiven." I include the old timers in this letter for they have known the truth of God a long time and I include the young people for they are strong and vigorous and need to be able to learn to overcome evil.

Don't get too interested in the world and the things in the world for fear of putting such interests ahead of God. The desires of the flesh, the temptations which are seen, the pride of accomplishment; these things are not God's goal for mankind, and so all such things will perish and only those who love God and obey his will have access to eternal life.

You have all been told that there will come an anti-christ, and by golly there are already a bunch of anti-christs. Some of these were members of our church who left us and went out on their own pursuing some wierd tangents of thought. Those preachers and lay leaders declared themselves to be separated from us.

You people know that there is only one Christ. I am writing this way to you because I know that you know right from wrong and that you know about Christ.

Anyone who denies that Jesus is the Christ is automatically an anti-christ. A person who denies Christ, the Son, by implication denies God the Father. You people stick to the basic, Jesus Christ, the Son of God, crucified and risen from the dead, and he is the one who promises to believers eternal life.

I am writing to help prevent you from being mislead by leaders or speakers who do not accept Christ. If you are strong in your belief then you will have inner strength and you will be full of confidence and excited rather than ashamed when Christ comes again to claim the world. You know that Christ is full of understanding and completely righteous, so those that follow Jesus also develop understanding and grow in righteousness.

Chap.

3

It is great to know that we are now considered sons of God even though it means that those who refute God also refute us. We know that we have eternal life, but we are not clear as to the form we will have, except that we shall be somewhat like Christ himself and that we shall be able to see him as he really is. Every person that has this hope is on the right trip.

If anyone sins, Christ is able to forgive the sins, but a person who follows Jesus should not sin. You don't sin when you are conscious of the presence of Jesus.

Don't be fooled, for persons who are good do good things and persons who do wrong are working for the devil. The Son of God has arranged to destroy the devil and his works. A person who does not have real concern for other people is a devil worker and not on the side of the Lord. It has always been the same old story of God saying, "love one another."

Cain blew it when he killed Abel because he was jealous. The big difference in life is the matter of attitude toward other people. If you really care for others you would be willing if necessary to give your life for someone else even as God gave his life for all of us. If you love other people you live, enjoy life, and join Christ, while if you hate others you are subject to bitterness and death.

It is impossible for a person who loves God to be stingy or a tightwad, for the love of God will cause a person to give to the needy and to share his own blessing.

You don't just talk about love either. You have to practice it. You can't fool God for God knows whether or not you act from love or from some ulterior motive. If you are truly good hearted then you feel at ease about God.

If we are sincere in our love for others and for God, then we can make requests to God and he will do anything we ask that suits his plan. The whole thing can be summarized in the commandment to believe in God's Son, Jesus Christ, and to love one another. The spirit which has been left to dwell in us testifies to the fact that we are in Christ and he in us.

Let me warn you again about phonies. There are some real smart fellows that will try to tell you of new inspirations. There is only one test of reality and that is belief in the fact that Jesus came to earth, in the flesh, and was from God. Anybody who denies the deity of Christ is an anti-christ, and is in the wrong.

You are in a position to handle life because the spirit of Christ that is in you is more powerful and more effective than the supporters of the earthly group that worships mankind. People that respond to straight preaching are of God and those who won't listen belong to the devil.

Love one another, for love is of God, and leads us closer to God. If a person does not love people and life, such a one does not love God, for God is love.

The essence of the miracle of love is not that we love God but that God loves us and that he sent his only Son to pay for our sins. No one, however, has seen God, but God may be sensed in the operation of the spirit of love.

Whoever affirms that Jesus is the Son of God will find that God dwells within such a person.

There is no fear in complete love, and we can look forward happily to the day of Judgment. We love God because he first loved us. A person must love other people or such a person is not capable of loving God. How can you love God whom you have not seen unless you love those persons that you have seen. The commandment then is to love God and love people also.

The commandments of God are not tough,[1] but if we really love God we will grow into enjoying the keeping of his commandments. If we believe in Jesus Christ, we are then conquerors of the world with Jesus.

The spirit of truth testifies to us that Jesus came both by water and by blood, fulfilling baptism and sacrifice, and there are three persons that witness to this, the Father, the Word, and the Holy Spirit, all those three are also one. These bear witness in heaven.

The three things that bear witness on earth are the spirit, the water, and the blood and these three also are one.[2]

The witness of God is found in those that believe on Jesus Christ, and those who don't accept Christ are just flat wrong.

---

[1]The writer was admittedly getting old.
[2]I don't know what this means, at least not exactly.

The record explains that God has given us a chance at eternal life through Christ, and you are either in with Christ forever or separated forever from God.

My whole purpose in writing is to get you to reaffirm your faith in Jesus in order that you might live forever.

There are sins in life that are against God and Jesus and which result in permanent death and then there are sins which are "excuse me" sins and are easily forgiven.

If a person is sincerely dedicated to the works of the Lord the devil can't get anywhere with such a person.

Don't get sucked into any idol worshipping, my children, but believe in Christ. Follow God and his Son Jesus Christ and you will find the true God leads you to life eternal. Amen.

Yours truly,

John

Dear Mrs. Logan and Family:

There are many things that I would like to write to you but writing is tough duty and so I'll try to come and talk directly to you.

In the meantime, remember to love one another, to affirm your faith in Jesus Christ. Keep your faith active and don't pay any attention to any speaker that does not believe in Christ as the Son of God.

Grace be to you all, mercy, and peace from God the Father and from the Lord Jesus Christ, the Son of God. Amen.

Amen.

Your friend,

John

3 JOHN

Dear Randy:

My big wish is that this letter finds you prosperous and in good health. It was a great thrill to hear the report that you walk in the truth. There is no greater thrill to a teacher than to learn of the success of a student.

It is reported that you are considerate of strangers as well as the needy ones in your area. We all need to support the cause of Christ.

I wrote to the church but old Sage[1], who wants to shine all by himself, let my offer to come to preach get lost in the mail.

If I come anyway I'll remember Sage and I'll have my say to him, for I understand he is really hard on good Christians.

Pursue good things, for all such are of God, while evil things are of the devil.

Ben Rose[2] is reported to be a top notch person and a speaker of the truth. I hope to see you soon and be able to talk at length with many of you. Peace be with you. Tell my friends "hello."

Sincerely,

John

[1]Diotrephes   [2]Demetrius

Dear Believers:

This letter is to those who have committed themselves to Christ, and led by God into the life of a witness. May mercy, peace, and love be multiplied in your life.

The main reason I am going to all this trouble to write[1] is to warn you about some unorthodox people who are turning the grace of the Lord Jesus into permissiveness, and even denying that Jesus is the Lord of all.

Let me refresh your memory about the Lord delivering his people from Egypt, and then destroying those that rejected him. They are probably now with the fallen angels, chained in darkness, awaiting the day of judgment.

This new 'do as you please' crowd is following the path of the cities of Sodom and Gomar, where there was no restriction and every form of loose living was commonplace. These people who are loose today are not subject to any authority and recognize no decent or duly constituted control.

Remember, however, that when Michael, the archangel, argued with the devil about the body of Moses, Michael refrained from accusations but merely spoke to the devil and said, "The Lord will tend to you."[2]

There are people on the scene today who denounce things or conditions or doctrines about which they know nothing, but rely on their own beastly desires as a basis of their behavior.

Woe to them. They are going down the same road as Cain, and they are chasing the dollar worse than Midas.[3] It hurts me to see some of these folks at the Family Night Supper, eating without fear, when really they are just as useless as clouds without water, or withered fruit trees, already plucked up by the roots. Some are like raging waves, just foaming at the mouth, or similar to a shooting star that disappears forever in the night.

Did you know that ole J.P.,[4] who was only about seven phases behind Adam, prophesied about some of this saying, "The Lord will come with about ten thousand saints and execute proper judgment. At that time all the ungodly actions and speeches will be pointed out to the ungodly. The chronic complainers will get it, so will the big phony lip artists, and the people who take advantage of the unfortunate."

You want to be sure and remember the words of Jesus Christ when he warned the apostles about mockers, about persons who are concerned only with worldly desires and their own interests. As for

[1]No ballpoint pens, no smooth paper, etc., in those days.
[2]This has got to be a great sentence to remember.
[3]Balaam   [4]Enoch

you, be certain that you grow in the faith, praying under the guidance of the Holy Spirit, keeping yourself joyfully under the love of God, and anticipating eternal life through the mercy of the Lord Jesus Christ.

Use common sense, too, helping some persons with real compassion and understanding, while with others you will have to scare them with hellfire, but save people.

Now to the only one who is able to keep you from falling and to present you clean in the presence of his glory with great joy, to the only wise God, our Saviour, be glory and power, majesty, and dominion, now and ever more. Amen.

Yours truly,

Jude

REVELATION
TO THE CHRISTIANS

Now get the picture. God tells Jesus about the general plan and various circumstances that must take place before the second coming of Christ in glory. Jesus tells all this to an angel who goes and tells it to me, John, a witness to the first coming and one who, having received the word, testifies to it.

Naturally it must be said that I am getting the information fourth hand, and you're getting it fifth. Also I am writing in such manner that having this letter won't get any of you arrested. In addition, my revelation came in vision form, and you should bear this in mind also.

Nevertheless, listen to what I have envisioned and prepare yourselves for the Lord's day, when Christ comes in great glory.

First off, I bring you words of greeting, expressions of peace and concern from God the Father and from the seven angel spirits which are on stand by duty near the throne of Grace. Jesus Christ also sends this regards. Jesus is the faithful witness to the good news, and he is the one that has washed away our sins, the one that loved us, and that enables us to be eligible for eternal association with God the Father.

When Jesus comes this next time he will come in prominence and great glory and every one shall see him. Those fellows who crucified him will see him and recognize him and so shall all those through the years who have denied him or defied him.

God has proclaimed that he is the beginning and the end, the A to Z, the all powerful, almighty One. As for me, my name is John, I have suffered for the sake of the cause, and I am at present living on the island of Patmos. The other day I dropped off into a trance or whoozy period and an angel spoke or at least I heard a voice telling me to watch my vision and write down the messages to the various divisions of churches that are forthcoming, the Baptists, the Presbyterians, the Catholics, the Methodists, the Reformed Jews, the Episcopalians, and the Pentacostal group.[1]

In my vision I saw the seven lights, each representing a different one of the church divisions and in the middle of the symbols of all the churches was a great central figure, whose power was so obvious that he appeared to hold all the galaxies of stars, and the brightness of his being prohibited the determining of any specific features.

Although I was already in a trance, in my trance I went kerplunk down on my face. The voice then said to me, "Don't be afraid. I am the first and the last. I am the resurrected Lord and I will live forever. I have the keys that will open heaven and hell and I will

---

[1]Feel free to change these divisions around a bit, or add your own.

explain partially some of your vision.

"The seven candles or symbols represent the seven great divisions of the church and the full deck of stars represents the great spirit of these churches and the bringing of light to all portions of the world."

The first message, and these are not necessarily in order of importance or on a rating scale, but this message goes to the Catholics.[1]

Here is the message: "You are faithful people, with great patience, and you are unalterably opposed to evil. Bully for you!

"You are also tough on phony priests and will not tolerate variance from the rules of the orders. That's the good news.

"The bad news is that you have forsaken your original zeal of complete devotion and absolute faith. Repent and reform or I will destroy your church system.

"Nevertheless, you are opposed strongly to the same evils that I oppose. Be encouraged. To those that overcome evil I will give to such eternal life, and you will get to live in a paradise created by God."

Now to the Reformed Jewish Churches,[2] listen to this message. "The good news is that I know about your good deeds, about your terrible suffering and persecution, and about your moaning of being poor, though you birds always wind up in good financial shape.

"I know also that you have a problem with a lot of joiners who claim to be Jews and they aren't. Forget them; they are from the devil.

"Don't get too distrubed about your terrible mistreatment. I know it is bad, but it won't last but about 10,000 years, during which time you'll be arrested, deported, put in concentration camps, and have general miseries.

"If you are faithful even to death I will personally present you with a crown of life and you will be exempt from the second death and you will live with me forever."

Now let me pass along a message to the Baptists.[3]

"I know all about you Baptists. I know where your weak spot is, but I also know that there are many faithful among you. There are Baptists who have clung to their faith in the face of death, and many who remained faithful in spite of periods of evil leadership.

"The bad news for you folks is that I know how you have let your church loosen your rules so that anything is permissive. Some of your leaders have even advocated the doctrine of expediency.

"You need to reform. If you don't, I'll work against your

[1]Church of Ephesus [2]Smyrna Church [3]Church of Pergamos

church and it will dissappear. If you've got ears, you better listen.

"Nevertheless, for the Baptists that keep the faith, I have prepared a special I. D. card which will provide you with an access to an exclusive area in heaven, which is what you want."

Now comes the message to the Church of England and its off-spring the Episcopal Church.[1]

"The good news is that I am acquainted," says the Lord, "with many fine things that you have done, your charity, faithfulness, patience, and good deeds. Admittedly you have been better about doing good deeds than about being generous with your money.

"The bad news is that you let Queen Elizabeth control your church. No one person should ever be permitted to do this and as a result almost anything became acceptable if it suited the Queen. The Queen didn't repent and the church didn't reform. Needless to say, all such who use the church for selfish ends will be punished. That is for sure!

"I expect to reward people in accordance with their works. For the Episcopalians who have not fallen into evil and have not worshipped only the form and liturgy, I'm prepared to ease your pains. For those of you who keep the faith in the right spirit, I will give to you all special powers in the day of judgment and you good Episcopalians shall be as bright a signal as the morning star, and your presence welcome in the family of God."

Chap.

3

Now here is the message from Christ to the Presbyterians.[2]

"You have a reputation of being a real live church, but you are near dead. You are substituting mechanics and organization for belief and good works. Get with it!

"You are well educated. Remember what you have been taught, repent of your shortcomings. If you don't get back with the basics, I will destroy your name.

"You've got some mighty fine people with you, they are very worthy, and they shall walk with me in heaven. Those Presbyterians that keep the faith shall have their names written in a book, which is what they like, and I will nominate these people to God for life eternal."

The next message is the Pentacostal Churches,[3] it is also from Christ, the controller of the gate to heaven.

"I know all about you Pentacostal people. I know about your many fine works and I have given you the open door policy. You have not been a church that was really affluent or politically prominent, but you have kept the word of God as a precious gift and you have not been ashamed of the name of Jesus Christ.

---

[1]Church of Thyatira   [2]Church of Sardis   [3]Church of Philadelphia

"I plan to make a lot of the members of Satan's church come and join yours. Because you have kept my word as a church, I will protect you from the temptations that come with great growth. Keep the faith!

"Be sure that when the end comes the faithful among the Pentacostal groups will receive written upon each, the new name of Christ, also the name of the new city of God where the saved will live."

Now listen to this message to the Methodists,[1] which comes from the one great faithful witness, the one who was with God from the very beginning.

"The big trouble with you Methodists is that you are neither hot or cold. You're just lukewarm. I can't stand that. If you don't get with the program I'll bring your whole church to a screeching halt.

"One of the troubles with your thinking at the leadership level is that you think you have it made. You don't. What you need to do is to really sacrifice. You never really press yourselves with your gifts of time or money. Take a look at yourselves. You need to suffer a bit. You've got it too easy.

"Yet remember I always am standing at the door and knocking. If any of you come to me, I'll meet you more than halfway.

"When you do come to me I'll let you Methodists sit right by my throne. That's a firm offer." Amen.

This is what my vision seemed to reveal as messages to the churches. My writing is necessarily subtle so think carefully about what I am saying and use your head.

Chap.
4

Following this vision about the future development of the churches, I was summoned into another section of heaven and the spirit of God was fully in control of me.

You wouldn't believe what I saw! First, there was a great throne, surrounded by Saints in brilliant white garments.[2] The whole scene was awesome. The one sitting on the throne was so bright that I could only think of some exotic jewel.

There were four beast like beings with at least six wings and many eyes, apparently space craft of some type, and all present were there to worship the being on the throne.

The scene itself seemed to be full of crystal glass, rainbow colors, and was more spectacular than anything anyone could imagine.[3]

The whole impression was of power, majesty, beauty and joy. That's the way it struck me.

[1]Church of Laodicea   [2]Not doctors.
[3]Beat anything Hollywood has ever devised as a spectacular.

The one who was on the throne, the Lord himself, held the Book of Life in his possession.

At this juncture I saw an angel of tremendous strength and the angel asked, "Is anyone strong enough or pure enough to open the Book of Life?"

Not only was it noted that no person or creature was able to open the book and see into the future[1] but no one could even look at the book.

Naturally I was greatly dissappointed because I was plenty curious about the future, which is natural. I cried a little.[2]

One of the Saints near the throne then spoke to me and said, "Don't be so upset, John. Christ, the Lord of Life, can open the book."

Then Christ appeared, in a different form than I had known him, but he represented all the fullness of all the Saints and all the churches and he took the book.

When the Lamb of God took the book, the Saints, the choirs, the recordings of the prayers of the people, all joined in a mammoth song of praise and glory to Jesus, who redeemed us from our sins. I never heard such singing and such commotion. The voices of the believers of all time were raised and the countless thousands sang the praises of Jesus Christ.

In my vision I could see and hear all creatures, all those who had died and all those yet to be born, all singing the praises of Jesus, for in time it is a dead cinch that Jesus will be acknowledged by everyone as the Lord of Life.[3]

The spacecraft people, the Saints, the church leaders, all acknowledged Jesus and worshipped the one who had made possible eternal life.

There were seven chapters all sealed in the Book of Life and these chapters pertained to all the various things that would in time occur in accordance with the will of God. No time sequence was mentioned, except that there was always the assurance that victory belonged to Christ and his followers.

The first chapter just appeared to me to say that there would be leaders who often under the guise of saving the word of Christ, like the Crusaders, would go forth to win some battles and lose some battles. Seems a shame, but true.

The second chapter dealt with the matter of world unrest so that man could be seen plunging occasionally into something similar to World War II.

[1] That goes for Jeanne Dixon etc.
[2] The crying fad for men is gradually returning.
[3] I get the impression that church in heaven is not solemn.

The third chapter indicated that there would be periods in the life of mankind when everything was business, and mankind tried all manner of schemes to see that he had oil for energy using machines and wine for his pleasure.

The fourth chapter indicated that there would be a time when at least 25% of all the people of the earth were in turmoil, and there would be war, and hunger, and endangered species among the animals.

The fifth chapter gave a run-down on the mighty martyrs and witnesses for Christ, who had sacrificed greatly, some giving their lives for Christ. Naturally, they wanted to know when Christ was going to punish the wicked and bring peace on earth. These wonderful people were told to cool it, then they were given fresh white garments and assured that the time of justice was coming. In the meantime, these great ones were to rest.

The sixth chapter dealth with natural disasters. The book explained that the Lord would occasionally seem to shake the earth and there would be earthquakes, floods, storms, total eclipses of the sun and moon, stars falling in unusal abundance, mountains would disappear and islands would be swallowed by the ocean.[1]

There is no doubt but that during such times as these people will have the willie-nillie scared out of them, and they will hide in caves and storm shelters and worry themselves silly. Well, it will simply be a way of God telling people that he is not happy with their behavior and materialistic tendancies.

Chap.
7

The next portion of my vision was at first a little scary as I saw the four angels who handled all the winds and they seemed to be planning to blow the whole earth away. About that time the angel in charge of protecting all the people who loved the Lord appeared and told them to hold up the blowing and commotion until all the people to be saved were secured by the protective identification mark and all had their passes into heaven.

I was greatly impressed with the number of those saved,[2] those being 144,000 Jews, which is our asiatic way of saying a big bunch. All twelve tribes were represented. Then I saw countless thousands of non-Jews, from every nation, so many that you could not count them, and this great multitude stood in purity before the Lamb of God, and with palms in their hands, and they were praising God with a loud voice.[3]

The angels were also involved in the worship as were the spacecraft groups. These participants were praising God, and exclaiming over God's wisdom and glory, thanking God, honoring

[1]Atlantis? [2]This is very encouraging.
[3]Apparently heaven is fairly noisy.

the Almighty One, and saying may His power be forever and ever.

One of the old time inhabitants of heaven then asked, "Who are all these characters dressed in white? Do you know?"

"I sure don't known," I said.

"I figured you didn't," said the old timer.[1] "These you see in white are those who have become pure through suffering for Christ and remaining faithful under trying conditions. These are permanent residents here and they serve God day and night in complete happiness and Christ associates with them all the time. This bunch will never hunger or thirst again, they will never know pain or distress, and there shall be no tears in their eyes, for the Lamb of God will have taken away all their sorrows and troubles."

Chap.
8

My attention was then directed to the seventh chapter in the book and when this chapter was opened there was a great silence in heaven. It didn't last long.[2]

About this time seven angels appeared and each was given a trumpet as a symbol of limited power. Another angel appeared who was in charge of staging and this angel saw that the prayers of the Saints arose with a sweet smell up to the throne of God.

The seven angels then each took a turn revealing what they planned to do on earth. The first angel planned to bombard about one third of the earth with hail, meteorite showers, and grass fires.

The second angel planned to throw a huge mountain, a real live volcano, into the sea. This would cause many fires, and a great tidal wave.[3] The tidal wave and explosive volcano would kill many fish and cause great loss of life.

The third angel took a portion of a star, a meteor, and socked it to the earth, contaminating many streams, causing lots of people to die of the plague.

The fourth angel resorted to using an eclipse to attract man's attention to the power of God. This caused great confusion on earth and many people became greatly perplexed and were as confused as if there were a new daylight savings plan instituted.

Then an angel came zooming by calling forth, "Look out, earth. There are three more terrible natural disasters yet to come."[4]

Chap.
9

Next came the revelation of the activity of the fifth angel, a real lulu. First thing this angel did was to touch off a whole bunch of volcanoes and create a major air pollution problem. Then a bunch of

---

[1]This is exactly the way old timers talk.
[2]I tell you, it's a noisy place for sure. Good noisy!
[3]Krakatoa?   [4]Not all angels are good, happy new angels.

super-bugs began to run loose over the whole earth. These bugs didn't live on grass, but they thrived on stinging people. Although the sting was not fatal it created almost half a year of pain and aggravation. The fascinating part seemed to be that the bugs only bit the bad people or unbelievers.

These super-bugs were really fierce, steamed up as horses ready for battle, and they looked like men with gold caps on their heads. The super-bugs had long hair and big teeth, and they looked almost exactly like a Lear jet. The king of this crowd had an odd name. Anyway, this outfit caused a whole mess of trouble.[1]

This was the first big world wide problem. The second was under the jurisdiction of the 6th angel. The sixth angel then took charge and released the four angels who handled all the winds and told them to get busy creating havoc. In the process there came into being World War III.

The fighting was mainly with planes shooting from the nose and the stern and about one third of the people of the earth were killed in the war. In spite of this, the people did not have sense enough to realize that God was trying to get them to simply worship Him, and so the people still did not repent of their sins, their greed, their false values, and their thirst for money. The nuts couldn't see that all the wars and natural disasters, small and great, were God's signs urging the people to repent and call on the Lord.

Chap.
10

The next thing I saw was another angel, a real biggie. This angel was quite spectacular, using a rainbow for a hat and she[2] had a small book in her hand. She stood as if she had one foot on land and one on the sea and she spoke forth firmly saying, "Now hear this!"

When the angel said this there suddenly broke forth into song a seven voice choir and they sang of the secrets of life. I was not permitted to write these down.[3]

The rainbow headed angel then said, "The time has come for the final scene is to be staged."

A voice then directed me to go and to take the little book from the Ms. Angel.

I went to the angel and said, "Please, ma'm, would you give me the book?"

She said, "Take it and eat it."

As a result I took the little book, being glad it was little, and I ate it. It tasted real good, like a Hershey bar. When I had swallowed it, however, my stomach turned bitter.

"You are to go and prophesy to all the nations and all the people throughout all the world," said the Ms. Angel.

---

[1]Sure sounds like the Chinese.   [2]No man would wear a rainbow for a hat.
[3]If he had, Jack Anderson would have schemed to get them.

Next I was given a tape measure and told to mark off the measurement of the temple of God as a sign that there would always be a remnant of the Jews left protected and faithful, and that a portion of the holy city Jerusalem would always remain intact. The non-Jews, however, will often control the major portion of Jerusalem. All these things were preliminary to the beginning of the time when the end of the world was imminent.

The angel then said, "There will be two who come along some time in history and they shall be great, profound prophets. If any man tries to hurt them the men will be swept back by fire from the mouths of the preachers.[1] If any man hurts either of these two such a person will be executed.

These two prophets will be given power from God to control rain[2] and also the power to spread disease. When these two have finished their period of over three and one half years of great preaching, then a representative from the devil shall arise and have them killed. Their dead bodies shall lie in the street in Jerusalem.

The bodies shall lie in the street for three and a half days and this will give ample time for full T.V. coverage so that all the people will know that the prophets are dead. The hundreds and thousands of people all around the world with guilty consciences who were embarrased by the preaching of the prophets shall lead a time of great celebration, exchanging gifts as if there were another Christmas.

After three and a half days the spirit of God will return to the prophets and they will stand on their feet. People everywhere will be astounded and terrified. A voice from heaven will then say, "Come on to the heaven, boys."

The two prophets shall be lifted in a space cloud and their enemies will witness it.[3]

When this happens the earth will react in the form of a huge earthquake, and ten per cent of the city of Jerusalem will be destroyed, and over 7,000 people will be killed. Many thousands will then worship and glorify God.

This is the second big period of conflict and trouble preparatory to the end of the world.

There is a lull here in time and then the third period is stated to arrive. The seventh angel explains this saying, "The voices of the chorus of heaven are singing 'the kingdoms of this world are become the kingdoms of our Lord and of his Christ and he shall reign forever.' "

The elders gathered around the throne of God then chanted their songs of worship, chanting in this fashion, "O Lord God Almighty, who is past, present, and future, your power is tremendous, and because of it the nations of the earth were jealous.

[1]Bad breath at its worst? Something yet to be invented?
[2]They haven't come to Texas yet.   [3]Probably on the Today Show.

"Now is come the time of judgment. This is the time when the servants of Christ will be rewarded, as will the prophets, and all that fear God, little or big. There will also be destruction for those who pollute or destroy the earth."

At this point I could see into the temple of God; there was the ark of the covenant, the holy scriptures, and great lightening and thunder, hail, earthquakes and other manifestations of the power of God.

Chap.

12

There appeared then a tremendous wonder and the sight I saw was the act of creation which appeared, of course, as a woman, bright as the sun, and naturally being in a state of creative motion, as any woman in the process of childbirth.

Then I saw another wonder, and the form of this wonder was a red and murderous dragon, the old devil himself, and he was furious at the Creative Process, and he stood ready to destroy the result of the creation.

The woman, the symbol as I saw her, produced a son who was immediately taken to God, and this must have been near the very beginning. The woman, the process, having accomplished the great miracle of all, dissappeared for a while.

Then war broke out between the angels under Michael and the dragon, the devil, and his crowd of angels. The devil and his bunch were defeated, and Satan was exiled to the earth along with his group.

Then there was posted on the bulletin board in heaven a notice which said, "Now is the beginning of the kingdom of God and the power of Christ. The devil is gone and he cannot present his cases to God any longer. The devil is overcome and is continaully defeated by the faithful who love Christ. Heaven is cleared of the contentious devil and his gang. Hurrah!"

Not so on earth. The people on earth now have to contend with Satan and his bunch. The devil is also mad as he knows he has only a limited time before he's going to be a real goner.

Naturally the devil began to cause as much trouble on earth as he could cause to the woman, who represented the Creative Process. The devil tried everything, such as trying periodic floods, but the earth swallowed most of the water. Since the devil couldn't stay the Creative Process he then started working on the people who were the result.

Naturally the devil focused his attention on those people who loved God and followed Christ. That's how the earth situation came into the condition of the war between good and evil.

After this I began to see all the many conflicts and difficulties that would beset mankind.

One thing I saw that was awesome was a sea monster that seemed to have been made by a committee with a body like a leopard, feet of a bear, and the mouth of a lion. The devil gave him power to conquer and people were afraid of him, and many worshipped him, and some thought there was no way to oppose him. This powerful, influential leader also spoke against God, but he died young. People who are not dedicated to God are always following some such leader, but God puts a limit on such a ones activity. This one lasted 42 months of prime time.

Think about this. No one can defeat the system of God.

A fellow who takes captives himself eventually becomes one. If a person starts killing, such a person gets killed.

Apparently I was to be shown a number of samples of this type for next I saw a second beast.

This second beast praised publicly the activities of the first beast and this started the same old routine of grabbing power, intimidating people and the like. This second one had managed to come along with overhead bombers and he had a great following. This beast like leader had everyone killed that didn't support him.[1]

This fellow wouldn't allow anyone to do business of any kind with a person who didn't have a mark of identification.[2] Once again, though, the leader finds his days numbered and he dies. Another war against God lost. That's the bad news about life, man foolishly turning against God.

Then some good news! I saw the Lamb of God, surrounded by 144,000[3] with special armbands, for these were the pure ones, virgins in thought and deed, and they joined in a song accompanied by a lot of harp players, and the song was their alma mater and no one else knew the words.

About this time an angel came flying by, one of the good ones, and this angel was responsible for seeing that the gospel of Jesus Christ was preached throughout all the world, to every nation, and in every language.

"Fear God," sang forth this angel, "for the hour of judgment is close. Worship God, for he made heaven and earth."

Then another angel came flying by saying, "Babylon, the symbol of sin and corruption, has perished."

A third angel appeared and said, "Now hear this, if any person has worshipped an ungodly leader, and pledged himself to an

---

[1]I think he had a mustache.   [2]Swastika, Rising Sun, Oil derrick?
[3]Round number — no way of John counting that many — he means a <u>bunch.</u>

ungodly cause, such shall be subject to the wrath of God. God will pour out fire and brimstone on these evil ones and they shall be tormented. The angels will be spectators.

"The smoke of the burning of the evil ones will rise to heaven and be seen by the faithful who stayed with the commandments of God, and kept their belief in Jesus Christ."

Then I heard a voice from heaven saying to me, "John, write this as encouragement to the people, 'Very fortunate are those who die in the Lord, for they will be relieved of all their hard work, and their good deeds will come with them to heaven as a blessing.' "

Again, I saw a new sight. This time the Son of God was sitting on a cloud with a sharp sickle. An angel came zooming by and said, "The time has come. The earth is ready, and now you are to reap."

Then another angel appeared with a sharp sickle and the angel in charge of fire said to the one with the sickle, "At last you can reap. Take your sickle and get all the liquor and the beer and the wine and bring it near the city of God and it will all be destroyed."[1]

Chap.
15

The scene changed and I saw another revelation. This vision appeared to be seven angels and each of them was given a special power to work some hardship on the anti-godly people. I also saw at this time a great group of those who had been faithful and who had withstood the onslaughts of the devil and they were singing,[2] and their song was praising the Lamb of God, and chanting 'holy, holy, holy, glory to the one great God.'

The doors of the temple then seemed to open and the seven angels came out and each one had a handbag. One of the four spacecraft people came and put into the handbag of each the special instructions for showing the wrath of God toward the evil people. The temple was so full of the manifestations of the power of God that no one could enter the temple, and it was to remain this way until all the angels had done their thing on the earth.

Chap.
16

Next I heard a voice out of the temple saying to the angels, "Go do your thing. Use your power when and wherever you so desire, for you are showing here and there down through the years that God means business."

One of the angels then started visiting the earth and using diahorrea as a means of humbling persons and making them aware of their weakness.[3]

Then another angel was put in charge of the red tide that would be used at sea to kill thousands of fish and contaminate vast areas of

[1] I wish we had sense enough to do it ourselves.
[2] Choirs and singers really have an inside track. [3] It works, too.

the oceans.

The third angel socked the fresh water areas and made the water unfit to drink. The angel enjoyed doing this, feeling that this was a way of getting even with the evil people who dealt in violence and hatred.

Then there was an angel who had the power to initiate heat waves. During some of these periods of extreme drouth and extreme heat many persons cursed God, and they failed often to take advantage of the opportunity to repent.

The fifth angel went after the communists and great inner turmoil came into being with them and the communists would bite their tongue in frustration and anger, but they did not repent and turn to God.

The sixth angel hit the Middle East.[1] I saw three major powers here showing all manner of signs and with much big talk they all three went out intent on starting an all out war.

Remember that the Lord said that he would come as a thief in the night. Very happy is the person who keeps his faith in good shape until Christ comes again.

The three great evil powers then gathered all their forces together in a triple entente, and met at Aspen[2] for some plotting and skiing along with it. These three powers are devils and furnish promises, promises, promises.

The last angel then opened his handbag and simultaneously a voice from heaven said "This is it!"

Along with all this were major natural disasters in the form of thunder and lightening, a great earthquake, and as a result Jerusalem was split into three sections and many other cities were torn to pieces.

Then came the hail, worse than in West Texas, and men cursed God instead of repenting.

Chap.
17

"Come here, John," said one of the angels to me. "I'll let you have a look at some panoramic history and I'll show you the woman who represents thirst for power. She is the one that has caused so many world leaders to stumble and fall and she has made many persons drunk with the wine of ambition."

I went with the angel and the angel showed me a real knockout of a woman, dressed in gaudy garments, and the woman had seven heads and ten horns.[3]

Written on the headband which the woman wore was "Mystery. Babylon the great mother of harlots and abominations of the earth."

---

[1] I think this angel is there now stirring things.   [2] Armageddon
[3] She must have had a real good figure though.

The woman was saturated with the blood of many who had died for Christ and been victims of the greed that comes with thirst for power.

I admit I was impressed. The woman was really stunning.[1]

"Why are you so impressed?" asked the angel. "I'll tell you about the woman and about the spirit that propels her, which is represented by the seven heads and ten horns.

"The beast which the heads and the horns represent is the old enemy Satan, who gets released from the bottomless pit for temporary activity on the earth. Those who do not believe in Christ and the limitless power of God don't understand how Satan was, is not, and yet is.[2]

"The seven heads represent seven kings. Five of them were before you were born, John, one of them is alive now, and one is yet to come.

"There will be an eighth, the worst one, and he really will be the devil himself and he will come close to the end of the world. The ten horns are ten rulers who are like presidents or dictators, as the king bit will have passed along, but these ten will line up all their power to pitch in with the devil and they shall combine their strength to fight the Lamb of God.

"The ten rulers will pretend to despise the thirst for power, and will pose as leaders for the people, but all this is part of the plan of God. God knows the whole scene. Still the woman has a great influence being as important as a huge city."

Chap.
18

"After absorbing most of this, I saw another angel with great power and this angel called forth, "Big news! Babylon the great is fallen. This is what happens to all great cities that lose their faith.[3] These cities actually become a gathering point of evil doers. The big city ambitions and scramble for money makes it a rat race."

Then I heard a voice from heaven saying, "You people in the big cities, if you're smart, you'll get out and not get hooked on the evils of city life. God has no intention of allowing the concentration of evil to exist indefinitely. The worse a city becomes the greater the burdens the Lord will put on the city.

"The merchants will howl long and loud when a place like New York goes bankrupt. The trading will stop. Then the merchants will moan and groan but they won't come to the rescue of the city; they will just lament the loss of a great place.

"The ship captains shall view the city from a distance and talk of its great past, but they will no longer dock their ships in the harbor area.

[1]Now I know she had a good figure.
[2]Satan has had it and doesn't know it.
[3]Look out, New York. You're in tough shape now.

"This is really always the history of a great city that becomes wicked and selfish. One such city was so obnoxious that an angel threw a huge stone in the ocean and the waves washed over the city and it sunk from sight.[1] After this there were no more sounds of the craftsmen in the city, the lights of the city were out, there were no marriage feasts, and the city was no more. The cities have often been responsible for the death of Saints and prophets.[2]

After witnessing all this symbolism of history, I heard a great chorus singing and chanting, and they said, "Salvation, glory, and honor to God. Hallelujah. True and right are the judgments of God for He had judged the woman that with ambition corrupted the earth and God has avenged his Saints."

Chap. 19

The four spacecraft became active again and worshipped God, and the chorus sang, "May the smoke of the burning of the evil ones continue to be seen."

A voice then came from near the throne saying, "Praise God. Praise him all his servants and stand in awe of his greatness."

Then I heard another mighty chorus, sounding like the roar of rapids, with thunder in the background, saying, "Allelulia, the Lord God Omnipotent reigns. Let us be elated. For the Lamb of God is prepared for his marriage to the church, for the church is finally purified."

"Write this down, John," said the angel. "Happy indeed are those invited to the marriage of the Lamb of God. These are direct statements from God."

At this point I fell down and bowed at the feet of the angel.

"Quit that, John, I'm one of your own brethren," said the angel. "I am one also that witnessed for Jesus. When you worship, you worship God."

Then the heavens opened again. I saw a white horse and on the horse was the one who has always been faithful and true, and he judges in fairness and make war only out of necessity.

The eyes of the rider of the white horse were like flames and he had many crowns of recognition. He also had a name, but no man was allowed to see it. The name turned out to "The Word of God."

All the armies of heaven followed the one on the white horse, he was given power over the whole earth and on his belt was engraved "King of Kings and Lord of Lords."

Next I saw an angel standing in the bright light of the sun and the angel was calling to all the birds to come and prepare to feast on the bodies of men and animals that are to be killed in the great war between Christ and his angels and the devil and his.

I saw the beast-like-person who represented the devil and all his

[1]Atlantis? [2]I wish our cities and our nation would unashamedly turn to God. It would save us.

gang and they gathered to fight against Christ and his angels. The beast was captured, and his PR man was taken and the two of them were thrown into the lake of burning brimstone.

The vast array of supporters of the devil were killed by flame throwers and bombs, and the birds came and ate their decaying flesh.

Another incident was shown to me, but with no dates. I saw an angel come down from heaven and the angel had the key to the bottomless pit. The angel, a real #1 draft choice, grabbed Satan and chained him to the side of the bottomless pit and told him to cool it for a thousand years. The plan was to let him out at the end of one thousand years to have another try at deceiving mankind.

Then I saw a whole series of thrones which were actually judgment seats, real seats of authority. These places were occupied by those great persons who had given their lives for Christ, who had never worshipped the beast, and they lived and ruled the earth with Christ[1] for one thousand years while Satan cooled it in the pit.

All other persons who had died previous to the one thousand year period remained at rest. The first resurrection involved only the actual martyrs. Particularly blessed are those who participate in the first resurrection for they don't have to worry with the second one, having already defeated death. This select group simply live and reign with Christ for a thousand years.

When the thousand years are finished, the saying is that hell breaks loose, for Satan gets out of hell, the bottomless pit, and goes out to get every person he can to fight on his side. Satan organized his outfit and surrounded the Saints of the Lord who were meeting in the Holy City.

The Lord sent fire down from heaven and wiped out the whole crowd.

The devil was thrown into the lake of fire and brimstone where the beast and his PR man already were, and they were scheduled to be tormented day and night forever.

Then I saw a great white throne and no one could look upon the one who sat on the throne. Then I saw the small and great, all risen from the dead, and the books of life were opened and the dead were all judged based on the notations in the book.

The sea gave up its dead, the buried ones came forth, and the lost, burned or separated ones also appeared and every one was judged according to the works recorded.

Death and separation were declared eliminated and whoever was not found written in the book of life was cast into the lake of fire.[2]

---

[1]Or in Christ's name.　[2]No clerical errors possible.

Then came the beautiful part. I, John, saw a new heaven and a new earth. The old arrangement was a goner. I saw a new city being lowered down from God dressed as a bride spruced up for her husband.

I heard then a great warm voice from heaven saying, "The dwelling place of God is with mankind, and God will associate with people, and shall be with people and shall be their God.

"God will wipe away all tears. There shall be no more death, nor sorrow, nor crying, for all these things are gone forever."

The Almighty who sat upon the throne said, "I make everything new. Write that down, John, for it is true."

"It is all arranged," God said to me. "I am the beginning and the end. I will give to anyone who thirsts for the water of life, and I'll give such that is wanted. The faithful shall come into everything and shall be as one of my children. I will be God.

"The unbelieving, the murderers, the wicked ones, liars, all these shall get tossed into the lake of fire."

About that time there came to me another one of the seven angels and the angel said, "John, come with me and I will show you the bride of the Lamb."

The angel flew me to a high mountain and showed me the new Jerusalem, having the glory of God, and appearing as a precious gem. The city had a wall around it and twelve gates representing the twelve tribes of Israel, 3 gates to each side.

There were twelve foundation stones upholding the city and each was named for one of the apostles. The city was really fantastic. The angel measured it. The city was made of gold, jasper, and clear glass. The twelve foundation stones were made of precious jewels. The twelve gates were pearl. Actually, no expense was spared.

I was surprised to see that there was no church there, but I immediately realized that God and Christ were there; so no church was needed. The city didn't need a sun or a moon.

The saved of the nations can walk always in light and the gates are never shut and there is no night there.

Some of the glorious treasures of nations shall be shown in the city but there will be nothing allowed that defiles or contaminates. No persons shall enter except those whose names are written in the book of life.

There was a beautiful stream flowing in the middle of the city and trees grew on the banks. The leaves of the trees were tasty and the eating of the leaves brought understanding to the nations.

In this city of God or heaven, there are no female periods, no curse or difficulty of any type. The throne of God and of Jesus will be in heaven and there will be no night there; so no need to pack a flashlight or worry about daylight saving time. The Lord is the light and his rule is forever.

The angel said to me, "Everything you've seen and heard is true, John. The Lord ordered us to reveal all this to you. It won't be too long. Jesus is coming. Remain faithful!"

I, John, saw and heard these things, and when it was all shown I fell on my knees at the feet of the angel of God.

"Quit it, John," the angel said. "I am one of your brethren. I am just one of the believers. When you worship, you worship God."

"Don't keep all this poop to yourself. The time is coming faster than many might think."

When Christ comes action comes.

"I will come suddenly," said Christ, "and unexpectedly. The evil will be doing evil and the good doing good. I am also the beginning and the end. Happy are those who follow the commandments of God for they will have the privilege of eating from the tree of life, and they will have access to the city of God.

"Outside heaven there will be wicked ones, murderers, women chasers, liars. I, Jesus Christ, have sent my personal angel to show you these things so that you can publish the words in the churches. I am the offspring of the line of David, the bright and morning star."

The spirit of God says "come," the church says "come." Let everyone that hears say "come." Let everyone that is thirsty for the refreshing life come and drink freely.

I want to testify here and now that no one is to try to add or subtract from what I have said. You may make it clearer but don't change it. If you try to leave out or take away a part of this book you will have your part in the kingdom removed.

Jesus says, "I'm coming. It will be sudden. Be ready." Amen.

Come, Lord Jesus.

The grace of our Lord Jesus Christ be with you all. Amen.